The Collected Columns Vol. II
Crisis & Conceit, 2006-2009

Books by Vox Day

Non fiction

The Irrational Atheist
Return of the Great Depression
SJWs Always Lie: Taking Down the Thought Police
SJWs Always Double Down: Anticipating the Thought Police
Cuckservative: How "Conservatives" Betrayed America
(with John Red Eagle)
On the Existence of Gods (with Dominic Saltarelli)
On the Question of Free Trade (with James D. Miller)
The Collected Columns Vol. I: Innocence & Intellect

Selenoth

Summa Elvetica: A Casuistry of the Elvish Controversy
A Throne of Bones
A Sea of Skulls

Quantum Mortis

A Man Disrupted (with Steve Rzasa)
Gravity Kills (with Steve Rzasa)
A Mind Programmed (with Jeff and Jean Sutton)

Eternal Warriors

The War in Heaven
The World in Shadow
The Wrath of Angels

Collections

The Altar of Hate
Riding the Red Horse Vol. 1 (ed. with Tom Kratman)

VOX DAY

The Collected Columns Vol. II

Crisis & Conceit, 2006-2009

CASTALIA HOUSE

The Collected Columns Vol. II
Crisis & Conceit, 2006–2009

Vox Day

Published by Castalia House
Kouvola, Finland
www.castaliahouse.com

Cover: Castalia House

ISBN: 978-952-7065-73-0

Contents

Foreword

WORLD NET DAILY. I had never heard of it. I watched Fox News regularly and got at least 40 minutes of Rush Limbaugh every day during lunch. What more can a guy need? I can't remember really having another news and opinion source before then. World Net Daily, huh? So I checked it out. Here I am, minding my own business and enjoying life's rich party with the recreational drug of talk radio and then someone, peering from behind a cracked door with strange voices and smoke seeping out, says to me, "psst! Come on in here. Try some of this".

Upon entering the world of WND, I felt I had just been dropped into the deep end of the pool. There was plenty there that reinforced what I already knew to be absolutely 100% true. *Hey! There's Ann Coulter. Look Michelle Malkin. Awesome! Oh hey, that guys fills in for Rush! Nice.* Still, looking around, there were plenty of faces and ideas I had never seen before. Wow. This woman is a Jew from South Africa living in Canada and she's talking about this guy named von Mises, whoever that is.

Just as I was starting to get used to my new friends, I spotted a stranger in the corner. Sitting alone at his table, a man with a Mohawk and a metaphorical cigarettehanging from his mouth beckoned me to join him. He was wearing shades like the Matrix's Morpheus – we were indoors. I could tell this man gave zero f^*#s!

He didn't introduce himself, but WND's party organizer had provided name tags. I could see it peeking out from behind the lapel of his trench coat: Vox Day. He spoke in a more courteous tone than his appearance suggested. "Hve a seat".

I feel like I've joined a conversation that has been going for a good while already.

"George W. Bush is a traitor to the American people and their Constitution." Bam! Like a punch in the nose from a left jab you just did not see coming. "But John Kerry is a fraud, so..." he continued. "Michelle Malkin is an ignoramus". I stared wide-eyed for what seemed like weeks. Just then a party attendant dropped off his drink, a bright blue drink in a high-fluted glass. It sported an umbrella.

I pressed him. "Do you like anybody!?"

"Yeah. You know Joseph Schumpeter, right?"

"What?! Who?!" Perplexed, then resigned, I had to admit: I had no idea what he was talking about. How could I have gotten this far in life and never have even *encountered* the ideas or concepts he was telling me about?

I managed to get caught up on the previous conversation that I had missed to that point. Every now and then I had to run out and look up a reference, but mostly I just took it all in.

Each week thereafter, like clockwork, we met at his table. Bright and early each Monday we sat there together and hashed out the latest geo-political event or, sometimes discussed a new topic I had not thought about before.

To look back through the compilation of Vox Day's WND columns is to look into a time capsule. It is the freeze-frame photography of the evolution of a man and of a nation. As you read through the columns, you will be swept back to the thoughts and feelings you had at the time, only now they will be filtered through what you know, or what you *think* you know now: 9-11; arguments about freedom and privacy; war in multiple theaters; presidential elections. Sometimes you'll feel validated. Often, you'll realize that you just didn't get it then.

You'll also find a number of columns that will make you say, "what the hell were we talking about then? Who cares? But these entries are just as significant as those addressing the topics that are still relevant. They remind us that it's fairly easy to caught up in the ephemeral topics of the day – those items and issues and problems which don't last and which won't really matter in the near future. Fast forward 15 years from today: can you believe anyone even gave ten seconds of their precious life discussing if President Trump's inauguration was as well-attended as President Obama's?

By then, the Great Wall of Trump will be erected, Kek willing, and we will be tired of all the winning.

In this second volume of collected columns, you can see clearly the evolution of a man. While still liberty-oriented, Vox Day no longer considers himself to be a small-l libertarian. You will find here several references to that now-abandoned libertarianism, and speaking of ephemeral things, even an endorsement of one Michael Badnarik.

You will also see the rumblings and percolations, of ideas that eventually came to the fore many years later. Vox Day began pointing out the demise of the EU long ago, observing how more than 80 percent of all the laws and regulations affecting the British people were emanating from Brussels, not the British Parliament. This was eleven years before Brexit! Vox was the first Christian I heard to say that our current civil and legal structures give young men no incentive to marry. It was this bluntness, uncloaked in Chistianese, that made me take note. And he was right. You'll recognize these columns as forerunners anticipating those who hand out red pills today.

There was one idea against which I held out longer than I should have. I was sure the Democrats and liberals were bad and that Republicans and conservatives were the good guys. But Vox was right again. He wrote about conservatives in 2005:

"But nothing dissuades the Three Monkeys from screeching and howling their enthusiasm for their Dear Leader's every action. They have redefined conservatism to be the actions of one known as a conservative, so the individual is no longer defined by his ideology, the ideology is defined by the individual." September 2005

Of course, looking back now, it makes sense. At the time, I thought he was just trying to be edgy. I can see now that he was planting the seeds to one of my favorite Vox Day works, *Cuckservative: How "Conservatives" Betrayed America*, ten years prior.

Like talk radio was a gateway to WND, WND was a gateway to the world of Vox Day. Vox introduced me to *The Irrational Atheist*, the four horsemen of the Bukkakelypse, Sam Harris, free will, omniderigence, Steve Sailer, Austrian Economics, dialectic vs rhetoric, John C. Wright, #gamergate, Derb, TENS, Milo, the Alt-Right, Scalzi, and so much more.

Welcome to his mind.

Andrew Urban,
Toledo, Ohio

Introduction

B Y 2006, I had found my groove as an editorialist and blogger. Although the Universal Press Syndicate's attempt at nationally syndi-
cating my column had failed, my WorldNetDaily column continued to grow in popularity, regularly ranking third in the weekly readership
charts behind only Ann Coulter and Patrick J. Buchanan. Other columns,
some written by popular media figures who are now considerably better
known than me, such as Michelle Malkin and Ben Shapiro, never saw traffic
that came even reasonably close to mine at the time.

The moral of the story: television appearances trump the written word.

Although my column was popular and I never lacked for ideas or subjects
to write about, the period from 2006 to 2009 was a time of personal and
professional turmoil for me. On the personal side, my father's long-running
battle with the Internal Revenue Service, a battle which dated back to 1989
and a PCB-manufacturing facility in Ireland, finally came to a close with his
arrest and subsequent conviction on five counts of tax evasion, one count
of conspiring to impede an officer in violation of 18 U.S.C. §372, and
one count of aiding and abetting the obstruction of justice. After a not-
inconsiderable amount of legal drama, he was sentenced to 15 years and 2
months in U.S. federal prison; as of 2017 he is still serving out his sentence
in a Texas prison.

On the professional side, I had been forced to come to terms with the
fact that my politics and my fame, scanty though it was, had rendered me
completely unpublishable in the mainstream science fiction world. In 2005,
Patrick Nielsen Hayden, the award-winning editor of the largest science fiction publisher, had expressed his horror that I had been named to the Science
Fiction and Fantasy Writers Association's Nebula Award novel jury, in a post
on his personal site entitled "New Heights of Prestige for the Nebula Award".

Interestingly (in light of his remarks about Jews), Day is actually a "Christian
libertarian" novelist named Theodore Beale. Interestingly (in light of his remarks

on female science fiction writers), what Day writes is science fiction. Interestingly, the Science Fiction Writers of America, **"not constrained by conventions and formulas…as open as the speculating human mind"**, *has rewarded Mr. Beale by making him one of the seven jurors for this year's Nebula Award.… The humor of the situation, in my opinion, is the ongoing degradation of the prestige of the once-coveted Nebula Award. Certainly if I were running a literary award that was widely perceived as being increasingly tarnished by arcane rules, unabashed logrolling, and general ridiculousness, my next move would definitely be to recruit me a yawping borderline anti-Semite and woman-hater for the award's jury. Just as an exercise in branding, if nothing else.*

Science fiction writers eager to curry favor with the influential editor at Tor Books dutifully piled on, including John Scalzi, Scott Lynch, Jonathan Vos Post, Charles Stross, Laura Mixon, Steven Gould, and Elizabeth Bear, just to name a few. Never mind that I had been an SFWA member in good standing for years, and had previously served on two Nebula Award juries without incident, that single point-and-screech session over a single column was sufficient to put the brakes on my science fiction career. As Charles Stross correctly observed, *"The people who live and work and pitch their tents in this field have long memories. You'll have to share the same field with them for a long time – decades, maybe – if you want to be in it at all. And you've just offended 75% of them? I think you just made a career-limiting move."*

I had indeed. Nor were the science fiction writers the only people I mortally offended. In 2006, a group of four authors were marketed heavily to the pop intellectual crowd as "The New Atheists". These authors, also known as "The Four Horsemen of Atheism", were Richard Dawkins, Sam Harris, Daniel Dennett, and Christopher Hitchens. Like many of their godless fans, I read their books, unlike many of their godless fans, I was distinctly unimpressed.

A series of critical columns grew into a book, *The Irrational Atheist: Dissecting the Unholy Trinity of Dawkins, Harris, and Hitchens.* The book became influential as a result of its debunking of the atheists' ahistorical "religion causes war" argument, a conclusive dismissal that was later cited everywhere from *Nature* to the *New York Times*, and has largely, though not entirely, seen the once-popular argument disappear from the public discourse.

The most significant event of this period was the global financial crisis of 2008. As you will read in these columns, the crisis was not a surprise to me, and indeed, I was one of the few economics observers who saw it coming. Sadly, unlikely the financial wizards whose actions were chronicled in *The Big Short*, I was only able to profit modestly from correctly anticipating the crisis, but my interest in the situation did result in *The Return of the Great Depression*. The book, published in 2009 by WND Books, was well-received and is still considered by many to be an excellent introduction to the basic schools of economics.

But possibly the most surprising development was the transformation of my personal blog, Vox Popoli, from a convenient place to address multiple emails about the most recent column into a lively intellectual community of readers. Begun at the behest of a fan in 2003, by mid-2009 the blog was seeing traffic of over 300,000 monthly pageviews. Although that is less than one-tenth the traffic the blog now receives, it was enough to lay the groundwork for what has turned into a number of projects undertaken in cooperation with the readers, including the WarMouse, Alpenwolf, Castalia House, Rabid Puppies, and InfoGalactic.

The conceit to which the title refers is the last gasp of the Western triumphalism that began with the fall of the Soviet Union in 1989. Just as the idea that the victory of liberal democracy had led to the end of history was soon to prove unwarranted, the "permanent Republican majority" and multicultural globalism were destined to disappoint those who had vested such confidence in them. The astute reader may note an air of increasing concern, if not exasperation, beginning to creep into the weekly columns, as my own ability to believe in these ephemeral, and in some cases, fatal, conceits was destroyed by events.

Although I did not yet fully grasp the extent to which America, and Western civilization, were endangered by immigration and dyscivilizational ideologies, the period from 2006 to 2009 was an important one in my development from an abstract libertarian to a far more realistic and pragmatic nationalist.

As I mentioned in the previous volume, I had initially favored sorting the following columns by category, putting all the economics columns in one section, the columns devoted to presidential campaigns in another, and so on. I'd also considered annotating them. But upon further reflection, I decided that it is much more useful to read them in the order they were originally published, because doing so serves as an educational glimpse into a period of recent history that is now not only gone, but already appears almost unbelievable, even to those of us who lived through it and can still remember it clearly.

Vox Day
24 May, 2017

Athenian America

January 9, 2006

AMERICA owes much of its national identity to Athens. From our ruthless military supremacy to our quasi-democratic political system, we are in debt to the principal polis of the ancient Greeks. But as empires are wont to do, Athens reached too far and fell, and it is this fascinating tale of war and human hubris that classicist Victor Davis Hanson tells again in *A War Like No Other: How the Athenians and Spartans Fought the Peloponnesian War.*

Hanson is also a columnist for *National Review*, but unlike the vast majority of books published by members of the commentariat, VDH actually knows whereof he writes. His familiarity with Thucydides, the primary source for the greater part of the war, is intimate, and his deep knowledge of the politics, events and their underlying causes is inescapable. Moreover, as he previously demonstrated in *Carnage and Culture*, he is an engaging writer, as he brings to life what in the hands of other, lesser authors would be dry and dusty bones.

Rather like the war it describes, *A War Like No Other* is not a conventional history. (The Peloponnesian War of Thucydidian fame is actually the second Peloponnesian War and encompassed several wars, some of which did not involve one of the primary belligerents.) The author clearly recognizes this, and indeed, recommends no less than five more traditional histories to the reader. Instead of chronicling events according to their order of occurrence, VDH structures his history around the various martial elements involved, dividing the book into sections with deceptively simplistic names such as Armor, Horses, Walls and Ships.

While this leaping around the timeline can be confusing at times, especially when one can never be entirely certain whose side Alcibiades is on at the moment, it is a colorful and effective way of communicating the war and its vagaries to the modern reader. The horror of the many merciless sieges, the arrogant madness of the Athenian Assembly and the prickly obstinance of the Lacedaemonians comes shining through the text—no author of fiction could ever hope to get away with so many wildly improbable twists of plot.

The work is not unflawed. While VDH's frequent comparisons to more recent historical events are usually apt, his use of modern political terms—he sprinkles words such as "right-wing" and "conservative" about—to describe politics circa 420 B.C. is as inaccurate as it is annoying. And like most classicists, VDH's focus is Athenocentric and the reader's comprehension of Spartan thinking and war-making suffers accordingly.

But these are minor defects, and *A War Like No Other* makes for a welcome addition to any thinking man's library. For all that it addresses ancient events, the book is a timely one and its analogical relevance is particularly illuminating given the situation in which the intellectual heirs of Athens currently find themselves. While VDH touches lightly on America's Global Struggle Against Violent Extremism and ancillary events, the many similarities between the actions of two imperialist democratic non-empires separated by 2,436 years will be more than a little haunting to the perceptive reader.

Like Athens before her, America is a rich and militarily superior democratic state seeking to forcibly bring democracy to a diverse group of non-democratic peoples. She is engaged in hostilities with an asymmetric and multifaceted foe, who can neither defeat her nor be conventionally defeated by her. And while there are dissimilarities too—for all his friendliness toward Islam and the Saud family, it seems improbable that George Bush will actually switch sides—Americans contemplating the wisdom of the Iraqi occupation as a pillar of the war against the global jihad should keep in mind VDH's dry critique of the Athenian invasion of Sicily.

"In the last analysis, one does not defeat the proximate oligarchic enemy by sailing 800 miles distant to attack a democratic neutral."

The dark and dirty secret

January 16, 2006

A few years ago, my publisher reminded me that a synopsis of my next novel was due. For no particularly good reason, I found myself thinking about the rather difficult question posed to the writer by vampires. And while I was familiar with every spin on the genre from Bram Stoker and Anne Rice to Buffy and V:TM, I'd always been bothered by one massive logical flaw, namely, where are all the dead people?

Consider the following. The FBI's Uniform Crime Report for 2004 states that there were 16,137 murders in the United States. If one omits the 70 percent committed with firearms—for surely no self-respecting vampire would ever use a gun—that leaves 4,787 annual corpses. Assuming a vampire only requires sustenance every third night and that every murder performed sans high-velocity lead injection can be blamed on vampires, the maximum number of vampires in the United States is 40.

Being immortal and all, they must be really sick of each other by now.

But then it occurred to me: There is another readily available source of non-frozen human blood that does not show up on the Uniform Crime Report. In fact, the nation is nearly awash in the blood of children who are brought into the world by the hands of their murderers. Research soon revealed that because it is a cash business with enhanced privacy protections, there are often some very sketchy characters involved with your friendly local children's abattoir. A plot began to suggest itself…

Two weeks later, I could practically hear the blood drain from my publisher's face as I described the gripping story to him. "Let me just get this straight," he said, sounding rather as if he'd been kicked in the stomach. "You're writing a Christian vampire novel that revolves around the abortion industry? That's certainly original. Do you think you could throw in some insults to the religion of peace while you're at it?"

Being not completely unskilled in the dark arts of human communication, I correctly interpreted this to indicate that he would very much prefer something a little less controversial. And so I returned to the drawing board and came up with something involving a divine intelligence agency, an insane prince of angels and a political sub-text that perhaps one reader in a hundred will correctly grasp. I daresay it may be the first fantasy novel to be inspired by Camille Paglia's *Sexual Personae*, specifically, the bits about Spenser.

But that's neither here nor there. What's significant is what I discovered during my process of researching precisely who profits from continued abortion in America. Some of the parties are obvious, but one in particular is rather less so. Indeed, it is possible that no party has profited as greatly from the abortion industry as the Republican Party. When one considers the political situation in 1973, with a long-time Democratic Congress, Nixon's resignation just around the corner and a Supreme Court full of liberal Republicans, it is amazing to consider how the righteous anger of millions inspired by the Roe v. Wade decision has helped reshape the American political landscape.

So, it was intriguing to read the uncharacteristically insightful Eleanor Clift making the following observation in Newsweek:

> Now that the GOP is within striking distance of overturning Roe, they're having second thoughts.... "Any activist will tell you they'd rather have the issue out there than to have it resolved," says this pro-choice Republican, who has worked on the Hill and for various Republican interest groups. "If Roe were overturned, we'd be electing Democrats as far as the eye can see."

There has been a Republican majority on the Supreme Court for over a decade. We are currently blessed with a Republican House, Senate and White House as well. Republicans are likely approaching the zenith of their political power, and they will probably never be more able to act to end the national shame than they are today. The fact that two pro-abortion figures, Giuliani and Rice, are being openly bruited about as presidential candidates in 2008 tends to indicate that they will never be more inclined to do so either.

But the dark and dirty secret of the Republican Party is that it is only nominally pro-life. Given the history of the last 33 years, voting for vocally pro-life Republicans has proven to be as ineffective a way to stop the slaughter as voting for abortionette Democrats would have been. Keep this in mind before you get too excited about Supreme Court Justice-in-waiting Alito sailing through his Senate confirmation.

Beating the war drum

January 30, 2006

To THE CASUAL OBSERVER, it might seem utterly ludicrous to imagine that the administration is seriously contemplating yet another invasion of a Middle Eastern nation when it is still losing troops every week in an occupied, but unpacified Iraq. But the war drums are again being beaten by the talking heads and the signs are unmistakable.

One of the most reliable indicators is the inevitable flying of the Hitler flag. Slobodan Milosovic was the first in the recent string of Second Comings of Hitler; after the Serbian surrender the dread title was passed on to Saddam Hussein. Now that he has been unceremoniously removed from power, (and following a brief consideration of fellow Axis of Evil member, North Korea's Kim Jong Il), Hitlerhood has been finally been conveyed upon Iran's president, Mahmoud Ahmadinejad.

Other obvious signs include Iran pulling its funds out of Swiss banks before they can be frozen. And closer to home, a blog regular who often drives on a major interstate highway recently made the following comment:

> *I travel regularly for business and have noticed a marked increase in flatbeds hauling new Humvees, tanks and armored vehicles over the past couple of weeks. Something is going on—haven't seen this much since the war started.*

Unfortunately, the public rationale for what appears to be an incipient war is nearly as nonsensical as those used to excuse the last one. We must attack Iran, we are informed, or those mad mullahs will attack Israel! And certainly, insane or not, the Iranians have been rattling their sabers in that direction. But have we not provided more than $64 billion in military aid over the years for just that very purpose? If all of those F-16s and M-16s and Sidewinders and Patriots do not permit Israel to defend herself against a regional military threat, then what was the point of providing it in the first place?

And if the mere possession of active nuclear power plants is grounds for an invasion, why are we not looking to invade Taiwan? Or Finland, for that matter? It seems strange to argue that Iran, a nation that was civilized long before America was discovered, is significantly less stable than either North Korea or Pakistan. One begins to wonder if there will soon be an incident like the sinking of the battleship Maine or the Gulf of Tonkin, to which an American invasion of Iran will be the only reasonable response.

As I suggested in November 2002, one of the few proposed explanations for the Iraqi invasion that has held up over time was the preservation of American financial hegemony, which had been threatened by Saddam Hussein's decision to require payment in euros for Iraqi oil rather than U.S. Federal Reserve Notes. I can't help but note that although there have been rumors about the readiness of Iran's nuclear program for years, the war drums only began beating in earnest not long after Iran announced the establishment of the Iran Oil Bourse, an alternative oil market traded in euros.

Is it possible that the Bush administration—not exactly innocent of the oil industry, its financing and the subsequent ramifications for the national economy—is regarding this as anything less than an act of economic war? And is it possible that the federal government would simply accept this major shift of financial power from the Federal Reserve to the European Central Bank? I am skeptical.

While a recent poll showed that 57 percent of Americans believe that an invasion of Iran would be justified, the media did not report that 52 percent likewise believe that an invasion of Canada would be equally justified and that 84 percent believe that an invasion of France is not only justified, but long overdue. Let's face it: A sizeable minority of Americans believe that invading any country at any time is our national birthright by virtue of our superpower status and inherent human decency.

And this boldness of national spirit is not necessarily a bad thing. There is a certain, straightforward honesty, even beauty, in the American breed of patriotism. Of course, that does not mean it is always wise for a nation's leaders to freely make use of that spirit, lest it be dissipated and unavailable for when it is truly needed.

So, if the administration is prepared to plunge the nation into its third foreign invasion in five years, the president owes it to the American people to be honest with them about what they actually are fighting for. It may be true that war is required to preserve America's unique and privileged financial position in the world, and if that is indeed the case, George Bush should remember that this is not a decision for the American president to make, but the American people.

Afro-abortion

February 6, 2006

WHEN NEW ORLEANS MAYOR Ray Nagin lamented how a once-chocolate city had gone vanilla after being washed by the whitening winds of Hurricane Katrina, the pathos did not escape me. I was thinking how hard it would be to get those hundreds of thousands of African-Americans to voluntarily concentrate in one central location again.

But then I cheered up, as the anniversary of the 1973 Roe v. Wade decision—that liberated women from the tyranny of their biology—got me thinKKKing about the blessing that abortion has been to this country for the last 25 years. After all, what does it matter where the former residents of Nestle Orleans go, so long as they continue to exercise their emanative and penumbrad reproductive rights?

Consider that less than 30 years ago, a pregnant colored woman was almost certain to inflict more dark chocolate upon an unwitting vanilla America. But thanks to the Supreme Court, progress has been indubitably made, as every day now, another 1,452 black babies are no longer permitted to grow up to become rappers, basketball players and welfare recipients.

Lemony Snicket notwithstanding, one cannot really consider this a bad beginning. Indeed, Dr. Kelly Hollowell estimates that were it not for the brave decision of these heroic Negresses to exercise their long-established and unrevisitable right to privacy, America would be inflicted with 14 million more black citizens than the country presently endures today. However, Americans cannot truly rest content until black women are collectively removing 3,030 non-human lumps of hyper-melaninized tissue from their bodies on a daily basis.

Only then can we be sure that the long, national nightmare of racial relations will finally come to an end.

The great challenge facing America now is that abortions are still expensive, and since so many black women are lazy and unemployable in addition to being fat and physically unattractive, they often do not have the money to pay for these operations, which are so vital to the progressive vision of utopian America. But we cannot permit mere dollars to stand in the way of progress!

Ironically, there is a source of wealthy black individuals whose personal financial interests lie very much in common with this vision. Every NBA player is well aware of the personal risks presented to him on a daily basis by the honeys, whose life's goal is to entrap an innocent young man whose only crime is to possess unusual height, athletic ability and tremendous financial upside, so it is in their interest that I propose an NBA-wide Gestational Tax Pool, from which funds will be directed to abortion clinics located in every city which possesses a Martin Luther King Boulevard within its limits.

This Gestational Tax Pool will thus spare young black men from having unwanted financial burdens imposed on them, while allowing young black women who might otherwise be robbed of choice to exercise the only constitutional right that is really important for them.

Some benighted folk might argue that not all black women should not enjoy Choice—some would even argue that black women should not be permitted this most sacred of women's rights—but this is obvious nonsense. It is illogical, as I will demonstrate:

1. Human Rights are good.

2. Abortion is a human right.

3. Therefore, abortion is good.

Q.E.D.

It is clear, therefore, that those who wish American blacks well will not hesitate to contribute to the Gestational Tax Pool, in order to make sure that no black fetus goes unaborted.

And if you happen to encounter a pregnant black woman, do not hesitate to encourage her to exercise her fundamental woman's right to terminate her potential progeny. After all, Margaret Sanger's vision of America depends upon it!

Europe is not America

February 13, 2006

I F THERE IS ANYTHING to be learned from the Cartoon Riots, it is the following:

1. American commentators are largely clueless about events outside the United States.

2. Liberals will not actually defend to the death your free-speech rights, their bold prediliction for Voltaire quotes notwithstanding. As a matter of fact, they won't even defend their own free-speech rights if you scare them enough.

3. Muslims have learned from Western feminists how to successfully use victimhood to silence their opponents and advance their agenda.

4. The Bush administration is unlikely to win its hearts-and-minds battle. The ease with which the jihad was able to stir up Muslims around the world on such a slender rationale does not bode well for the administration's strategery.

But we shall, for today, content ourselves with addressing the first point.

It is surpassingly ironic that the talking heads and scratching pens of the opinion pages, many of whom seldom set foot outside the city limits of New York, Los Angeles and the District of Columbia, consider themselves to be sophisticates explaining the realities of a complex world to the heartland. In truth, the vast majority are as parochial as the proverbial country bumpkin, a fact which immediately reveals itself every time they decide to ignorantly bloviate upon events in Europe, Asia, Africa or the Middle East.

As anyone who has met more than two or three journalists can testify, the grand illusion of journalism is the belief that having heard about something is equivalent to knowing it well. Thus, the columnist who has done the Venice-Florence-Rome circuit once—and loved Firenze—and has learned that Barolos have more cachet than mere Chiantis, will consider himself an expert on all things Italian evermore. Hence the "Torino" Olympics now taking place in the city home to the Shroud of Turin.

The contretemps inspired by the now-notorious Danish cartoons have been the subject of much media discussion of late. Some of it has been intelligent and appropos, especially the criticism directed towards institutions such as the *New York Times* and the ABCNNBCBS cabal, organizations which have never been slow to print or broadcast material offensive to American Christians which nevertheless see fit to avoid reproducing the cartoons even while covering it as a news story.

However, most of the discussions regarding the European aspects have been, as is almost always the case, illuminating only with regards to the ignorance of the opinion-writers. Only Patrick Buchanan has seen fit to notice that Europe is not America, that American constitutional rights do not apply in European countries and that all discussions which assume they do render themselves irrelevant on that score.

"Of course they should have been published," is the opinion of those who are complacently innocent of European law. "The Sacred Freedom of the Press demands it!" argue those who are clearly unaware of the jailing of revisionist historian David Irving, of the fact that in Austria, Belgium, the Czech Republic, France, Germany, Lithuania, the Netherlands, Poland, Romania and Slovakia it is against the law to question the historical accuracy of the claim that 6 million Jews were killed by Germany's National Socialists, and of the Bundesrepublik's announcement last week that World Cup fans— especially the English– who by word or by gesture should remind Germans of their most recent defeat at their national sport would be arrested and face a punishment of up to three years in jail.

Consider, for example, Switzerland, the most democratic country in the world, a wealthy European nation which ranks No. 1 in the Reporters Without Borders' annual Worldwide Press Freedom Index, 43 spots higher than the United States. No doubt an American writer wishing to pontificate on press freedom and the Islamic cartoon riots would think himself safe in assuming that the Swiss have the same liberty to publish religiously offensive material enjoyed by First Amendment-protected Americans.

And that American writer would be completely wrong, due to Section 311, Article 261 of the Helvetic Confederation's federal code:

STÖRUNG DER GLAUBENS- UND KULTUSFREIHEIT

Wer öffentlich und in gemeiner Weise die Überzeugung anderer in Glaubenssachen, insbesondere den Glauben an Gott, beschimpft oder verspottet oder Gegenstände religiöser Verehrung verunehrt, wer eine verfassungsmässig gewährleistete Kultushandlung böswillig verhindert, stört oder öffentlich verspottet, wer einen Ort oder einen Gegenstand, die für einen verfassungsmässig gewährleisteten Kultus oder für eine solche Kultushandlung bestimmt sind, böswillig verunehrt, wird mit Gefängnis bis zu sechs Monaten oder mit Busse bestraft.

DISTURBANCE OF THE FREEDOM OF BELIEF AND OF THE RELIGIOUS COMMUNITIES

Who publicly and in a vile manner insults the conviction of others in matters of faith, (particularly the faith in God), or denigrates a subject of religious admiration, who disturbs or maliciously prevents a constitutionally-protected religious ceremony, who violates a place or an article which are intended for use in such religious ceremonies for a constitutionally-protected religious community, will be punished with prison for up to six months or be charged with a fine.

Interestingly enough, and unlike the United States, it seems Christians are not considered to be second-class citizens by the Swiss media, as an editor at Blick discovered in 1971 after being convicted for publishing a painting of a pig being crucified in the place of Jesus Christ. The truth is that Muslims who have argued for the prosecution of the various European newspapers that ran the cartoons may very well have a case in many countries—not necessarily a clear-cut one, but a legitimate and reasonable claim worthy of due consideration in many European courts of law.

It might be worthwhile to keep this embarrasing little incident in mind the next time you read an opinion-page writer expressing his two cents with regards to Japanese electoral politics, the French legal system or women's rights in the Middle East.

Air power and low probability

February 2, 2006

T HE WAR DRUMS are beating, and yet the administration is uncharacteristically reserved. Is it possible that it has learned a degree
of humility at last? Even a world-straddling empire has its limits,
as the Khans and Caesars learned in their days, and to ignore them can be
fatal.

While there is no widespread agreement regarding the extent to which the
U.S. military is taxed—opponents of the Afghani and Iraqi occupations claim
that it is "exhausted," while the Pentagon insists that it is merely "stretched"—
even the most hawkish neocons appear to recognize that a sequel to the Iraqi
conquest is probably not in the cards. And for good reason, as there are other
factors that enter into the invasion equation beyond the present state of the
American armed forces.

Iran is larger and more populous than Iraq and its population is less het-
erogeneous, so the tactics of divide-and-conquer that worked so well with
the Northern Alliance and the Iraqi Kurds are unlikely to be effective. The
mountainous terrain does not lend itself to a fast-moving blitzkrieg of the
sort that took Baghdad in record time, and Iranian military history suggests
that its army is considerably less intimidated by mass casualties than Saddam
Hussein's cardboard Republican Guard.

So, the whispers of late have been of precision air strikes launched in
combination with special forces operating inside Iran. This sounds very high-
tech and impressive, and while the Fox News analysts are no doubt eager to
draw some imposing arrows on computerized maps (complete with little red
explosion graphics indicating targets) an attack of this sort is only likely to
succeed in Hollywood.

For the history of strategic bombing is a history of complete failure. Every
USAF strategist since the the Air Force was called the Army Air Corp has

either been deluded or deceitful about the ability to win a war from the air. With one notable exception, the atomic attacks on Hiroshima and Nagasaki, aerial bombardments have never won a war.

There are numerous historical examples. Goering assured Hitler that the Luftwaffe could bomb the British into submission. Five years later, Germany surrendered. Knowing how little the Pearl Harbor raid could accomplish, Adm. Yamamoto wisely advised the Japanese generals against it, but he was overruled, much to Japan's eventual detriment. The USAF dropped 6.1 million tons of explosives on 5 million sorties against North Vietnam that not only left the North Vietnamese undefeated, but apparently didn't even retard their economic development. NATO's 78-day air war against Serbia did not stop the ethnic cleansing taking place there, nor, as was later learned, did it significantly degrade Serbian military capabilities.

Air power has always been overestimated by its advocates. A crucial tactical element, it is strategically toothless. In August 1941, at the request of President Roosevelt, the U.S. Air War Plans Division created a strategic document laying out the design for "an unremitting and sustained air offensive against Germany" called AWPD-1. The strategy "assumed that airpower could achieve strategic and political objectives in a fundamentally new way."

However, the AWPD planners might as well have been writing fiction. Despite launching 98,400 sorties against German industrial targets, including a 7-day bombing campaign called Big Week which utilized 3,800 heavy bombers operating around the clock, German aircraft production actually rose 279 percent from two years before. And this was despite having the benefit of Britain's earlier, failed strategic bombing campaign to serve as an example.

It seems wildly optimistic, then, if not actually insane, to assume that an air war against Iran's nuclear facilities can be any more successful than its conceptual predecessors.

The historican Carroll Quigley wrote that the centralization of government power tends to ebb and flow according to the availability of military technology. If his theory is correct, the impotence of the United States in the current situation will likely represent a watershed moment in history. The great trend of the post-World War II era has been one of increasingly centralized power, primarily due to the expense and technological expertise required to produce weapons of mass destruction. However, events in Iran appear to suggest that this 60-year trend may be nearing an end.

Precisely what that will mean for America is unknown, except that its hegemony, financial and otherwise, is likely to be challenged. One need not be enthusiastic about Iran acquiring nuclear weaponry to understand that it may—may—not be possible to prevent them from doing so.

The war against blondes

February 27, 2006

I WILL FREELY ADMIT that I am perhaps more partial than most to the Nordic beauty. This may be due in part to growing up in Minnesota, where one is surrounded at all times by blondes named Johnson, Nelson and Olsen, where "ON or EN?" is a most commonly asked question, where "swedegians" are considered half-breed mongrels and where girls who look exactly like Scarlett Johansson do not receive Maybelline contracts, but work as janitors at the local health club instead.

Minnesota is, perhaps, the only state in the Union where there are more Kirstins, Kjirstins and Kjerstins than Christines of either the "C" or the "K" variety. For my first six months at the East Coast university I attended, every woman named Kristin was under the impression that I had a speech impediment.

Now, none of this is intended as any slight to the non-blonde, you understand. A man would have to be struck blind in order to fail to appreciate the powerful African beauty of Tyra Banks, the delicate Asian appeal of Lucy Liu or the allure of the dark-haired English rose as exemplified by Kate Beckinsale. There is also much to be said for the Celtic redhead, the Latina and the Italiana, to say nothing of the Brazilian melange.

Even so, I think you will understand why I am deeply troubled by the horrifying news that blondes may soon be an endangered species, if they are not already.

A study by the World Health Organisation found that natural blonds are likely to be extinct within 200 years because there are too few people carrying the blond gene. According to the WHO study, the last natural blond is likely to be born in Finland during 2202.

Understandably, the notion of blondeness as something worth preserving is more than a little tainted by the memory of a certain infamous Aryan enthusiast, whose record of respect for genetic human heterodoxy marks what one hopes is the definitive low. But one need not argue for racial superiority— or even admit to the existence of race—in order to favor the survival of genetic diversity within the race as a whole, however superficial the genetic marker.

During last year's brief media uproar over "Prussian Blue," I found my-self wondering what was so wildly outrageous about two young girls whose primary interest appeared to be perpetuating their blondeness. Regardless of whether the National Socialist Hess was or was not a man of peace—and the fact is that the Allied powers thought well enough of his quixotic mission to spare his life when others lower in the National Socialist hierarchy were executed—how is it any worse to profess one's concern for the perpetuation of one's genetic kindred than to "fight" publicly against the effects of assimi-lation and intermarriage on one's ethnicity, to give but one example?

As we live in a profoundly oversensitive age wherein the profesionally offended are ever looking to take offense, let me state for the record that I am in favor of the continued existence and well-being of both Jews and blondes. (Ironically, and no doubt this is another Minnesota thing, the Jewish family I know best happens to be three-fifths blonde anyhow, so it's not as if the two are completely incompatible.)

Perhaps it is only my imagination, but it seems to me that the ubiquitous celebration of diversity that began in the '90s has taken an insidious turn of late. These days, one has to look hard to find an advertisement featuring a black man paired with a black woman, an Asian man paired with an Asian woman, and, if two white individuals are paired together, you can just about be certain that they will both be of the same sex. I see nothing inherently evil in cross-cultural or cross-racial relationships, but it seems very strange to assert that there is somehow something inherently virtuous in them, and even stranger to imply that they are the historical norm.

Indeed, if one were to possess the hyperactive imagination of a feminist, one might well conclude there is a secret war against blondes. Could it be that the producers of hair-color kits are seeking to eliminate the natural competition?

Now, I am not calling for government action, eugenics laws, intermarriage bans or even activist groups with silly acronymic names. I am a libertarian, after all, and I am merely expressing my opinion that it will be a true aesthetic loss to mankind if, one day, the only blondes are those produced by hydrogen peroxide.

The myth of the servant leader

March 6, 2006

FOR ALL that God has not given Christians a spirit of fear, it seems that most church leaders in America today are governed by one. Barna gives us to understand that although they know God hates divorce, Christians are as likely to file for it as non-Christians and it is the rare church where the pews are not filled with practicing and unrepentant adulterers.

Nowhere is the disconnect between the ideal Christian life as described in the Bible and the quotidian practice of American Christians greater than with regard to marriage and the structure of intersexual relations within it. Indeed, the modern church is now far more accepting of the "Love That Will Not Shut Its Mouth" than it is of the biblical concept of submission.

After almost four decades of feminist indoctrination, it is understandable that women who have been told their entire life that they can do anything, be anything and possess the absolute right to obtain the full measure of their momentary desires on demand would react to the doctrine of marital submission as if they were being asked to drink a brimming cup of venom milked from Oxyuranus microlepidotus. Being submissive, after all, is directly contradictory to being a Strong, Independent Woman, and submitting oneself to another individual puts a certain cramp in one's ability to pursue one's passing whims at all times by any means necessary.

And yet, distasteful or not, one's personal feelings on the matter are irrelevant. No doubt there was a Roman or two who thought it entirely possible that a certain Nazarene had risen from the dead and in doing so saved mankind, but looked askance at unseemly demands that he abandon his vomitous banquets and slave-girl orgies. And so it is perhaps worth remembering that Jesus Christ described His way as being a hard and narrow path, not a wide, easy, politically-correct and culturally-approved one.

Even in these latter days, it still occasionally occurs to a pastor to gently remind his congregation that the duty of a married Christian woman is to submit to her husband in all things as the head of the household. As one can expect, this does not tend to go over well in an audience where the women understand themselves to need men about as much as marine dwellers require two-wheeled transportation.

However, before the outraged audience has recovered from its shock, stormed the pulpit and revived the ancient rites of Cybelline, this delicate reminder is almost always quickly followed by a long dissertation on how the leader of the household should not be interpreted as being an actual leader per se, but rather as a servant one, and if the ladies will just refrain from committing violence long enough to listen and reflect upon the matter, they'll soon realize that a servant isn't all that different from a slave, and therefore submitting to a husband's servant leadership is merely a matter of giving him his orders, so please, please don't hit me, just keep doing what you're doing and God will be happy, world without end, amen.

This creative doctrine is loosely supposed to be based on the command for husbands to love their wives as Christ loved His Church. But sacrificial love is not synonymous with servanthood, much less servitude. The soldier who leaps on a grenade to save his buddies is not their servant, nor did Jesus Christ's humility in washing His disciples' feet alter the fact that He was still the Master and they the followers. It is unlikely, for example, that even with his clean feet Peter would take it upon himself to inform the Messiah what He would be teaching the next day.

It is true that there is a sacrificial element in all leadership. The true leader must always put the interests of the family/business/team ahead of his own desires. He must accept responsibility for failure and deal with the consequences, even when it is not his fault. It is C.S. Lewis who may have described the concept best when the king of Archenland explains the burden of kingship to his newly-discovered heir in *A Horse And His Boy*:

> *"Hurrah! Hurrah!" said Corin. "I shan't have to be King. I shan't have to be King. I'll always be a prince. It's princes have all the fun."*

> *"And that's truer than thy brother knows, Cor," said King Lune. "For this is what it means to be a king: to be first in every desperate attack and last in every desperate retreat, and when there's hunger in the land (as must be now*

and then in bad years) to wear finer clothes and laugh louder over a scantier meal than any man in your land."

The doctrine of the servant leader is little more than the attempt of the American Christian church to accommodate feminism within its body, in much the same way that its predecessor once transubstantiated pagan gods into Catholic saints. It is neither rational nor biblical, and the poverty of its fruit can be seen in the continued fraying of the bonds that hold Christian marriages together. Christian husbands, wives and their so-called leaders alike would do well to honestly consider a variant of Joshua's great question: Who do you serve, your culture or your God?

Sheep's clothing and Adam Smith

March 13, 2006

HOW DOES ONE resolve the question of the presumably cataclysmic meeting between the hitherto immovable rock and the
historically unstoppable force? Perhaps by reversing the logic
of the famous question: "Who are you going to believe, me or your lying
eyes?" Is the rock truly immovable? Or, alternatively, is the force actually
unstoppable?

I mention this because I have long been a vocal advocate of free trade. I was
raised on Adam Smith, inoculated against the usual collegiate flirtation with
Marxism by controlled doses of Schumpeter taken in combination with *Das
Kapital* and *The Communist Manifesto*, and eventually found in the Austrian
School of von Hayek, von Mises and Rothbard an intellectual home.

My first serious questions about the free-trade doctrine arose during the
NAFTA debates. The fact that Democrats and Republicans were coming
together in bipartisan support made me suspicious, as bipartisanship is a
reliable sign that the American people are about to get screwed over in a big
way, and it seemed very strange that a genuine free-trade agreement would
require documentation exceeding the size of the average encyclopedia.

Thirteen years later, the honest observer is forced to admit that it is the
opponents of NAFTA whose predictions have been proven to be correct. Free
trade has not improved the Mexican economy enough to dissuade millions of
Mexicans from coming to America, it has not improved the American wage
rate and it has significantly reduced American industrial capacity. The base
concept behind Smith's doctrine of free trade is a nation that stops protecting
its inefficient sectors will turn its resources toward those sectors in which it
has a genuine competitive advantage—apparently selling houses to each other
is America's great strength.

Moreover, the recent history of the European Union demonstrates that free trade is the sheep's skin that clothes a very savage wolf indeed. The European Common Market was sold to the people of the formerly independent nations of Europe as a free-trade arrangement, and while it has not significantly benefited the economic welfare of those nations, it has managed to subjugate them to an unelected commission that rules over them, taxes them and from whose ever-more-invasive dictates they enjoy no appeal.

Can trade be free when the people aren't?

Now, it is certainly possible to argue that the free trade of the NAFTA variety is actually nothing of the sort and that the Third Way social engineering of the European Union is wholly distinct from the free-trade doctrine from which it was birthed. In fact, this is precisely how I have previously attempted to resolve the dilemma.

However, that reasoning is all-too similar to that of the public-school teachers who insist that merely spending more money on teachers will lead to better public schools, and socialists who argue that despite dozens of failed historical examples, the One True Method of communism has not yet been applied. At some point, even the most lovely theory has to pass the more prosaic test of practice or else be relegated to the children's nursery of daydreams and wishful thinking.

I am not arguing, yet, that it is time to do so with regard to free trade. However, for the first time in years, I find myself forced to re-examine the merits of this long-hallowed doctrine, and to do so with a jaundiced and critical eye. It is certain that there are false prophets of free trade—that they exist neither confirms nor denies that the god itself is false.

The deeper question is this: In a globalist world that denies not only the sovereignty of the nation-state, but even its right to exist, is there any fundamental relevance to a doctrine that is defined by the asserted benefit to the nation-state and its citizens? If there is no nation-state and there is no freedom for the individual, then where is the free trade and to whom does it apply?

Sheepskin scam

March 20, 2006

EMOCRACY AND EDUCATION are always good. That is perhaps the most fundamental core belief of the vast majority of American parents; certainly more of them hold to it than believe in God, the sanctity of marriage or the tuck rule. But just as American faith in democracy has been shaken by the election of Hamas in the Palestinian Authority and by what appears to be the looming failure of the Orange Revolution in Ukraine, the belief in higher education as a universal panacea will be severely tested in the coming decades.

The belief in a near-sacrosanct prime directive to pursue education is primarily rooted in the ability of the more highly educated to command higher wages from their employers. This has long been true, but the advantage was significantly compounded during the last four decades, when machine automation, computers and outsourcing enabled U.S. employers to replace skilled, highly paid but less-educated American workers with machines and inexpensive foreign workers. This resulted in the current situation where a college-educated worker can expect to earn twice the income of a worker who possesses only a high school degree over an average lifespan.

But that trend has largely run its course. So much of the American industrial base has already been exported that much of the remaining blue-collar labor is the sort that cannot possibly be outsourced. While it is much cheaper to find workers to assemble electronic hardware in Taiwan or Mexico, it is not cost-efficient to hire a Korean plumber, security guard or retail clerk, because regardless of how low the hourly wage might be, airplane tickets are more expensive.

However, the development of the Internet and a reliable global communications infrastructure means white-collar office workers, those for whom a college degree is almost always considered a necessity, are increasingly replaceable, regardless of their level within the organization. Location is all but irrelevant in an age of conference calls, project management software and e-mail, and if an executive can hire a newly minted MBA from India for a fraction of the salary of an American graduate of Harvard, he would be a fool to not at least consider the costs and benefits.

While there are a number of barriers to white collar outsourcing, including cultural and language barriers, these are far less daunting than they might appear at first glance. When I was the CEO of a technology company a few years ago, I ran it one time zone and several latitudes away from my entire employee base. I happened to do so from within the United States, but could have as easily run the operations from the Bahamas, Mexico City or anywhere else with telephone lines and decent Internet connections.

Remote management makes group meetings all but impossible, but as anyone who has ever worked in an office knows very well, intra-corporate meetings are negatively productive and cause more problems than they solve. Shunning the office also tends to cut down on other productivity-enhancing, profit-building activities such as water cooler conversations, sexual harassment and the daily commute. And while one might not get to know one's fellow employees quite as well, it's not as if the addition of a few cubicle-dwelling corporate rats to one's social circle is likely to make a significant difference in one's quality of life anyhow.

It is interesting, then, to note that what two economists at the Economic Policy Institute, Lawrence Mishel and Jared Bernstein, call the skill premium shrunk 6.8 percent between 2000 and 2004. As Geoffrey Colvin of Fortune notes:

> *The real annual earnings of college graduates actually declined 5.2 percent, while those of high school graduates, strangely enough, rose 1.6 percent.*

Meanwhile, even as the compensation advantage it brings is reduced, the cost of a college education is quickly rising. A comparison of statistics taken from CNN/Money shows that the total cost of a four-year public degree has increased from $8,086 in 1999 to $11,354 in 2004, a 40 percent rise, while the cost of a degree from a private university has gone from $21,339 to $27,516, a smaller but still hefty 29 percent increase.

And the trend has just begun, as few higher-level executives realize just how eminently replaceable their management staffs may be, most likely because it requires recognizing the possibility of their own inherent superfluousness. Once the old school begins retiring and are replaced by technologically savvy executives who understand the irrelevance of location to intellectual labor, one should expect to see radical changes in the world of white-collar employment rivaling those that rocked the blue-collar world in the recent past.

Of increasingly questionable quality, it is probable that a college degree has never been of lower value. Parents and prospective students alike should seriously investigate the matter before blithely assuming debt in order to follow the educated lemmings on a path that appears to be ever more outmoded.

Rainbow mutations

March 27, 2006

W HAT DOES the shape of a Minneapolis stripper's naked bottom have in common with a landmark of English finance? And how is it possible that the color of the roadside prostitutes in Italy can harbor any implications for the ability of a New York woman to stay home with her children? The point of commonality, as it happens, is historical patterns of migration.

In 1990, Umberto Eco wrote an article titled "Migrazioni", which was published in L'Espresso. In that essay, he presciently noted that what Europe was undergoing at that time was not a phenomenon of immigration, but of migration. The difference is significant and one of degree—an individual can immigrate or emigrate, but only a people migrate.

Eco observed that migrations result in inexorable changes to the region of destination, changes to the normal form of dress as well as changes to the color of skin, eyes and hair. A secular humanist in good standing, he adroitly avoids committing the grand faux pas of criticizing this hybridization, fatalistically accepting the inevitability of a new Afro-European culture. For to even hint at criticism would, of course, be crude racist ethnocentrism of the first degree, and not even the reputation of one of the world's leading intellectuals could survive accusations of that.

But what the great dottore mentions only in passing, and what the defenders of the diversity faith avoid discussing like sorority girls pretending not to hear a bulimic sister purging her caloric sins in the neighboring stall, is that changes to the political culture as well as the physical mean are likewise unavoidable. For 40 years, the people of nations such as Denmark, France, Germany, the Netherlands and the United Kingdom believed it was possible to bring Muslim immigrants into their countries in order to replace their declining workforces. They believed their governing elite's assurances that prolonged exposure to the French or English way of life would suffice to turn these immigrants into ersatz Frenchmen or Englishmen.

What they did not realize was that their governments were not permitting immigration, but were instead inspiring a mass migration. Now, there are demands for Sharia in the land which once mobilized against a Catholic armada, the French are showing signs of wishing to revive Maurice Papon's practice of baptizing Algerians in the Seine and even the notoriously tolerant Dutch are beginning to question the once-sacrosanct notion that all cultures are created equal.

While in the United States, Islam is still an issue of immigration, not migration, this does not mean that Americans are not facing their own migrational challenge. With the importation of 30 million immigrants of varying degrees of legality in the last 35 years, most from Spanish-speaking countries that have never known individual liberty or free markets, combined with 34 million native women listening to the siren song of feminism and putting family life on the back burner, the probability that America will be able to retain its unique political identity and the tattered remnants of its Constitution are rapidly decreasing.

For example, the vast majority of native-born Americans of African and European descent consider the notion of a supranational American Union with Canada, Mexico and various Central American countries to be unthinkable and would oppose it if they recognized it to be the natural progression from NAFTA and the FTAA. But is the same true of the growing Spanish-speaking population across the Southwest, an outspoken segment of which is already calling for closer ties with Mexico? As recent events in Afghanistan and the Palestinian Authority have demonstrated to all and sundry, democratic institutions are not capable, by themselves, of moderating ideology, religion or cultural identification.

It is unlikely that Europe can solve its demographic problems without violence—Eco seems uncharacteristically untroubled when he notes that periods of mass migrations are not known for being peaceful—but it is not necessarily too late for the United States. The answer is simple, but it will require inspired leadership that is conspicuously lacking today. If America is to remain America, sovereign, liberal and free, then her people must completely turn away from the ideologies of multiculturalism, immigrationism and feminism. If they do not—and continue on the present path—she will not be sovereign, liberal or free within four decades.

This country, like her Old World progenitors, stands on the brink of precipitate change. In embracing the rainbow, America has been engulfed in its lethally mutating rays and the resulting cancer will surely kill her if it is not removed in the near future.

Metasexual society

April 3, 2006

L AST WEEK, I attended a lecture given by a friend of mine who can perhaps best be described as a mediatective. Part semioticist, part interpreter of electronic entrails, he presented a compelling case of how the medieval symbology of the Catholic Church has been turned on its head by the iconic language of corporate advertising.

Whereas a millennia's worth of art once spoke of a vast and comprehensive order rising from the muck and mire to eventually approach the rarified heights of the Almighty God dwelling on His throne, corporations have made the profane sacred, and the sacred profane, in their never-ending campaign to seduce via shock value.

It is possible that this has happened for no reason in particular, that there is no meaning behind the great symbolic tearing down and that it is nothing more than a natural reaction to the public announcement of God's death and public burial. It is possible, but it is not probable, and anyone who rejects the Accident Theory of history is unlikely to find this lack of an explanation convincing.

It is also interesting to note that this iconic revolution has sparked little alarm in conservatives, especially considering their powerful reaction to what some have described as the "porning of America." (We shall leave for another day the fact that it is only visual porn of primary appeal to men that is so troublesome, while the emotional pornography of television and romance novels is considered less offensive, if it is considered at all.) And yet, it seems likely that the two phenomena are related when considered from a neurosomatic metaprogramming perspective.

Consider this description of a theoretical programmed sexual environment conceived by Robert Anton Wilson in 1983:

Let us call this, in memory of Hermann Hesse, the Magic Theatre. We start with what is concurrently available in high-priced brothels in the Sun Belt section of America. Massage, a first-circuit tranquilizer, has all the advantages of the opiates without being habit-forming. Our Magic Theatre, then, would include computerized body-relaxers-and-energizers better than current massage techniques.

Porn movies are available, for stimulation, in the better brothels. Our Magic Theatre would have them in 3D on all four walls, obviously. Marijuana and stimulants like cocaine or speed are available in brothels everywhere. Our Magic Theatre would have better chemical rapture-agents....

A strange thing has happened in constructing this cyberneticized brothel. We seem to have gone beyond sex to something that might be called meta-sex.

While Wilson believed this experience was available in one's brain as the end result of neurosomatic reprogramming—the true Philosopher's Gold of the alchemists—I imagine he would still be very surprised to see the similarities between his ideal brothel and the current reality of porn-surfing Ritalin kids whose mothers are stoned on Xanax and Dr. Phil, while their fathers get off on Viagra and sympathetic adrenaline rushes.

Like the Marxists, the neurosomaticists placed their faith in a god of human progress, although in the place of awakening class consciousness they hoped to awaken the full potential of the individual human brain. Unfortunately, like the Marxists, their vision of Utopia is far more likely to turn out to be yet another dystopian second-circuit trap, albeit a particularly mind-bending one.

Now, it is certainly possible that this column is nothing more than a second-circuit response to a perceived threat to my extant fourth-circuit imprint, or perhaps my third circuit has gone somewhat haywire. But shining the light of semiotic analysis on today's dominant media culture appears to indicate that someone, somewhere, was taking Mr. Wilson's eccentric but extremely interesting ramblings very seriously indeed. What else, one asks, is rising in company with Prometheus?

Insourcing & amnesty

April 10, 2006

I N 1986, Congress passed an amnesty that was, the American people were informed, going to end the invasion of illegal immigrants. As with most government solutions, it exacerbated the problem that it was nominally designed to solve, thus leading for Jorge Bush's call for a second "one time only" legalization of the millions of illegal immigrants already present in the United States.

Jorge and his fellow Republican traitors—for what else can one call those who look the other way while the nation is invaded by a force more numerous than the Europe-conquering Wehrmacht—attempt to justify their treason by arguing that immigrant labor is necessary to the economy. This is not only completely untrue—as the American economy will not only exist, but will also continue to be the largest in the world even if every legal and illegal immigrant went back to Mexico tomorrow—but also serves to distract Americans from a more damning realization.

As I have previously written, the primary reason for the decline in American real wages since 1973 is the mass entry of middle-class women, approximately 31 million in all, into the workforce. The secondary reason, and one that is nearly as significant, is legal and illegal immigration.

Two things must be kept in mind when dealing with deceptions of pro-immigration, corporatist commentators. First, the statistics they use are so incomplete that they amount to intentional dishonesty. For example, the 4.7 percent unemployment rate trumpeted so loudly last week does not count those who are in jail, have given up looking for work or are unwilling to work at the prevailing wage rates. It also equates part-time jobs with full-time jobs. But even using these flawed metrics, the Bureau of Labor Statistics reveals that the unemployment rate is far higher than is usually reported in the press, for example, the 6.2 percent rate of the second quarter of 2003 was actually 10.5 percent, by the BLS' own reckoning.

Of course, a simple comparison of the number of employed Americans to the total American population over 16 reveals that the real unemployment rate is much, much higher. In 2002, the employed labor force was 136.5 million, while the officially unemployed (8.4 million) plus the "Not in labor force" (72.7 million) was 81.1 million. Add to that the 1.9 million incarcerated who are not counted in the government figures and it becomes clear that the true American unemployment rate is 38 percent.

While it is true that not all of those unemployed wish to be employed, it is also true that one cannot assume that they would be similarly disinclined to work if their employment was better compensated. For as the law of supply and demand dictates, lower prices will always inspire a lower level of supply. Thus, given the large supply of untapped employment among the American citizenry, it is clear that legal and illegal immigrants are only reducing the price of labor, they are not supplying a resource that would otherwise be nonexistent.

Corporate support for increased immigration and the legalization of illegal workers can best be summarized as insourcing. Think about where illegal immigrants tend to work—almost always in the service industries. These are the sort of jobs that cannot be exported via outsourcing, because they require a physical presence at or near the customer. So, goes the corporatist thinking, if the service industries cannot go to the cheap labor, the cheap labor must be brought to the service industries.

Jesus Christ once asked what it profited a man to gain the world at the cost of his soul. It would be wise for Jorge Bush to consider what it will profit him to gain cheaper wages for the service industries at the cost of his country. Treasonous by nature and economics-challenged, one cannot expect Democrats to see any political downside to supporting immigration, especially as an influx of poor, uneducated "minorities" accustomed to overbearing governments can be safely expected to add to the Democratic vote totals. Pro-immigration Republicans, however, are committing long-term political suicide, and if the reaction of the nation to the recent Mexifornia protests is any indication, quite possibly short-term political suicide in 2006 as well.

Jorge's No Illegal Alien Left Behind agenda, as Mickey Kaus so aptly named the amnesty that dare not speak its name, has now struck out twice in three years. But Americans had better understand that it is not yet out, the con game is not yet over, and if they are foolish enough to bite on the next proposed bipartisan immigration reform bait, they will deserve the loss of their country that will soon inexorably follow.

In, but not of

April 17, 2005

THE RISE of the Religious Right was one of the more significant political stories in the last 20 years of American history. Unfortunately, its ultimate failure was preordained from the start, even if the moral and spiritual bankruptcy of the party it brought to power has only become widely understood in the last two years.

A desire to end the national abomination of abortion was the primary driving force behind the Religious Right's entry into politics. The theory was that electing a Republican president, House and Senate would lead to a pro-life majority on the Supreme Court. But 25 years and seven Republican Supreme Court justices later, no progress has been made on that front.

In fact, from a national perspective, it is clear that an invisible counterforce has made far more headway than the great bogeyman of the Democratic Party's fund-raising letters. Gay marriage was not an issue in 1980, now merely halting its advance is hailed as a great victory of sorts. Divorce rates are down, but only because fewer couples are bothering to marry in the first place. Now it is not only God and prayer that are banned from the public schools, but the Boy Scouts and anyone else insufficiently enthusiastic about men inserting foreign objects—safely covered in latex, of course—into their rectums.

Who would have ever imagined, 25 years ago, that the very words "Christmas" and "Easter" would be banned by government bodies and assiduously avoided by soulless corporations? If every action inspires an equal and opposite reaction, surely it would have been better if the Religious Right had remained in the churches.

Many recent political and social developments are rightly considered unwelcome by any sane Christian, and yet, they are no cause for individual despair. For if the fate of the nation and the prospects for the freedom of its citizens are all but sealed already, these things matter little, if indeed they matter at all, when viewed from an eternal perspective.

Time and space, the scientists tell us, are an illusion. So, too, are the mass hallucinations to which so many Americans still cling, from "democracy" and the fiction of our money to the so-called rule of law. But some verities remain. Christians in America must remember what Christians living under governments from ancient Rome to Communist China all knew very well: Earthly authority is evil. This does not, however, mean that it is illegitimate, indeed, the Apostle Paul writes precisely the opposite on several occasions in the New Testament.

Consider this apparent dichotomy. In Romans 13:6, Paul notes that "the authorities are God's servants." And yet he later notes in Ephesians 6:12 that the Christian struggle "is not against flesh and blood, but against the rulers, against the authorities, against the powers of this dark world and against the spiritual forces of evil in the heavenly realms."

But nowhere does Paul state the human authorities are good or that the spiritual authorities are illegitimate. Indeed, Jesus Christ never disputed Satan's ability to deliver on the promise to give him all the kingdoms of the world, if only he would bow down. So, we must struggle against God's servants?

This seems confusing, but perhaps a fictional example from *The Lord of the Rings* might help sort through the confusion. In the absence of Aragorn the King, the Steward of Gondor, Denethor, rules the White City. Denethor is not only mad, but he is arguably evil, being soft on Mordor as well as harboring a certain patricidal inclination. Does this make his rule illegitimate? As Paul would say, by no means! The evil Steward is still due the same honor and respect that is normally due the rightful king in his royal absence.

The key, I think, is that we are to give nothing that is not owed, and the Christian does not owe obedience to the state, but to God alone.

As the current president repeatedly insists, Americans live in a democracy, or possibly in the tattered remnants that remain of their former constitutional republic. Christians, however, are citizens of an eternal monarchy and they must never forget that loyalty to the Risen King always comes before any lesser loyalties.

Patriotic anthems notwithstanding, America is, like Rome, merely another fallen earthly power, and one day she too shall fall amid chaos and fire. Render her the honor and respect that she is due, but place not your trust in her. The way to the Father, after all, does not come through two-party systems and ballot boxes, but through the Son.

Nike University

April 24, 2006

OW THAT hundreds of thousands of parents have discovered for themselves how the public school system is an incredibly inefficient and ineffective means of providing children with an education, it is interesting to note that some of them are beginning to turn skeptical eyes on the hallowed institution of the university.

I've written before regarding my own doubts about the logic of college, but a conversation with a friend who attended the Minnesota Association of Christian Home Educators annual conference last weekend got me thinking about the issue again. My friend, whose wife homeschools their children, had attended a workshop titled "Credentials without College," which resonated with him when he realized that he had never once had an employer ask for his diploma or review his college transcript.

What's particularly interesting about my friend's perspective is that he graduated from one of the more expensive and exclusive private universities in the country (picking up keys from Phi Beta Kappa and Tau Beta Phi in the process). But not only did he find his education there to be largely superfluous, it actually got in the way of his career development, for as he informed me during our conversation, his senior year was largely a matter of taking philosophy courses while waiting to graduate and work full-time for the company he'd been with for the three previous summers.

My experience was similar. I remember being called a few years ago by a European headhunter who was looking for a technology executive. The headhunter was puzzled by the way in which my career did not coincide with my education, wondering how I had learned the management skills that brought me to her attention when my degrees were in economics and Asian literature. But learning and formal education are not synonymous, and any correlation between what we study in college and what we subsequently do to earn a living is often mere coincidence. Even in the case of the more technical fields and the professions, the vast majority of that which is taught in college is outdated by at least a few years. One need merely look at the equipment in any university computer lab to see that.

When confronted with these facts, university cheerleaders often like to say that a college education, especially a liberal arts education, is not about preparation for a specific career, but learning how to learn and think critically instead, providing skills that are useful in any job. While this may have been true 100 years ago, it is certainly not true now. A 10-minute conversation with any recent Ivy League graduate will suffice to reveal how even very bright young individuals are not being taught how to think critically or logically, and worse, are permitted to continue wallowing in their parochial ignorance of the world and its history.

What college boils down to is a brand name stamped on the graduate for the benefit of corporate consumers. The large international corporations, like wealthy, upscale shoppers, prefer to make their selections from among the elite brands—the Harvards, Oxfords, Stanfords and Yales. At the other end of the scale, the small businesses paw through resumes from the Wal-Mart equivalents, hunting for bargains in the public universities and no-name two-year institutions.

Still, it is vital to note that to say something is merely a brand is very different than asserting it is without worth. One need merely look at Microsoft or Nike to understand that there is inherent value in a brand because consumers harbor such regard for them. If Man was a perfectly rational being, no one would buy Microsoft Office for $499 when OpenOffice 2.0.2 provides compatibility and 98 percent of the functionality for an infinitely better price, being a free download.

So, what is a brand worth to my child? That is the important question that every parent should ask when considering college applications. And university presidents will soon be forced to wrestle with that question themselves, as the gap between the perceived value of the brand and its actual value to the corporate consumer becomes more obvious with every inflated grade, every graduate with an English, sociology or philosophy degree and every new Women Talking About Feelings program.

Technology has an uncanny way of puncturing such structural vacuities. Already universities are flirting with various forms of Internet-based distance education, and once a brand-name university realizes that it is far more profitable to charge $1,000 per class to 10,000 online students than $40,000 in annual tuition to 1,000 on-campus freshmen without harming the brand, the next great revolution in higher education will begin.

Striking at the heart of the schools

May 1, 2006

THE LEVEL OF ENTHUSIASM varies from region to region, but there is no question that sports is more important than education to most high-school students. This is as true of homeschooled children as of their private- and public-school counterparts. For while personal instruction tailored to the individual is a much superior method of learning algebra, Latin and Shakespeare, it is impossible to play football alone unless a Playstation is involved.

The laws vary from state to state, but in those school districts where homeschool participation in sports is banned, parents who wanted to give their children the chance to participate in team sports often opted for lawsuits and political lobbying in the interest of forcing public schools to allow athletes not attending those schools to play on their sports teams. However, this is a short-sighted and sub-optimal strategy for five reasons.

First, it teaches reliance on the courts and legislatures to correct a perceived injustice rather than personal initiative. Is running to Mommy Government at the first sign of difficulty truly the lesson most homeschooling parents wish to teach their children?

Second, by creating an emotional involvement with the local public school, athletic participation strengthens the very institution that should be encouraged to wither away.

Third, even if such efforts are successful, the ability to participate is unlikely to be permitted for long, as what a legislature can give under pressure, it can also take away.

Fourth, it fails to build an alternative structure for future generations of homeschooled children.

And fifth, it often doesn't work.

And while it may be churlish and unjust to deny homeschooled children the right to play for the same institutions that are funded by their parents' taxes, one can hardly expect coaches and athletic directors who belong to the National Education Association to embrace what is quite literally the competition and a potential threat to their financial livelihood.

So I found it encouraging to note in the *Washington Times* that just as their predecessors did not shirk from providing children with an academic option, modern homeschoolers are beginning to work together to offer their children sporting options as well:

> *Home-schooling parents in Frederick County, learning that their children could not play on high school football teams, decided not to punt. They formed their own squad instead. "My son and daughter have not been able to play football or cheer because the [community] programs end at eighth grade," says Terry Delph, who with fellow home-school mother Nancy Werking co-founded the Central Maryland Christian Crusaders....*

> *The Crusaders and their cheerleader squad for girls yesterday held their second informal practice at St. Stephen's Reformed Episcopal Church in Eldersburg, Md. Official practices are set to begin July 31. The football team currently includes 28 boys, while nine girls have signed up as cheerleaders.*

The separation of school and sport is hardly a new concept. Already, some of the most elite teams in the country have very little to do with school— the basketball academies that regularly send players to the NBA and NCAA Division One programs aren't exactly devoted to academics—and in Europe nearly all sporting competition revolves around athletic clubs, not schools, which has likely helped Europe surpass the United States in both academic and athletic performance.

Public schools that can't teach children how to read or speak English are nothing new, but when a team full of NBA All-Stars can't even medal in basketball, then one must truly fear for the future of America.

Some thinking outside the conventional will no doubt be necessary, but allies may well be found in the churches, community centers and even professional sports teams. For example, some of the richest and most famous professional teams in the world hail from multi-sport athletic clubs, including Real Madrid and FC Barcelona, which also sponsor numerous children's squads from the first grade level on up.

It will not be an easy or a short-term endeavor to recreate an entire sporting infrastructure, but it can be done, and with the energetic growth of home-schooling, it is quite likely that it will be done. And as with standardized tests and spelling bees, success in the field of sports will eventually attract the best athletes to these extra-curricular sporting organizations, thus furthering the American enthusiasm for the development of children devoid of government control.

Hot-air Republicans

May 8, 2006

WHILE THE WORD is not yet devoid of all meaning, the last five years have been witness to a corruption of the word "conservative" that earlier rotted out the once-noble concept of liberalism. To be liberal once meant to be pro-freedom and skeptical of state intervention. Now, it signifies limits on free speech and free association, no limits on government spending and state intervention.

If a verb such as "to be" can be called into doubt, (or at least its present tense, third-person singular), how much easier it is to redefine an adjective!

Keen political observers will note that what passes for the "conservative" commentariat follows opinion as much as it leads. With the exception of a few mavericks such as Michelle Malkin and John Derbyshire, they followed the pro-amnesty, open-borders party line until quite recently, when the mood of the American people began to turn very ugly at the sight of a horde of illegals marching and demanding more of the non-existent rights they have been claiming for decades.

It is ironic that such "conservatives" argue that illegal immigration is good for the American economy, given that they are theoretically adherents of Adam Smith's capitalism, which states, among many other things, the Law that as supply goes up, that price must go down, given constant demand. One would have to be a serious sophist indeed to miss the application of that law to labor prices, which have declined more than 16 percent while 30 million legal and illegal immigrants have entered the country and provided that price-suppressing supply of which Mr. Smith speaks so highly.

So, the economy is healthier while Americans are making less money. Pro-immigration economists will point out that household income is higher, but this is only because more married women are working than in 1973, the year real wage rates peaked. It is interesting to note that these "conservative" commentators are therefore defending a practice which is directly linked to the profoundly non-conservative value of removing mothers from their children.

No doubt the next thing these "conservatives" will be championing is government-funded day care.

It's also remarkable to mark how poorly the so-called conservative commentariat seems to understand its principles. For example, Mark Alexander wrote on TownHall, while complaining of how the president had failed conservatives domestically:

> As the titular head of the Republican Party, President George W. Bush has distinguished himself as a conservative when it comes to foreign policy....

But as real conservatives once said of a Reichsfuhrer, circa 1933, "tell me one thing he wanted to conserve?"

There is nothing inherently conservative about a willingness to wage war. Indeed, the presidents responsible for World War I, World War II, the Korean War and the Vietnam War were all Democrats of a distinctly liberal—in the modern American sense—stripe.

And Jorge's jihad for democracy isn't conservative in the slightest—it is Woodrow Wilsonism gone mad and transferred from Europe to the Middle East. Interestingly enough, some of the current World Democratic Revolutionists have strong links to Trotsky's World Socialist Revolution, which raises some real questions about just who, precisely, is zooming who?

It is time for conservatives to abandon their allegiance to the Republican Party, which in its tripartite power has revealed itself to be far from the party of freedom and small government it billed itself to be when it claimed the presidency in 1980. Yes, this means that the Democrats will win in 2008, which they are sure to do anyhow when the Elder Gods of the Inner Circle dig up the corpse of Bob Dole, rename him and offer him as a sacrifice to the Lizard Queen.

Power draws scoundrels like rotting flesh draws flies. With the success of the Republican Party and Fox News, you can be sure that half of the "conservative" commentariat and three-quarters of the "Republican" politicians are in service to no higher principle than their own advancement.

And while conservatives can continue to play along and serve these frauds if they wish, at least they need not do so in ignorance. As Trent Reznor urged: "Bow down before the one you serve. You're going to get what you deserve."

Against a fence

May 15, 2006

DEAR JORGE plans to address the nation tonight, a speech wherein he will almost surely attempt to deceive citizens into believing that he does not wish the mass migration from Mexico to continue unabated. He will likely offer some negligible resources for law enforcement and border security—resources which will never materialize—in return for an amnesty program that will grant American citizenship to the Mexican nationals who have helped lower America's wage rates by 16 percent over the last 32 years.

And he will be lying, again, just as he lied when he said: "Massive deportation of the people here is unrealistic—it's just not going to work."

It couldn't possibly take more than eight years to deport 12 million illegal aliens, many of whom don't speak English and are not integrated into American society. In fact, the hysterical response to the post-rally enforcement rumors tends to indicate that the mere announcement of a massive deportation program would probably cause a third of that 12 million to depart for points south within a week.

The complete absurdity of stating that enforcement of the national immigration laws is unrealistic, while simultaneously insisting that reshaping the entire Dar-al Islam to the liking of the World Demokratic Revolutionists is perfectly feasible, should be obvious. Dear Jorge's deceits are not only transparent, they are downright insulting to anyone capable of considering two concepts at the same time.

Unlike the Libertarian Party, I do not subscribe to a two-way open-borders policy, for reasons I explained previously. I do, however, believe that the chief hallmark of a free society is the freedom to leave it, as evidenced by the "no exit" policies so often adopted by socialist and other totalitarian governments.

The problem with a fence is that it works both ways. As it stands today, the only government agency that objects to an American leaving the country is the Internal Revenue Service, which weirdly attempts to claim income tax for up to 10 years after an American leaves the country and his citizenship behind. This is mostly because apart from the farsighted Fred Reed, few Americans now wish to leave what is still a wealthy and relatively free country.

But that may not always be the case, especially given the increasing probability that the Lizard Queen will be squatting on the Cherry Blossom Throne three years from now. And a government that believes the importation of low-skill, low-income Mexicans is necessary is not one that is likely to smile benevolently upon the departure of high-skill, high-income Americans.

Dialectic has long been the political elite's favored means of manipulating public opinion. They push and the people pull. Action-reaction-synthesis. In this case, the action is government-abetted illegal immigration, the reaction is the massive outcry for a fence and the synthesis is a self-imprisoned people.

A fence is not necessary, for there are other means of efficiently resolving the problem without resorting to such an obviously dangerous measure. Instant deportation policies, employer fines and bounty programs combined with the denial of all social services to non-citizens would suffice to settle the matter without the need to imprison the American citizenry. As the Minutemen have proven, again, unleashing the power of motivated private citizens is far more efficient than relying on government bureaucrats.

A conspiracy uncovered

May 22, 2006

FOR YEARS, Italian soccer fans have watched skeptically as Juventus collected scudetto after scudetto, winning nearly twice as many Serie A championships than its closest rival, AC Milan. But spectator cynicism grew with each last-minute penalty gifted to the team from Turin whenever a goal was needed to avert an unexpected defeat—I myself watched in disbelief when Juve, maintaining a narrow one-game advantage over the surging rossoneri with two games left in the season, scored three goals in the first eight minutes against a Siena team that had only given up 24 in 17 previous games.

The fact that eight of Siena's players, plus their assistant manager and another assistant coach, were all on loan from Juve was merely a coincidence, fans were assured by the Italian sports media, which often complains about the public's tendency to see conspiracies everywhere.

But, as it turns out, even the most paranoid fan's suspicions proved to be far too conservative compared to what was really going on behind the scenes. Over the last two weeks, Italian front-page headlines more commonly associated with wars have been announcing astounding revelations in what may prove to be one of the biggest sporting scandals in history.

Imagine if it was learned that Patriots coach Bill Belicheck had engineered New England's recent run at dynasty status by suborning the head of NFL officiating through bribes and threats. Imagine that in the place of solitary hit ref Dick Bavetta, David Stern was found to have 25 made men dressed as referees fixing the results of 82 games over the course of two seasons.

That's the American equivalent of what Juve's general manager, Luciano Moggi, is now known to have done. Magistrates in four cities are investigating further shenanigans even as transcripts of Moggi's cell-phone conversations are being published daily in the newspapers. Here's an excerpt from one of his discussions with Paolo Bergamo, the man responsible for referee assignments in Serie A:

> *Moggi: Bertini, Paparesta, Trefoloni, Ragalbuto, I had put in Tombolini, but before he screwed up with Lazio (a Roman team), I don't know about him here, he messed up, he gave a penalty…*

> *Bergamo: …uh…*

> *Moggi: So those were the referees I put the heat on!*

> *Bergamo: Rodomonti in the place of Tombolini, OK?*

> *Moggi: Or Rodomonti in Tombolini's place, that's all right.*

> *Bergamo: However it's done, it's the same, you see… And honestly, I wanted to hold Tombolini out for a turn because he messed up. If we don't do it this way, wouldn't you punish him?*

> *Moggi: Yes… yes…*

The repercussions have already been impressive. Juve's entire board has resigned, its publicly traded shares are down 50 percent and the club that Fortune Magazine rated No. 6 in the world is now worth $350 million less than it was two weeks ago.

So, why is any of this of interest to Americans, who care little about Italy and even less about Serie A soccer? I believe there is a lesson to be learned here, in the way the scandal offers a momentary glimpse behind the veil of the world according to the mainstream media—a glimpse into the way in which the real power and money games are played around the world.

Conspiracy theorists are accustomed to being scoffed at, even as their paranoid predictions prove to be more reliable than the sober analyses of mainstream experts. To be sure, not all of them can be true—I'm particularly skeptical of those involving UFOs and aliens myself. But before you scoff at the next wild assertion you encounter, remember that only two weeks ago, all the experts were insisting that the game of calcio was clean, too.

3rd-party freedom lovers unite!

May 29, 2006

And for Republicans, the most shocking, most shameful thing of all is that this act to vastly swell the number of future Democratic voters, to bring about "the greatest expansion of the welfare state in 35 years" (Robert Rector), to kick working-class Americans in the teeth, to render meaningless the very concepts of our nation and our citizenship—in fact, to shove U.S. citizens off the sidewalk so that foreigners can be awarded special privilieges not available to us—this appalling monstrosity was cheered through by a Republican Senate at the urging of a Republican president. For shame, for shame, for shame.

—John Derbyshire, *National Review Online*, May 26, 2006

Congress had a chance to come out swinging against corruption—to demonstrate, amid a slew of tawdry scandals, its recognition that public officials are subject to the same laws as ordinary citizens. The Republican leadership in particular should have seen an opportunity to redirect attention from its caucus' lapses to a Democrat's crude criminality. They chose, instead, to rally around an apparent swindler. We can think of 100,000 reasons why this will be remembered as an unparalleled blunder.

—The editors, *National Review*, May 25, 2006

FOR FIVE YEARS, Republicans have been wondering what in the world is going on inside the minds of their leaders. To be sure, there were no shortage of treacherous stabs in the back even before the current president's father was asking the American people to read his lips, but those could be explained away as political strategies—however incompetent—and individual failings.

And the Republican leadership always found the grass roots willing to swallow such betrayals in the name of the long march toward power. Conservatives were able to tolerate much in the name of expanding the big tent and obtaining Republican majorities in the House, Senate and Supreme Court to provide a Republican president with what Ronald Reagan lacked, effective partnership across the three branches of federal government.

But Republicans have looked on, aghast, as the man they believed would be Reagan's heir instead turned out to be the illegitimate heir to Woodrow Wilson and Lyndon Baines Johnson. From his bizarre dabbles in Islamic theology to his enthusiastic embrace of activist, ever-expanding central government power, George W. Bush has sold out every Christian, every nationalist, every constitutionalist, every libertarian and every conservative in the Republican Party.

Still, while this was tremendously disappointing to the naive grass roots, it wasn't entirely unexpected. It is a family tradition, after all. But what appears to have finally proven to be the last straw for even Republican die-hards is the way in which the entire Republican congressional leadership joined him in his rush to sell out America's national sovereignty and, even more mystifyingly, defended Democratic politicians—their nominal enemies—from the consequences of their criminal actions.

As Arthur Conan Doyle once wrote, "When you have eliminated the impossible, whatever remains, however improbable, must be the truth."

It is now impossible to argue Republican politicians are any different than Democratic politicians with regard to their intrinsic ideology or their long-term goals for the nation. The intraparty debate merely concerns the speed with which the Constitution is abandoned, the sovereign rights of Man are eliminated and global federalist government is instituted.

Reform is impossible. One can no more reform a political party than one can reform a Fortune 500 corporation. Competition is the only answer; if one does not like IBM's computers, one does not apply for a job in IBM's mail room in the hopes of one day becoming CEO and changing the company's direction, one starts a company selling rival computers. There are a plethora of examples of successful reformations by competition in the corporate world, and one can even find them in American political history; where are the Whigs today?

There are certainly ideological differences between "third" parties such as the Libertarian Party, the Constitution Party and the current American Party, but these pale in comparison with each parties differences with the bi-factional ruling party of Democratic-Republicans. It is time to set differences aside and form an American Alliance that subscribes to the following three arch-principles:

Could not even a conscientious Green sign on to that? Everything else is secondary, because without those three principles, all else can be modified at the momentary whim of those who hold the levers of power. Yes, the birth of a competitive new party will take time; yes, it would mean a Rodham presidency in 2008 (although since the Lizard Queen's victory is already in the cards, that's a feeble objection), but the reality is this:

You are either with the concept of American liberty or against it. The Democratic-Republicans have proven themselves to be firmly against it. Either an American Alliance will restore America to herself, or her people will be swallowed up by the bureaucratic Brussels on the Potomac that is now aborning.

God's plan for America

June 5, 2006

A PASTOR at a church I occasionally attend preached an interesting series of sermons a while back, as is his wont. In the sermons, he taught that politics is not a central concern for either individual Christians or the church, that God is neither a Democrat nor a Republican and that George W. Bush is the Antichrist.

(OK, I made that last one up. Everyone knows the Lizard Queen makes a much more likely candidate for the Antichrist. At least "W" doesn't eat puppies.)

The pastor's sermons were more effective than the usual Sunday lectures in that they inspired a powerful response from the church membership. Unfortunately, that response was for 30 percent of the church members to leave the church.

Now, I have no problem with anyone leaving a church for any reason; it's one of the many ways to demonstrate how the freedom in Jesus Christ is greater than that of any worldly government. But I do find it peculiar that there are so many people who make national politics a central part, if not the central point, of their theology. And I'm saying this as a member of the Christian right by blood; when Ralph Reed was in town with the Christian Coalition, he stayed at my parent's house.

While it's true that the vast majority of the Founding Fathers were Christians—nearly half of the signers of the Declaration of Independence were theologians—it's also obvious they understood the difference between a nation of Christians and a Christian nation. It is without question that America was once a nation of Christians; it is rather less obvious that it is still one.

Consider the state of the seven deadly sins in America:

1. Lust: Pamela Anderson and the Pussycat Dolls are famous. Enough said.

2. Gluttony: 64 percent of Americans are overweight.

3. Avarice: The concept of bling-bling was not invented in France.

4. Sloth: We pay farmers not to farm, we pay workers not to work.

5. Wrath: 5.5 murders per 100,000 is better than in the past, but still a high rate by world standards.

6. Envy: The basis for our progressive tax system and most advertising concepts.

7. Pride: Ask anyone from Argentina to New Zealand about this.

None of this should be taken as a criticism of the country. After all, America has rather more reason for harboring a sense of national pride than, say, Uzbekistan. But if we judge the nation by the Christian measure, its metaphorical fruits, one finds it very difficult to believe that the land of 40 million abortions and cradle-to-grave feminism is in the good graces of the life-affirming, children-loving God the Father.

There is, I suspect, an unconscious stream of omniderigence underlying the concept of divine American exceptionalism. Either God has inordinately blessed America because of the unique qualities of her inhabitants or because He has a special plan for America. The problem with the first possibility should be obvious in light of the character and behavior of said inhabitants; the problem with the latter is that it requires believing that the Christian God is responsible for the death of millions of unborn children, the establishment of transnational globalism and Paris Hilton.

If you believe that George W. Bush is the president because God wanted him to be, you must also accept that God also wanted Bill Clinton, Jimmy Carter and Franklin Delano Roosevelt in office as well. Moreover, those who believe possessing supreme military power for the last 60 years proves divine favor would do well to remember that God's word expressly tells us about

His plans for past superpowers when He sent the Assyrian and Babylonian empires against the kingdoms of Israel and Judea.

And then recall the U.S. military is now occupying the land in which the crumbled remnants of those long-vanished empires can be found.

The vanishing conservative

June 12, 2006

I AM NOT A CONSERVATIVE. While I respect genuine conservatives and appreciate the value of conserving cultural traditions, the Judeo-Christian ethic and the foundations of civilization, conservatives have always struck me as the political equivalent of *catenaccio*.

Invented by the Austrian coach of the Swiss national team, the defense-oriented system was embraced by the Italians and used in Italy for over three decades, hence the name. But over time, attack-minded strategies were developed in response, most notably Holland's famous Total Football System, which broke down the bolted door. No manager actually implements *catenaccio* today and references to it are mostly ironic and situational, made, for example, when a team is protecting a lead or is overmatched and playing for a tie.

The problem with both *catenaccio* and conservatism is that any positive movement is largely the result of luck, not purpose. They are defensive strategies, and as any military historian will tell you; defense never beats offense, it only staves off defeat for a time. In the end, even the most intrepid defenders will weary and the gates will finally fall to the barbarians.

Although it sounds ludicrous in a time when conservatives nominally rule the airwaves, the legislative, judicial and executive branches; 2006 may well be one day viewed as a low point for the American conservative. For politics is not mathematics and it knows no transitive law. It is true that many institutions and individuals are Republican, and certainly the Republican Party is supposed to be America's conservative party, but this does not equal conservative dominance of the political scene.

For neither the institutions nor the individuals can be relied upon to work toward conservative goals. Most of the conservative actions taken in the last 20 years can be best described as holding actions, not actions intended to lower the rising tide of central government influence or combat societal devolution.

The malaise is movement-wide. Indeed, it is debatable as to which group is in worse shape, the "conservative" politicians or the "conservative" commentariat. While the leftward drift of the administration and the Congress have not escaped notice despite the best efforts of its cheerleaders to play it down; the abandonment of principle in favor of pragmatism has caused many in the so-called conservative media to do the likewise.

Just this week, one could listen to Michael Medved playing the left's favorite game of denouncing another commentator—me, actually—as a Nazi while watching nominal conservatives falling all over each other in the competition to be the most outraged by Ann Coulter's precision-guided comments about the ever-grieving "Witches of East Brunswick."

(Given that there are thousands of people who lost loved ones in the September 11 attacks who Coulter did not criticize, it is more than a little disingenuous to pretend that her criticism is somehow inappropriate or misplaced. And just what is the statute of limitations on celebrity-victim status anyhow?)

Indeed, what with Michelle Malkin pushing FDR's internment program, Ben Shapiro, Sean Hannity and numerous others pushing Woodrow Wilson's foreign policy, Larry Kudlow pushing Richard Nixon's monetary policies and the editors of *National Review* harboring a Harry Truman-style crush on the United Nations, one has to wonder if a liberal media is redundant these days.

The word "liberal" once meant something very different than it does today. It rather looks as if the concept of a "conservative" is in the process of undergoing similar etymological evolution. Regardless, it appears the bolted door has been unlocked and is hanging open on loose hinges.

Sucked in by Saracens

June 19, 2006

F EW REMEMBER that events in the Middle East, despite the seeming chaos, are going according to plan. Unfortunately, that plan is the one ascribed to Osama bin Laden and it remains in effect regardless of whether the first great bogeyman of the 21st century is still alive or not.

Americans have seemingly forgotten that according to bin Laden, the primary purpose of the September 11 attacks was to lure America into an engagement with the forces of the Dar al-Islam that would ultimately cause the USA to abandon its involvement in the Middle East. This plan would appear to have gone horribly awry, of course, following the lightning-like conquests of Afghanistan and Iraq and the subsequent military occupations.

However, I was recently re-reading an old favorite, Sir Charles Oman's *A History of the Art of War in the Middle Ages, Volume One, 378 to 1278 AD* and a chapter on the grand strategy of the Crusades caught my attention. It contained a pertinent passage in which the historian laments the failure of Christendom's crusaders to avail themselves of the lessons learned by the Byzantine generals and criticizes them for ignoring the instructions recorded for fighting Muslim armies by the Emperor Leo in his classic *Tactica*.

> *Most notable of all is the evident inability of the Franks to learn from the unhappy experiences of their predecessors. The thousands of veterans who drifted back from the East did not succeed in teaching their successors the precautions appropriate to Turkish warfare. Fifty years after the first Crusade, Conrad III and Louise VII committed exactly the same mistakes as the contemporaries of Godfrey and Bohemund... It seemed that the art of learning by experience hardly existed in the military circles of the West. The description of the faults of the Frank as a soldier which Maurice wrote in*

580, and Leo the Wise repeated in 900 might still be utilised almost word for word in describing the Crusaders of 1150.

Now, this would be an unfair criticism of the U.S. military's tactics in the Middle East as no doubt every West Pointer at the Pentagon has read both Leo and Oman. Certainly the American forces in Iraq and Afghanistan possess more accurate knowledge of the ground than Sir Charles would have believed possible thanks to GPS systems and air supremacy; they make the most sophisticated use of combined arms ever known to Man, they do not abandon their strong points without caution and they are always kept well-supplied with provisions.

And yet, there is a close and defining relationship between a culture's preferred tactics and its strategies. As Victor Davis Hanson pointed out in *Culture and Carnage*, the extreme lethality of Western tactics stems at least in part from the intrinsic desire of Western strategists to engage the enemy and bring matters to a speedy and decisive close. The Eastern way of warfare, by contrast, revolves around deception, false retreats and constant attempts to entrap the enemy into making fatal blunders through overconfidence. It is a much more patient concept designed to painstakingly wear down an enemy over time instead of seeking to destroy him through a single, crushing blow.

Thus, it seems oddly familiar to read complaints of how the insurgents will not fight fair, how they pop up to fire their rocket-propelled grenades and disappear in much the same way Turkish horse-archers once similarly—and just as harmlessly—annoyed the mailed Frankish knights against whom they could not stand in close combat. The ubiquitous placement of IEDs is reminiscent of the old practice of burning the grasslands in order to deny forage for the Crusaders' horses and making troop movements more dangerous.

And it is striking to see how American troops have been forced to remain inside fortress-like defensive positions in Baghdad's Green Zone and the other coalition bases in Afghanistan and Iraq, from which they only emerge on heavily armed patrols. Indeed, it would seem morbidly fitting to name these bases after Acre, Antioch, Montferrand, Krak and Akkar, the great castles that allowed the ill-fated Kingdom of Jerusalem and the three other Crusading principalities to survive much longer than might have otherwise been expected.

It is important to remember that America is not the first nation to occupy territory in the Middle East. The Russians controlled more of Afghanistan than we currently do, and yet they were forced to withdraw after only a decade. The Crusaders held Acre, the key to the Holy Lands, from 1104 to 1291, (except for a four-year interlude from 1187 to 1191), but as Christendom's will gradually failed, even this strong point fell in the end. As the following passage from Ludolf of Suchem shows, the more things change, the more they stay the same.

> As the Mongol armies began their advance into the Near East, there was for a time some hope that they might cooperate with the Christian powers of the Near East against the Muslim armies of that area. St. Louis, in fact, continued to cherish the hope—not entirely without foundation—that the Mongols might in time become Christian converts.... The battle of Ain Jalud was of major importance, for it demonstrated both the prowess of the Egyptians and the vincibility of the Mongols.... The hope of joint Latin-Mongol cooperation in Palestine had failed.

> Egyptian campaigns against the Latin kingdom came thick and fast. In 1265 Caesarea, Haifa and Arsuf all fell to the Sultan. The following year saw the loss of all the important Latin holdings in Galilee. In 1268 Antioch was taken.... Pope Gregory X (1271–1276) labored valiantly to excite some general enthusiasm for another great Crusade, but he labored in vain. The failure of his appeal was variously ascribed by the pope's advisers to the laziness and vice of the European nobility and to clerical corruption. Though each of these factors may have been in part to blame, a more basic reason for the failure seems to have been the debasement of the ideal of the Crusade itself.

It is possible that the democratized Muslims of Iraq and Afghanistan will prove more helpful to the West's cause than the Mongols of yore, but given that public enthusiasm for the neocons' World Democratic Revolution has never approached a crusading zeal and is flagging already, a similar retreat is surely in the cards. Reclaiming the initiative and striking out at Iran may look appealing to the neocons' nervous strategists, but then, King Guy was of the opinion that pushing on to Tiberias was a good idea too.

The Brothel or the Burqah

June 26, 2006

O NE OF THE SURPRISES of the 21st century is the revival of slavery around the world. From the Chinese laogai to the brothels of Berlin, from Darfur to Darby, humans are being bought and sold as property. In fact, it is estimated that 27 million individuals are currently enslaved, nearly double the number that were owned as slaves throughout the entire history of American slavery.

This revival of slavery is more than a little ironic, especially in the West, considering it comes at a time when the equalitarian dogma of sexual sameness is taken for granted and millionaire descendants of African slaves demand reparations for acts committed over 14 decades ago, while ignoring Africans enslaved today.

In examining this issue, it is important to understand that slavery has been, throughout most of human history, an accepted institution. Every culture and every religion has embraced it, from the civilized Egyptians, Greeks and Romans to the barbarian Celts, Mongols and Zulus. Slaves have been owned by Christians, by Jews, Muslims, Hindus, Buddhists and atheists alike.

There are only two cultures of which I am aware that have banned slavery without external pressure. One is Japan during the Momoyama Period of the 1580s, the other is early nineteenth-century Britain. But while the Japanese ban was inspired by one man's dictate and did not long survive his successor, the British ban was inspired by Protestant Christianity and was spread by the daunting influence of Imperial British arms, everywhere from Europe to Asia, Africa and America.

But much has changed in the 199 years since William Wilberforce and his alliance of Quakers and Evangelicals led parliament to pass the Abolition of the Slave Trade Bill of 1807. Great Britain is no longer a devoutedly Christian empire, it is now a post-Christian province of the avowedly secular European

Union where only 1.2 percent of the population bothers to attend Anglican services on a weekly basis. And the rest of Western Europe has seen a similar decline in religious belief, from Iceland to Italy.

Some insist it is merely a coincidence that this descent into post-Christianity has seen a concomitant rise in slavery, but this fails to recognize that slavery is the historical norm, even as hundreds of thousands of women are enslaved throughout the countries of the West.

> *In Europe alone, officials estimate more than 200,000 women and girls— one-quarter of all women trafficked globally—are smuggled out of Central and Eastern Europe and the former Soviet republics each year; the bulk of whom end up working as enslaved prostitutes. Almost half are transported to Western Europe. Roughly a quarter end up in the United States.*

—Preston Mendenhall, *MSNBC*

At the same time, women are turning to Islam at a surprising rate. While many have heard Islam is the fastest-growing religion around the world, fewer are aware that eighty percent of converts to Islam are women. Islam For Today even maintains a website with testimonies from Irish, Slovak, German and American women who have reverted, to use the Islamic parlance.

The reason for these seemingly senseless trends is that the godless faith of secular humanism, of which feminism is but one aspect, is a barren one. It offers neither the moral guidance and aspiration that is required by men nor the sense of security and affirmation that is sought after by women. Rejecting outdated notions of good and evil in its determined relativism, modern neopagans find it impossible to explain to the slaver why it is wrong for him to seek the profits to be gained by enslaving another individual, much less offer him a worthier goal.

And in an increasingly amoral and brutal environment, it is not difficult to understand why women deprived of the protections offered by traditional Judeo-Christian society—indeed, the very notion that they might need such protection is now perceived as an insult—should turn to a religious structure that guarantees them a place, however inferior, where at least they will be valued for themselves and not as inexpensive property.

When one considers that a pretty young blonde sells for between $700 and $2,500, it's no wonder that aging feminists rage about the low value men place on them. You could probably get Gloria Steinhem for less than the price of a decent bottle of scotch and Catherine MacKinnon for a Red Bull and a pack of chewing gum. Naomi Wolf would run a bit more, of course, since a discerning master would no doubt appreciate her ability to advise him on his wardrobe.

The usual liberal canards about changing society and education are hopelessly irrelevant in the face of amoral greed, lust and fear revealed by these twin trends. This is not to say that there is no answer for them, but a fallen world that has already rejected the transformational power of Jesus Christ in favor of godless philosophy and unprincipled moral pablum is unlikely to consider it, let alone embrace it as the logical solution.

The human spirit, like nature, abhors a vacuum. It is looking increasingly likely that the spiritual vacuum of the 21st century will offer women a choice between the brothel and the burqah as their equalitarian dream shatters around them.

In defense of the *New York Times*

July 3, 2006

I AM NO FAN of the *New York Times*. It is a pompous, outdated media organization that combines a dedication to poisonous ideology with a predilection for mediocre art and faux eurostylism. Its reporters are columnists who write opinion columns that pass for news stories, while its columnists are talentless divas whose ignorance of politics and economics is only exceeded by their unfamiliarity with world history.

The *New York Times* is the fever swamp from which a myriad of infectious and debilitating memes spread throughout the mainstream media and into the mind of America. All of this is obvious to even the occasional observer, I merely mention it so that the reader will understand that my defense of the old hag is a reluctant one.

Like many of the commentators who have waxed apoplectic following the *New York Times'* revelations of the administration's financial spying on the SWIFT system, I was surprised by the breaking news. However, my surprise was due solely to the fact that it passed for news, considering the panoply of data-mining operations in which the U.S. government is already known to be involved.

From Carnivore and Echelon to the giant government database currently being constructed by the credit card companies—in fact, at first glance, I thought that's what the *New York Times* was reporting—the Clinton and Bush administrations have made great strides at turning America into the Panopticon of dystopian science fiction visions. Indeed, much of what went into Patriot Acts I and II was first conceived by the Clinton administration in 1993, as Al Gore's concept for a Directorate of Central Law Enforcement presaged George Bush's new Department of Homeland Security.

The only significant difference is that the shock of 9-11 enabled the Bush administration to do what its predecessor could not in ramming a giant, pre-prepared assault on American liberties through the Congress. And like the Patriot Acts, the SWIFT program will do nothing to protect national security, despite all of the posturing and ignorant howling on the part of the administration's defendants in the supposedly conservative commentariat.

Arnaud de Borchgrave of the *Washington Times* reports that the total expenditure for the attacks on the two U.S. embassies, the USS Cole, 9-11, the Madrid train system and the London Underground was $625,000, spent over a period of eight years. SWIFT transfers amount to $6,000,000,000 daily, so this spy program isn't comparable to looking for a needle in a haystack, it is closer to looking for a needle in Nebraska. It defies credibility to argue that this program will locate a single terrorist given the way in which Muslims prefer using the Islamic hawala system to wire transfers, much less that its exposure somehow threatens American national security. And despite all the barking by the media hounds, no one has even tried to argue that this "vital program" has, in fact, done so.

According to the administration's logic, every dollar spent by terrorists justifies subjecting $28 billion to U.S. government oversight. Needless to say, it will not be long before that oversight will be expanded to search for everything from deadbeat dads to tax evaders and to perform industrial espionage in the age-old tradition of expanding government power. Only 100 years ago, federal agents were unarmed and possessed no arrest powers. Now, in the name of protecting us, they are claiming carte blanche to stick their federal noses into every financial transaction in the world.

In fact, the outrage expressed by the administration and its apologists most likely stems from the way in which the exposure of this program eliminates any possibility of European support for the neocons' much-sought war on Iran. Since European banks seldom issue checks, most transactions are done via cash, postal account or bank transfer, and some of those transfers now undergoing U.S. review belong to the very European people and politicians whose support for an Iranian excursion is being sought by the administration. That support, always unlikely, would appear to be nonexistent now given this latest demonstration of the administration's total disregard for their laws and property.

One can only imagine how Americans would shriek in understandable fury if it were the United Nations or the Chinese going through their financial transactions with a fine-toothed comb. The SWIFT program is a useless, ill-conceived and ultimately dangerous abuse of power by a government so heavily dependent upon foreigners financing its gargantuan debts.

International terrorism requires little financing, but a spendthrift government requires an almost unthinkable amount on a daily basis. The *New York Times* did well to report on how the Bush administration is running the foolish risk of infuriating those who finance its fiscally irresponsible ways in nominal pursuit of terrorists it will never catch.

The futility of arms control

July 10, 2006

The first ordinance bearing on military matters in the Capitularies of Charles the Great is one showing his anxiety to keep as much armour as possible within the realm. In 779 he orders that no merchant shall dare to export byrnies from the realm. This order was repeated again and again in later years, in the Capitula Minora, cap. 7, and again in the Aachen Capitulary of 805; the trade in arms with the Wends and Avars is especially denounced in the last-named document. Any merchant caught conveying a mail-shirt outside the realm is sentenced to the forfeiture of all his property.

—Sir Charles Oman, *A History of the Art of War in the Middle Ages, Volume One*

A S THEY SAY in France, "Plus ca change."
While the very public fizzle of North Korea's long-feared missile program has been viewed with a sigh of relief by some, no doubt the World Democratic Revolutionists will use it to argue that the United States must take advantage of this unexpected reprieve to attack Iran and bring its nuclear weapons program to a forcible end.

But as a brief review of Charlemagne's military ordinances shows rather clearly, arms control has been nothing but an exercise in futility for over 1,200 years. Law after law threatening brutal retribution didn't prevent the Avars, the Vikings or the Magyars from obtaining the iron armor that allowed them to meet the Franks on equal terms.

The most fundamental rule of technology is that once the genie has escaped the bottle, it is all but impossible to recapture it. Humanity can no more pretend it does not know how to split the atom than it can forget how to forge an iron-mail shirt. The only effective limitation on the spread of military technology is that of cost; the United States is able to prevent the proliferation of cruise-missile armed nuclear-powered submarines because very few countries or individuals possess the 4.4 billion dollars required to make one, let alone the werewithal to hire and train 133 individuals to staff it.

And of those few who do possess the necessary resources, it is obvious that none of them see any point to doing so. No law is necessary, indeed, any law banning the ownership of boomers would be easily ignored by anyone with the ability to buy one.

As diverse countries have demonstrated over the past decades, it is neither prohibitively difficult nor expensive to construct a nuclear weapon and a long-range delivery system. The French have done it, the Israelis have done it, the South Africans, the Indians and the Pakistanis have done it. If North Korea, a nation of 22 million people with a Gross Domestic Product of $1,700 per capita, can successfully pull it off, then anti-proliferation activists shouldn't be worrying about Iran doing it, as they inevitably will. They should instead probably start worrying about Ingvar Kamprad, Bill Gates or Roman Abramovich deciding to go nuclear.

It has never been possible to control human beings for an extended period of time. This holds true for nations as well as individuals. The fact that a probable event is seen as undesirable, even dangerous, should not lead those hoping it will not come to pass to resort to violence, at least not in a foolish cause that history has repeatedly proven to be completely ineffective.

There may eventually come a time when each and every man holds within his hand the power to destroy the world. Should that doomsday scenario ever come to pass, perhaps then we will finally find ourselves able to treat others as we would ourselves be treated.

The beautiful idiocy of liberals

July 17, 2006

S INCE I WAS A WEE LAD watching the Vikings lose Super Bowls, liberal-minded sportswriters have waged a war against racial injustice in the huddle. Every fall, like clockwork, one could count on copious columns calling for more black quarterbacks, early examples such as James Harris, Joe Gilliam and Vince Evans having been deemed insufficient.

The sports media concocted a legend that the reason for this outrage was that racist coaches and fans were opposed to black quarterbacks, a myth that persists today. Not so long ago, one Pittsburgh writer blamed racism on Steelers' fans unwillingness to embrace Kordell Stewart as a starting quarterback and a Minnesota writer even claimed Vikings fans similarly rejected Culpepper when he started as well."

Of course, this ignores the small fact that Kordell Stewart had a negative touchdown-interception ratio as a starter, and except for one marvelous year in 1997, was pretty much a disaster behind center. Indeed, the year after the Steelers gave up on him, he threw nearly twice as many interceptions as touchdowns for Chicago before getting benched for good. Current Steelers QB Ben Roethlisberger, on the other hand, had a 1.7 TD-to-INT ratio, in addition to leading the team to a Super Bowl win, which perhaps factors slightly into his popularity.

As for Culpepper, the accusation is simply fiction. A Minnesota fanbase that enthusiastically supported both Warren Moon and Randall Cunningham, (to say nothing of Tony Dungy, who was a very popular four-year starter at quarterback for the Golden Gophers), had no absolutely no problem with starting a black quarterback. We were all, however, very nervous about Denny Green deciding to go with a second-year quarterback who not only had not thrown a single pass during his rookie season, but also looked really bad during the 1999 preseason.

By the time Daunte threw three touchdown passes and no interceptions against the Bears in leading the Vikes to a 6-0 start, everyone was on board with the big guy.

Of course, the debate has moved on of late. Although the sporting media continues to be, in Rush Limbaugh's words, "very desirous that a black quarterback do well" and continues to consistently overrate black quarterbacks, (not only has Michael Vick failed to reinvent the position, but the Falcons unwillingness to trade Matt Schaub makes one wonder just how long he'll even remain a starter), the new racial crusade is the "growing problem" of too few black coaches. How the problem is growing when there are more black NFL head coaches than ever before remains a mystery.

For years, it was Tony Dungy who was the face of coaching discrimination, then it was Marvin Lewis, and after him, Lovie Smith and Romeo Crennel. Now that all four men hold head coaching positions, it is Jim Caldwell of the Colts and Donnie Henderson of the Jets who are being unfairly oppressed by The Man. As one Philadelphia columnist writes: "When it comes to hiring black coaches, the NFL doesn't need to regress, they need to progress."

Now, all of this is absurd. The U.S. Constitution happens to guarantee the Right of Free Association, which means an NFL owner or an NFL coach has the perfect right to hire whoever he wants, for whatever stupid reason he likes. Indeed, blacks are statistically overrepresented in the NFL head-coaching ranks, and anyone truly concerned about racial equity in the league would be agitating for more Hispanic or Asian head coaches, of which there are currently zero.

Furthermore, there's no question that racial equity demands more white players, who are shockingly underrepresented in the NFL. But where is the sports media on this vital question of racial imbalance?

About to be hoist on their own petard, that's where. I couldn't help but smile upon reading Scoop Jackson's recent call to arms regarding the lack of blacks in the sports media, in which he cited the *Washington Post*'s calculation that only four of the 305 Associated Press sports editors were black. I'm with Mr. Jackson 100% on this one, although his reasoning is little more than the usual whining about numbers. Still, this third stage of the long march toward total sports domination should be entertaining; I can't wait to see the white liberal reaction when a black editor is hired at a major sports publication and pulls a classic Denny in immediately purging most of the white staff.

The beautiful idiocy of liberals is their total inability to think through the probable consequences of their actions. For years, white liberal sportswriters have waged war against white quarterbacks and white coaches, so justice will be well served when their jobs are turned over to blacks in the name of cosmic justice. One merely wonders, at what point white liberals will deem equity to have been reached. When all the quarterbacks, coaches, sportswriters and spectators are black?

Still, it is true that the late Ralph Wiley could write a better column from the grave than Michael Silver can manage on his best day, while even Jason Whitlock's lesser musings on hazing in women's soccer are to be preferred to Peter King's homoerotic NFL panegyrics. So, why not march with Scoop on this one? Come on, people, you know the words. WE SHALL OVER-COME....

The myth of the coathanger

July 24, 2006

I T IS INTRIGUING to learn that even now, some educated and intelligent individuals worry that restricted access to abortion will lead to a large number of women dying as the result of illegal abortions. Indeed, the coathanger remains a favored icon of feminists, who brandish it as a symbol of anti-abortion activists' purported indifference to women's lives.

What is so amusing about this is that abortionettes might as reasonably brandish a narwhal's horn for fear of the unicorns that will inevitably reappear when abortion is banned. And it will eventually be banned, of this you can be sure, as the demographics curve begins to threaten age- and income-based transfer payments, as Third World migration pressure increases and as sex selection technology becomes cheaper and more reliable.

For as we have already seen in India and the United Kingdom, the realities of prenatal sex selection technology are capable of overwhelming the enthusiasm for abortion of even the most die-hard women's rights advocate.

But those concerned about the consequences of the coming abortion bans need not trouble themselves about the theoretical problem of women surreptitiously scraping out their insides with coathangers. Not only is there no evidence of numerous American women having died from self-inflicted abortions in the past, there is no evidence of women who live in countries where abortion is currently banned dying from them either.

This is easily demonstrated in a variety of ways. In 1973, there were approximately 106 million women living in the United States, of whom 876,208 died that year. If 20,000 women had died by coathanger, it would have been the seventh leading cause of female death at 18.8 per 100,000, putting it right between diabetes mellititus and arteriosclerosis. In fact, a mere 10,000 deaths by coathanger would have still made the top ten, beating out suicide by a comfortable 2,090 female corpses.

Of course, it is always possible that these deaths were disguised or improperly reported. There were, after all, 19,782 women recorded in the "All other accidents" category, and it's also possible that sympathetic coroners might have made a habit of misrepresenting the actual cause of death in such cases. In order to deal with this possibility, it is necessary to examine the female death rate in toto.

If women had been dying of complications related to illegal abortions, one would expect to see a decline in the female death rate starting in 1974. And that is exactly what an examination of the statistics shows! From 1971 to 1973, the female American death rate averaged 806.13 per 100,000. But in the seven years after the landmark Roe v. Wade decision, that rate declined to an average of 768.25 deaths per 100,000 women. This would seem to indicate that 4.9 percent fewer women were dying, which could suggest that coathangers were responsible for almost 43,000 annual deaths!

Of course, the key word in that sentence is "seem." Statistics are always dangerous in the hands of the half-informed, to say nothing of the disingenuous and dishonest.

What blows that notion away is that as female deaths declined by about 5 percent, male deaths declined even more rapidly, by 8 percent, in the same time frame. So, unless sapient, murderously minded coathangers were wreaking havoc on men and women alike before disappearing mysterously in 1974, one can only conclude that there were other explanations for this reduced female mortality. And sure enough, the delta in the death rates for cancer, murder and heart disease are more than enough to account for the overall decline.

Unfortunately, the fact that there were never any significant number of American women dying from illegal abortions has not prevented abortionettes from repeating their favorite and second-most effective lie as they do their best to bring the gift of infanticide to the rest of the globe.

From abortionfacts.com:

On June 18, 1989, CNN World Report, in an hour-long documentary, stated that in Brazil there are six million illegal abortions each year and 400,000 women die. But the U.N. Demographic Yearbook of 1988 lists only 40,000 women, age 15–44, dying each year of all causes.

That's an astounding number of abortions, especially considering that in the United States, a country with 50 percent more inhabitants, there were about one-fifth that many abortions in the same year. But, as Barbie informs us, math is hard for women and the evidence suggests it's harder for abortionettes than most.

So, the next time a feminist tries to slide the myth of the coathanger past you, don't hesitate to ask her precisely how many women suffered a death-by-coathanger prior to 1973. And don't be surprised when the answer is the female equivalent of "hrair."

Who's really riding the weaker horse?

July 31, 2006

When people see a strong horse and a weak horse, by nature, they will like the strong horse.

—Osama bin Ladin

IN EXAMINING the events of the past five years, it is increasingly apparent that Western leaders and commentators alike have fundamentally misconceived the relative positions of the primary parties in this third great wave of Islamic expansion. While there are nearly as many grand strategic recommendations floating around the Internet as there are editorialists, it is intriguing to note that virtually none of the Western analysts have grasped the basic reality that from the perspective from which a clash of civilizations must be considered, it is the West that is the weak horse.

The overwheening confidence which so often colors statements from men such as bin Laden and Mahmoud Ahmadinejad always rings strange in Western ears. It stands so powerfully at variance with what we know of Western wealth, technology and military advantages that it seems to be indicative of false bravado at best, at worst, clinical insanity. The fact that this sort of thing sounds exactly like Baghdad Bob's surreal rantings only makes it that much more difficult for anyone to take it seriously.

And yet, history is rife with examples wherein a wealthy or more technogically advanced society is defeated by its lesser rival. Despite its lack of a navy, the intrepid Romans defeated Carthage on both land and sea, while the technical superiority of its machine guns, tanks, submarines, rockets and airplanes were not enough to allow the Germans to overcome the allies in World War II. The knights of Western Europe lost numerous battles and a number of wars to Mongols, Magyars, Turks and Saracens even though none of their enemies could stand before an armored cavalry charge.

Neocon ravings notwithstanding, national will, (or more accurately, cultural will), is not the issue at hand here. The majority of Americans are largely indifferent to the Bush administration's Global Struggle Against Violent Extremism while an ovewhelming majority of the rest of the West is openly against it. But most Muslims are similarly indifferent to this third round in the great clash of civilizations too. An anecdote from William Manchester's biography of Winston Churchill is most informative in this regard:

> *During the early 1950s, when this writer was living in Dehli as a foreign correspondent, social scientists began a comprehensive poll of Indian villages to determine how many natives knew British rule had ended in 1947. The survey was aborted when it was discovered that a majority didn't know the British had even arrived.*

And while it might be tempting to dismiss those Indians as ignorant illiterates, it might be illuminating to ask your neighbor if he knows the name of his congressman, his state representative or his city councilman.

Christendom has twice previously endured periods of Islamic expansion and even managed to roll back Islamic gains with the Reconquista, and, more temporarily, during the Crusades. But that was when the Christian West saw Islam as an enemy and bitterly contested it on every side. Now, a secular West no longer sees itself as a player in the great game, but as a referee, and views Islam as being merely one of the various contestants.

The unavoidable challenge is this. In the same way that atheism provides no moral basis for an individual to resist evil, secular, religious-neutral government provides no practical foundation for opposing Islamic expansion. If Congress funds no mosques, neither can it prevent them from being constructed by militant Saudi Wahhabists. If the Supreme Court requires no one to pray towards Mecca, neither does it allow the banning of immigrants on the basis of a religious adherence to jihad. The range of options accessible to the leaders of the West are formidable; they are also irrelevant.

Bin Laden's statement about horses can perhaps be best understood thusly: Unlike its Christian predecessor, the secular West is structurally incapable of resisting an Islamic expansion due to its demographic disadvantages and philosophical weaknesses. If this is an accurate characterization, one can only conclude, unfortunately, that his statement is logically, historically and psychologically sound. Certainly the actions of the West's leaders, especially those of the Bush administration, have done nothing to disprove the assertion, the establishment of a modern-day Kingdom of Acre in Iraq notwithstanding.

None of this means that Islam cannot be turned back a third time; it does, however, suggest that the concept of Western secularism is doomed to failure one way or another. Secularism does not inspire, it enervates. The spirit which led to the sapping of British spirit and the decline of the Raj has been at work in America for decades, it should surprise no one that the lion's heir is following the mighty tracks of its predecessor.

The impotence of secularism is only the first of several realities that must be recognized if the West is to survive its third test of character. Here are some other important verities:

1. Democracy does not reduce radicalism or inhibit religion.

2. Exposure to Western culture does not eliminate radicalism. Even complete immersion in it does not guarantee its elimination.

3. Western shock and awe cannot impose permanant defeat upon an Eastern culture of retreat and regroup.

4. Technological proliferation is inevitable. This includes nuclear weapons.

5. Internal dissension, not external force, ends offensive expansion.

The West turned back the forces of an expansionary Islam twice before. Those hoping to see it turned back a third time would be wise to examine precisely how it was accomplished on the previous occasions.

Stockpiling Jews for Jesus

August 7, 2006

AMONG THE SILLIER ACCUSATIONS made by non-Christians about those they like to describe as "fundies" and "Bible-thumpers", is the notion that Christians only support Israel because they want to bring about the Apocalypse and kill them all. This is deeply and profoundly ignorant, right up there with the asinine "most wars are caused by religion" assertion of which maleducated atheists are so fond.

Now, there's no question Christians are rather more enthusiastic about the Jewish return to Israel than they have historically been about the Rothschild family's influence with the London Stock Exchange, but it is worth recalling that without Christian Zionists in positions of influence in the British Empire, Israel might never have come to pass in the first place. Thus, Christian interest in Israel is neither new nor unnatural.

The primary reason Christians are fascinated with Israel is that its existence lends support for the verity of Scripture, which is the doctrine of the faith. For many years, the absence of Israel was cited by non-Christians as proof that the Bible could not be true, in much the same way that the absence of any archeological evidence of the Assyrians and the Hittites was once considered testimony to Biblical inaccuracy.

But what in its absence is testimony against truth becomes supporting evidence for Biblical accuracy upon its appearance. Once the ruins of Nineveh and Hattusha were discovered, doubters were forced to concede that the Bible was a valid historical document more reliable than the historians of the day. Since 1948, its value as a predictive model has become apparent too, as with the exception of students in the Middle East and the American public schools, no one points to a globe and asks where Israel can be found anymore.

The non-Christian confusion stems from the events prophesied in the Revelation of St. John. There, Israel is predicted to be a primary player, and it is written that during that time, the Jews, having returned en masse to Israel, will finally come to recognize Jesus as their Messiah. Apparently it's the fact that he's returning as the conquering king that they were expecting the last time that will prove conclusive. Considering this, non-Christians have concluded that because the return of the Jews is a precursor to the second coming of Jesus Christ, Christians are therefore trying to summon Jesus Christ by a) supporting Israel against Islam, and, b) stockpiling Jews in Jerusalem.

Most Christians would plead guilty to (a). (And it is Islam, not Arabs, since Iran is Persian, not Arab, and is arguably Israel's most dangerous enemy at the moment. It's not pan-Islam, however, since Muslim Turkey has proven to be an Israeli ally of sorts). Islam has declared war on Christendom too, after all, and alliances often begin with a common enemy. But Christians don't support Israel against its enemies because they are concerned about it disappearing again, after all, Christians believe in an Almighty God, who, as the architect of human history, is perfectly capable of protecting His Chosen with or without our help. No, Christians primarily support Israel because God says in His Word that He will bless those who bless Israel and curse those who curse it. It's that simple. Most Christians don't question the imperative to bless Israel any more than they question "thou shalt not kill."

And certainly, if you compare the life of the average Israel-cursing Muslim with that of the Israel-blessing Christian, there would appear to be some truth to be found in that particular verse.

One of the quirkier things about non-Christian critics of Christianity is how they will take a verse or two from the Bible, build an uninformed interpretation around it, and then completely disregard every other verse that makes it clear that the interpretation is hopelessly incorrect. Just as the absurd argument that "an atheist only believes in one less god" ignores the first of the Ten Commandments as well as Psalm 82:1, Jesus' words in Matthew 24 make it clear that the concept of the Eschaton being immanentizeable is ridiculous.

For in that verse, it can be seen that the hour had already been chosen and was known to the Father two thousand years ago. And furthermore, Jesus tells his followers: "Then you will be handed over to be persecuted and put to death, and you will be hated by all nations because of me. At that time many will turn away from the faith and will betray and hate each other."

So, one can only conclude that these eschaton enthusiasts are so clueless that they are actively working to bring about something that is already proceeding according to a fixed schedule, something that they don't realize will reward them with hatred, persecution and death. And while some bold Christians might seek the martyr's crown being awarded even today in the Dar al-Islam, in North Korea and in China, does that fit the description of the average Christian in America today?

No Christian is seeking to speed up the Apocalypse, because there isn't a Christian in the world who believes he can. Indeed, the most any Christian can do is to repeat the words of the author of Apocalisse when he writes "Amen. Come, Lord Jesus."

Riding the Weak Horse II

August 14, 2006

ILITARY HISTORIAN Victor Davis Hanson recently wrote that he detected a whiff of the 1930s in the air. And he is correct, there are a host of similarities between the bizarre appeasement practiced by Baldwin, Chamberlain, Dadalier, and Halifax and the inability of Tony Blair and George Bush to identify the enemy, much less wage effectual war against it.

Nor is Hanson the only one to draw a '30s analogy. Robert Tracinski, in an excellent, if misguided article entitled Five Minutes to Midnight catalogs similar analogies attempting to equate the current situation with that faced by the Western Powers in 1936, 1938 and 1939. However, like the recalcitrant world democratic revolutionists, Tracinski follows the analogies to an incorrect conclusion in arguing that a strike against Iran is the correct next step required to fight the war on terms advantageous to the West.

The problem is that like the generals of the old epigram, the media hawks are hoping to fight a previous war, in this case one more than sixty years past. Suppose, for a moment, that Iran was successfully invaded and occupied. How would this prevent future Sept. 11 attacks by Saudis visiting the United States on legitimate travel visas? If the conquest and occupation of Iraq did not prevent British citizens funded by Pakistani jihadists from plotting to bring down jets flying out of Heathrow, how would the elimination of the Iranian regime make any difference at all?

What the hawks have failed to understand is that one cannot end an internal threat through external measures. Just as there is no number of dead Iraqis that will protect America from Saudi Arabians, there is no magical number of dead Iranians that will preclude a threat from Pakistan or any other Islamic nation.

As I pointed out more than two years ago, Iran is only one of the two centers of global terrorism and it is the lesser of the two. As violent incidents everywhere from Spain to Seattle have demonstrated, the main threat posed to the people of the West is an internal one and that internal threat is funded by Saudi Arabia, not Iran. In fact, invading Iran will likely increase the internal threat, not reduce it.

While neocons hail with quivering excitement the president's recent adoption of their term "Islamofascist", this actually represents an attempt at continued linguistic appeasement in the cringing tradition that produced the ludicrous Global Struggle Against Violent Extremism, the Council on American-Islamic Affairs' protests notwithstanding. There is, quite simply, nothing that is Fascist about "Islamofascism", as even a brief perusal of the Manifesto of the Fascist Struggle will conclusively demonstrate. For example, one rather doubts that the imams would stand for "The seizure of all the possessions of the religious congregations...."

However, the '30s analogy does hold true in at least one respect. While reading the second volume of Manchester's biography of Winston Churchill, I came across the following passage which described the situation in London at the time of the German invasion of Poland in Sept. 1939:

> It was still His Majesty's Government's policy to avoid offending Germany; although Great Britain and the Third Reich were at war, Reith's BBC was uncomfortable with criticism of the enemy regime.

—William Manchester, *The Last Lion—Alone 1932–1940*, p. 583.

Plus ça change, plus c'est la même chose. In light of that, it was interesting to read the *Sunday Times* which writes: "Muslims have to be persuaded that we are on the same side, that there is no witch-hunt against Islam and that the wars involving British troops are about stopping Islamists and the corruption of their religion."

But persuading Muslims that the West is on their side is not the responsibility of the West or its leaders. This is pure appeasement at its most insidious. And how can the current jihad be a corruption of a religion that has always been a religion of the sword?

The only responsibility of the West is to its native inhabitants, to demand that those non-Westerners who wish to reside in it will live by its standards, by the cultural norms of the West. Likewise, Western leaders have a duty to recognize the enemy as all of those who have declared themselves to be at war with the nations of the West and to give them what they have demanded, regardless of whether they live in Baghdad, Boston or Buckinghamshire.

Riding the Weak Horse III

August 21, 2006

WHEN WATCHING events unfold, it is customary to assume they will continue to proceed in a linear manner. Thus, it was impossible for most observers of Operation Barbarossa, seeing the Red Army retreating in disarray before the onslaught of the Wehrmacht, to imagine that in only four years, positions would be reversed and the Soviets would be marching through the streets of Berlin.

Such action, however, invariably inspires a reaction, while the vagaries of a dynamic situation always triggers complicating factors that tend to come into play on the side of the reaction. This is one of the most fundamental limits on exercising power, which has hampered victorious conquerers from the Hittites to the Bush White Houses.

In my first column in this series, I wrote:

The West turned back the forces of an expansionary Islam twice before. Those hoping to see it turned back a third time would be wise to examine precisely how it was accomplished on the previous occasions.

The first great wave of Islamic expansion ranged from 632 to 732 A.D. During this time, Arabia, Persia, northern Africa, northern India and Spain all came under the domination of various Islamic powers; a succession of defeats at Byzantium, Toulouse and Tours finally exhausted its momentum. The disintegration of the great caliphates into rival emirates and taifas began almost immediately, starting with Berber revolt of 740.

The second great wave came under the Ottoman Empire, which rather like the current situation, began with a migration into the West. The migration was transformed into an imperial sultanate by Osman Gazi in 1299 and the growth of his empire saw Islamic forces expand throughout the Christian lands of the Byzantines, until Mehmet II finally took the great city of Byzantium itself in 1453. Large parts of Eastern Europe fell to Turkish scimitars and without the navies of the European Powers, the Mediterranean would likely have become a Turkish lake.

As with the previous wave, however, the climax of this second expansion was marked by failures, first with an unsuccessful siege at Vienna, followed by the naval defeat at Lepanto 42 years later. By the time the second siege of Vienna was beaten back in 1683, imperial decline had already set in.

It is important to note that successful Western aggression against the Dar al-Islam always took place during a time of Islamic quiescence due to decadence or internecine struggles. The Crusades, the Reconquista and the Colonial era were all marked by powerful rivalries between various Muslim potentates, indeed, had the Holy Lands been entirely in possession of the Seljouk Turks instead of divided between the Seljouks, the Sultanate of Roum, the Egyptian Fatimites and the emirates of Aleppo, Damascus, and Mosul, it is very unlikely that the First Crusade would have ever survived to set eyes on Jerusalem.

The strategists of the jihad understand that internal division is their greatest weakness, which is why they are at war with the national leaderships as well as the West. They have consciously offered a pan-Islamic vision, which in an ironic mirror of the secular EU's post-Christian pan-Europeanism, transcends the nation-state. It is this vision which has allowed the jihad to escape its colonial shackles and explains why a jihadist is at home in Indonesia or Somalia as he is in Saudi Arabia or Iran.

Or in the nations of the West. And this is the great challenge facing Western leaders, for the jihad cleverly takes advantage of the secular tradition of religious neutrality to provide it with protective cover for its ongoing Kriechskrieg. A future attack on Iran will no more solve the problem than did the conquest of Iraq. Bin Laden outright welcomed Western attacks on Islamic nation-states, for he knew they would primarily harm his nationalist rivals and strengthen the globalist jihad, moreover, the jihad cannot possibly lose so long as Islam continues to grow in the West.

Christendom twice turned back jihad. There is good reason to doubt the post-Christian West can likewise do so, unless it is willing to abandon its commitment to religious neutrality and return to the colonial policy of fostering the inevitable intra-Islamic rivalries.

The value of marriage

August 28, 2006

WHEN I WROTE my first column on the subject of the growing unsuitability of the modern American woman for marriage back in 2003, it was unusual enough that I received requests for radio appearances from Toronto to Texas. At the time, it tended to fall into the category of something every man of experience knew, but didn't discuss in public for fear of scaring the horses and children.

So, Forbes editor Michael Noer's recent article pointing out the wisdom of not marrying a career woman was more refreshing than enlightening, more interesting for the reaction to it than its content. For there was nothing "downright frightening" about it except perhaps to career women being forced to confront a reality they have long attempted to deny. When Cosmopolitan begins publishing articles on the subject, then we'll know the societal tide has truly turned.

Marriage is one of two things. For the Christian, it is a religious sacrament, a vow before God and Man that no power on Earth has the ability to set aside. That vow can be broken, of course, and it all too often is. But the vow stands as the foundation of a new creation, the family, which for all its flaws has not been improved on despite centuries of experimentation.

We are informed that it is good for the Christian to marry and that a wife of noble character is worth far more than rubies. But the priorities of such a woman are rather different than those of most career women. The Christian wife's priorities are God, family, self, whereas the career woman's are job, self… and then maybe the trophy child if the injections work. A woman's heart can be discerned by her priorities; if Powerpoint demonstrations rank anywhere in the Top Ten, a man will do well to look elsewhere for a companion.

But marriage is not only a religious vow, it is also a state contract designed to prevent the state from being forced to provide for unproductive women and children. That this is the true purpose underlying the marriage contract can be seen from the way the state has no interest in ascertaining whether the proper man's financial resources are tapped for child support. Indeed, not even proving the complete impossibility of any relationship through DNA testing is enough to sever that state-enforced bond.

In light of this, a man must be either a fool or a weakling to enter into such a contract, especially given that the traditional reason for doing so has been eliminated by societal devolution. The end of the dowry system meant that the primary motivation for marrying was sexual, but the Sexual Revolution has significantly lowered the sexual value of women by increasing the available supply.

One reason that career women are so shocked to hear of their lack of desirability to men is that their comparatively high incomes mean that they are bringing something to the marriage table, in effect a form of modern dowry. But they tend to forget that in addition to their salaries one must assess their sexual values, which can be computed thanks to data collected on average American sexual practices which state that the average sexual encounter lasts 28 minutes and Americans average 58 such encounters per year.

Therefore, the sexual value of a woman can be computed according to the formula $(P*(E/60)*(N*12))$, wherein P = price per hour, E = length of average sexual encounter in minutes and N = number of monthly encounters. Assuming realistic maximums, this value can be expected to range between 0 and $1.67 million on an annual basis. However, if one assumes that P for the average woman is one-third the overnight rate of a pretty, but non-elite 20-year-old call girl, the sexual value of the average American woman works out to only $1,353.33 per annum.

So, the problem faced by career women, then, is that while they do bring their modern dowry to the table in the form of a salary and a health insurance package, they bring little else, and money does not buy happiness. However high their original sexual value, their time commitments and job stresses tend to reduce it, while they are at a disadvantage with regards to other relationship aspects valued by men, such as providing children, child care and various household services.

But what of love, you ask? How can one put a price on love? One can't, but then, marriage is not love, most marriages in history have taken place for reasons other than love and some of history's most famous lovers have been unmarried. And as post-Christian Europe increasingly demonstrates, merely being in love and having a child or two is no reason to marry.

While putting a price on marriage might seem distasteful to some, it is an important consideration for any man contemplating the commitment. Because if you don't make a realistic assessment of marriage's value to you prior to entering into it, the probability is that a divorce court will be doing so for you on the other end.

The ideology that isn't

September 4, 2006

THE CONTINUED RELUCTANCE of the Bush administration to name its enemy after five years of so-called war long ago crossed the border of the absurd. First, there was the War on Method, then there was Gathering Silly Acronyms Vice Execution. Throughout, the president demonstrated his hitherto unrevealed linguistic expertise in assuring the people that Islam did not, as is commonly supposed, mean "submission", but peace.

To the delight of neocons of all religious persuasions, George Bush annoyed his fellow Islamic experts by referring to "Islamo-fascism" a few weeks ago. He publicly backpedaled in the face of criticism from the Council on American-Islamic Relations as is his wont, but not before inspiring a chorus of praise from the bloodthirsty revolutionaries who want to attack "Islamo-fascists" in Iran, Syria, Lebanon, Gaza and the West Bank.

It is strange that neocons seldom have a word of criticism for the only Islamic nationals who are actively planting mosques throughout America and the West, the Saudi Arabians. Apparently jihadists in Baghdad and Tehran are a problem, those in Boston and Terre Haute, Indiana are not. All of this dancing around the subject makes little sense until one realizes that the term "Islamo-fascism" is not intended to identify a particular enemy, but rather to create an artificial distinction between "Good Muslims" and "Bad Muslims."

This is ludicrous, not because all Muslims are either good or bad, but because there is no such thing as a fascistic strain of Islam. Fascism is more than a synonym for evil, it is a coherent and structured political ideology and the fact that it was not perfectly implemented in its most pure fashion should confuse no one living in a modern Western democracy where the power of the people's vote is strictly hedged on every side.

The principle elements of Fascist ideology are laid out in the Manifesto of the Fascist Struggle and are as follows:

1. Nationalism

2. Economic centralization with progressive taxation

3. Subordination of Church to State

4. Expansionist militarism

5. Political equality for women

With the partial exception of number four, none of these points apply in any way to the expansionist Islam of today. The global jihad is pan-nationalistic and is more genuinely diverse than the fraudulent multicultural-ists of the West. So long as the strictures of Sharia are respected, it is equally at home in a socialist or capitalist economic structure. It is precisely the opposite of Fascism in subordinating the State to the Mosque. While there is certainly a military element to the jihad, this is actually a secondary line of attack; its primary line rests on a quiet and peaceful migration that lays the groundwork for future victory through demographics and democracy.

As for the last point, while the Islamic disregard for Western "women's rights" is no secret, rather less well-known is the fact that political equality for women was the very first point in the Fascist manifesto. Furthermore, it was a woman who founded Britain's first Fascist organization and famous suf-fragettes such as Mary Richardson, Mary Sophia Allen and Adela Pankhurst all became leaders in Fascist organizations subsequent to their successful campaigning for women's suffrage.

Finally, Fascism was not anti-Semitic. The anti-Jewish laws of 1938 were imposed under pressure from Nazi Germany and more than 40,000 of Italy's 50,000 Jews survived the Holocaust despite the National Socialist occupation that began five years later.

The nonsensical, chimerical nature of the neocon term is further under-lined when one considers the way in which the historical Fascists regarded Fascism itself. Giordano Bruni Guerri writes in "Fascisti":

La solidarietà fascismo-Vaticano non può stupire, anche se—idealmente—Mussolini e il fascismo originario erano anticattolici e anticlericali perchè consideravano se stessi una religione. La Chiesa però aveva in comune con il fascismo tutti i nemici: la democrazia, il liberalismo, il comunismo, la massoneria.

—*Fascisti* p. 146

The solidarity between Fascism and the Vatican cannot astonish one, even if Mussolini and the original Fascism were ideally anti-catholic and anti-clerical because they considered Fascism to be a religion in itself. The Church, however, had in common with the Fascists all of these enemies: democracy, liberalism, communism and Masonry.

Were Fascism not a defunct historical ideology, it would be a rival to Islam, not a variant form of it. And indeed, considering the numerous ways in which Tony Blair's Third Way and George Bush's Strong Government Conservatism echo the principle elements of Fascism, future historians may even see that as having been the case.

Regardless, a review of history and the tenets of the actual ideology prove that it makes no more sense to refer to "Islamo-fascism" than it would to talk about "Catholo-fascism" or "Judeo-unicornism". Jonah Goldberg, who has been writing a book on Fascism for quite some time now, notes: "The problem with "Islamo-fascism," as many have noted, is that ? historically ? Fascism is at war with traditional religion, while the Islamists believe that they are loyal to the true tenets of their faith."

It is a positive sign that some of the most prominent members of the conservative commentariat are beginning to reject neocon terminology; here's hoping they will soon come to reject the neo-trotskyite World Democratic Revolution as well.

When the black hat doesn't fit

September 11, 2006

I N THE RESPONSES to last week's column, it has been intriguing to see how neocons and confused conservatives seduced into supporting the Trotsky-Wilsonian World Democratic Revolution have attempted to defend the intellectually incoherent concept of "Islamo-fascism."

Strangely, the most common response to my demonstration that violent expansionist Islam shares very few similarities with the historical Fascists of Italy that could not be as easily applied to anyone from Alexander the Great to Tiglath-Pilasar was to supply a list of purported similarities between the Nationalsozialistische Deutsche Arbeiterpartei and the violent global jihad of which Osama bin Laden is the primary figurehead.

This seems bizarre until one realizes that in the maleducated mind of the average, public-schooled American, Fascism and Nazism were not merely 20th Century totalitarian ideologies which happened to share a fondness for central authority, mass rallies and designer uniforms, but were in fact the same.

This bait-and-switch defense is a mendacious and cynical attempt to take advantage of American historical ignorance, especially since the two major elements of Nazism which are shared by the global jihad, virulent expansionism and anti-Semitism, simply don't apply to the Italian Fascists. Space does not permit a detailed comparison of the ideological differences between the two totalitarianisms, but suffice it to say that they were no more identical in theory than in practice.

And personal relations between the two dictators aside, the relationship between Italian Fascists and German Nazis was actually much closer to the ancient one between Roman legionaries and barbarian German tribesmen than the fraternally authoritarian one that is commonly assumed by the historically challenged.

Austrian Nazis assassinated the Fascist Chancellor of Austria, Engelbert Dollfuss, in July 1934, in revenge for his banning their party in the previous month. Benito Mussolini then thwarted Hitler's first effort at Anschluss by sending 50,000 troops to the Italian-Austrian border and forcing the Germans to back down. It is ironic that prior to Churchill taking power, il Duce was the only European leader who ever dared to call one of Hitler's many bluffs.

Even the Fascist-Nazi military alliance, the infamous Rome-Berlin Axis, was an accident of diplomacy that should never have come to pass. It seems few have heard of the Stresa Front, the anti-German Anglo-French-Italian alliance of 1935. It collapsed primarily due to an astounding diplomatic blunder by British Prime Minister Stanley Baldwin, who betrayed both of Britain's allies by reaching a separate and contradictory accord with Germany, the Anglo-German Naval Agreement, only two months later. This error was compounded by British hypocrisy and incompetence in addressing Italy's colonial aspirations in Abyssinia at the League of Nations.

Winston Churchill wrote of His Majesty's Government's alienation of a historical ally thusly: "In the fearful struggle against rearming Nazi Germany which I could feel approaching ... I was most reluctant to see Italy estranged and even driven into the opposite camp." His biographer William Manchester adds: "England had chosen 'to depart from the principle of collective security in a very notable fashion.' The French would moan but cling desperately to Britain, their only sure ally. The Italians could go elsewhere. And, he [Churchill] predicted, they would."

Furthermore, it is worth noting that when the Fascist Grand Council deposed Mussolini, the Nazis immediately set up a military occupation of northern Italy, a puppet-state called the Republic of Salò. The Fascist government of Pietro Badoglio, on the other hand, signed an armistice with the Allies and subsequently declared war on Nazi Germany.

Now, it must be said that there are some who admit "Islamo-fascism" is unrelated to Italian Fascism but insist that the lower-case "fascism" merely indicates a reference to the secondary definition provided by the American Heritage dictionary: "oppressive, dictatorial control." The fact that unemployed Islamic schoolboys in Britain and jihadist insurgents in Iraq are not in a position to oppress anyone, control anything or dictate to anyone doesn't seem to have occurred to these linguistic apologists.

The reason that the media propagandists do not attempt to push the term "Islamo-Nazi" is because it is quite obvious to everyone that the enthusiasts of violent expansionist Islam are not Nazis, notwithstanding their similar inclination for Judenhassen. But the Fascists were not Nazis either, just as the global jihadists are neither Fascists nor fascists.

The bestial Bush administration

September 18, 2006

I N RECENT CENTURIES, war has reliably accomplished three things: kill vast quantities of individuals, expand the size and scope of the central state and degrade the traditional values of Western Civilization. As the historian Paul Johnson points out in *Modern Times*:

> *The effect of the Great War was enormously to increase the size and therefore the destructive capacity and propensity to oppress, of the state. Before 1914, all state sectors were small, though most were growing, some of them fast. The area of actual state activity averaged between 5 and 10 percent of the Gross National Product.*

According to the CIA *World Factbook*, the five leading members of the Coalition of the Willing, the multinational force purportedly bringing "freedom" to occupied Iraq, feature state sectors averaging 34.9 percent of Gross Domestic Product, a five-fold increase in less than 100 years. It is sobering to realize that for all of our technological riches, citizens of modern democracies possess far less economic freedom than did the average subject of Kaiser Wilhelm II or King George V.

But this is not the only way in which Western Civilization has significantly devolved. The social degradation that accompanied the Sexual Revolution of the late 1960s has been much-lamented, and there is little doubt about which political party has been the standard bearer for what Robert Bork so eloquently described as "slouching toward Gomorrah." Ramesh Ponnuru decries a "party of death," although a more unwieldy but accurate appellation might be "the cult of the death of Western Civilization."

Sadly, it is not only Democrats who have sold their souls to barbarism. Not content to rest with their betrayal of the once-central concept of small government, at the behest of George W. Bush, Republicans have likewise abandoned one of the core hallmarks of civilization itself. Consider the words of Winston Churchill, a man not well-known for shirking confrontation or combat, written after World War I while he was secretary of state for war:

> *All the horrors of all the ages were brought together, and not only armies but whole populations were thrust into the midst of them. The mighty educated States involved conceived—not without reason—that their very existence was at stake. Neither peoples nor rulers drew the line at any deed which they thought could help them to win. Germany, having let hell loose, kept well in the van of terror; but she was followed step by step by the desperate and ultimately avenging nations she had assailed.... When it was all over, Torture and Cannibalism were the only two expedients that the civilized, scientific, Christian States had been able to deny themselves: and they were of doubtful utility.*

It is those last words that most completely damn the Bush administration as barbarians unfit for leadership of the free world. Few would find appeals to national security very compelling if the president insisted that victory in the War That Dare Not Speak Its Name required feeding the armed forces on the flesh of fallen Iraqis, and yet there is very little evidence, historic or current, that indicates torture will be of any use in turning back the forces of expansionist Islam.

Enthusiastic use of the most brutal torture did not help the French hold Algeria against Islamic rebels, nor did it bring victory to the Soviet Union in Afghanistan. Debates about whether "water boarding" is more acceptable than the rack or thumbscrews are meaningless; the point is that civilized societies do not indulge in such activities since they are evil and effectively useless.

It's not as if the administration possess a shred of credibility when it comes to national security in the first place. It cannot be denied that 9/11 happened on the Bush administration's incompetent watch; it is arguably on the verge of losing control of Afghanistan; and it is definitely threatening to compound failure with more failure by rattling an impotent saber at Iran. Meanwhile, it turns a blind eye to increased Muslim immigration, hands out entry visas to Saudi nationals and holds border control hostage in an effort to grant U.S. citizenship to millions of illegal aliens.

And yet Americans are somehow supposed to believe that if only the president is allowed to order the application of electricity to the genitals of a few captured jihadists, all will be well. This is absurd, and yet one can easily imagine that if George Bush suddenly decided that the state interest dictated serving Long Pig at the next state dinner, today's torture enthusiasts would immediately begin flinging accusations of disloyalty and insufficient patriotism at those cowardly critics of cannibalism.

As long as its nominal defenders consist of Devolutionary Democrats and Three Monkey Republicans, it is eminently possible that Western Civilization will not survive its barbaric enemies.

The shadow of the torturer

September 25, 2006

COGNITIVE DISSONANCE and logical contradiction are trusty indicators of inferior thought processes. It is not consistency that is the hobgoblin of small minds, after all, but "a foolish consistency." Those claiming to possess large and superior minds should therefore be capable of consistencies that are not foolish.

But fear exerts a strange influence over the human mind. Fearfulness is a form of foolishness, indeed, it is one of its more powerful forms, capable of overruling reason and wisdom alike. The evil, the lazy and the intellectually corrupt make habitual use of fear in their arguments, because unfortunately, the ease with which fear can be inspired makes it an irresistably tempting instrument for politicians and commentators alike.

It has been disgusting to see the enthusiasm which conservatives supposedly adhering to concepts such as limited government, human liberty and Western civilization have been cheering the Bush administration's attempts to circumvent the limits of the Geneva Convention. Worse, they have urged it to altogether cast off the strictures of human decency and civilized behavior. They argue, with fearful lips aquiver, that if America does not assert the right of the Executive Branch to indiscriminately kill and torture, the Dread Terrorist Osama will rule from the White House as an iron-fisted Islamic dictator.

Or at least "win," although somehow the pro-war brigade never finds the time to define what victory for one side or the other would be. Never mind, for have we not always been at war with Osama?

If the pro-war argument often borders on lunacy, the pro-war plus pro-torture position leaps into mad irony with the ease of undocumented workers crossing the Rio Grande. On the one hand, the hawkish torturists assert, it is cowardly for Americans to refuse to fight back after having been attacked. On the other, they declare it is imperative that we abandon centuries of civilized behavior for fear that there might one day be a bomb ticking somewhere at the same time that the perpetrator of the attack fortuitously happens to be in American custody.

This is an ontological argument for torture and the rational individual will find it less convincing than its kindred case for the existence of space aliens.

Last week in WND, one could almost picture Craig Smith's hands shaking in terror as he wrote the following:

> *I would give the interrogators whatever they need to get the info we need. They are the professionals. They face these animals each day knowing that they want us dead. They know the information they hold will allow us to keep these murderers from killing more people. So let's take the gloves off.*

I don't know how Mr. Smith knows the Iranians or Saudi Arabians want us dead any more than the Germans, Japanese or Soviets once did, but I do know that jihad's ability to kill large quantities of Americans is arguably lower than that possessed by any American enemy since the war of 1812.

Rusty Humphries, meanwhile, is so frightened of not only terrorism, but crime as well, that he wishes to provide even your local police with the legal right to torture:

> *As for the police who have one of the kidnappers of your daughter, let's be honest. If we do not give them the tools, leeway and permission to do whatever is necessary to prevent her brutal murder, we are a society not worth saving.*

The Apostle Paul writes that we are not given a spirit of fear, but Americans certainly appear to have acquired one from somewhere. And while there are a number of things that one might argue make our society not worth saving, a dearth of torture is seldom numbered among them.

The poverty and contemptible nature of these arguments for torture can be seen by the ease with which they can be as accurately applied to those for rape or cannibalism. After all, a terrorist might be more easily persuaded to inform on the whereabouts of the ubiquitous "ticking-bomb" if forced to watch his prepubescent daughters raped by federal agents and a thief might be more prone to confess his theft were his fingers gnawed to the bone by a policeman with a taste for human sashimi.

Why, with a sufficiently enthusiastic application of these post-civilized principles, Americans could not only reduce terrorism and crime, but dispense with that annoying and outdated concept of trial-by-jury altogether!

The reality is that America, like most great powers, is far more likely to fall to internal rot of the sort exhibited here than to external attack. We have far more to fear from these frightened intellectual descendants of Malcolm X and the Marquis de Sade than from a planet full of terrorists.

Gay Old Pedophiles

October 2, 2006

THE CRINGE FACTOR is back in American politics. It suddenly doesn't seem all that long ago we were wincing over the significance of a stained blue dress; now, one finds oneself looking back on Mr. Clinton's proclivity for porcine young women with a certain nostalgia. Hummers, interns, cigars and "I did not have sex with that woman" suddenly seem almost respectable, even statesmanlike, compared with underage pages, Internet chats and "do I make you a little horny?"

Republicans may find the concept of the big tent as well as its implications for electoral success to be appealing, but few conservatives previously understood that the party elders envisioned a tent so big it encompassed fifty-year-old ephebophiles. Mark Foley isn't a fringe figure on the perimeter of the party; at the time of his resignation last week, he was a six-term congressman from Florida expected to easily win election to a seventh term in office.

But despite the lingering aftershocks from a media quake that will continue to reverberate for some time from a scandal that is at least a 4.0 on the Rupert scale, Mark Foley is not the central issue here. Foley is merely the latest symptom in a disease that has been evident for quite some time now in a Republican Party that values power over principle and the perquisites of politicians over the God-given rights of the American people.

The elections of George W. Bush and Arnold Schwarzenegger were also symptoms of this disease. They were significant primarily due to the way long-held conservative principles and candidates were cast aside, even derided, by the national Republican establishment in pursuit of pragmatism. The conservative commentariat hailed this newfound electoral realism and defended it as a necessary evil, unfortunate, perhaps, but justified by the moral imperative to keep the irresponsible perverts in the Democratic Party out of power.

But evil is evil, regardless of how necessary one deems it to be, and the result of this unprincipled pragmatism was not only unsurprising, but eminently foreseeable, as evidenced by a column I wrote during the California recall election entitled Satanic Schwarzeneggerians.

What is particularly contemptible about the Foley case is the way in which House Speaker Dennis Hastert, House Majority Leader John Boehner, John Shimkus of the Page Board and other Republicans, including the boy's own parents, all knew about Foley's attempted homosexual predation and in the interests of the party chose to keep it in the closet rather than confronting and disciplining the former congressman. Hastert and Boehner didn't even ask Foley to quietly step down from his position as head of the House Caucus on Missing and Exploited Children, which would at least have removed a portion of ironic sting from the scandal.

Although in truth, Foley's leadership of that particular caucus is rather less ironic than it appears, given the way in which other gay pedophiles gravitate toward positions as school teachers, scoutmasters, sports coaches and other occupations that offer close contact with their favored prey. I haven't checked the Congressional Record, but is there any doubt as to which way Rep. Foley voted on the issue of subjecting public school children to strip searches by the school authorities?

No doubt the congressman will want to look into the possibility of teaching civics at his local high school. After six terms in Washington, he surely has a lot to offer the youth of America.

Now, none of this is to say the other half of the bi-factional ruling coalition is any better. Democrats may not be as hypocritical as Republicans, but then, it's rather difficult to fall short of a nonexistent standard. If Foley were a Democrat, he'd still be in Congress and the NEA would be giving him an award for his efforts to interest students in political science.

Nevertheless, it is long past time for conservatives to begin judging the Republican Party for its deeds and not its promises. The current collection of unprincipled reprobates are incapable of governing themselves, still less a sovereign nation of 300 million individuals. There is no lesser evil and following the Republican Party over the cliff will prove no less fatal than if it were the more openly appalling Democrats at the wheel.

Any genuine conservative would have to be blind, deaf and cognitively challenged to continue to support the Republican Party. The Foley scandal is simply one more proof that the Gay Old Pedophiles cannot be reformed, they can only be abandoned.

Draping the devil

October 9, 2006

IT SEEMS that the exposure of unseemly Republican aides and politicians, along with the concomitant improvement in odds that Democrats will take the House and Senate, has caused a certain influential New Media Democrat to become overly giddy at the prospect of a return to Democratic rule. But it's not that Markos Moulitsas' notion of godless mega-churches is completely pointless—although one has to wonder if those more committed to aborting and abusing children than raising them will actually see child care as a major draw—only that it's redundant.

After all, hundreds of "real-world destinations for progressives and liberals throughout the Midwest, 'cultural outposts' designed to attract thousands of like-minded liberals" with "a vast left-wing conspiracy component" already exist. They are called "universities" and "colleges," and they are becoming increasingly irrelevant to modern life thanks to their ongoing transformation from centers of learning to centers of left-wing indoctrination.

Even more quixotic than this vision of organized secular religion, however, is Moulitsas' notion of the Libertarian Democrat, an ideological creature every bit as polygeneric as the gryphon, the centaur, the chimaera or the hippogriff, and as mythical. Kos described this incredible creature in an blog post this summer. Incredibly, he even claimed to have located a few of these rare beasts hidden away in the El Dorado of the Mountain West, presumably feral descendants of the lost menagerie that once belonged to Mr. Braddock Washington.

While Kos correctly ascertains that unlike the Reagan-era Republican Party, modern Republicans are no friends of libertarianism or small government, his discovery of a mutated Third Danger is based on a common and overly simplistic political Manicheanism. He writes:

Traditional "libertarianism" holds that government is evil and thus must be minimized.... The problem with this form of libertarianism is that it assumes that only two forces can infringe on liberty—the government and other individuals. The Libertarian Democrat understands that there is a third danger to personal liberty—the corporation. The Libertarian Dem understands that corporations, left unchecked, can be huge dangers to our personal liberties.

Kos here commits the same error as columnist Eric Alterman, who continually advocates expanded government as a much-needed check on the otherwise untrammeled powers of the mighty multinational corporations. And in doing so, the great mind of the New Media Left ironically shows himself to be trapped in the same 19th century socialist mindset of the Old Media. For, as I have previously explained, corporatism is not capitalism, and there is no inherent rivalry between the great corporations and the national governments.

Indeed, such a rivalry is impossible, since corporations are nothing more than creations of the state, artificial persons created from the clay of legalese and given life in the form of a tax identification number by the secretary of state. As children of the state, they are subject to their masters and helpless before them, not even a corporate giant like Microsoft can hope to stand against the smallest state in the Union, much less an international government, as evidenced by almost $1 billion in fines being levied against it by the EU.

The true relationship between government and corporation is a symbiotic one, with the latter often acting as an agent of the former in preying upon the wealth of the population. Take the insurance industry, for example. The insurance corporations lobby the government for laws requiring automobile insurance to be purchased from an insurance company to receive a license plate from the government. This causes money to flow first to the insurance company, with a cut of the profits then paid to the government in the form of corporate and employee taxes. The partnership between the state and its corporations is necessary, because without the use of government force to deny the roads to unlicensed vehicles, safe drivers who seldom crash their cars and generate pure profits for the public-private partnership would likely never bother to purchase insurance against a low-probability event. And without corporate participation, the revenue collection would simply amount to an overt tax.

Since the relationship between state and corporation is symbiotic, the state will only act as a check on corporations when their activities contravene the state interest, not individual rights or the interests of the populace. This is why online gambling was recently banned, because it primarily benefited foreign corporations without generating income for any domestic governments. The fact that many forms of state-sponsored gambling are unaffected by this gambling ban proves that protection of the financial well-being of individual gamblers was never a factor, the noble rhetoric notwithstanding.

Government cannot be relied upon to act against corporate interests because in most cases, it shares those interests and possesses a direct financial stake in them. Because the Kosian concept of the Libertarian Democrat relies upon the false presumption of rival interests, it is a logical dead end and does not represent "progressivism for a new century" so much as yet another attempt to drape the devil in angel's robes.

Oh ye of little faith

October 16, 2006

THE JIG IS UP. The non-proliferation bluff has been called by a second-generation socialist dictator and the nuclear powers who so jealously guarded their destructive privilege for decades are revealed to be holding nothing. This really should not be surprising, given that none of the countries who developed or are believed to have developed nuclear weapons had ever had their programs attacked during their various development periods.

Furthermore, of the 15 nations which possessed significant nuclear weapons programs but did not go on to complete a functional weapons system, only Iraq was ever attacked. So, the odds that the Nuke Club was speaking loudly and carrying nothing were always weighted heavily in Kim Jong-il's favor, the infamous Axis of Evil speech notwithstanding.

North Korea's nuclear test—assuming that it was, in fact, nuclear—was not merely a massive blow to the credibility of the Nuke Club, but also highlighted the nonsensical nature of the case for a military strike against Iran. Indeed, when one takes the time to consider the justification for the current Iraqi occupation, it quickly becomes apparent that the Iranian nuclear program can be as easily justified and on the very same grounds.

The neoconservative World Democratic Revolution is predicated on two basic concepts. The first is the Wilsonian notion of a people's right to self-determination. While not a primary justification of either the Afghani or Iraqi wars, it is the main basis of both continuing occupations, which are theoretically in place to allow the people of those two countries to peacefully and democratically determine the way in which they will be governed now that the oppressive regimes that previously ruled over them have been removed by American force.

While the Bush administration's insistence on an undivided Iraq raises some serious questions about its genuine commitment to this right of self-determination, it nevertheless remains the primary rationale for the continuing occupation there. The reason the insurgency remains a concern is not due to any threat it poses to the USA, but to that which it poses to the infant Iraqi democracy which theoretically represents the collective will of the Iraqi people.

However, it is impossible to claim that a nation has a right to determine how it will be governed and simultaneously deny that a nation has a right to determine how it will defend itself, let alone supply its power needs. Even if a nation does not possess a democratic government, it is entirely possible that the will of the people would support its government possessing nuclear weapons, perhaps on the basis of national pride but more likely out of a preference for the familiarity of dictatorial rule over the violence and chaos of a military invasion and occupation by a foreign power.

The second pillar of the World Democratic Revolution is the idea that people everywhere want to be free. This, unfortunately, is arguable even in the United States due to its current flirtation with a host of abominable government powers ranging from domestic spying to secret trials and torture. If Americans, with their Constitution and a tradition of liberty that spans hundreds of years, are perfectly willing to accept an all-powerful central state that intrudes upon the lives of its citizens at will for fear of a terrorist attack on a single city, it should not be hard to imagine that the autocratic religious dictatorship of the mullahs does not seem unbearable in comparison with the thought of tactical nuke strikes on dozens of locations around Iran.

But the most important reason that the United States should accept Iran's acquisition of nuclear weapons is that it simply has no other choice. The technological imperative can be delayed for a time, but it cannot be denied. Not even the powerful idea behind so much of the support for the United Nations, that world government can prevent the mass destruction caused by a nuclear war, will suffice to prevent anyone with the means and the desire from acquiring the weapon that endows the owner with autonomy on the world stage and freedom from fear of American military action.

Finally, many Republicans argue that an attack on Iran is justified due to the perceived probability of an Iranian attack on Israel. But George Bush, being a Christian, should know better than to worry about Israel even if there was anything he could do about the Iranian bomb. If the modern Jewish state truly is the prophesied Israel of the Bible, then it will survive by the grace of the Lord God of Israel even if every single Arab and Islamic state in the Middle East launches nuclear missiles against it.

It takes an amount of faith to believe that North Korea and Iran are more interested in inoculating themselves against American military force than in immolating the world. But it takes a very blind faith indeed to believe that there is any effective means of permanently preventing a nation-state from going nuclear once it decides to do so, without resorting to utter barbarism.

The pope of Princeton

October 23, 2006

HAVING PREVIOUSLY informed us that infanticide, if performed in a timely fashion, is compatible with die Neue Ethik of which he is a champion, the professorial pride of New Jersey is now turning his attention toward correcting the moral misapprehensions of Middle America.

In a recent column in the Guardian, Singer draws on the philosophies of John Stuart Mill and HLA Hart, the sexually explicit temple carvings of India and international anti-discrimination laws in a meandering attempt to disguise the fact that he has no intention of even beginning to explain why the view that homosexuality is immoral is incorrect. Considering that the assertion of this flawed legal foundation is supposedly the central point of his article, the omission is astounding and its curious absence goes a long way toward explaining some of Singer's other, equally convincing lines of reason.

After skating very lightly past Islamic objections to homosexuality on the basis of their lack of secular democracy and habit of incorporating religious teachings into law, Singer first turns to Mill's and his principle that "the only purpose for which power can be rightfully exercised over any member of a civilized community, against his will, is to prevent harm to others" as a foundation for his moral argument. But rightly sensing that this principle of individual sovereignty would forbid a veritable host of actions he deems acceptable, such as abortion, public education and the income tax, Singer quickly drops Mills in favor of Hart's hair-splitting division of legal paternalism and legal moralism.

No doubt the unsound foundation of Mill's formation for his case encourages this speedy departure, as it is far from clear that homosexuality, in all its disease-ridden, suicide- and violence-prone glory, does no harm to others. Indeed, on the sole basis of J.S. Mill, one possesses a better case for the morality of necrophilia, cannibalism and rape.

Hart's primary departure from Mill is his acceptance of the idea that the state may interfere with an individual if it does so on behalf of his physical well-being, hence the intrinsic morality of seat-belt and helmet laws. But Singer leaps from Mill's frying pan into Hart's fire here, since there can be no doubt that forced restraint from homosexual activity will cause far less physical harm to an individual than such activity permitted unrestrained. Hart's legal paternalism actually provides a irreligious moral basis for the illegality of homosexuality, and Singer's perverse citation of it only highlights the poverty of his reasoning.

Singer then turns, even more fruitlessly, to address the reproductive objection to the harm that homosexuality does to societal continuity. While it is fair to point out, as he does, that this objection has little weight in overpopulated India, he is silent about its obvious applicability to dying Europe, especially to a Britain possessing a 2002 birth rate of 1.64 per woman, 22 percent below the rate required for a stable population.

But Singer's biggest blunder is to ignore the obvious and direct connection between morality and legality, especially in secular democracies such as the United Kingdom and the United States which feature no shortage of religious teachings incorporated into their laws. While laws and morals are not the same and should not be confused with each other, as the Founding Fathers made explicitly clear, the laws of the land stem from the moral sensibility of the people. Modify the latter and the former will, in time, inevitably alter. This blunder stems from Singer's desire to avoid confronting the ultimate source of the view that homosexuality is immoral, namely, the written foundation of the Judeo-Christian ethic which is an implacable enemy of Singer's Neue Ethik, the Christian Bible.

This atheistic discomfort with directly disputing the religious ethic is all too typical, because if they admit that Judeo-Christian morality stems from nothing more than its mythical sky deity, they risk casting aside centuries of civilization-sustaining belief in favor of dancing with Darwinian nihilism. What is right for the philosophers and the Pope of Princeton is, as Voltaire noted, all too dangerous a seed in the minds of hoi polloi.

And yet, Singer's bulls notwithstanding, if sin is nothing more than a perception instilled by social tradition, is it not remarkable how its Biblical wages are so reliably paid?

The clowns of reason

October 30, 2006

THIS MONTH'S Wired Magazine featured an interesting article by Gary Wolf entitled "The Church of the Non-Believers." Considering that it was written by a self-confessed disbeliever, it was remarkably free of the foam-flecked rhetoric that dribbles so freely from the New Atheists featured in the article, Richard Dawkins, Sam Harris, and Daniel Dennett.

It's hard to decide which of the images painted rather skillfully by Wolf is the most informative. The painful naivete of Harris, the bitter celodurismo of Dawkins and the avuncular arrogance of Dennett are all sketched in brief, but vivid detail, but in the end, I found the comparison between the grim, pedestrian joylessness of Atheists United and the "moving spectacle" of a charismatic church service to be the most damning.

Of the three jesters at the Court of Reason, Harris is clearly the sad-faced slapstick and pratfall guy. His ignorance is profound; he opens *The End of Faith* with a convincing demonstration of his lack of knowledge of the history of suicide bombing. After painting a clichéd portrait of an Islamic bus bomber, he writes: "Why is it so easy, then, so trivially easy—you-could-almost-bet-your-life-on-it easy—to guess the young man's religion?"

It is easy, so trivially easy—one-finds-oneself-cringing-at-the-punctuation easy—to display Harris' superficiality. Having already rejected Pascal's Wager, the hapless Harris seems prone to staking his life on foolish bets since he has apparently never heard of the Tamil Tigers, "an adamantly secular group with Hindu roots" that University of Chicago professor Edward Pape, the author of "Dying to Win: The Strategic Logic of Suicide Terrorism," describes as "the leading purveyors of suicide attacks over the last two decades."

Of course, it's understandable that such a deeply profound public intellectual like Harris would never have heard of this obscure little group, since they don't blow up buses in global media centers, they merely assassinate prime ministers of the world's second most populous nation.

Harris also demonstrates reasoning skills that are as poor as his historical knowledge. Indeed, he is so rationally incompetent that he inadvertently makes a case against that which he wishes to defend instead of his intended target. In describing the growing danger that religious belief poses to mankind, he writes:

Our technical advances in the art of war have finally rendered our religious differences—and hence our religious beliefs—antithetical to our survival. We can no longer ignore the fact that billions of our neighbors believe in the metaphysics of martyrdom, or in the literal truth of the book of Revelation, or any of the other fantastical notions that have lurked in the minds of the faithful for millennia—because our neighbors are now armed with chemical, biological, and nuclear weapons. There is no doubt that these developments mark the terminal phase of our credulity. Words like "God" and "Allah" must go the way of "Apollo" and "Baal," or they will unmake our world.

But this is a neo-Luddite attack on science, not an atheist argument against religion. As Harris admits himself, these "fantastical notions" have been around for millennia without imperiling the world, it is the chemical, biological and nuclear products of Reason encapsulated in the methodology of science that pose the actual danger. Even if one could magically sweep out every fragment of religious faith and supernatural superstition from every human mind, the clear and present physical danger to the world from those weapons would remain exactly the same.

And when one considers that an estimated 89.2 percent of all the wars in history were fought for reasons unrelated to religion, one cannot even argue that the probability of those weapons being used would be significantly reduced in a perfectly secular scenario.

Harris then goes on to assert that two myths protect religious faith from rational criticism, first that "there are good things that people get from religious faith that cannot be had elsewhere", and second "the terrible things that are sometimes done in the name of religion are the products not of faith per se but of our baser natures."

One is tempted to respond by stating that it is a demonstrable absence of rational critics that protects religious faith from rational criticism, but even a clown deserves a fair critique. First, anyone who has attended an American university in the last 40 years knows that religious faith receives more than its fair share of rational criticism, and it is evolution that is legally protected from uncomfortable questions by the courts in the United States, not Christianity, Judaism or Islam.

Second, the myths themselves are simply not mythical. For individuals and nations alike, the advantages of religious faith are increasingly being made manifest in a manner amenable to scientific study. And one would have to be unaware of 100 years of events ranging from the French revolutionary terror to the killing fields of Kampuchea to even consider taking his second myth seriously.

Sam Harris may be last and least in this trinity of clowns, but I have to confess, I'm rather looking forward to his new book, *Letter To A Christian Nation*. I think he has a real shot at replacing Scott Adams as the leading American comic of the 21st century.

The clowns of reason, II

November 6, 2006

Looking for art in science
Is a peculiar aspiration,
For there is little wonder
Once Man denies Creation.

And his reduction to mere numbers
O'er the passing of the years,
Leaves us with naught but the aesthetics
Of damned chess-club engineers.

U NLIKE SAM HARRIS, Richard Dawkins possesses a formidable mind. And unlike the ploddingly hapless Harris, Dawkins is an engaging, even charming writer. It is impossible to dislike anyone so utterly sound on the poisonousness of post-modernism, still less one who harbors such a genuine appreciation for beauty and the literary arts.

Richard Dawkins, in short, has a soul, even if he would be the last to credit it.

What he does not possess, strangely enough, is a firm grasp of the very Reason he champions. It is a great irony that the world's foremost spokesman for secular science, a method founded upon the primacy of empirical evidence, should totally disregard mountains of evidence in favor of mystical pronouncements about ontological possibilities.

In *Unweaving the Rainbow*, Dawkins writes:

Keats, too, complained that Newton had destroyed the poetry of the rainbow by explaining it. By more general implication, science is poetry's killjoy, dry and cold, cheerless, overbearing and lacking in everything that a young Romantic might desire. To proclaim the opposite is one purpose of this book, and I shall here limit myself to the untestable speculation that Keats, like Yeats, might have been an even better poet if he had gone to science for some of his inspiration.

This speculation is as improbable as it as untestable, given the ample evidence that science is simply not capable of providing the inspiration for passable poetry, much less great art. Forget Irish astronomical telescopes and D.H. Lawrence's hummingbirds, what could be more profoundly poetic than the dystopian prospect of Man's suicidal annihilation by the deadly fruits of his mind? And yet, in six decades of the Atomic Age, the only memorable pronouncement is J. Robert Oppenheimer's invocation of the Bhagavad Gita!

While one can envision Byronesque epics dedicated to the tortile beauties of the DNA helix and dolorous quatrains lamenting the darker aspects of apoptosis, it would require Oscar Wilde's proverbial heart of stone to do so with a straight face.

At Richard Dawkins' core is a band geek who is unable to accept the reality that marching tubas will never impress the girls. For all its passionate and detailed explanations of water droplets and whole new kinds of suns, *Unweaving the Rainbow* ultimately amounts to little more than an unconvincing and repetitive refrain: "This one time, at band camp..." Still, Dawkins' belief in the artistic possibilities of science is rather sweet. It is, as I believe I have read somewhere, the substance of things hoped for, the evidence of things not seen.

If Dawkins' failure to assemble empirical evidence in support of his belief in science-inspired art is harmless enough, the same is not true for his making the same mistake in postulating civilized behavior and morality without a basis in traditional "superstitions". In a 2003 article in the Guardian entitled "Bin Laden's Victory", Dawkins wrote:

Like sin and like terror (Bush's favourite target before the Iraq distraction) Evil is not an entity, not a spirit, not a force to be opposed and subdued. Evil is a miscellaneous collection of nasty things that nasty people do.

But substituting "nasty" for "evil" explains nothing, it solves nothing and in this context, the substitution is wholly meaningless. Dawkins states that evil is not a force to be opposed but does not bother to explain what nastiness is nor why it should be opposed either, even though he recommends the modification of Western institutions, constitutions and electoral systems specifically in order to oppose it.

In his latest book, *The God Delusion*, Dawkins commits the very error he lambasts in clinging to the common atheist delusion of religion being a primary cause of war in the face of the vast quantities of evidence recorded to the contrary. If religion was an integral element of warfare, one would think that Sun Tzu, Caesar, Vegetius, Machiavelli or Clausewitz would have noticed and commented upon it. And the professor's strange comment that nations "whose infantrymen act on their own initiative rather than following orders will tend to lose wars" will be met with no little amusement by those familiar with USMC war fighting doctrine.

The Marine Corps' style of warfare requires intelligent leaders with a penchant for boldness and initiative down to the lowest levels.

—*MCDP1: Warfighting*, the United States Marine Corps

It is the combination of his anti-empirical approach with an inability to perceive the obvious consequences of his assertions that leaves Dawkins in the position of a tone-deaf singer who cannot hear how out of tune he is. He confesses his surprise at how often he is asked why he bothers to get up in the mornings; clearly his readers understand the logical implications of his ideas much better than their author.

Richard Dawkins is an interesting and thought-provoking writer and I am informed that he is an excellent evolutionary biologist. As historian, logician and philosopher, however, he makes for a most amusing clown at Reason's court.

3-monkey massacre

November 13, 2006

F OR THE LAST DECADE, ever since the failed implementation of the Contract With America, Republican moderates, Rockefellerites and the mainstream media have preached that in order to maintain its grasp on the electorate, the Republican Party would have to move to the center and establish a Big Tent. This wisdom was embraced and repeated ad nauseam by most of the conservative commentariat, which with only a few exceptions was quite happy to "carry the water" (in Rush Limbaugh's term) for the party's political pragmatists.

This Republican pragmatism came at the price of Republican principles. Conservatism was replaced by compassionate conservatism. Small government was replaced by strong government. National defense was replaced by the defense of Middle Eastern democracy. National sovereignty was replaced by the Free Trade Area of the Americas. Congressional declarations of war were replaced by permission slips from the United Nations. The Department of Education was not closed, but the Department of Heimland Sicherheit was created.

The pragmatists claimed that all of these betrayals of conservative principles were nothing more than the necessary price required to establish a long-term electoral supremacy that would enjoy a life span expected to rival the Democratic Party's 41-year reign from 1954 to 1995.

But last week, the unprincipled pragmatists were proven to be completely wrong. And worse than wrong, they were shown to be counterproductive, as the only thing more useless than selling one's soul for temporal power is giving it away in exchange for nothing at all. Nor can pragmatists convincingly claim that the Republican defeat was the result of unpredictable incidents such as the Foley scandal or even rather more predictable events such as the failing military occupation of Iraq, since this unlooked-for turn of fortune was not only predictable, it was predicted:

> *Pragmatism in politics is self-defeating in the long run. It is a euphemism for the slow sacrifice of one's principles. The constant substitution of "electable" moderates for principled conservatives is what repeatedly kills the Republican Party and prevents it from ever realizing even a small part of its platform when it is in power.*

—"Satanic Schwarzeneggerians", September 15, 2003

> *Genuinely conservative Republicans are dismayed by the president's unveiling of his core liberalism and rightly fear for the future of a party which has likely seen its high-water mark already.*

—"The Coming Conservative Collapse", September 19, 2005

By the pragmatic logic, both Gerald Ford and George Bush were more electable than Ronald Reagan. But when Reagan finally got his chance in 1980, he won in a landslide, with a margin of 440 votes in the Electoral College. By the same pragmatic logic, Bob Dole was considered far more electable than his conservative rival for the 1996 nomination, Patrick Buchanan. Despite that electability, he lost by 220 Electoral College votes to an incumbent who was never popular enough to win a majority of the popular vote.

Unfortunately for conservatives, the Republican Party is still held closely in the grasp of the unprincipled. Calls for accommodation have already rung out from the highest circles, under the mistaken assumption that most Americans would rather see more government action, even if it is misguided, than gridlock. And even if one accepts that notion at face-value, one has to wonder at the bizarre strategery of those political experts who believe that making a Democratic Congress look good in comparison with its predecessor will somehow aid future Republican fortunes.

Conservatives should resign themselves to recognizing that 2008 is already a lost cause for them. Even if the Pelosi-led Democratic Congress badly overreaches, on immigration, for example, chances are good that they will be insulated from blame by a complicit President Bush. That, combined with the fact that three moderate-to-liberal Republicans, Romney, McCain and Giuliani, are the current front-runners for the presidential nomination, all but ensures the Lizard Queen's ascension to the Cherry Blossom Throne.

(Speak no ill of her, lest she unleash the full fury of the Patriot Acts upon thee!)

But there is a silver lining in the dark clouds on the horizon. Defeat has caused even some of the most blind, deaf and dumb Three-Monkey Republicans to begin to reconsider the conventional wisdom that they hitherto accepted so blithely. The lesson is not yet learned, not fully, but the crushing sting of a Clinton victory in 2008 should prove sufficiently salutary to convince the party's rank-and-file that a return to Reagan Republicanism is in order.

Running with the turtles

November 20, 2006

MAN CAN PROVIDE a reasonable defense for almost any idea he dreams up. We are not rational creatures so much as we are rationalizing animals, creating post-facto defenses for what we have chosen to believe due to its emotional appeal.

The human mind has a powerful tendency to cling to its beliefs, regardless of how they have been acquired. We are loyal to them in much the same way we hold to our sports teams, and often with as little reason and as little reward. (There speaks the Minnesota Vikings fan, still bitter about Drew Pearson and the most infamous no-call in NFL history… and don't even mention Gary Anderson).

Most beliefs are based on underlying assumptions, which come in varying degrees of validity. But even the most invalid assumption will remain a solid foundation if it goes unquestioned. And while it is often uncomfortable to question the assumptions that underlie our beliefs, it is the best way to strengthen those beliefs… assuming that they pass the test.

Indeed, the anger often expressed by those whose beliefs are being questioned reveals their fundamental lack of faith in them, in their confidence that their assumptions will survive the questioning. The more insecure the belief, the less the believer can afford himself any questioning of his base assumptions.

Two of the basic assumptions that underlie public schooling is that mass education is beneficial to society and that group education does not inhibit the intellectual development of the individual student. While I am not entirely sure that the former is true, I am content to leave it unmolested for the time being. I am, however, interested in questioning the logic of the latter assumption.

An American child is the recipient of 13 years of group schooling, assuming that he has been to kindergarten. But consider, for example, a non-elite, but above-average child who is more intelligent than three-fourths of the student population, but less intelligent than the highest quartile. If he is limited to the performance of the average, as is necessarily the case in a classroom environment, in the first year he will only be advancing at 62.5 percent of his capability. And by the time he finishes third grade, he will be at only 15 percent of where he could be if he had been permitted to advance at the pace at which he is capable.

This may sound absurd, of course, and it is, but there is an element of truth in it. When we do not permit our children to test their limits, when we impose limits upon them, we rob them of the chance to experience the fullness of their potential. What is lost will not necessarily be made up as time passes, since it is impossible for us, as adults, to know what a child, with that child's imagination that we have long forgotten, will choose to do even at a very young age.

There is no shortage of empirical evidence suggesting that homeschool is a better means of allowing children to develop their intellectual capabilities than public school. This is not to say that it is the ideal means of doing so, much less that developing a child's intellect is one of the most important aspects of parenting or that such development can or should be forced.

Many parents are content if their children simply grow up to be healthy, happy and normal. There is nothing wrong with this, this world would be a better place if every child could be so blessed. But it would be a pity to waste the potential being thrown away every year by parents allowing their children to be held back by professionals whose primary interest is maintaining order and a uniform level of advancement where no child is left behind.

It is important to remember that Aesop only wrote fables and the tortoise cannot always run with the hare. No educational system that forgets that can hope to truly educate either.

The clowns of reason, III

November 27, 2006

SEVENTY-FOUR YEARS AGO, the great inventor Nikola Tesla accused scientists of practicing metaphysics rather than science, of engaging in ontological speculation rather than empirical experimentation. Apparently science is rather hard work, since despite Tesla's very public accusations in his letter to the *New York Times,* many so-called scientists today continue to demonstrate a tendency to assiduously avoid doing anything that can be legitimately described as science.

But not even Tesla could accuse Daniel Dennett of shirking his scientific responsibilities, for he is simply a professor of philosophy despite the scientific trappings that surround his books and his reputation. Still, it is interesting to note that of the three New Atheists lauded as champions of Science, only one is an actual scientist, the other two hailing from a modern discipline now better known for copious bong usage than anything intellectual.

Now, Dennett is no Harris, which is to say that he is not prone to making factual errors in nearly every paragraph he writes, but like Harris, he is an inept logician. Consider the following statements Dennett made in a 2003 interview with Salon:

Tell us the story from your new book about the ant and the blade of grass.

Suppose you go out in the meadow and you see this ant climbing up a blade of grass and if it falls it climbs again. It's devoting a tremendous amount of energy and persistence to climbing up this blade of grass. What's in it for the ant? Nothing. It's not looking for a mate or showing off or looking for food. Its brain has been invaded by a tiny parasitic worm, a lancet fluke, which has to get into the belly of a sheep or a cow in order to continue its life cycle. It has commandeered the brain of this ant and it's driving it up the blade of grass like an all-terrain vehicle. That's how this tiny lancet fluke does its evolutionary work.

Is religion, then, like a lancet fluke?

The question is, Does anything like that happen to us? The answer is, Well, yes. Not with actual brain worms but with ideas. An idea takes over our brain and gets that person to devote his life to the furtherance of that idea, even at the cost of their own genetics. People forgo having kids, risk their lives, devote their whole lives to the furtherance of an idea, rather than doing what every other species on the planet does—make more children and grandchildren.

It seems to have escaped the professor's notice that it is not the religious portion of the population that is demonstrably having trouble doing what every other species on the planet does, but rather, the fungus among us, the godless. If there is a metaphorical lancet fluke to be blamed for anti-evolutionary human behavior, then it is atheist secularism which most accurately fits the profile now that the Shakers and Skoptsi are no more. Indeed, the demographic performance of secular Western societies over the last fifty years suggest that from a grand historical perspective, modern secularism will be seen as a fluke indeed.

But if Dennett's weak logic merely provides some small ironic amusement here, it threatens to become downright dangerous when he attempts to solve the Darwinian dilemma of morality by positing an evolved free will that gives humanity the opportunity to usurp the Blind Watchmaker of natural selection and begin to guide its own evolution.

For this concept points inevitably to what Charles Stross fans will recognize as transhumanism, which is nothing more than Eugenics 2.0. Little wonder, then, that in light of the transhuman meme currently percolating in science fiction circles, another clown of Reason, Richard Dawkins, should publish an open letter calling for a reopening of the eugenics question, a question previously answered firmly in the negative following the ugliness resulting from certain German eugenics enthusiasts and their famous experiments in guided evolution.

Like Dawkins and his Watchmaker, Dennett is blind to the probabilities of where this guided evolution is likely to lead, or the way in which it is likely to be inimical to the very evolved human freedom he champions. For when asked where society will find its moral foundation if not from religion, Dennett responds with a tautology:

> *Rules that we lay down ourselves.... Now we can continue to expand the circle and get more people involved, and do it in a less disingenuous way by excising the myth about how this is God's law. It is our law.*

But even if Dennett is correct and there is no magician behind the moral curtain, this assumes that the positive consequences of revealing his absence will outweigh the negative ones. Needless to say, philosophers from Socrates to Voltaire and Nietzsche have strongly disagreed with this optimistic proposition, despite their similar skepticism about the truth of God's existence.

Dennett is also an enthusiastic promulgator of the crudely propagandistic term "bright", which is the atheist's would-be self-serving term for himself. (Why he didn't go directly for "super handsome sex machine to all the chicks", I'll never know.) But while one must respect every intellectual's right to label his own beliefs, in light of Dennett's "stubborn and complete intolerance of any creed, belief, or opinion that differs from [his] own," it would be more accurate to follow the pronunciation of the guard at the castle of Guy de Loimbard in making use of the term.

And contrary to Dennett's declaration in *Breaking the Spell*, thinking theists have nothing to fear from this insubstantial bigot or his Darwin-inspired memes. As Leon Wieseltier pointed out in his review of Dennett's book in the *New York Times*, "It will be plain that Dennett's approach to religion is contrived to evade religion's substance."

Dennett does not use the tools of science to analyze religion, he merely misuses the tools of philosophy to sketch caricatures of an imaginary concept which bears only a vague and superficial resemblance to genuine religious faith. While some of his philosophical questions are not without merit, his evasive answers and fraudulent assertions reveal him to be little more than a bearded jongleur attempting to avoid dropping plates as he dances before the throne of Reason.

Godless criminals

December 4, 2006

ONE OF THE MORE UNEXPECTED THEMES in the critical responses to my three "Clowns of Reason" columns was the counterintuitive assertion that atheists are more moral than religious individuals in general and Christians in particular. This assertion was usually supported by various rationalizations, one historical, one theoretical and one statistical.

The historical argument for atheist morality is the most easily addressed, as it is simply a variant on the demonstrably false "religion causes war" claim. The critic usually pointed to the Spanish Inquisition or the European witch-burnings and said: "See, atheists don't burn people at the stake." Well, that's technically true, although since atheists are currently crushing Christian skulls with bulldozers in North Korea and beating them to death in China, it's an argument that is as nonsensical as it is outdated.

The theoretical argument is that since atheists don't require the threat of punishment in the afterlife to behave morally in the here and now, they are better, more moral individuals. Of course, this would be true, if it could be established that they were, in fact, better behaved—and that they possessed a universal morality to which their behavior could be reasonably compared.

Now, some atheists have claimed that the irreligious are better behaved in terms of Christian morality, but little evidence to support this has been offered, while John Stossel and Arthur Brooks have both found that "the single biggest predictor of whether someone will be charitable is their religious participation"; religious people give four times more than the non-religious.

Charity, of course, is far from the only measure of morality. And this leads us to the third argument, the statistical one. It should come as a surprise to no one that the last and least of Reason's clowns leans heavily upon it; in his latest proselytistic pamphlet, *Letter to a Christian Nation*, Sam Harris writes:

> *While political party affiliation in the United States is not a perfect indicator of religiosity, it is no secret that the "red states" are primarily red because of the overwhelming political influence of conservative Christians. If there were a strong correlation between Christian conservatism and social health, we might expect to see some sign of it in red-state America. We don't. Of the 25 cities with the lowest rates of violent crime, 62 percent are in "blue" states and 38 percent are in "red" states.... Of the 22 states with the highest rates of murder, 17 are red.*

As with so much that Harris writes, this immediately triggers the thinking man's bovine ejectus detector. Since Christian conservatives aren't generally known to be big-city dwellers, the implication would seem to be that Texas Christians are driving into Houston, Dallas and San Antonio to wreak lethal havoc. Of course, as with his blatant errors on war and suicide bombers, it's easy enough to prove that Harris not only has it wrong, but backwards.

Consider Florida, which went Republican in 2004. It has 67 counties, and the 10 that supported John Kerry most heavily (thus, by Harris' reckoning, the least religious) were home to 367 murders in 2006. The 10 counties wherein Bush found his strongest support, on the other hand, had only 19. Even taking population differences into account, the murder rate per 100,000 in the "blue" counties was more than twice that of the "red" counties, 4.7 to 2.0. And the two most murderous counties in the state, Gadsden and Madison, averaged a murder rate of 13.9 to go with their 60 percent support for the Democrat.

It is clearly perverse, bordering on the intellectually dishonest, to attempt charging these godless "blue-county" murders to the religious "red-state" account.

Nor are American statistics the only means of demonstrating a godless proclivity for crime, the inherent problem of equating legality with morality notwithstanding. A comparison of a 2000 survey of the British prison population with the 2001 national census revealed that whereas individuals claiming atheism or no religion make up only 15.5 percent of the British population, they comprise 31.9 percent of those imprisoned.

Of course, it stands to reason that those who do not believe in biblical morality would not subscribe to it. The fact that so many atheists behave as well as anyone else is not testimony to superior atheist morality, but rather, the moral inertia fortuitously intrinsic to Western civilization.

Brownshirts are marching

December 11, 2006

THE INCREASINGLY LAWLESS behavior of the pro-immigration forces in America is both informative and telling. It is a clear warning of precisely what these forces stand for as well as what they hope America will become. For the problem is not that America is being invaded by millions of semi-civilized aliens with no cultural or historical ties to American traditions and liberties, or respect for them, but that America is being transformed by these invaders.

As Umberto Eco pointed out in his 1990 essay entitled "Migrazioni," there is a crucial difference between immigration and migration. In the case of immigration, it is the immigrant who is transformed. This was the case in historical immigrations from Ireland, Germany, Italy and Scandinavia, where the immigrating generation quickly adapted to the language and culture of its new land and the second and third generations were all but impossible to distinguish from Americans who could trace their roots back to the original colonies.

This adaptation was made possible by three factors. First, the desire of the immigrants to become Americans. This can be seen in the readiness with which past immigrants changed their names and quickly adopted English, to such an extent that the third generation rarely spoke more than a word or two of their grandfather's tongue. Second, the similarities between the Western, Christian cultures of Europe and the Western, Christian culture of the United States. Third, the number and the proportion of immigrants was smaller, for example, 3.5 million Irish immigrants arriving over a 60-year period versus more than 9.8 million Mexicans entering in the last two decades.

Obviously, this is not immigration, this is a migration, and in the case of a migration, it is the destination that is transformed, not the immigrants.

Destination transformation is a perverse, but common consequence of migratory behavior. While it seems counterintuitive to leave one place in favor of another, then seek to recreate the very situation one previously fled, this is actually normal human behavior. And despite the inflammatory attacks on those who very reasonably oppose this transformation, there is nothing wrong with opposing it. Does it make a Washingtonian racist to oppose the Californication of his state? Is a Naples, Fla. resident bigoted simply because he dislikes sitting in gridlocked traffic all winter as his city is temporarily transformed into a southern suburb of Minneapolis?

Of course not. The real distinction between Brown America and America is not racial, but rather cultural and ideological. The problem with Brown America is not that sunscreen sales will take a hit, but that Brown America will be indistinguishable from every other semi-civilized third-world country in its disregard for human liberty, its contempt for law and limited government, and its short-sighted abuse of society's most productive classes. One can already see this situation developing in Mexifornia, and the fact that Brown America's most enthusiastic proponents so readily demonstrate their disdain for elemental American concepts such as the freedom of speech and the right to free assembly highlights the great ideological divide.

There is nothing moral about the pro-immigration position. Would the Michigan brownshirts argue that America must also be willing to accept the importation of 10 percent of the Chinese or Indian populations? If not, on what basis could they possibly argue for granting citizenship to masses of Mexican nationals while denying the claims of the Chinese and Indian masses to the same? The truth is that even the proponents of Brown America believe in immigration restrictions, they would merely set the numerical limit much higher than those who value historical America and its freedoms.

Given that their position is so nonsensical and the way in which any serious discussion will reveal that fact, it is little wonder that the brownshirts are so desperate to stifle all debate on the matter. But they will not be able to hide long behind disingenuous accusations of racism and "hate," not when even a shameless multiculturalist such as British Prime Minister Tony Blair is being forced to retreat from his long-held pro-immigration extremism: "Failure to talk about multiculturalism is not politically correct, it's stupid.... Very good intentions got the better of us."

Unfortunately, the fact that most Americans support immigration restrictions and alien deportations in order to preserve their nation does not mean that the Democratic Congress or the Republican White House will cooperate, either now or in the future. Brown America is not the chance result of huddled Mexican masses yearning to breathe free, it is simply the bi-factional ruling party's Brechtian solution to the problem of American liberty; dissolving one people and electing another.

The war they can't win

December 18, 2006

EVERYONE from Americans United for Separation of Church and State to Wonkette swears up and down that there is no unholy alliance of Jews, atheists and African-American Marxists waging war on the Christmas holiday. According to a 2005 survey by Media Matters, no fewer than 14 newspaper editorials and 48 signed opinion pieces expressed the view that "the war on Christmas is bogus."

This list of newspapers assuring us that there are no holiday hostilities included the *Boston Globe*, the *San Francisco Chronicle*, the *Philadelphia Daily News*, the *Austin American Statesman* and the *Toledo Blade*. Opinion writers included Adam Cohen, Nicolas Kristof and John Tierney of the *New York Times*, Joel Stein of the *Los Angeles Times*, Ellen Goodman of the *Boston Globe* and Cynthia Tucker of the *Atlanta-Journal Constitution*.

Well, that is surely a relief! Christians and non-religious keepers of the Western cultural tradition across the nation must have been delighted to receive this powerful vote of reassurance from such an elite group of editorialists. Now we know that we can in all good conscience wish everyone a Merry Christmas without wasting a moment's concern for the possibility of offending anyone. We can sing Christmas carols at school, throw Christmas parties at the office, and generally share the Good Tidings of the Savior's birth with all and sundry without hesitation.

In the extremely unlikely event that anyone should object to all of this Yuletide good cheer, one need merely refer them to any of the aforementioned opinion writers, who will no doubt be more than happy to set them straight as to the fact of their nonexistence. I recommend Joel Stein in particular, who is always good for a snappy and sarcastic comment demonstrating his thumb on the pulse of popular culture. Or, if this hypothetical anti-Christmas jihadist is especially hostile, one might consider putting him in touch with Ellen

Goodman, a lady who can mercifully end anyone's psychosomatic holiday depression with a dose of her lethally tedious prose.

It is with some trepidation, however, that I consider the dangerous depths of "Happy Holidays." For if it is insulting to wish a "Merry Christmas" to an individual who does not celebrate Christmas, then how much more offensive is it to simultaneously pile on a "Happy Hanukkah," a "Sunny Saturnalia," a "Felicitous Festivus," a "Kameradschaftlichste Kwanzaa" and a "Happy New Year" as well? After all, even an Messianic Jew of African-Chinese descent who loves Seinfeld might rightly take offense at all of this, given that the Year of the Pig does not start until February. Indeed, the only reasonable response to "Happy Holidays" is: "Which one?"

As for me, I have decided to reach an accommodation with American holiday diversity by celebrating five out of the six seasonal holidays each year. This year I'll be celebrating Christmas by decorating a tree and giving gifts to my loved ones, Hanukkah by taking eight days off work, Festivus by bitching about the Fed's decision to stop reporting M3, Saturnalia by letting Promporn and Sunisa tie me up for a change, and Kwanzaa by holding up the liquor store on Martin Luther King Boulevard using a piece of corn carved into the shape of a Glock 9mm.

(Of course, every day is Kwanzaa as 47,700 of my African-American co-celebrants got their Ujamaa on in like manner last year.)

This means, of course, that I have no choice but to join my Chinese co-non-celebrants in bristling angrily at anyone who is so insensitive as to wish me a "Happy New Year" or even a "Happy Holidays" that includes a "Happy New Year." Which I don't celebrate in this, the Year of the Dog.

So, dear readers, with the very best will in the world, I wish you all a Happy Hanukkah, a Felicitous Festivus, a Sunny Saturnalia, a Kameradschaftlichste Kwanzaa and a Propitious Year of the Pig.

I seem to have forgotten something… ah, yes, and a very Merry Christmas, too. May God bless us.

Tidings of Comfort and Joy

December 25, 2006

THE PROTESTATIONS of the mainstream media notwithstanding, it is undeniably and demonstrably true that the institution of Christmas is under siege by secular culture in America. However, as annoying and petty as this is, it is merely a minor reflection on the wider, more serious war on Christians that is taking place worldwide:

In Nigeria, the Hekan church in Kano is being facing the seizure of its property by the local government, only two years after its previous building was destroyed.

In Cuba, pastors are being detained and imprisoned without being charged with any crime, while their churches are being closed by the Castro regime.

In Peru, the government has finally ordered the arrest of its "counter-terrorist" soldiers who murdered five young men and a boy at a church service... only 22 years after the murders were committed.

In China, four house church leaders were sentenced to years of "re-education through hard labour" on July 25. They will be forced to serve their sentence at the Langzhong Detention House, which, according to its director, was "built for Christians."

In Belarus, Pastor Georgi Vladimirovich Vyazovsky was arrested and sentenced to jail for "holding systematic religious meetings in his home without permission from the local authorities."

In India, Christians were attacked in two locations on December 17 by Hindus, after which the police registered a formal complaint against pastor Philip Jagdalla for "hurting the religious sentiments of Hindus," a violation of section 295A of the Indian penal code.

In Australia, two pastors were found guilty of "vilifying Muslims" under the Racial and Religious Tolerance Act, required to publish a statement in several newspapers acknowledging their guilt, and avoid making statements about Muslims and Islam in the future.

In Iran, members of a house church movement were arrested on December 10 by the secret police. Seven men and one woman remain in custody; the authorities instructed church members remaining at liberty not to send news about the arrests to anyone outside the country.

In Iraq, an Evangelical Presbyterian elder was kidnapped and murdered on November 30, just after his body was found, on December 5, Father Samy Abdulahad was kidnapped after leaving his church in Baghdad.

In Egypt, former sheikh Bahaa el-Din Ahmed Hussein el-Akkad was transferred to another prison on October 21, despite his release having been ordered after serving 18 months of provisional detention for "insulting Islam" by converting to Christianity.

In Germany, Christian homeschooling mother Katherina Plett was arrested and sentenced to ten days in prison for violating the 1938 Nazi law against homeschooling.

These are only a small portion of the outrages being committed on a regular basis against Christians by religious individuals and secular governments alike. And while America has not yet attained the post-Christian status of countries such as Germany and the United Kingdom, nor incorporated Sharia into its federal or state laws, the general direction in which the nation is headed can be seen quite clearly if one considers the great changes that have taken place here in the last 25 years.

But if this developing antipathy towards Christmas and all things Christian is something that can be regretted for a variety of reasons—for even the most militant atheist might well mourn the loss of a few days off work in late December—it is not necessarily to be feared or even lamented. For Jesus Christ said:

> If the world hates you, keep in mind that it hated me first. If you belonged to the world, it would love you as its own. As it is, you do not belong to the world, but I have chosen you out of the world. That is why the world hates you.

American Christians have long been the beneficiaries of a cheap and easy grace. There has been little cost to claiming the name of Jesus Christ and even less hindrance to our worship; as a result, we possess a weak and tenuous allegiance to the very faith which defines us. Today, even our greatest church leaders are corrupted by dreams of secular power when they aren't openly fallen into sin, speaking blatant lies as readily as the evil rulers with whom they consort.

This Christmas, remember that Jesus Christ did not promise us an easy way, but a hard and rocky one. He did not promise that we would be loved and admired, but that we would know hatred and scorn. He did not instruct us to seek the approval of the world, but to stand firm to the end.

The War on Christmas will continue, as will the War on Christians, until eventually it expands to encompass what was once a Christian nation. But there is nothing to fear, be of good cheer, for the War on Jesus Christ has already been fought and won by Him whose birth we celebrate today.

Merry Christmas, every one.

Selling Out America

January 8, 2007

I N HIS RECENT ATTACK on Joseph Farah and every other individual in America who thinks it is a stupendously bad idea—to say nothing of treason—to create an EU-style superstate on this side of the Atlantic, Michael Medved assured us that these concerns were imaginary, that no one "anywhere near the Bush administration, the Congress of the United States, Cabinet departments or even major think tanks" has had the mere thought even begin to speculate about the merest possibility of crossing their minds.

It goes without saying that the plans for the North American Union are almost certainly located in an abandoned bathroom with a sign on the door saying "Beware of the Leopard."

But if it is a daring concept to base one's argument upon the integrity of a political leadership that began by fraudulently representing itself as conservative and is best known for lying repeatedly about the nature of the Global Struggle Against Virtually Everyone it is waging, it must nevertheless be said that this is unlikely to prove terribly persuasive.

Moreover, anyone who is even remotely familiar with the evolution of the European Coal and Steel Community into the European Union is well aware of how the EU was built upon a foundation of lies piled upon lies. It is telling to note that the European Union celebrated its 50th birthday on May 6, 2004, which the naive observer might think to be somewhat curious considering the EU was established only 12 years ago, by the Treaty on European Union in 1992.

Even if the politicians are telling the truth in professing their innocence of any treasonous plans to merge the United States of America with Canada, Mexico and anyone else willing to kick into the kitty this doesn't mean that the process is not taking place. Back in 2002, I wrote a column noting how the Eurofascists managed to hoodwink the prime minister of the United Kingdom, as Lady Thatcher herself confessed in her memoirs:

Nor have the lies ended, as the Bundeskanzlerin Angela Merkel recently vowed to revive the European Constitution which was rejected twice last year, as per the vote-until-you-get-it-right philosophy that has been established as a basic principle of union. And though this well-known European history does not prove that the American political elite is involved in similar skulduggery, I suggest that Michael Medved is perhaps not the observer most likely to perceive it.

For while Medved does sport a righteous stache that would be the envy of many a '70s gay porn star, his judgment in other matters has never been what one would be tempted to describe as keen. During a rant last summer about my opposition to a fence on the southern border, he first displayed his inability to distinguish between National Socialist totalitarians and anti-government libertarians, then followed that embarrassment up with a hilarious demonstration of intellectual acumen in an exchange with a caller on his radio show.

From the June 8th transcript:

> *Medved: He [Vox] was talking about the idea of deportation.... Okay, the Germans didn't deport Jews, they murdered them.*

> *Listener: So what? You're comparing the final example of the Jews, what he's talking about is deportation.*

> *Medved: No, he is not talking about deportation!*

From this exercise in conversational self-contradiction, we can conclude that either the furious denials regarding the existence of the North American Union mean that Medved is telling us, in secret mustache-speak, that there really is a treasonous conspiracy to hand over American national sovereignty, or that the man is simply a hysterical Republican Party cheerleader with less consistency and intellectual depth than clam chowder.

While some conservatives believe that his reaction indicates he is on the take, as per Armstrong Williams, I rather doubt this is the case. Had Michael Medved been living in 1937 Germany instead of 2007 America, I'm confident that he would have similarly dismissed rumors about "some malevolent, hidden agenda" on the part of Germany's political leaders as "a paranoid and groundless frenzy."

And given the history of the 20th century, it is deeply ironic indeed that it should be a Jew who takes the lead in insisting upon the innocuous nature of the surreptitious actions of an expanding central government with international aspirations.

Iraqi Roulette

January 15, 2007

Never reinforce failure.

AN ADAGE that is as old as its parentage is uncertain, it nevertheless leaps insensibly into the mind when considering the President's recently announced New Way Forward. It is, of course, unlikely that an additional 17 percent more troops will turn out to be the critical mass required for the pacification of the Sunni and Shiite combatants, much less the peaceful democratization of a collection of ancient peoples who have never known, or even shown any signs of wanting, democratic rule.

And for a situation that, we were repeatedly assured, bears absolutely no similarity to Vietnam, there are what certainly appear to be Vietnamic vibes resonating throughout Washington, as what had been whispers of a Bush-approved military coup that would remove elected Prime Minister Maliki from power are now being openly discussed in *National Review*, in ominous echo of the Kennedy-approved assassination of South Vietnam's president, Ngo Dinh Diem.

This "new" plan appears to be right out of a rather old playbook, and involves an ugly combination of betrayal, hypocrisy, additional cannon fodder and micromanagement of the military operations from Washington. While President Bush is unlikely to be issuing orders to lieutenants in the field as President Nixon so famously did, it's clear that even if American troops are going to be given more tactical freedom with which to operate, the generals will still be on a tight strategic leash from the White House.

Not only is this no way to win a war, history suggests that it is a dependable way to lose one.

The truth is that Iraq is not winnable, at least not by the terms in which the president has defined winning, and moreover, it never was. America is still attempting to fight fourth-generation warfare with troops, officers and strategies beholden to second- and third-generation military concepts. It is looking for a knockout punch, that one climactic battle, that will never come.

One cannot defeat a pool of water with a stone, and one cannot defeat an insurgent campaign with conventional military operations. If, to paraphrase Mao, the people are the sea through which the insurgents swim, one will need to drain the sea in order to be sure that the insurgency has been defeated, otherwise, one has likely achieved nothing more than to delay the inevitable.

The backlash from the failure in Iraq is only beginning. American enthusiasm for the neocons' World Democratic Revolution has never been at a lower ebb, and not even dire predictions about the inevitability of an Iranian attack on Israel is enough to revive it. One wonders how many Americans who supported the war would have supported it had they known that hundreds of thousands of Iraqis are expected to immigrate to the United States, (and if Thomas Friedman's advice is followed, given U.S. citizenship) as a direct result of the invasion and occupation.

Considering the extreme displeasure the citizenry is already expressing over the administration's immigration policies, the revelation of an Iraqi immigration program may well have the Republicangrass roots clamoring for an impeachment of President Bush.

Like Mao's Great Leap, the New Way Forward is almost certain to end up in another direction altogether. About the only positive thing one can say about it is that it is highly unlikely that the New Way will cost as many lives as the Great Leap Forward did, although given its low probability of sparking nuclear conflict in the Middle East, one can't entirely discount the possibility.

The Sunni-Shiite conflict is far from the only conflict in what used to be known as Iraq. The Kurds are biding their time and busily preparing for their bid for independence, one possible effect of which would be to cause Iran and Turkey to ally against the United States. The situation is a puzzle, not a nail, and unfortunately, a hammer is simply not an effective instrument for puzzle-solving.

In his recent admission that his actions have increased instability in Iraq, President Bush missed an opportunity to confess the bankruptcy of the World Democratic Revolution strategy, announce the immediate withdrawal of

American troops and declare that his focus would be on defending America, not Iraqi democracy. Instead, he has foolishly decided to squander his last remnants of credibility on one more spin of the Iraqi roulette wheel.

Braveheart's dream

January 22, 2007

F OR ALL THAT American pseudo-sophisticates enjoy pretending that they are more European than American, usually on the basis of the biennial 10-day vacations to London, Paris or Florence, they neither know much about Europe nor do they pay any attention to what is actually happening there. This is particularly true of the American media elite.

For example, it is currently en vogue to insist that European anti-Americanism is at an all-time high, thanks to the manifest evils of the Bush administration. While it pains me to defend this fraudulent and disgusting White House, this is one charge that cannot be reasonably laid to its door. Bush is personally unpopular, true, and the futility of the Iraqi occupation is widely recognized, but the vast majority of Europeans are not particularly interested in the details of whatever madness the Americans have gotten themselves into now.

And it's not as if President Bush is particularly popular here in the United States, either.

This is not to say that Europe's political and media elite are not somewhat anti-American, at least in their public pontifications. But the opinions of Jacques Chirac, Angela Merkel, Romano Prodi and Tony Blair are becoming increasingly irrelevant, to Americans and Europeans alike, as they represent the last gasp of the European transnationalists, a generation whose constitution has been rejected, whose euro is an economic disaster and whose bureaucratic mandarins have proven to be as corrupt as they are unpopular.

The common people of Europe have bigger concerns striking much closer to home. In Italy, the Juventus scandal and an unexpected victory in the World Cup have occupied everyone's minds, when they are not contemplating the idea of escaping the rigors of the euro in favor of a return to the cheerful chaos of the lira and an Italian-run central bank. Prodi once told the Danes that "the euro is forever", and yet the currency may not survive its second decade intact.

The French are more concerned with the burning of their inner cities and the marital vicissitudes of Ségolène Royal and François Hollande than which side America is currently supporting in the Sunni-Shiite struggle. The British are far less anti-American than anti-Polish, anti-Romanian and anti-Bulgarian these days, mostly because six hundred thousand unemployed Americans have not immigrated to Great Britain in the last two years. While the American invasion of Iraq has commanded more headlines and engendered more lethal violence, it is significantly smaller in scale than the New European invasion of Britain, so it should come as no surprise if Iraq is not foremost in the thoughts of the junior partner in the Coalition of the Willing.

But even the European invasion is not the greatest matter for concern in Great Britain these days, because for the first time since the Blitz and Operation Sea Lion, the very survival of Great Britain is in question. In 1999, after an abeyance of 292 years, a Scottish Parliament was seated for the first time, and a 2006 poll by the Scotsman newspaper indicated that 51 percent of Scots favored full independence. Intriguingly, 59 percent of Englishmen declared themselves to be in agreement, for once, with the Scots.

This move toward Scottish independence is naturally opposed by the traditional political powers, especially the British Labour Party, which relies heavily upon the left-leaning Scots for its current electoral majority and only granted the partial step of "devolution" as a means of harmlessly blowing off the pro-independence pressure building in Scotland. The move appears likely to backfire, and badly at that, because the Scottish National Party has been making its gains at Labour's expense and is expected to win the election scheduled this May. And if the SNP takes power, no doubt one of its first acts will be to pass a referendum allowing the Scots to decide if they wish to continue to abide by the Act of Union, or to fulfill Braveheart's dream instead.

Such an act will have profound reverberations throughout Europe and may even have an impact on U.S. foreign policy. It will be very difficult for the President to explain how Iraqi freedom and democracy is worth billions of dollars and thousands of American lives, but Scottish freedom and democracy must be denied. And this dichotomy would be even more difficult for Tony Blair, Gordon Brown and David Cameron to explain away.

It seems clear that as the political and media elite grow ever more transnational in outlook, they are inspiring increasingly more powerful nationalist reactions among the voters. This means that either the elite will have to become less responsive to the democratically expressed will of the people—and therefore more authoritarian—or abandon their goals.

Unfortunately, the Bundeskanzlerin has already indicated that the former is the strong preference of the European elite, while President Bush's insistence on continuing both the ironic war for Iraqi democracy and the mass importation of Mexicans indicates that he and the new Democratic Congress will stand shoulder-to-shoulder against the American people until the time when we, too, are blessed with a Bundesführrette we can call our own and no longer need trouble our pretty little heads with such lofty concerns.

One wonders why one never reads of the looming Scottish secession in the American media, despite its breathless, front-page enthusiasm for the Ukrainian Orange Revolution and the Purple Fingers of Iraq. I suppose maybe because seeing freedom in the West might give Americans the terrible idea that they, too, possess the right to self-determination.

Ashes of conservatism

January 29, 2007

C'ERA UNA VOLTA... This is the way that Italian fairy tales begin. There was a time.... It's a little less nebulous than the familiar "once upon a time" that usually begins the American equivalent, containing as it does within the statement the implicit reference to a genuine moment in history.

And there was a time when conservatives only dreamed of power, when the thought of a Republican White House, Senate and House of Representatives were little more unthinkable than the idea of a wooden boy coming to life or a sleeping princess dead to the world for a century being woken with a kiss. Nevertheless, the fairy tale came to pass, only to be revealed as bearing as little relation to the conservative vision as Tanith Lee's devilish spins on the Brothers Grimm do with the original versions.

In her brilliantly twisted "When the Clock Strikes", Lee writes of Ashella, who is the last descendant of a noble line usurped by the ruling duke. Like Cinderella, Ashella has lost her mother, who was a witch sworn to Satanas that committed suicide after swearing Ashella to Hell and vengeance. When her father eventually remarries, Ashella's step-mother and two step-sisters treat her kindly but the girl rejects their friendship in order to hide her dark purpose under a veil of seeming madness. And when the invitations to the ball arrive, Ashella waits until the others depart before summoning demons to prepare her for the dance.

> *"If it were only so simple," said Ashella, smiling, smiling. "But the debt is too cruel. Justice requires a harsher payment."*
> *And then, in the ballroom, Death struck the first note on the golden bell.*
> *The girl smiled and she said: "I curse you in my mother's name."*
> *The second stroke. "I curse you in my own name."*

The third stroke. "And in the name of those that your father slew."
The fourth stroke. "And in the name of my Master, who rules the world."
As the fifth, the sixth, the seventh strokes pealed out, the prince stood non-
plussed. At the eighth and ninth strokes, the strength of the malediction
seemed to curdle his blood. He shivered and his brain writhed. At the tenth
stroke, he saw a change in the loveliness before him. She grew thinner, taller.
At the eleventh stroke, he beheld a thing in a ragged black cowl and robe. It
grinned at him. It was all grin below a triangle of sockets of nose and eyes.
At the twelfth stroke, the prince saw Death and knew him.

This story came to mind when I was reading The Corner at the *National Review* website over the weekend. As disastrous as the last six years have been for American conservatives, with Three Monkey Republicans joining neoconservatives in shrieking for ever-larger government and ever more for-eign entanglement, it seems that last year's self-inflicted electoral suicide was not enough for certain members of the conservative media.

For example, Mark Steyn, the Canadian who is the current darling of the conservatariat now that Ann Coulter has been banished for Excessive Conservativism, announced the following prior to his star turn at the NRI's Conservative Summit in Washington D.C.: "In the modern world, your civil service, judiciary, agriculture and treasury expertise need a capacity for global projection, too."

In other words, it's not enough that domestic spending has exploded, but Americans should be forking out the funds necessary to establish overseas offices for the Department of Justice, the Department of Agriculture and the U.S. Treasury. And instead of being tarred, feathered and shipped back to Canada for advocating this "Compassionate Crusaderism", Steyn was actually seconded by Kate O'Beirne and Newt Gingrich, who lament the fact that the Pentagon is "carrying virtually the entire burden" of the Iraqi occupation.

And this is what passes for leading conservative opinion? Surely this would never have happened if William F. Buckley were still alive!

Actually, the compassionate Canadian and company just might have a point. Sending herds of fat, bitter federal bureaucrats over to Iraq would not only get them out of our hair and our wallets, but they'd soon cause the war-ring Sunnis and Shiites to band together against an enemy even less palatable than each other. Come to think of it, Iraq could probably use more education and equality too, so perhaps we can unload the Ivy League professoriat and a few spare pods of feminists to accompany the compassionate crusade.

Sure, we'll probably have to reinforce the Air Force's C-130s, but with any luck, the endeavor will turn out like the People's Crusade of 1096.

Fairy tales don't always end well, but this one has gone beyond imagining. It's beginning to make Tanith Lee look like Walt Disney.

The logic of the Lizard Queen

February 5, 2007

I T IS ALWAYS INTERESTING to watch the media shape the electoral possibilities during the early stages of the presidential campaign. Those who still operate under the illusion that America is a democracy, even the limited form of democracy known as representative democracy, would do well to study the process by which prospective candidates are divided into permissible and not permissible categories.

The media's preferred term is, of course, "electable" and "unelectable", but it is easy enough to show that these are inaccurate and intentionally misleading terms. For example, a reasonable observer would conclude that the two most unelectable candidates of the apparent field are Rudy Giuliani and B. Hussein Obama.

It's worth noting that Giuliani couldn't win a Senate race against a carpet-bagging Hillary Clinton, holds a panoply of views that are expressly contrary to his nominal party's platform, is a poor speaker and has no record of achievement except for having successfully fought crime in a single city. His candidacy is primarily based on his grand accomplishment of "holding the city together after 9/11", which is about as nebulous as an accomplishment can get and still be articulated; it's not as if New Yorkers were on the verge of breaking into civil war or fleeing the city en masse and leaving an empty, depopulated shell behind.

Moreover, there's a reason Newt Gingrich didn't dare list New York City and Washington D.C. among his list of potential targets should Iran ac-quire only three nuclear devices. Considering the very low esteem in which those two cities are held by a substantial minority of Americans, Gingrich's attempted scaremongering would have had the opposite effect. Indeed, if Ahmadinejad would only promise to take out Hollywood with his third nuke, he'd probably find it easier to raise funds across America than UNICEF.

(We pause here for a moment to allow the professionally offended to take a deep breath and commence with the shrieking.... The point, which will no doubt be ignored, is that "saving New York City" isn't necessarily the big national plus that the New York-based media believes it to be.)

Amazingly, B. Hussein's candidacy is even less credible than the sometime drag queen's. While Obama is, as Sen. Joe Biden informs us, an exemplary Negro who can be trusted not to break into inopportune rap or be found in the company of young women with an unaccountable predilection for poop-rolling, there are a few small matters such as the cocaine use, the Muslim schooling and the mysterious biographical gaps to be taken into account. And given that the American electorate has not hitherto been prone to electing many blacks, senators or people named Hussein as their president, his oft-asserted "electability" is more than a little suspect.

A comparison with Tom Tancredo is illuminating. Rep. Tancredo is an elected politician of no particular achievement in the forefront of one of America's most popular political movements, the anti-illegal-immigration wave. Obama is an elected politician of no particular achievement primarily known for being black and taking showers. Which one sounds more "electable" to you? Naturally, the media has announced that America is pining for a leader who doesn't fear running water, and they will repeat this ad infinitum until it becomes sufficiently true.

Of course, as the recent polls demonstrate, no one actually intends to vote for Obama. He is merely a feel-good candidate, one who allows white liberals to engage in their ritual demonstration of moral superiority prior to voting for whoever the party machinery decides will be its standard bearer. Since the Democratic anointment has already fallen upon the Lizard Queen, Obama merely serves as a much-needed distraction for the next eighteen months, for which his reward will likely be the vice-presidency.

Since the Republicans are showing every sign of nominating the only sort of candidate who could lose to Ms. Rodham-Clinton, a pro-war moderate Republican guaranteed to keep conservatives home on election day, the only way Hillary can blow her chances of becoming President Rodham is by failing to tack right on immigration during the general campaign. Whichever party runs anti-Iraq and anti-illegal-immigration will claim the Cherry Blossom Throne. At this point, the only candidate likely to do so is the Lizard Queen.

And don't forget that none of this means either of those policies will change once she has ascended the throne, changed her name and shed her human skin. She'll be far too busy making use of the Patriot Acts and other liberty-enhancing tools which the present regime has so helpfully constructed in preparation for her coming.

As for me, I tend to agree with those who argue that Americans deserve better and shouldn't be content with settling for the lesser evil. *Fa'thagn Cthulhu! Cthulhu 2008!*

Free speech follies

February 12, 2007

I T WOULD TAKE a heart of granite not to laugh at the overwrought Victorian reactions of students at Central Connecticut State University to a satirical piece about the societal benefits of rape published in their school newspaper.

Sarah said she couldn't keep her knees from buckling and the tears from welling in her eyes when she picked up a copy of the student newspaper at Central Connecticut State University this week. "I couldn't believe anyone in this day and age would write something like that, and that other people would let it be published."

After all, humanity has witnessed the death of God and has progressed beyond good and evil, haven't we evolved past satire and free speech yet? Certainly some of her fellow students saw no amusement in Sarah's knee-buckling reaction to what must have been some very frightening ink assembled into a series of threateningly occultic glyphs on paper. One specimen in particular seems rather unlikely to find much humor in anything.

"There are some things that just aren't funny, and rape is one of them," Griffin [one of the students protesting the article] said. "I mean, what's next? The Holocaust? Slavery? There's nothing funny there, I'm sorry."

I'm sure we shall all anticipate receiving a list of humor-approved subjects from Mr. Griffin. Apparently we can also look forward to seeing three Oscars being rescinded from Roberto Benigni and Nicola Piovani, to say nothing of the public flogging of Mel Brooks. As for slavery, I have to confess that I tend to find it rather amusing when the historically ignorant make melodramatic references to the historical American slave trade while failing to realize that a woman can be purchased for a few hundred dollars in nearly any country in the world today.

For there is a tremendous amount of dark humor to be found in the post-Christian era, where it is ironically far easier to argue for the moral and scientific imperative of rape than it is to make the case that rape should still be considered a crime, much less a moral offense. As Daniel C. Dennett writes in *Darwin's Dangerous Idea*, the full extent of precisely how dangerous the idea of natural selection is has not been understood, much less accepted, by the vast majority of those familiar with Darwin's theory of evolution.

For who are you, dear reader, to declare that one reproduction-oriented act is superior to another? Do you not know that there is no God? Are we not merely vehicles for our selfish genes?

But whether we consider ourselves to be vessels for amoral genes subject to the reproduction imperative or containers of an immortal soul subject to future Divine judgment, atheists and Christians alike can agree that the removal of Nick Gilburn's videos from YouTube is a direct offense to free speech as well as being the latest revelation that Google's "don't be evil" slogan is nothing more than meaningless words.

Gilburn is a poor-man's Richard Dawkins, whose YouTube videos are popular with and considered marvelously enlightening by the sort of 10th-grade boys who seriously believe that no Christian has ever read the Bible. This is a common theme in the sort of science fiction they read, wherein the scene featuring the atheist hero stunning the Bible-thumping bigot into silence with a devastating quote from John 8:7 is as mandatory as the sex scene with the seductive female scientist/space alien. Of course, only an author who knows nothing about the ubiquity of Christian Bible studies could posit such a scenario, moreover, they invariably leave out John 8:11.

But it is only a weak and fragile faith that cannot bear to be questioned, however incompetently. So while Gilburn posted his anti-Christian videos on YouTube without a problem, his posting an anti-Islamic video met with a speedy response from the Google-owned company. Gilburn's account was permanently disabled and his videos were removed due to the "inappropriate nature" of the video. Slashdot's coverage of YouTube's action spurred the geek community into action; the result was that while most of Gilburn's videos were permitted to be uploaded again, the Islam-related one remained banned.

Now, this is not censorship. Google is not the government and there is no constitutional right to have YouTube or your college newspaper publish your speech. However, it is important to note that Google, college administrations and American liberals all proudly claim to be supporters of free speech when the evidence demonstrates quite clearly that they are actually its enemies.

Inevitable failure

February 19, 2007

NICCOLO MACHIAVELLI, the famed author of *The Prince* and *The Art of War* was once given the opportunity to put his martial theories into practice by Giovanni de' Medici, the captain of the Black Bands, an elite mercenary company. As Bandello relates the story, things did not exactly go according to plan, in fact, it required the de' Medici's intervention to unsnarl the tangle of hopelessly confused troops.

As this example suggests, (to say nothing of 15 centuries of post-Roman military history), it is more than a little dangerous to look to Italy for advice on military matters. So, it is disheartening to see the way in which the Bush administration looks as if it is increasingly interested in the long-discredited air power theories of Giulio Douhet.

For 86 years, air power advocates have been overpromising and underdelivering. While no one could possibly deny that air power is a vital tactical element necessary for military victory in most situations, it is no more a decisive strategic weapon than armored cavalry, indeed, it is demonstrably less capable of delivering strategic victory than sea power alone. Ironically, this important tactical aspect of air power in support of land and sea forces, which is its only reliably successful application, has been disavowed by air power advocates from the start.

And yet, since no one would seriously argue that strategic victories can be won by using nothing but tanks and self-propelled artillery, it is very strange that armchair strategists and politicians still cling to the myth that they can be won with air power alone. For the history of air power is a long and ignoble history of failure piled upon utter failure.

The air raid on Pearl Harbor not only did not knock the United States out of World War II, but the historical ignorance of overwrought columnists notwithstanding, it barely damaged the U.S. Navy at all, either in terms of ship numbers or overall tonnage. The AWPD-1 and AWPD-2 plans to destroy German industrial capacity were such a complete failure that Germany actually managed to increase its arms production despite the incessant Allied bombing; while the fire-bombings of Dresden and Tokyo managed to kill massive numbers of civilians, neither attack did significant damage to the ability of Germany or Japan to continue to wage their hopeless wars.

Strategic bombing did not conquer London or North Vietnam. In fact, without nuclear weapons, it is hard to think of a single example where strategic bombing served as a reasonable substitute for force on the ground augmented by tactical air superiority.

And while Desert Storm is often cited as one of air power's few smashing successes, that success turns out to be a mirage according to the detailed post-facto evaluation of the air campaign. For example, the Air Force's F-117 Nighthawks completely missed 40 percent of their targets on the first night, and 72 percent of the targets they were assigned to knock out were deemed to require repeated additional strikes over the next five days.

It is easy to forget that President Bush is a former fighter pilot himself. And while it is true that he saw no combat during his time in the Texas Air Reserve, there is no reason to believe that he is not subject to the same misguided belief in the strategic capacity of air power that is shared by so many past and present Air Force officers.

As WND reported this weekend, the Pentagon has announced that its wargaming predicts the unfeasibility of a ground assault on Iran. While this could be simple misinformation, it corresponds with the assessment of many other military experts who are cognizant of the limitations of the military force available to the U.S. commanders in the Middle East. The U.S. could surely stage an invasion that would smash through the conscript-heavy, unprofessional Iranian ground forces, but it would fare poorly against the inevitable insurgent campaign that has proved so difficult to quell in Iraq.

This leaves air strikes, always popular with politicians who itch to take bold and drastic action without risking a large number of American casualties. But the idea that air strikes are risk-free is based on the assumption that the Iranian strategists who are causing such havoc in Iraq and Lebanon are incapable of thinking asymmetrically, that they can't possibly envision any way of effectively striking back against a nation full of disarmed urban centers with open borders to the north and south. Of course, it's remotely possible that none of the estimated 12 million illegal aliens currently resident in America are Iranian agents, but that strikes me as a very low probability indeed.

Douhet's strategy of victory through attacking industry, transport, communications, government and civilian morale from the air has not been successful since it was first envisioned in *The Command of the Air*. The improvements in air strike technology notwithstanding, this strategy is no more likely to be successful in 2007 than it was in 1942, 1965 or 1991.

Ducking Darwin

February 26, 2007

Darwin's Dangerous Idea: Evolution and the Meanings of Life
by Daniel C. Dennett
Rating: 9 of 10

IN DANIEL C. DENNETT'S excellent book, *Darwin's Dangerous Idea*, he walks the reader through some of the aspects of Man's intellectual development by the 19th century, so that the reader might better understand both the full measure of Darwin's conceptual achievement as well as the contributions of other intellectuals upon whose ideas Darwin drew in formulating his own landmark ideas. It is a brilliant book, although it might be going a bit overboard to describe it as a surpassingly brilliant one.

The historical aspects of the book are genuinely interesting, but more interesting by far are Dennett's thoughts regarding the importance and the applicability of that dangerous idea to the future direction of Man. And an even more fascinating aspect is the way in which Dennett constantly flirts with the obvious dangers that are created by the logic of this dangerous idea without ever being able to precisely articulate them, much less accept them as a Darwinian reality.

The regular reader has probably noticed that I have steeped myself in a good deal of atheist literature of late; this is only the most recently read. Since I have been reading on the matter, I have naturally been blogging on the matter, which led to a number of heated debates as well as finally providing the world with a succinct and definitive distinction between the concepts of "agnostic" and "atheist."

> *Agnostic: I very much doubt there is a God. Because I haven't seen the evidence.*
>
> *Atheist: There is no God. Because I'm an asshole.*

But the point around which every atheist vs. theist debate seems to revolve endlessly is that of morality. Theists, of course, have a perfectly logical argument for the application of their god-based moralities which even the most die-hard rational atheist will not reject given the postulate that God actually exists and created the universe. In short, God's game, God's rules.

Atheists, ironically enough, enjoy no similar logical advantage, and are usually reduced to arguing that they are personally behaving in a moral manner based on a morality that someone could invent if he just sat down and thought about it enough, although strangely, none of them ever claim to have actually done so himself. So, they decry the evil done by Muslims and Christians for adhering to moralities based on the dictates of imaginary beings on the basis of their own hypothetical morality.

The imaginary aspect of his morality does not stop every atheist with a web site from stamping his cute little feet and citing ontological proof of its existence, to say nothing of its obvious superiority to Christian morality because, you know, he hasn't personally engaged in any Crusades or Spanish Inquisitions. And yet, not only do we know these reason-based moralities don't exist, we are informed from a reliable source that it is "quite obvious" that they do not exist and have never existed.

> *I do not intend this to be a shocking indictment, just a reminder of something quite obvious: no remotely compelling system of ethics has ever been made computationally tractable, even indirectly, for real world moral problems. So, even though there has been no dearth of utilitarian (and Kantian, and contrarian, etc.) arguments in favor of particular policies, institutions, practices, and acts, these have all been heavily hedged with ceteris paribus clauses and plausibility claims about their idealizing assumptions.*

Those aren't my words, that's Prof. Daniel C. Dennett his own godless self writing thusly on page 500 of the hitherto-mentioned book. In fact, in that particular passage, Dennett sounds rather more like the great anti-socialist F.A. von Hayek demonstrating the impossibility of socialist calculation than like a committed socialist desperate to prove socialism is beneficial to the economy.

But one must give Dennett his due for his honesty in admitting that Darwin's dangerous idea tears a huge and gaping hole in the moral fabric, and he deserves credit for manfully attempting to lay the groundwork for a means of addressing that hole in the last two chapters of his book. And if he falls into the very same trap he describes so eloquently, well, it has happened to many an intellectual before.

One finds it hard to blame evolutionists for wishing to hide the most dangerous aspects of their hero's idea from the general public, even if one must decry their attempts to do so. After all, the Edwards' blogger fiasco has already demonstrated how normal people who still possess at least some remnants of a functioning moral conscience regard the final conclusion of evolutionist morality:

> *Abortion, not just the right to abortion but the actual procedure, is a moral good that helps women and families and should be honored as such.... Pleasure is a moral good. I think people who oppose pleasure are the real anti-lifers, because what's life for if not for living it?*

Of course, the Satanist Aleister Crowley said the same thing rather more succinctly: *Do what thou wilt shall be the whole of the Law.*

The case against science

March 5, 2007

S CIENCE, we are repeatedly informed by scientists, possesses a unique claim on truth due to its self-correcting nature. And this is certainly true in theory, although it is not difficult to demonstrate that scientific history is littered with a long list of honest mistakes, not-so-honest mistakes and outright lies.

And this merely refers to the cases of which we know, scientific frauds that have been caught and exposed. But even if we politely avert our eyes from this well-chronicled inability of scientists to live up to their scientific ideals—a nicety seldom granted to religious idealists—there is real cause to doubt the continued benefit of science to modern society, or even its right to a respectable place within it.

For the common belief in the beneficial nature of science rests on an underlying assumption that knowledge of all truth is desirable in all circumstances. But this is far from settled, as intellectuals from Plato to Daniel C. Dennett have frankly expressed their doubts on this score. Even lesser thinkers who have witnessed a child losing its innocent illusions or a family torn apart by the exposure of a long-hidden secret might well share this skepticism.

For if all knowledge is inherently good, then it is a moral imperative to scientifically determine the relative intelligence of Asians and Zulus once and for all. But is everyone really comfortable with the possibility of determining that men are, in scientific fact, intellectually superior to women? Or vice-versa? The cowardice of scientists regarding such controversial subjects, their nominal dedication to absolute scientific truth nothwithstanding, is powerful evidence of their lack of faith in the inherent beneficence of science.

Moreover, for a group of individuals claiming a right to act as a secular priesthood on Man's behalf, scientists demonstrate an aversion for personal responsibility that would shame a child. Consider how the same militant atheists who claim that religious individuals are somehow responsible for the past actions of other religious individuals who do not even happen to share their beliefs simultaneously assert that scientists are not responsible for their personal actions even when those actions provide the means of mass murder or the motivation for embarking upon mass slaughter.

If "religion" is to be held culpable for the Inquisitions and the jihads, "science" is certainly no less culpable for the historical ravages of scientific socialism, the gassings of World War I, the National Socialist Holocaust, the fire-bombings of Tokyo and Dresden and the American abortion atrocity, to say nothing of the possibility of nuclear devastation as well as the inconvenient perils of global warming.

I have previously demonstrated that religion does not cause war. But even if it did, the number of Americans killed by medical science in the last ten years far exceeds the total number of Americans killed by war in U.S. history. If medical science can justly claim to have saved many lives, it must also take responsibility for the estimated 783,000 annual iatrogenic deaths it now causes every year.

Furthermore, the benefits of science are hugely exaggerated. Most of the advances in human technology are a function of the wealth produced by capitalism and human liberty, as may be seen in the retarded technological development in countries with no shortage of education and scientists, but handicapped by anti-capitalist, anti-libertarian ideology. Most inventors are not scientists and most scientists are not inventors; whereas Oppenheimer and Einstein gave us the nuclear bomb, Steve Wozniak gave us the personal computer and Al Gore gave us the Internet. It's worth noting that the inventors of what is considered to be the most significant invention of the century, the silicon chip, were not scientists but electrical engineers.

Science advocates may argue that while scientists may not do much inventing, inventions are merely a practical application of the principles discovered by scientists. And while this is true in many cases, it is false in even more. From vulcanized rubber to the microwave oven, accidents combined with fortuitous observations by non-scientists have accounted for a surprising number of advances in human knowledge, advances to which the scientific method of hypothesis and experimentation may claim no credit.

Sciencists (those who believe in science as a basis for dictating human behavior, as opposed to scientists, who merely engage in the method), like to posit that Man has evolved to a point where he is ready to move beyond religion. A more interesting and arguably more urgent question is whether science, having produced some genuinely positive results as well as some truly nightmarish evils, has outlived its usefulness to Mankind.

Man has survived millennia of religious faith, but if the prophets of over-population and global warming are correct, he may not survive a mere two centuries of science.

The case against science, part II

March 12, 2007

I T WAS INTERESTING to see the plethora of reactions to last week's column, wherein I demonstrated that the arguments commonly made against religion cannot only be made against science, but can be made more conclusively against science than against religion. And it was particularly amusing to see how individuals who attack religion with these sorts of arguments were incapable of recognizing their own logic when applied to a different target.

Here are a few of the more common responses engendered by the column:

It is not fair to blame all scientists, or science itself, for the evil actions of a few scientists.

Of course it is not. And therefore it is obviously not fair to blame everyone who possesses religious faith, or religion itself, for the evil actions of a few religious people. Yet anti-religious individuals such as Sam Harris actually attempt to blame Christian moderates for the actions of Islamic extremists.

You are a lunatic/kook/Luddite/nut if you believe that science is not inherently good.

A most persuasive argument. I somehow find it hard to believe that any of the individuals making this argument would seriously consider an identical case made for the existence of God to be conclusive. While I am always a fan of a creative slur, I suggest they are best used in addition to making a substantive case, not as a substitute for one.

Science can't be blamed for the atomic bombings of Hiroshima and Nagasaki, because scientists only designed and built the bomb, they didn't actually drop it themselves.

If we accept this reasoning, then the Catholic Church should no longer be blamed for either the Spanish Inquisition or the Crusades, since the Church only pronounced guilty verdicts in the Inquisition's heresy trials and publicly advocated the recovery of Jerusalem, it neither burned anyone at the stake nor invaded the Holy Lands.

Furthermore, I note that this attempted defense of science is inaccurate anyhow, since there was a scientist, William Parsons, who was a member of the Enola Gay's flight crew and served as the bomb commander and weaponeer when Little Boy was dropped on Hiroshima.

Science is good because antibiotics and vaccines it has developed have saved millions of lives.

And science is bad because the weapons it has developed have ended millions of lives. It's important to remember that scientists only create antibiotics and vaccines, they don't personally administer them any more than they personally go out and shoot people with the weapons they create. If scientists wish to claim responsibility for the good things they have contributed to mankind, they must take responsibility for the evil things they have contributed as well.

Science can't be blamed for scientific socialism or Nazi science because socialism and Nazi science weren't really true science.

Then how can religion be blamed for patently irreligious actions carried out "in the name of God"? If religion is responsible for every evil carried out "in the name of God," then science must be likewise responsible for every evil carried out "in the name of science." Therefore, scientists must be held responsible for scientific socialism, scientology and the Jim Rose Circus Sideshow; perhaps we can agree to split the difference on Christian Science.

As for Nazi science not being science, it seems rather strange that the U.S. should have made a priority of acquiring the non-scientific talents of so many of the non-scientists who worked on the V2 rocket program.

There may be frauds in science, but science is self-correcting. When was the last time we heard of religious frauds being exposed by someone in the fold?

Jim Bakker was exposed by investigative journalists and auditors hired by Jerry Falwell. Many, if not most religious frauds are exposed by other religious individuals connected to the person committing the fraud.

Doctors only kill 225,000 people per year. And they're trying to save lives, so that doesn't count.

The specific number depends upon how you define iatrogenic deaths. If you are inclined to take issue with the 783,000 statistic, I suggest you take it up with the authors of this report. As for the 225,000 number, I simply note that Wikipedia has been known to be less than entirely accurate.

If one does not accept the "I had to destroy the village in order to save it" logic from soldiers, why would one accept it from doctors?

It's the stupidity of people like Vox Day that's preventing humans from progressing.

That's interesting—just how does that work? And toward what, precisely, are humans progressing?

Al Gore didn't invent the Internet, you idiot!

No, really? I stand corrected.

Ron Paul and the naked Pajamas Media

March 19, 2007

I WAS NOT ASKED to be a part of *Pajamas Media*. That was just as well, as I would have declined to participate for three reasons. The first was that I regarded it as a stupid business plan, about as well-conceived as the idea of selling dog food over the Internet. While there is some genuine demand for news and opinion, the supply approaches that post-scarcity vision of which neo-Marxian economists happily dream.

The second reason was the much-publicized involvement of various individuals I neither like nor respect. That's completely subjective, of course, but is closely connected to the third reason, which is not. This third reason was that it was clear from the start that many of those involved with *Pajamas Media* saw the mainstream media as a club to which they hoped to be admitted, not an unnecessary evil better disrupted and left for dead on the roadside of technological advancement.

The chief role of the media in modern American society is to act as an intellectual gatekeeper, determining which thoughts are to be deemed permissible and which are not. To give one of many possible examples, it is considered unacceptable to doubt the verity of the Holocaust or global warming, lest one be labeled a "denier," whereas identical doubts about other, equally well-established facts merely causes one to be described as a "skeptic."

With regards to politics, the rule applies to the concept of "electability." Electability has nothing to do with whether a candidate is actually considered electable based on any rational grounds such as his achievements, electoral record or appeal to the voting public, but rather how acceptable he is to the gatekeepers. Thus, a comedian, a lisping, thrice-married man holding political positions diametrically opposed to his nominal party's or a confirmed satanist serving time for child rape and murder will all be described as being more "electable" than a popular congressman without a hint of scandal whose best-known political cause is supported by 80 percent of the American public.

"Electable" in this context merely means "acceptable."

As I wrote nearly two years ago, it is the Democratic faction's turn to take over the White House, which is why the ruling party's other faction is, according to the rules of the great game, staunchly determined to nominate a wildly unelectable individual in the Bob Dole mode. It doesn't matter if it's Giuliani and his speech impediment, McCain and his speech-banning impediment or Romney and his sacred underwear impediment, none of these men have a ghost of a chance of beating any Democratic candidate for president, let alone the Lizard Queen and her scorched-earth political destruction machine. Ironically, that's precisely what makes them "electable" for the purposes of the nomination.

Conservative Republicans understand this on some level, which is why so many are depressed about polls showing that the lisper has a lead on the speech banner. No one ever took the Mormon seriously, except those who get overexcited about executive hair. Our presidential selection process would be about as genuinely democratic, and would definitely be more fun, if we simply had Romney and Edwards stage a Zoolanderesque hair-off for the White House.

And the truth is that there are alternatives, genuine alternatives to the three-part multiple choice quiz, but the mainstream media is, as always, doing its best to prevent anyone from considering them. And in their best freshmen-at-the-frat-house fashion, *Pajamas Media* is playing precisely the same game, as evidenced by their 2008 Pajamas Media Presidential Straw Poll.

> *The eighth week of the PAJAMAS MEDIA PRESIDENTIAL STRAW POLL has officially begun. Bill Richardson and Rudy Giuliani were again winners in the seventh week with over 70,000 votes now cast. Barack Obama and Newt Gingrich (undeclared) were runners-up on the Democratic and Republican sides respectively.*

What the headline fails to mention is that in the Feb. 19 *Pajamas Media* poll, Ron Paul, the Texas congressman and now a declared candidate for the Republican nomination, roundly defeated Rudy Giuliani, 43.1 percent to 20.1 percent. Moreover, he did so by winning more votes, 1,769, than Giuliani subsequently did in winning the Mar. 4 (1,431) and Mar. 11 polls (1,158).

The innocent observer might wonder how Ron Paul could slip so much in three weeks that Giuliani could surpass him with fewer votes, or that a disgraced adulterer and non-candidate for president like Newt Gingrich could claim second place. Did his actual declaration of his candidacy on March 11 somehow inspire a backlash against him? No, the truth is much more simple.

Because they didn't like the results, *Pajamas Media* simply dropped Ron Paul from the poll, while retaining the likes of George Pataki, Tommy Thompson and other no-hopers who aren't even running for president!

Pajamas Media has thus declared Rep. Ron Paul to be unelectable on the basis of his demonstrated respect for the United States Constitution, his allegiance to Republican ideals and his commitment to human liberty. This speaks rather better of Ron Paul than it does of *Pajamas Media* and their naked ambition to tell the American people what they are, and are not, permitted to think.

Republicans create own Frankenstein monsters

March 26, 2007

I T WASN'T all that long ago that Republicans were looking to Arnold Schwarzenegger as a pumped-up version of Ronald Reagan, who but for the unfortunate fact of his Austrian birth, might have ridden the coattails of a Republican revival in California to an eventual victory in the White House. They spurned a man with genuine conservative credentials and spent much effort convincing Republicans in California and around the country that Arnold was a conservative at heart, his connections to Hollywood and the Kennedy clan notwithstanding.

And, in fairness, Gov. Schwarzenegger demonstrated that he does have some genuinely conservative inclinations. But a man's personal inclinations and his ability to stand by them in public are two entirely different things, especially when that public is hostile. It didn't take long for Arnold to capitulate to the girly men, of course, surprising no one except perhaps Hugh Hewitt, whose Panglossian approach to life must be envied.

For life is at its most entertaining, after all, if every day brings a new surprise with the sunrise.

It is a pity that there is no pithy aphorism that assigns shame to those who are fooled neither once, nor twice, but every single time. It does not take a keen observer that the California recall election is serving as a bellwether for the 2008 Republican nomination, as three non-conservatives are fraudulently being pushed on the conservative base of the party on the basis of their supposed electability.

To his credit, Rush Limbaugh appears to be ready to sit this election out. His recent criticism of his friend, Gov. Schwarzenegger is not necessarily linked to his announced lack of enthusiasm for the anointed bunch, but it's hard to believe a man of Rush's intelligence does not see the obvious parallels between Schwarzenegger's governance and the probable result of a Giuliani, McCain or Romney administration. And yet, I doubt Rush will have the fortitude to maintain that stance once the Lizard Queen wins the Democratic nomination and the familiar, frantic chants about "the most important election ever" begin again.

All of this, of course, is academic. There will be no Giuliani, McCain or Romney administration. Giuliani is many things, first and foremost he is a class one jerk. A jerk can win in New York City, where the natives pride themselves on their unpleasantries, but he can't win a national election, especially not against a woman who isn't afraid to switch gears at will and play the "don't hit a girl" card just before slamming the dagger into the jugular vein. No one actually likes McCain except the press, least of all Republicans, and liberal Massachusetts ex-governors don't win presidential elections when they run as Democrats, let alone Republicans.

If I were a conventional commentator, this is the part where I would begin to make the case for how my guy was the answer, and that only by supporting him would the Republican Party be able to unite despite its differences and forge ahead to victory in November. But the truth is, no one can. Eight disastrous years of George W. Bush in the White House have depressed and divided Republicans; his lasting political legacy will likely be surprisingly similar to Jimmy Carter's. Bush barely won re-election as an incumbent president when the Iraq War was going well, I am beginning to suspect that Hillary's electoral totals may have more in common with Ronald Reagan's landslide than her husband's plurality.

This is the cost of political pragmatism: a landscape barren of credible candidates, a discouraged base and the expectation of defeat. The counter-intuitive truth for conservatives is that principle is the ultimate pragmatism. No sports team has ever won a game by committing to move the ball in the direction of the goal that it is defending. Conservatives cannot win moderates to their cause by becoming moderate, they can only win them over by demonstrating confidence in the superiority of their ideas, principles and ideals.

The wrath of women

April 2, 2007

FOR YEARS, the media has chronicled the phenomenon of the "angry white male." This is not unreasonable, since a story about a school shooting or a violent resignation from the U.S. Postal Service almost invariably reveals the culprit to be an individual who is male, white and very, very angry about something.

But if the vast majority of us are fortunate enough to never have any degree of contact with such explosively angry individuals, we encounter a less violent and more pervasive form on a much more regular basis. While it may contradict the feminist dogma which states that men and women are exactly the same except for women's complete moral superiority, inability to lie and greater monetary value per hour of labor, no one who has actually spent more than a week in the vicinity of one or more women will be surprised by the results of a recent British study on anger and the sexes.

In that massive survey, researchers interviewed more than 20,000 people in determining that women are more likely to feel a sense of persistent anger. This is, of course, inherently subjective but then who is better qualified to report on the presence or absence of an emotion than the individual feeling it? And it also corresponds with most adult experience; while male anger tends to be more calamitous and is more likely to produce headlines and criminal charges, female anger is more ubiquitous and more likely to produce lingering psychological fallout.

It is good to see that this issue is finally being opened to public discussion, as the myth of female martyrdom is a pernicious one and damaging to men and women alike. The destructive cycle of female verbal aggression provoking male avoidance which then inspires more female hostility and verbal aggression is a very familiar one to every marriage counselor and divorce lawyer. Without a serious and dispassionate examination of this sort of cycle, it will be difficult for those trapped in one to break free from it, even with the benefit of the best intentions on both sides.

I don't pretend to know what so many women are so angry about. But it is ludicrous to pretend that it is the result of male oppression, considering that it is the politically and economically liberated American women who are the most poisonously furious women on the planet. One simply doesn't see the sort of ever-simmering hostility that is all but inescapable in suburbia when speaking with apartment-dwelling housewives in Japan or Muslim women in Britain.

And while the responsibility for their actions lies solely with women, since the mere fact of being angry doesn't excuse bad behavior for a child, let alone an adult, men must understand that they have been complicit in coddling and enabling this anger on the part of their mothers, wives, girlfriends, and daughters. As I have previously written, the Golden Rule is only a summary and a starting point, it is neither a comprehensive morality nor an effective guide to human behavior. Positive reinforcement is only half the battle and setting a positive example is pointless as a means of behavior modification if the other party has reliably demonstrated an unwillingness to pay it any notice.

In short, her anger isn't about you. And, in other news, the universe doesn't revolve around you either.

Both men and women use anger as a means to assert control within a relationship; the particular problem for men is that they are socialized to submit peacefully to this particular form of control. So, for men who find themselves dealing with a woman who uses the threat of her anger as a control mechanism, it may be useful to keep the following in mind:

- She is responsible for her feelings. You are responsible for your actions. These two things are not identical and in most circumstances are not even related.

- If she is angry no matter what you do, then her anger is unrelated to your actions and there is nothing you can do to resolve it.

- If she gets angry over crazy and petty things, she is using her anger to control you.

- Women despise men who allow themselves to be controlled.

- A no-win position is actually a can't-lose situation. If she puts you in a position where you cannot win regardless of what you do, then you are completely free to do whatever you want without taking her feelings into account at all. Enjoy the freedom.

- Life is too short to waste it with the angry. You're going to be spending a lot of time in avoidance anyhow, so you'd do better to avoid the entire relationship from the start.

- If a woman is always angry with her work, her family or her friends, she will always be angry with you as soon as you become a part of her life.

Is man worth it?

April 9, 2007

F OR GOD SO LOVED THE WORLD", begins the best-known verse of the New Testament. But today, most of us spend so much time wondering about what is right for us that it never even occurs to us to spend a single moment wondering if we are right for God.

Atheists often sneer that God, even if He exists, is not worthy of their approval, let alone their worship, due to His many manifest failures in their eyes. Surely, they often argue, surely an all-powerful God can do better than He has done with what is obviously a failure filled with war, disease, misery and death. And so they turn to their new god, Science, in the hopes that it will build them a better world.

Such individuals would do well to consider the book of Job, and consider God's answer to those creatures who would seek to judge the Creator.

Christians are little better. Their treacly pop-influenced "praise-and-worship songs" sing about nothing but ME, how Jesus died for ME, how God wants ME to be rich and own MY own airplane just like the greasy-haired evangelist who preaches a "Christian" prosperity message that is utterly indistinguishable from Oprah's Secret. Listening to them, you would think that the entire purpose of the Almighty's Creation and Jesus Christ's sacrifice was to create a satisfactory endorphin release in a single individual.

I expect, with no little trepidation, the eventual appearance of a similar "Christian" sexuality message which declares that since God wants us to be sexually fulfilled, we should have sex with everything and anything that appeals to us at every opportunity.

The gift of Jesus Christ is hope, not happiness. In a wealthy and decadent West, few lack for the essentials of life and it should come as no surprise that so many people today see Christianity as superfluous. We were warned, after all, that it would be hard for the rich man to enter the Kingdom of Heaven. Just as Jesus Christ was born in the blood and stink and shit of an animal-filled barn, Man's need for Jesus Christ is born of desperation, shattered dreams and the accurate perception of the reality that he is not the master of his own destiny.

Thus the arrogant and the self-deluded need not apply. They are free to act as their own gods, serve only themselves and reject the lifeline in the belief that they have the wherewithal to save themselves. And perhaps they are even justified in doing so, for only the least faithful need fear the possibility that our hope is nothing but a mirage. But better a mirage that brings hope to the hopeless, peace to the tormented and strength to the weak than an indifferent existentialism that promises nothing, delivers nothing and crushes the weak with more enthusiasm than regret. There is no inherent, scientifically determined virtue in truth, after all.

So, we are Narnians, whether Narnia exists or not. We will remain Narnians, whether men believe Narnia exists or not. And the fact that men hate us and are willing to kill us simply because we are Narnians only makes us that much more certain that Narnia truly exists.

There are doubts. There are always uncertainties. Only the dead know no doubts. If few doubt that humanity needs saving, whether it be from sin or anthropogenic global climate change, fewer still will seriously argue that humanity merits salvation. But without the humility required to recognize this need for unmerited grace, one will find it difficult to accept the hope which is on offer, not only this Easter Sunday, but every day.

Gesamtkunstwerk and games

April 16, 2007

THIS IS AN EXCERPT from "HALO and the High Art of Games,', an essay published in BenBella Book's latest SmartPop anthology, *The HALO Effect*. The full essay, complete with an interview with John Romero, can be read at Vox Popoli.

In 1849, the great composer Richard Wagner described what he considered to be the ideal artwork of the future, a holistic unification of the high arts he christened Gesamtkunstwerk. Wagner proposed this artistic vision as a "fire cure" for mankind, which would accomplish its miraculous effect by altering human sensibilities in the future from understanding to feeling. Gesamtkunstwerk was to be created by merging the distinct arts of music, poetry and dance with architecture, sculpture and painting, resulting in a revolutionary new form that would provide the audience with a sublime, purely emotional experience.

143 years later, Wagner's vision of Total Art saw what may have been its first partial realization by four young men working together in Texas. Inspired by a classic Apple II game about a prisoner attempting to escape from a Nazi prison, John Carmack, John Romero, Tom Hall and Adrian Carmack started id Software and produced *Wolfenstein 3D*, which was not intended as art but pure entertainment for adrenaline junkies. While it might be stretching metaphor too far to assert that *Wolfenstein 3D* incorporated poetry into the visceral violence it offered, the game definitely combined discernable elements of music, architecture, sculpture and painting in creating a sensual, emotional experience that was undeniably sublime.

And few who witnessed another individual attempting to escape from the dread Nazi stronghold's ten levels would attempt to argue that the art of dance was entirely absent. The non-stop, arrhythmic side-to-side motion of the player as he involuntarily mimicked the evasive motions of his on-screen avatar was a striking aspect of the game, one that bears testimony to the complete immersion of the player's consciousness in the virtual experience.

The power of that immersion is all the more impressive when one considers the crudity of the five Wagnerian elements involved in Wolfenstein 3D. While Bobby Prince's award-winning music was rivaled only by The Fat Man's within the game industry at the time, it consisted of nothing but 22 kilohertz synthesized electronics piped through an 8-bit Soundblaster. The architecture was a simplistic Bauhaus interpretation of a lab rat's maze, the sculpture was not only cartoonish but was not even truly three-dimensional and the painting was limited by the low-resolution VGA graphics and a palette of only 256 colors. Or 255, actually, since hot pink was reserved for transparency.

Neither the storyline nor the characters were exactly what one would describe as complex. If BJ Blazkowicz's motivation in escaping from a Nazi prison was not hard to understand, those of his antagonists, Hans Grosse, the evil Dr. Schabbs and robo-Hitler, remain a mystery. And yet, the whole was greater than the sum of the parts, for if the emotions inspired by the game were rather less lofty than those invoked by the Ring Cycle, they were arguably more powerful. While I have seen men and women cry at the opera, I have never heard more piercing screams than from an audience of one caught up in watching a session of *Wolfenstein 3D*.

But if *Wolfenstein* made id's two Johns, Romero and Carmack, successful, it was *Doom* that made them famous and confirmed that the first-person shooter was a bona fide gaming genre in its own right. Whereas the incorporation of fear had been largely incidental to the design in *Wolf*, it was an overt and intentional element of *Doom* from its moment of conception. From its ominous strings to the elements of madness in the storyline, from the terrifying appearance of the oversized monsters to the ghastly chainsaw-and-bazooka butchery in which the player is forced to engage, *Doom* was an awesome and overwhelming experience that didn't so much leave an emotional impression on the player as an intense psychic beating.

Doom inspired a host of imitators based on similar 2.5D technology, collectively known as *Doom*-clones. Unfortunately, too many publishers and game designers failed to understand that what made *Doom* such a visceral and absorbing experience was the way in which it provoked an emotional reaction from the player. The abrupt shift from silence and darkness, interrupted only by eerie strings and guttural breathing, to the roar of a saw carving through hordes of shrieking, flame-throwing demons could leave a player fired up and unable to sleep for hours after turning off the computer. These lesser game makers failed to see the art, they saw only the blood.

And while games and their machinimatic offspring are still currently well below the radar of the arts community, it is worth noting that there is no other medium which is so well suited for the expression of Wagner's Gesamtkunstwerk. There is no shortage of music in the genre, *HALO* even won a "best original soundtrack" from *Rolling Stone* magazine and award-winning composers such as John Williams have been writing music for computer games for more than a decade now.

The world may pray it never sees abominations such as *Quake: Swan Lake* or *Nutcracker 3D: Triumph of the Mouse King*, but the fact remains that first-person shooters such as *HALO* prove that Wagner's vision of Total Art is technologically feasible at last. It is impossible to say who will be the first genius to identify himself as a Total Artist and create a holistic work worthy of being proclaimed a Gesamtkunstwerk, but his appearance is all but inevitable now that the technological groundwork has been completed. The palm leaves are strewn, the ass awaits, only the identity of this first New Wagnerian and the nature of his creation remains to be revealed to Mankind.

The lesson of Cho Seung-Hui

April 23, 2007

I N RETROSPECT, all things become predictable. Some things, however, are easily anticipated. It did not take an hour before *ABC News* was attempting to connect the VTU murders with the assault-weapons ban, despite the fact that the "heavily-armed" murderer, Cho Seung-Hui, was actually armed with two of the smallest firearms known to Man. In fact, the only way to be less heavily-armed and still qualify as armed at all would be to carry two .22 pop guns instead of one with a 9mm.

Fortunately, after 20 years of similarly fraudulent anti-gun antics, the American people are no longer falling for such absurd tactics from those who wish to disarm them; *ABC*'s own online poll was running more than 2-1 against the utility of additional gun control measures even as the body count was still ticking upward on the cable news shows. While the irony of the fact that Virginia Tech is a legally gun-free zone may have escaped the empty talking heads of the news media, it clearly was not beyond the notice of the average American.

This may come as shocking news to some, I know, but it is true nevertheless: criminals do not obey laws.

It is true that we cannot know how many of the victims would have lived if those inclined to legally carry firearms had been permitted to do so by the university. What we do know is that maintaining a gun-free zone cost 32 lives and that at least two individuals who confronted the murderer were forced to do so at a significant disadvantage, being unarmed, and were unable to stop the killer.

As numerous commentators pontificated at great length about Cho and his decision to wreak havoc in the lives of his victims, an essay by Dinesh D'Souza engendered particular dismay among the atheist community by asserting that atheists have nothing to offer and are nowhere to be found when tragedy strikes.

The response to D'Souza was more than a little amusing, considering that none of his critics took any issue with the anti-gun crowd's similar use of the massacre to attempt to score political points; at least D'Souza's article was factually correct. When a tragedy occurs, atheists are silent because they have no intellectual comfort to offer the grieving, no hope of a hereafter, no glimmering of a silver lining that may one day penetrate the dark clouds. They don't claim to. However, I believe atheists should be congratulated for their circumspection in these circumstances, not castigated for it.

Still, one celebrated response to D'Souza posted on *Daily Kos*, written by an atheist VTU professor, was well worth reading for the mordant humor to be derived from it.

What eludes the VTU professor and makes his response so inadvertently amusing is the way in which he completely fails to understand the basic foundation of D'Souza's argument, which is that as an atheist, he has absolutely no grounds for condemning Cho's actions. His maudlin assertions are as touching as they are lacking in intellectual support; he rejects even the possibility of God's existence, presumably due to the lack of scientific evidence, but fails to inform us precisely where "complete and absolute" pain or "loss" can be found, what they weigh and what elements they consist of. And even if we agree that the professor's morality is more perfect and beautiful than Jesus Christ's, because it lacks any claim to universal applicability, it has no more standing for you or me than do the moral sensibilities of the murderous Cho.

And the professor clearly senses this on some level when he writes: "if not massacre then nothing could be wrong." But if human and animal history is reliable, massacre is as natural as sex. Therefore, in the absence of God, nothing is wrong.

Nietzsche, among others, articulated this long ago. Without the strictures of the Creator, we are all beyond good and evil and only the individual is capable of adjudicating the good or evil of his actions. Cho believed that he died giving hope to the hopeless, and it is unlikely that he was incorrect in believing this; no doubt there is somewhere an angry, bullied child taking savage satisfaction in the bloody events of last week, just as some did publicly in the weeks following Columbine.

Without good and evil, there is only strength, weakness and the will to power. And even the weakest among us can, for one brief, searing moment, let his will be done. That is the lesson of Cho Seung-Hui.

The war was won before it was lost

April 30, 2007

I T IS PERHAPS easier to understand the threat implicit in the Turkish Armed Forces comment last week on the Turkish parliament's battle over the presidency when one recalls that in 1960, 1971, 1980 and 1997, the Turkish military overthrew the democratically elected governments. It is clear from this polite, but unambiguous statement that the armed forces, operating in their self-appointed role as secular champions, see the election of Foreign Minister Abullah Gul to the presidency as presenting too much risk to the secular status of Turkey's "Guided Democracy."

The reason for this is that Mr. Gul is the candidate of the Justice and Development Party (AKP), the popular Islamist party which holds 353 of the 550 seats in the Grand National Assembly of Turkey. Since Prime Minister Erdogan is also a member of the AKP, the military not unreasonably suspects that given a second chance—both Erdogan and Gul served in the Islamist government that was overthrown in 1997—the AKP's leaders intend to oversee the transformation of the country from a secular democracy into an full-fledged Islamic republic.

Of course, the military's past actions and current threats make it clear that Turkey is not and has never been a secular democracy, it is merely a secular military regime sporting an amount of democratic window-dressing. The will of the Turkish people is quite clear, as the AKP claimed 34.3 percent of the 2002 national vote, nearly doubling that of the second-place party, the socialist Republican People's Party.

And yet, one rather doubts that President Bush will be calling for an invasion to build democracy in Turkey, even if a fifth military coup takes place there this summer.

While the conservative commentariat is waxing outraged over Sen. Reid's comments about his belief that "this war is lost" and the recent congressional votes to begin withdrawing American troops from Iraq in October, their ire should rightly be reserved for President Bush and his neocon advisors, who turned victory into defeat by their appallingly stupid decision to move the goalposts in Iraq. They changed what had been a specific and relatively reasonable objective of removing Saddam Hussein from power into a nebulous, unpopular and highly improbable vision of turning a fundamentally divided Islamic state into some sort of democratic Belgium on the Tigris.

In other words, the war was won before it was lost. Or, to put it in terms that even a child can understand, the president should have quit while he was ahead. The mission was accomplished.

A Baghdad blogger, Iraq the Model, is not pleased by the prospect of the coming withdrawal, and complains: " 'America's will can be broken, America is not invincible,' they will say in a thousand ways. Is this the kind of message you want to send to the enemy?"

But America is not invincible, any more than Rome or Great Britain or any great power of the past, present or future could ever be invincible. To suggest otherwise is to indulge in sheer fantasy. As for America's will, what does not exist cannot be broken; the American people were never asked to build a democracy in Iraq nor have they ever shown any signs of harboring any desire to do so. Should any Republican candidate be so foolish as to openly suggest that the American military take on the role of the Turkish Armed Forces in "guiding" Iraqi democracy by staging military coups every 10 years, the resulting Democratic landslide would make Ronald Reagan's 1984 thumping of Walter Mondale look like a photo finish.

And yet, that is precisely the position in which the president threatens to place the American armed forces assuming everything goes better than can realistically be expected!

The great con game of the neocons and their World Democratic Revolution is ending. One hopes that the Republican Party, especially its conservatives, will remember in the future that those nominal adherents who require an adjective seldom subscribe to the core values of the noun.

A landslide for the Lizard Queen

May 7, 2007

I FULLY EXPECT Hillary Clinton to be the next president of the United States of America. Check that. I expect Hillary Rodham to be the next president of the United States of America; she's already dropped the Rodham for the campaign, as I expected, and she'll surely bring it back and exchange it for the Clinton sometime between the election and the inauguration. Assuming, of course, that she wins.

And win she should. Last week's Republican debate demonstrated the massive problem facing Republicans in 2008, as Ron Paul was the only candidate with the constitutional fortitude to face up to the fact that the Iraq war is an electoral disaster waiting to happen. It's absolutely bizarre, as getting eviscerated in last year's congressional elections should have been more enough to convince the Republican Party that building Islamic democracies is not on the short list of the American people's most heartfelt wishes, but it's now clear that most of the Republican candidates are more committed to nation-building in Iraq than to the Constitution or preserving our own nation.

It's important to recall that in 2004, when the war was still supported by the majority of Americans, the presidential election was surprisingly close despite George Bush enjoying the benefit of being the incumbent, overseeing a friendly House and Senate and being popular within his own party. Now that the majority has turned against the war, or at least the idea of taking on the role of the Turkish Armed Forces in "guiding" Iraqi democracy, the House and Senate are in Democratic hands and the president's popularity has sunk to levels previously seen at the end of the Carter administration, an electoral landslide in favor of the Democrats appears highly probable indeed.

There are two recent positives for Republicans, though. The first is the way in which the debates unmasked Rudy Giuliani, as his first appearance on the national scene demonstrated that America doesn't have a mayor and that no one outside of the New York-based media actually cares that Mr. Giuliani saved New York City after 9/11. The idea that a Midwesterner, much less a Southron looking forward to an eventual Round Two, would support Giuliani on this basis was always cretinous and Republicans are fortunate that the myth is dissipating while there is still time to anoint a different frontrunner, preferably one who actually appeals to Republican voters.

The second is Ségolène Royal's defeat in France. There is normally little to be learned from French politics, but like the Lizard Queen, the Socialist candidate for the presidency was counting on her female appeal to women voters. Royal, as Hillary has done when pressed, wasn't afraid to pull the "poor little woman" card out of her bra, but it availed her nothing. In the first round of voting, Royal didn't even manage to win as many female votes as the eventual winner, Nicolas Sarkozy, who beat her 32 percent to 28 percent among women.

The important lesson here is that migration concerns trump sex. While women do like to vote for other women, they are even more inclined to vote for candidates who promise to do something about violent immigrants raping them and their daughters. Just as the violence in the banlieus doomed Royal, the unending reports of illegal aliens committing murders, driving drunk, molesting children and gang-raping women everywhere from California to North Carolina should give Republicans an opportunity to win the female vote.

Unfortunately, Republicans have stupidly lined up on the wrong side of the migration issue in their incredible championing of those who come to America to commit the crimes Americans won't commit. Given their other handicaps, it is far from certain that even a Republican taking a strong position on ending the migration and deporting all illegal aliens could beat Hillary or any other Democrat, but it is almost certain that a failure to do so will ensure a Democratic White House.

Obama, being an immigrant of sorts himself, probably can't afford to take a position opposing mass migration. But Republican abdication of this pro-American position leaves it open to the Lizard Queen and any serious move to claim the Lou Dobbs Democrats will probably guarantee her both the nomination and the election.

In the unlikely event that Obama shows any signs of giving Hillary a real run for her money, don't be surprised to hear her drop the southern accent and start talking like a Minuteman. And if she does that, prepare for a landslide of epic proportions.

The Mother's War

May 14, 2007

MOTHER'S DAY IS, to be honest, somewhat of an annoyance. It's manifestly one of those tedious Hallmark holidays wherein everyone is supposed to run out and support the revenue stream of cardboard manufacturers in the name of expressing gratitude to mothers, fathers, grandparents and anyone else to whom we might be related.

I imagine it won't be long until Sept. 18 is declared Anonymous Sperm Donor's Day, which will probably be celebrated by giving matching card sets to one's two mommies and lighting a candle for dear old anonymous sperm donor, whoever he might be.

Mothers are not only important, they are absolutely vital due to their position as front-line shock troops in the ongoing, centuries-long struggle for the survival of Western civilization. Despite the fact that their maternal instinct has been harassed, criticized, mocked, belittled and subjected to a 40-year effort to indoctrinate it out of existence, our mothers stubbornly continue doing the only thing we actually need women to do in order for our civilization to survive, bearing and raising children.

We don't need female doctors. We don't need female scientists. We don't need female entrepreneurs. We don't need female producers of PowerPoint presentations. And we really don't need female politicians.

While we can argue about whether such luxuries are beneficial or detrimental to society, there is no arguing the empirical evidence which proves that civilization has survived without them before and could easily do so again.

But without mothers, there is no civilization. Without mothers, there is no future for the civilized.

Europe is in the process of discovering what a world without mothers is like. It is an ugly picture, a brutal picture. It is a probable future that promises to be much worse than the most exaggerated images of past patriarchal oppression ever painted by Betty Friedan or Gloria Steinhem. Without mothers, there is only barbarism and the choice between the brothel and the burqa.

Motherhood is a sacrifice. It may mean putting off a college education and a career, or even giving them up entirely. It may mean sacrificing a flawless figure. It may mean sacrificing dreams. It definitely means putting two, three, four or more lives ahead of your own. But motherhood is also an expression of hope. Motherhood is a vote of confidence in the future of mankind. Motherhood is the brave voice of a woman saying, "I will not live life for today. I will create life for many tomorrows."

Cards, gifts and flowers are no adequate expressions of gratitude for this living statement of faith.

In the ongoing war against Christian civilization, it is the mothers who matter most. The sterile secularists don't fear Christian intellectuals or Christian pastors, they regard the former as petty annoyances and there's little need to worry about one weekly hour of Christian teaching on Sundays overcoming 40 hours of secular reprogramming from Monday to Friday. But they fear our mothers who can create children faster than they can manage to indoctrinate them. And they are downright terrified of our homeschooling mothers who rob them of their primary means of creating a new generation of secular barbarians.

Every time a woman says "I do," every time a wife turns to her husband and says "let's have another baby," every time a mother hugs her child and says "how would you like me to be your teacher?" she is striking a powerful blow in defense of her faith, her family, her church and God. We should celebrate these bold decisions—these audacious acts—as victories, not just for the family and the faith, but for civilization and mankind.

It is not enough to thank our mothers. We owe them a debt that cannot be repaid. But we can, and we must, love them, honor them, support them and sustain them as they faithfully continue to wage their mother's war.

The (Republican) party's over

May 21, 2007

Vox Day made the point during Bush's first term that he thought George Delano would do more damage to the Republican Party and conservatives than any Democrat could do. It turns out that he was entirely correct.

—The Physics Geek

I'M NOT PARTICULARLY interested in rubbing the White House's latest treachery in the faces of the Three Monkey Republicans, who are finally beginning to see and hear a little of the evil that has always been readily apparent in George W. Bush. What's more interesting than the fact that this latest attempt at a Mexican migration amnesty should seal the deal on Hillary Clinton's inauguration is the possibility that we may finally be witnessing the beginning of the end of the Republican Party.

This is far from certain, of course, as politics tend to swing back and forth like a pendulum, if rather less predictably. It's always possible that the Lizard Queen might overstep herself like she did at the beginning of her husband's presidency and revitalize the twitching corpse of the GOP. But although she is tone-deaf, Hillary isn't stupid, and I would be very surprised if she demonstrates a failure to learn from her previous blunders.

The president's Mexican migration plan could spell the end of the Republican Party in two different ways. The first is the obvious one, which is that Mexicans are significantly to the left of even moderate Republicans, as can be seen by examining the ideologies of Mexico's three major political parties, the National Action Party, the Institutional Revolutionary Party and the Party of the Democratic Revolution. Although PAN is considered to be the "conservative" party, it rejects adherence to right-wing principles in favor of the "adoption of such policies as correspond to the problems faced by the nation at any given moment."

In other words, it's the pragmatic party, similar to the Bush-Dole-Rockefeller wing of the Republican Party. Mexico has a parliamentary system, so although PAN's Calderón won the 2006 election, he did so with only 36 percent of the vote. That's why Republican support from Hispanics has never broken 40 percent, which means that granting amnesty to 12 million Mexicans likely means at least 8 or 9 million more Democratic voters in 2012.

The second and more intriguing possibility is that conservatives finally realize the pragmatists who run the party can no longer be trusted and leave. This is becoming ever more obvious, as the Republican commentariat and party elites support pro-abortion, pro-migration, pro-foreign intervention presidential candidates while the only pro-life, anti-migration, pro-American Constitution candidate, Ron Paul, is subject to constant attacks meant to marginalize and silence him.

Ronald Reagan is dead. There's no longer anything conservative about the Republican Party. It is merely the Democratic Party's away jersey.

So stand up for your principles for once in your life and leave the sinking ship to the moderates and pragmatists. Yes, Hillary Clinton will win in 2008, but she's going to win anyhow thanks to Iraq and immigration. Console yourself with the thought of how after eight more years of Bush-Clinton-Bush-Clinton rule, the nation will be more than ready to embrace real conservatives and a party genuinely devoted to human life, human liberty, and the American people.

If you're still not sure—if you're still not entirely convinced that the Republican Party is not on your side in any way, shape or form—then consider the following news excerpt from the Boston Globe about the migration amnesty:

A provision requiring payment of back taxes had been in the initial version of a bill proposed by Sen. Edward M. Kennedy, the Massachusetts Democrat. But the administration called for the provision to be removed due to concern that it would be too difficult to figure out which illegal immigrants owed back taxes.

America's strategic suicide

May 28, 2007

We're fighting a war on terror because the enemy attacked us first and hit us hard. Scarcely 50 miles from this place, we saw thousands of our fellow citizens murdered, and 16 acres of a great city turned to ashes.... These are events we can never forget. And they are scenes the enemy would like to see played out in this country over and over again, on a larger and larger scale. Al-Qaida's leadership has said they have the right to "kill four million Americans, two million of them children, and to exile twice as many and to wound and cripple thousands." We know they are looking for ways of doing just that—by plotting in secret, by slipping into the country and exploiting any vulnerability they can find.

And that's why the president of the United States is encouraging both houses of Congress to pass an immigration amnesty that will grant them Z-visas and probationary U.S. citizen status, because if we can't beat them, we might as well let them join us.

—Dick Cheney's commencement address at West Point,
May 26, 2007

O KAY, SO I MAY have added that last bit.
Nevertheless, that's exactly what the president and the U.S. Senate are attempting to do with their hilarious new comedy titled "Immigration Amnesty II: 21 Years After." It won't work, of course. It's only going to lead to importing more holy warriors, even as we provide the global jihad with legitimate justification for attacking the U.S. civilian population by continuing to occupy land that isn't ours.

Sure, it's possible that Rudy Giuliani wasn't lying when he said, "I don't think I've heard that before, and I've heard thome pretty abthurd exthplanathionth for Theptember 11th." He wouldn't be the first candidate for president whose grasp of foreign affairs and military history was nonexistent, and considering how little New Yorkers know about the American heartland, one can't expect them to have any clue at all about the Middle East.

As Robert Pape has demonstrated in a study of 315 suicide terrorist attacks from 1980 to 2003, 95 percent of suicide bombers are exploding themselves in an attempt to force democratic militaries to withdraw from occupied land.

This is true regardless of whether the terrorist affiliation is religious or irreligious. In fact, 75 percent of the attacks in Lebanon were made by Communist or Socialist Arab groups not known for religious fundamentalism. The reason for these attacks is a very simple and entirely secular one: they work.

In *Dying to Win*, Pape notes seven of the 13 historical suicide bombing campaigns resulted in forcing the withdrawal of the occupying democracy. Interestingly enough, there has been a sharp increase in the number of suicide bombings around the world since 2003; no doubt it is but a coincidence that the occupation of Iraq by a large, nominally democratic nation-state began at the same time.

And given that there are already rumors of a partial withdrawal from Iraq floating in the press, there is some reason to believe that the bombers' record of success will increase to 57 percent in the relatively near future.

The problem is occupation will no more end the jihad than amnesty will end the Mexican migration. Combining the two strategies is a recipe for disaster that will lead directly to civilian casualties within the United States, in the short term, and the destruction of American freedom and culture in the long term.

If Americans wish to preserve their freedom, economy and country, there are only two options that have historically proven successful. The first is to roll the dice with Roman-style occupations and establish hundreds of thousands of colonies in Afghanistan and Iraq. However, the French experience in Algeria argues that this option is less likely to succeed today. The second, much less risky, option is to withdraw the troops, repatriate the millions of criminal migrants to their homes and maintain a policy of friendly economic-only relations with the Middle East, Mexico and other nations of the world.

Globalization is far from inevitable. In fact, as mass-lethal weaponry becomes ever smaller and more affordable, techno-sociological history suggests that the nation-state will not be replaced with larger transnational government, as everyone believes, but by something more akin to the feudalism of the pre-modern era.

If America is looking increasingly unlikely to survive intact, thanks to the actions of her suicidal leaders, at least there is still some reason to believe that a number of the several states will be able to preserve many of the concepts that led to her original founding.

Letter to Rush Limbaugh

June 4, 2007

DEAR MR. LIMBAUGH,

    Last November, you said you were done with "carrying the water" for the Republican leadership. While one could argue that this was six years of the George W. Bush presidency too late, better late than never. And it was very heartening, indeed, to hear you denounce Amnesty II: 21 Years After as the Comprehensive Destroy the Republican Party Act, although it could just as accurately be described as the Comprehensive Destroy America Act.

I do not, of course, suggest what is good for the Republican Party is always good for America, or vice-versa, but in the case of ongoing Mexican migration, there can be no doubt what the Republican leadership is currently pushing is bad for both the Republican Party and America alike. It is encouraging to know there is at least one major conservative commentator who is neither politically insane nor culturally suicidal.

I also agree with you that Rep. Ron Paul's chance of winning the Republican nomination bears no little resemblance to the proverbial chance of the snowball in hell. And yet, as you well know, even the most wildly improbable event can take place. After all, we are reliably informed by physicists that the mere fact we are here on this planet today is in massive defiance of universal odds.

You are aware that you possess the power to dictate the Republican nominee, especially in this election cycle when the Republican leadership is trying to force Republicans to choose between three Democrats wearing away jerseys. And, you surely also recognize that Hillary will be the Democratic nominee, and Sen. Obama is merely media candy to keep reporters occupied until the two-horse race begins in earnest.

I very much doubt you believe either Giuliani or McCain can beat Hillary, given the way in which they share her views on headline issues such as immigration, national security and foreign occupation. As for Romney, I'm sure you recall how former governors of Massachusetts didn't fare particularly well in previous national elections, even when they ran as Democrats. I don't know if you're holding out any hope for Fred Thompson, but in light of the disdain he holds for the First Amendment, it is pretty clear that he is a conservative mirage in the mode of George W. Bush in 2000.

So, the probability is, regardless of which of the four "major" candidates are nominated, Republicans will not only lose in 2008 but lose in a landslide of epic, Reagan-Mondale proportions that will kill their chances in 2012 as well. In this case, aren't you free to make use of your power without any concern for "electability?" After all, "electability" means nothing but the approval of the mainstream media.

It's true that without your endorsement, Ron Paul cannot win the Republican nomination. But with your endorsement, I believe he has a shot. If you are willing to take him seriously, who else can refuse? And wouldn't you like to see a man who respects the Constitution in the White House for once? Can America really afford one more president who is willing to sell out the country to foreign interests and turn the American military into U.N. mercenaries enforcing United Nations' resolutions? Doesn't America need a genuinely principled leader who will put the rights and liberties of American citizens before everything else? Don't the American people at least deserve the right to choose between their historical freedoms and the socialist vision of Hillary Clinton?

You are 56 years old. You have accomplished many of your goals, and yet the country you dearly love is rapidly spiraling towards its ultimate destruction. If you do not make use of your power to save it now, will you truly be in a better position to do so in 2016, after eight more years of Bush-Clinton-Bush-Clinton rule? How much longer does America have before she is irretrievably caught in a web of transnational treaties violating her national sovereignty?

Mr. Limbaugh, I am urging you to do the right thing. I am asking you to set aside all of the pragmatic political considerations that have reduced the Republican party to its current state and to endorse the only candidate who is genuinely devoted to returning conservative principles to the party and liberty to the people.

I am asking you, Mr. Limbaugh, to publicly endorse Rep. Ron Paul for president.

With respect,
Vox Day

Fool me thrice

June 11, 2007

I WAS NOT WRITING this column during the campaign prior to the 2000 election, but I did follow the battles for the Republican nomination with some interest. I found it hard to believe after eight years of the William Jefferson Clinton circus, the American people would wish for symbolic continuation of his presidency.

Unfortunately, the Republican candidates on offer were a lightweight collection of conservative no-hopers, moderate Republican establishment figures and one popular governor of a large Southern state. That governor, George W. Bush, understandably looked like the only reasonable choice, and if his conspicuously non-ideological language was suspiciously protean, it made it easy for conservatives to see in him whatever they wanted to see.

I didn't buy it and did not vote for him. But I understand why many people did.

It is hard to condemn conservatives for supporting Bush in 2000, even if his "compassionate conservative" language sent a clear signal that he did not consider himself a proper conservative. And, if his disavowal of nation-building and advocacy of a humble foreign policy were misleading, it must be recalled that the vast majority of conservatives initially supported Bush's neocon-inspired world democratic revolution; indeed many still support it today. Nevertheless, Bush was portrayed as a conservative by the entire conservative commentariat—many of whom described him as the second coming of Ronald Reagan—and any blame for being fooled by Bush lies with Bush, his propagandists and his apologists.

There is no similar excuse for having supported Bush in 2004. Despite widespread optimism about his double-secret conservative plans, the Patriot Acts, the Medicare Drug Entitlements, No Child Left Behind, general subservience to the United Nations and his nation-building in Iraq made it clear that he was not only no conservative, but was markedly hostile to basic conservative concepts such as human liberty, small government and personal responsibility.

Now, when even the most blindly loyal Three Monkey Republicans are beginning to express some doubts about the president, and the three leading Republican candidates for 2008 appear to be shaping up to play the roles of Indonesia, Sri Lanka and Thailand in a replay of Southeast Asia versus the Indian Ocean, another apparently reasonable choice is being presented to Republicans. This time, however, the nominal Reagan cum Messiah is the laconic actor, Sen. Fred Thompson.

Like President Bush, the younger Sen. Thompson gives off conservative vibes. And as with Bush, those vibes are largely, if not entirely, misleading. According to the American Conservative Union's ratings, Sen. Thompson is little more conservative than Sen. McCain. He voted for Sen. McCain's attack on free speech, voted for first-trimester abortions and, despite his recent opposition to the Bush-McCain Amnesty act, has a mixed record on immigration. In light of his record on immigration and the extreme unpopularity of immigration amnesty, his disavowal of the amnesty act should be taken no more seriously than Bush's pre-presidential rejection of nation-building.

Thompson is actually one of the less conservative candidates; he is markedly less conservative than Tancredo, Brownback, Hunter, or Paul and only looks halfway conservative in comparison with the overt liberalism of Giuliani. Of course, it also helps that the so-called "conservative" commentariat is running interference for him and trying to burnish his appeal to the party polloi, as they did on behalf of George W. Bush in 2000.

Consider the way in which Sean Hannity intervened to prevent the senator from committing a gaffe that would have betrayed his true views on abortion to pro-life Republicans on Hannity's show:

After asserting he "always thought Roe v. Wade was a wrong decision," the actor-politician said: "I would not be, and never have been, for a law that says, on the state level, if I were back in Tennessee voting on this, for example, that, if they chose to criminalize a young woman, and ..." Co-host Sean Hannity then interrupted: "So, states rights for you?" Thompson replied: "Essentially, federalism. It's in the Constitution."

In other words, while Thompson believes, quite properly, that Roe v. Wade infringes upon states rights, he still opposes the criminalization of abortion on a state level. This means he is pro-choice; he is simply not rabidly pro-choice like feminists and other Democrats who are perfectly happy to use the Constitution as toilet paper if that will allow them to murder just one more unborn child.

First-time conservatives were fooled, and it wasn't completely their fault. The second time, they had no one else to blame. If conservatives are dumb enough to be fooled the third time in a row, and nominate Fred Thompson as the Republican candidate, they will not only deserve the Clintonian tidal wave that will likely ensue, they will fully merit their dismissal by the Left as a community simply not based in reality.

Interview with Ron Paul

June 18, 2007

What's your response to those who say you're not electable?

The idea of who is not electable is subjective. It's early. No one knows, and only one candidate will win, so everyone else will turn out to be not electable.

The nomination is completely open now because the party is in disarray, the base is unhappy and I offer them an alternative and a return to their tradition of true conservativism. I think I'm quite electable. I'm not placing any bets, but to argue that I'm not electable is just trying to dismiss someone they don't want to hear from. It's more rhetoric than anything else.

Do you believe in open borders? That's the libertarian position, after all.

Some libertarians believe in totally open borders. I don't. Remember, I was the Libertarian Party's candidate for president in 1988, and I ran as a right-to-life Libertarian. I don't support totally open borders because, although I think the federal government should be small, protecting borders and providing for national defense—which excludes occupying other countries—are two of its legitimate functions. I would beef up the borders and not worry about the borders in Korea and Iraq. It's ironic that we're taking border guards off our borders and paying them to go and train border guards over there. I do understand the libertarian argument. The more we deal with our neighbors, the better off we are. I like the idea of trade. I like the idea of free travel and friendship. When that happens, you're less likely to fight. But that doesn't mean anyone can come in and get easy citizenship.

My biggest argument is different than those who want to shoot anyone crossing the border. When you subsizide things, you get more of it, and we subsidize immigration. We need to stop that. I want to deny the benefits that draw people here.

Do you find the dichotomy between the excitement about your campaign on the Internet and the silence about it in the mainstream media to be a little strange?

I don't see it completely. I think that might be true of the three or four major networks, but on the national talk shows, the Bill Maher and John Stewart-type shows, we're getting a lot of invitations. I don't think we'd have that if we didn't have the Internet excitement. If we continue to do well, they'll be forced to follow and give us more attention. This is true of a lot of things; a lot of stories break on the Internet. The networks are usually pretty slow on picking up what's happening.

Do you think the endorsement of Rush Limbaugh would win you the nomination?

Oh, I don't think so.

Some Republicans criticize you for opposing the ongoing military occupations, since that's supposed to be a Democratic position.

There are some Democrats who oppose the war, although I oppose it in a different manner. They argue about tactics. My objections are strategic, philosophical and constitutional. The big debate recently was about whether you have a surge or not. I want to change the whole debate and not get involved in these insane alliances in the first place. There are a lot of arguments that support my position on non-intervention.

As a member of Congress, have you seen any evidence of attempts to merge the USA with Mexico and Canada?

I think they're working diligently for it, and that's why this administration is weak. They don't even believe in national sovereignty. It started with NAFTA, then SPP, and now they're moving to take the next step with this immigration bill. They're going to advance that effort to put the three countries together and have a single currency. Now that's something a president could do, is to let people know what plans have been made and express objection to them. I would work strongly against the North American Union.

Do you think being the only non-interventionist Republican helps your campaign?

I would think so. Of course, I see the philosophy as being very popular and commonsensical, and people respond to it. People like the message of the free enterprise system and letting people run their own lives with privacy. They are responding very favorably to minding our own business, and besides, we can't afford it.

One final, treasonous act before calling it a decade

June 25, 2007

WHEN TONY BLAIR swept to power on the red tide of New Labour, he promised that the British Labour Party had learned from its past mistakes. Most observers took this to mean the Labour Party now understood Marxist economics and centralized power were not compatible with a modern globalized economy, and Blair would basically pick up where Margaret Thatcher and the Tory Party had run out of steam.

But what began as Cool Britannia ended up as Londonistan. Instead of merely opening its markets to trade, Britain opened its borders to immigrants. Now, one can stroll down the streets of London's most exclusive boroughs and not hear a word of the language spoken by Shakespeare and Winston Churchill. One can wear a burqah without comment but find oneself facing legal charges for the inappropriate display of the Cross of St. George.

Instead of reducing central power, Blair expanded it dramatically. Instead of reducing the tax burden, New Labour embarked on a series of stealth taxes, raising the fees on a wide range of government services that had the net effect of reducing disposable household income while allowing the prestidigitator at 10 Downing Street to pretend that he had not raised taxes. The housing price boom accompanying the vast influx of immigrants mitigated those effects for a time, but now that those prices have peaked and begun to decline, the sting of those stealth taxes is beginning to be felt in earnest.

Blair's worst betrayal, however, was of British national sovereignty. Above all, this will be his lasting historical legacy. It was bad enough to increase central power in Britain itself, but far worse was his agreement to voluntarily abandon Britain's national veto in 40 distinct areas while denying the British people the opportunity to either confirm or reject this abase surrender of national sovereignty. What is particularly disgusting about this particular betrayal is all three major parties had agreed before the last national election that the British people must be consulted by referendum before any such surrender of sovereignty would be signed by their government.

In one treacherous act, Tony Blair appears to have achieved what the legions of Julius Caesar, Philip II, Napoleon and Hitler could not—the involuntary subjugation of the British people to a continental power.

The European Union is not an economic entity designed to further free trade. That stalking horse has been exposed once and for all by French president Nicolas Sarkozy's successful attempt—with Tony Blair's approval—to remove the treaty clause which describes one of the primary objectives of the EU as an "internal market where competition is free and undistorted." So, the long-standing excuse offered by EU apologists that the union is merely a means of fostering free trade is no longer viable, not that it was ever truly credible.

The significance of Tony Blair's betrayal of the British people to Americans is that their own political leaders are in the process of doing exactly the same thing to them. NAFTA and the Greater North America Co-Prosperity Sphere (or Security and Prosperity Partnership for North America, if you insist on literal, not metaphorical, accuracy) are analogous to the European Coal and Steel Community and the European Economic Community. Both the ECSC and EEC historically presaged the European Union as NAFTA and SPP are the entities designed to pave the way for the North American Union.

For those who are skeptical that either George Bush or the Democratic Congress would ever betray American national sovereignty, I simply note that the 50th anniversary of the European Union took place on March 25 this year, which celebrated the 1957 signing of the Treaty of Rome that established the EEC, not the 1992 signing of the Treaty of the European Union. If the North American model follows the European timeline, and there is every indication that it is doing precisely that, the end of the United States of America will take place before 2030.

The end of a free and independent England will be a great loss to humanity. It was the source of our language and our freedoms; the American Revolution was fought by those who proclaimed themselves to be free Englishmen. The Royal Navy ended slavery throughout much of the world, and the British Empire, for all its admitted faults, was a powerful force for civilization and human decency. And all that is on the verge of extinction thanks to the treachery of one man.

If this infamy succeeds, let Tony Blair's name never be forgotten. Let it be remembered with other history-damned names such as Benedict Arnold, Vidkun Quisling, Phillipe Petain and Judas Iscariot.

Prostituting science

July 2, 2007

FROM POLITICIANS to philosophy majors, everyone is feeling the need to defend reason these days. It seems that the 200-year failure of the Enlightenment to replace Christianity is finally beginning to seriously worry godless humanists on both sides of the Atlantic, as it appears to have belatedly occurred to a few of them that the moderate growth of atheism in a greying Europe is being outpaced by the incendiary growth of Christian evangelicalism in the growing societies of the United States, Latin America and Asia, to say nothing of the literally explosive growth of Islam around the world.

In a recent article in the *Chicago Sun-Times*, James Taylor, a senior fellow at a Chicago-based think tank, noted that Al Gore's recent book, *The Assault on Reason*, is full of assertions that have been refuted by the very science he claims to be defending. Taylor lists published refutations of Gore's unscientific assertions with evidence of Himalayan glaciers growing instead of shrinking, the number of hurricanes shrinking instead of growing, the retreat of African deserts instead of their expansion, temperatures in Greenland falling instead of rising and the enlargement of the Antarctic ice sheet instead of its reduction.

The reason for Gore's apparent carelessness isn't due to the fact that he's a politician, not a climatologist, but because he doesn't actually care about science at all. Gore is simply using the pseudo-scientific issue of global warming to justify his true goal of advancing democratic socialism. This is why every prescription to the various problems diagnosed involves transferring more power to the central government authority. If the scientific consensus flips again and global warming is abandoned in favor of warnings about an incipient Ice Age, one can be sure that Gore will be recommending precisely the same solution for global cooling that he has provided for global warming.

As shamefully abusive of science as Gore is, the New Atheists are arguably even worse due to the status of their nominal leader, Richard Dawkins, as a former scientist. Dawkins no longer engages in science, he is now little more than a professional propagandist for science, and the scientific method is entirely missing from his latest screed, *The God Delusion*. And yet, what Dawkins is selling under a fraudulent label is not science, in fact, it is not even atheism. The 1996 Humanist of the Year and vice president of the British Humanist Association confesses:

Dawkins, like Gore, is selling an unscientific product—an avowedly anti-scientific one—marketing it with the trappings of science in order to ensnare the unwary, the insufficiently educated and the too-easily impressed. There is no science to determine the optimal level of ice on the planet any more than there is one that will tell right from wrong or articulate the ideal system of government. Such things are not only beyond the capacity of current scientody, they are beyond the conceptual limits of the scientific method.

Science is very good at answering questions that begin with "what" and "how," it is significantly less useful for answering questions that begin with "should."

It is inherently dishonest to sell a political ideology through the use of science. Such efforts should be disregarded by laymen and decried by scientists, for the prostitution of their professional means in the pursuit of unscientific ends can only taint their profession in the cold eyes of history. What Gore and Dawkins are doing now is no different than what Trofim Lysenko and Otmar Freiherr von Verschuer did sixty years ago in the service of scientific socialism and racial eugenics. Their abuse of science on behalf of globalism and humanism will one day see both Gore and Dawkins repudiated by scientists of the future, as Lysenko and Verschuer are disavowed by scientists today.

Evolutionary evasion

July 9, 2007

> *Whether we call the early replicators living or not, they were the ancestors of life; they were our Founding Fathers.... The original replicators may have been a related kind of molecule to DNA, or they may have been totally different. In the latter case we may say that their survival machines must have been seized at a later date by DNA. If so, the original replicators were utterly destroyed, for no trace remains of them in modern survival machines.*

> —Richard Dawkins, *The Selfish Gene*

T HE ONE THING that must be confessed about Richard Dawkins is that he certainly knows how to make science entertaining. Only Wodehouse, Adams and Bethke can be guaranteed to be more amusing, although they can't top the heights of irony that Dawkins effortlessly leaps in a single, highly-evolved bound with his straight-faced discussion of the magic replicators which created all life on Earth before disappearing without a trace.

Evolutionary biology is one of the softest of sciences. It is largely dependent upon other sciences, as it cannot even date its own supposed processes without leaning on geology and cosmology. I find it fascinating how anyone asking an honest question about evolution can count on being immediately asked about a geological matter instead of receiving a direct answer.

Note: I have no opinion on the age of the Earth; I am an evolutionary skeptic, not a six-Earth-rotations Creationist or a geologist.

What is interesting is observable evidence shows that even professional evolutionary biologists are increasingly frightened to expose themselves to the ridicule that the softness of their science renders them liable. Consider this recent post at the science blog Pharyngula by Dr. P.Z. Myers, a biologist and associate professor at the University of Minnesota, Morris, entitled

Don't Debate Creationists. The good doctor approvingly quotes professor Charles Rulon's five points on why it is best for these academic champions of knowledge to refrain from sharing it in an environment wherein it will be questioned.

1. It pits oratory against science in a venue where you'll be judged on your rhetoric.

2. It gives publicity to creationists.

3. Creationists can generate more lies more quickly than you can refute.

4. Debates artificially give equal time to two sides, falsely elevating creationist trivia to equality with scientific substance.

5. The debates are often used to recruit members to fundamentalist Christian organizations.

Dr. Myers adds a few points of his own, most significantly, the importance of a lecture format and refusing to share a stage with the opposition. He is amenable to allowing the speaker representing the other side to attend the lecture but only as a member of the audience. This is very important, of course, because without control of the microphone, it might be difficult to cut off questions to which you cannot provide convincing answers.

But no one who is confident that they possess a strong case, which can be articulated in a manner capable of being understood by the average human being, has any fear of presenting it in public. I would not hesitate to debate a socialist economist in a room full of card-carrying Communists because I know that there is nothing that they can say, no matter how rhetorically well-honed, that will stand up effectively before the laws of supply and demand or the impossibility of socialist calculation. I am always delighted to debate the existence of God or to discuss the idiosyncrasies of religion with an atheist, even in a room where I am the only believer. It never bothers me to allow my opponent equal time; the more he talks, the more rope he hands me to hang him with.

New Atheist Daniel Dennett has some harsh words for the likes of Myers and Rulon in his book *Breaking the Spell*. He writes:

We wouldn't for one moment pay respectful attention to any scientist who retreated to 'If you don't understand my theory, it's because you don't have faith in it!' or 'Only official members of my lab have the ability to detect these effects,' or 'The contradiction you think you see in my arguments is simply a sign of the limitations of human comprehension...' Any such declaration would be an intolerable abdication as a scientific investigator; a confession of intellectual bankruptcy.

And that is precisely how this fear of debate should be regarded, a confession of intellectual bankruptcy on the part of evolution and its faithful adherents.

Christians vs. atheists: Who really divorces more?

July 16, 2007

C HRISTIANS WERE SHOCKED when George Barna reported in 1999 that married Christians were not only as likely to divorce as anyone else but actually get divorced more often than the godless hell-bound. Atheists, of course, were delighted and claimed they weren't the least bit surprised.

> *These findings confirm what I have been saying these last five years. Atheist ethics are of a higher caliber than religious morals. It stands to reason that our families would be dedicated more to each other than to some invisible monitor in the sky.*

> —Ron Barrier, national media coordinator, American Atheists

Thus demonstrating once more that an atheist is not primarily defined by any absence of any particular belief but by that sweet and pleasant nature that makes him so universally popular.

However, Barna's conclusions in his 1999 study were marred by a serious problem. The divorce rate he calculated was not based on the percentage of marriages that had failed within each religious affiliation but, rather, the percentage of divorcees out of the total population of the affiliation. Since one cannot get divorced if one has never been married, the conclusions presented a very misleading picture of the comparative likelihood of divorce for Christians, atheists and everyone else. This flaw may be why the study is no longer available on the Barna site; it is certainly the reason that Barna noted in a later study "One reason why the divorce statistic among non-born-again adults is not higher is that a larger proportion of that group cohabits, effectively side-stepping marriage, and divorce, altogether."

> *While the 2001 American Religious Identification Survey has the problem of any survey depending on the ability of the individual to correctly identify his own religion, its questions relating to marital status were asked in a manner devised to elicit more useful information. After demonstrating that its own results regarding marital histories were very similar to those reported by the 2000 U.S. census, ARIS appeared to support Barna's initial conclusion when it showed that 14 percent of Pentecostals and 12 percent of Baptists were divorced, compared to only 9 percent of those identifying as "no religion".*

But only at first glance, because ARIS also showed that 78 percent of Baptists and Pentecostals were, or had been, married, compared to only 34 percent of atheists. This means that 16.7 percent of Baptist and Pentecostal marriages ended in divorce compared to 26.5 percent of the irreligious marriages. If one takes the varying populations of the different Christian denominations properly into account, the result is that only one in eight of all Christian marriages, 12.5 percent, end in divorce. So it is not only an exaggeration, it is statistically incorrect to assert that Christian marriages are more likely to end in divorce, because atheist marriages are more than twice as likely to fail even though atheists are less than half as likely to get married in the first place.

Perhaps the seven combined marriages of the atheist champions Bertrand Russell and Richard Dawkins should have been Barna's first clue that his initial conclusions were awry.

George Barna's work is both interesting and worthwhile, but it is too often marred by inadequate question structures and other peculiarities. For example, one Barna study reported that 40 percent of Americans described themselves as evangelical Christians, another Barna study declared that evangelicals only represent 9 percent of the American population. While this is evidence that Barna is in the vanguard of statistical science through his demonstration of the unreliability of religious self-identification—it's both amusing and intellectually appalling to read of evangelical Christians who believe that everyone is going to heaven and atheists who believe in God— but it also renders his work susceptible to abuse by propagandists and misunderstanding by the statistically illiterate.

None of this excuses the frequency of divorce within the Christian body, but I await, with some anticipation, Mr. Barrier's declaration that atheist ethics are of a lower caliber than religious morals, and that atheist families, to the extent that they even exist, are less dedicated to each other.

Why Harry Potter can't survive

July 23, 2007

THIS ISN'T A SPOILER. While I have a copy of *Harry Potter and the Deathly Hallows*, I haven't read it yet. I will, probably sooner rather than later, and I expect to enjoy it too, the clumsy errors in logic and plot notwithstanding. (Has anyone ever designed a more ridiculous game concept than Quidditch, where all of the activity of most of the players is completely irrelevant to the outcome? It's as if there was a sixth basketball player standing just off the court and launching tennis balls from 94 feet away that count for 100 points and end the game if they go in.) And Rowlings has a gift for articulating emotion, for giving the reader a sense of how her young characters feel, which is no doubt one of the secrets of its huge appeal.

But there is a very big difference between a successful novel and a great novel. It is very rare that a great novel is also one that is hugely popular with the masses. Umberto Eco, one of the very few authors who is capable of pulling off the feat, describes "mass culture" as being an inherent contradiction bordering on an oxymoron, which is why an author is wise to decide early on if he wishes to pursue critical acclaim or sales numbers. Success at either is unlikely in any case, but it helps to know what your goal is, as Dan Brown's rather cynical approach to writing *The DaVinci Code* demonstrates.

I very much doubt, however, that the Harry Potter phenomenon will outlast this generation of children, because at the end of the day, there simply isn't any substance to the books. Books that last for generations have memes that resonate with the reader regardless of his distance from the social environment in which the book first became popular; the Christian parable of *The Chronicles of Narnia* will cause them to resonate so long as Christianity persists while the power of *Anna Karenina* will last as long as men and women are tempted by infidelity.

But what is the essential meme of Harry Potter? Being orphaned by a dark lord? Being special? Improbable friendships? The always-popular cliche of being true to yourself? There simply isn't one.

It's interesting to read books that were extremely popular in the past. Sometimes one can understand the appeal, more often one realizes that our predecessors had the same terrible literary tastes that we do today. *Day of Doom*, written by the Rev. Michael Bigglesworth in 1662, is considered to have been the first American bestseller, as its 1,800 copies sold represented 2.2 percent of the population, which in today's terms would account for 6.6 million book sales, roughly the number of Harry Potter hardcovers sold for each book in the series. But no one reads Bigglesworth today, just as they don't read *The Lady of the Decoration* by Francis Little, the best-selling novel in America 100 years ago.

Harry Potter is nowhere nearly as awful as *The Mammoth Hunters*, *The Bridges of Madison County*, or *Desecration*, to name three annual bestsellers from the 1980s, the 1990s and the 2000s. It's light and amusing reading. But it is neither a classic series nor a collection of great books. It is merely the popular entertainment of its day and should be enjoyed for what it is while it lasts. If you want to read a truly classic children's novel, I highly recommend reading *The Dark is Rising* by Susan Cooper before the movie from Walden Media appears in cinemas this October.

Let the woman drive!

July 30, 2007

I F YOU HAVE EVER held a position with decision-making authority or even driven a car with multiple passengers, then you are surely familiar with the irritation of the backseat driver. The backseat driver likes nothing better than to issue an incessant stream of orders, directions and commands to the driver, so long as he is safe from ever being held responsible for the consequences of the actions that result from them.

For decades, women have complained that they were being unfairly oppressed, deprived of the vote and of a voice in governance. This complaint was not unfounded, as they were most certainly deprived of both. But the significant point is not whether women were deprived of political influence or not, but whether they were wrongly deprived of it.

It is an interesting fact that many of those who believe solely in the material and empirical evidence nevertheless subscribe to a strange belief in an abstract notion of equality that is entirely contradicted by observation, both scientific and casual. Once the notion that all men are created equal has been rejected on the grounds that men are not created and that the immaterial does not exist, then what is the rational basis for equality?

There is none. One cannot measure equality, weigh it or taste it. In the material sense—which we are told is the only one that exists—two human beings cannot be compared in detail without constructing a massive compendium of near complete inequality. Even the current doctrine of evolution insists on fundamental inequality at the cellular level; at any given moment, every human being is either more highly evolved or less evolved than the human beings around him in terms of the genetic mutations that are the basis of evolutionary speciation. Some of us must be, in the immortal words of Rob Zombie, more human than human. And even in the very rare case of genetically identical twins, the equal are quickly rendered unequal by the environmental factors which shape them over time.

Modern democracy not only does not require that every individual possess a voice in government, it specifically denies the principle. The technology for direct democracy is readily available, however, the West continues to subscribe to a form of representative democracy specifically in order to prevent the perfect will of all the people from being realized. Even this limited form of democracy is further curtailed by unelected elites such as the Supreme Court in the United States or the European Commission in the European Union, for the presumed good of those who cannot be trusted to make their own political decisions. There is, therefore, centuries of precedent for denying political influence to whole classes of citizens who cannot be trusted to exercise it with discretion.

I have been one of the very few retrogradists openly calling for the elimination of women's suffrage in the interest of human liberty; besides Ann Coulter, I am unaware of any other reasonably popular columnist who is willing to publicly state such an iconoclastic position. However, once Hillary Clinton, D-N.Y., is elected president with the benefit of a democratic Senate and House of Representatives, I expect that it will not be long before there are other voices joining the small choir of the inequalitarians in defense of freedom, liberty and human dignity.

America's second president, John Adams, informed his wife that women would not be permitted to vote due to their predilection for what he described as the "tyranny of the petticoat". Like most men over the age of 30, he was familiar with the dictatorial manner in which most women exercise whatever authority they possess; anyone who has ever heard a woman speaking to an adult in a manner better suited to small children will understand what Adams was referring to.

If one considers the tremendous violations of human liberty that have taken place since the women's suffrage movement finally achieved success, if one thinks of the smoking bans and drinking prohibitions and hair-dressing licenses and gun registrations and then recalls that all of this has taken place when women were merely influencing the male politicians they helped elect, one may perhaps have the barest inkling of what a female-run government is likely to inflict on the citizenry. The intense public debate about acceptable cleavage that we are currently enjoying in the present campaign is merely the nipple on the tip of a very large and frigid iceberg.

The best way to shut up a backseat driver once and for all is to turn the wheel over to him and force him to live with the consequences of his own decisions. Of course, one would also do well to buckle one's seatbelt in the interest of surviving the inevitable crash. But it is not necessary, as Lenin advised, to accentuate the contradictions. I am supremely confident that President Rodham will show herself to be more than capable of doing her utmost on the inequalitarians' behalf.

Absence of abortion effect

August 6, 2007

I
T'S NOT OFTEN that I'm forced to admit I was wrong, but logic must always bow before evidence. Adhering to this basic rule would save many people, especially intellectuals, from much public embarrassment. The author of *Freakonomics* has established a lucrative literary career from exploiting the human tendency to forget this truth, demonstrating how what everyone "knows" to be the case is frequently wrong due to their application of reason to a foundation of incomplete or inaccurate data.

As with its digital counterpart, human logic is only as good as its input. Garbage in, garbage out.

I had long assumed that because nearly 800,000 abortions are committed in the United States each year, there must have been a statistically significant, negative effect on the U.S. population in the recent past. After all, it is reasonable to assume that the destruction of 27.2 million unborn children over the last 34 years must have had some depressing effect on the numbers, even if the population has continued to grow during that time. Are we not caught up in the throes of an immigration debate? Is it not reasonable to suppose that the negative effect of abortion has been more than counterbalanced by the increase in mass immigration, especially considering the ongoing Mexican migration?

It has even been argued that one of the reasons Americans must accept immigration is because of the lamentable habit of so many American women to exterminate their offspring in the womb. While I am a restricted borders advocate myself, I have to confess that I did take this argument seriously and considered it a point for the open borders crowd that restrictionists would have to surmount.

This was because I made the very same mistake so often made by those I criticize, which is to say that I completely neglected to examine the relevant evidence while trusting in a train of thought that made superficial sense to me, rather like a liberal arguing that gun control reduces crime or a militant atheist arguing that religion causes war. In this case, the relevant evidence is the U.S. live birth rates from 1973 to the present.

In 1973, when the so-called right to abortion was miraculously discovered within the emanations and penumbras of the Constitution, the American live birth rate was 14.9. Thirty years later, the rate was 14.7, very slightly lower, but essentially the same in light of how it had risen as high as 15.8 during the intervening decades.

This means that contrary to what is commonly imagined, abortion by itself does not reduce the number of children that are born each year. This may seem counterintuitive, but it is true. How can this be? The answer is simple. Given the plethora of contraceptive means, women who don't want to have children will not have them regardless of the nature of the precise means available to them.

Despite the near-religious rhetoric with which pro-abortion women hail their "right" to child-murder, abortion is nothing more than one of the many forms of birth control. If it is available, women will make use of it. If it is not available, they will find other methods ranging from condoms and contraceptive paraphernalia to prescribed pills and injections to the same net effect. Abortion, then, is literally nothing more than a personal preference for the appalling sort of woman who prefers participating in a live human vivisection to swallowing a pill.

While abortion does not provide a reasonable basis for an argument against immigration, perhaps this statistical proof of its complete lack of necessity may prove to be a useful argument in support of an eventual ban on this violent, dehumanizing and unnecessary act.

Join forces against the North American Union

August 13, 2007

R EPUBLICANS OFTEN COMPLAIN about the bias of the liberal media. Democrats complain about the right-wing airwaves. What neither of them understand is that there is no such thing as "liberal" and "conservative" anymore. The mainstream media is simply a massive PR organ for the single party that rules the country; this is true of both the "liberal" institutions such as the *New York Times* and the "conservative" ones such as *Fox News* and the *Wall Street Journal*.

This assertion may contradict your understanding of how politics is supposed to work in this country, but if you simply take the time to look around you and consider the evidence that is right in front of your eyes, it is impossible to reach any other conclusion. How else does one explain the fact that the first thing Republicans do when elected is to abandon their republicanism, while the first thing Democrats do upon taking power is to immediately embrace the policies of their predecessors? Why would the *Washington Post*, a nominally "liberal" newspaper, refuse to even mention Ron Paul's name when reporting the results of the Iowa straw poll, mysteriously leaping from the sixth place finisher to the fourth?

The ruling party is nameless. Paul Craig Roberts and Patrick J. Buchanan refer to it as the War Party, but that is only a description of one of its many interests, a better one would be the PoG, the Party of Government. Democrats and Republicans alike belong to it; the fact that more grass-roots Democrats are inclined to favor large government is irrelevant as members of the PoG are as happy to run roughshod over their campaign promises to Democrats as they are to those made to Republicans. One need only visit the many left-wing sites to realize that their sense of betrayal by the Democratic

House and Senate in supporting the continuation of the Iraqi occupation is as great as that suffered by Republicans who naively voted for Bush and his "strong government" regime.

The Republican and Democratic parties are best understood as two rival factions of one party working toward a shared goal. They may have slightly different ideas about the ideal way to get there, but their long term goals are identical. Democrat Bill Clinton labored hard for NAFTA, Republican George Bush has pushed for the Free Trade Area of the Americas, and it does not matter which faction is nominally in charge when the time comes to end American sovereignty once and for all in signing up for the North American Union. Mathematical probability suggests that it is not a coincidence that in a country of 300 million people, 2008 will see the election of the fourth Bush-Clinton-Bush-Clinton president.

The NAU is not a fiction; similar regional governments are already planned for other areas of the globe. The European Union is far ahead of its North American counterpart, but so is the lesser known African Union. The South American Union, on the other hand, lags slightly behind, while the Asian Union is so much less developed that it is still called the Asia Cooperation Dialogue. It seems the memories of how the last Greater Asian Co-Prosperity Sphere turned out has inspired a little more resistance in Asia than in the rest of the world.

This is the only issue that truly matters. All other subjects, from hot button 2008 matters such as immigration and the Iraqi occupation to traditional battlegrounds like abortion and civil rights, are irrelevant in comparison. Once the Union is established, an unelected commission selected by the various national congresses will make all of the significant political decisions; the democratic will of the people will have about as much influence on the commission as it has on Supreme Court judges today.

Of course, it is far too early to expect liberal Americans and conservative Americans to put their legitimate and very serious differences aside in the interest of defending their national sovereignty, their Constitution and their democratic rights. But it is manifestly in the interest of even the most left-wing cultural liberal to support a right-to-life Republican who stands for national sovereignty, just as the most right-wing tax crusader must understand that he is better off voting for a big-spending, affirmative-action Democrat who believes in national independence than a Republican like George Bush.

As the two factions continue to converge into one Unionist party, a third party will eventually emerge. It will be made up of left-wing anarchists and right-wing radicals; it will contain Communists and libertarians; it will have blacks, Jews and John Birch Society members. There will be atheists, and there will be Christians. The one thing, the only thing, they will have in common is that on this one, vital political issue they will be Americans first.

It's not too soon to start.

A lesson never learned

August 20, 2007

I N 1920, the Austrian economist Ludwig von Mises offered a proof of the impossibility of socialist calculation. This proof was based upon the idea that without information produced by market operations, central planners would not be able to establish prices at an equilibrium point that would adequately balance supply and demand. Friedrich von Hayek made a modified version of this argument in 1935, arguing that although socialist calculation was not theoretically impossible, it was impossible in practical terms.

Socialists rejected this argument by claiming it had been invalidated in advance by the Barone-Pareto equivalence thesis and subsequently by Oskar Lange in 1938. However, these arguments depended upon a static general equilibrium, not the dynamic equilibrium that is a more realistic approximation of the operation of a real-world economy. Needless to say, the performance of the socialist economies of the last seven decades, particularly their central planners' persistent inabilities to correctly anticipate the price-demand intersections, has offered copious evidence to support the Austrian position even though academics had declared the debate an intellectual victory for socialism.

But the dream of central planning springs eternal in the human breast. Only two years after the worldwide collapse of communism, Allin Cottrell and W. Paul Cockshott published a paper entitled "Calculation, Complexity And Planning: The Socialist Calculation Debate Once Again". This was a central part of their book *Towards a New Socialism*, which was reviewed by Len Brewster in the Spring 2004 *Journal of Austrian Economics*.

The essence of the "new" socialist argument is based on the idea that computers make economic calculation possible, providing both the necessary number crunching as well as data gathering. Cockshott and Cottrell write:

Admittedly, the above argument says nothing about the task of gathering the vast amount of data required to implement such a calculation – an issue of which Mises and Hayek make a great deal. We do not have space to address this issue here, but we have argued elsewhere (Cockshott and Cottrell, 1989, Appendix) that this should also be feasible, using an economy-wide network of cheap personal computers, running spreadsheets representing the conditions of production in each enterprise, in conjunction with a national Teletext system and a system of universal product codes.

One further relevant point should be mentioned here. Our argument for the technical feasibility of labour-time calculation clearly depends on both computer hardware and algorithms of fairly recent origin. It follows that those (both socialists and critics of socialism) who were arguing in the first half of the twentieth century that such calculation was impracticable, were probably quite correct at the time.

In other words, they are saying socialist critics who were ignored for 71 years were right all along, but now they're incorrect thanks to the wonders of capitalist technological advancement which make this "new" socialism possible. However, this betrays the same ignorance of the fundamental limits of computational modeling that is frequently demonstrated by those who attempt to model complex systems from climate change and the weather to macroecomics and macroevolution. In such complex, dynamic systems, the effect of each reasonable but inaccurate approximation is magnified by its multiplication with numerous other inaccuracies. As the butterfly effect shows, these systems are highly sensitive to even small changes in conditions, let alone the millions of inaccuracies inevitable in a massive centralized economy of the sort envisioned by the new socialists. The end result is hypothetical models which bear no relation whatsoever to the evidence derived from observing the actual process being modeled. Faster computers guarantee nothing but the ability to achieve the wrong answer more quickly.

This logical objection is strongly supported by evidence of persistent inability of the European health care systems to fix the supply and demand inadequacies inspired by their price perversions despite computerization. Unfortunately, neither the theoretical nor the practical failures of central planning have reduced the American enthusiasm for its expansion throughout the American economy.

Until Americans cease to indulge in the socialist fantasy that central planning is either desirable or even reasonably functional, they will risk seeing their health care system and their nation go the way of the Deutsche Demokratische Republik, the dodo and the dinosaur.

Communist deniers

August 27, 2007

OVER THE COURSE of the last week, I have been engaging in a debate of the theory of evolution by natural selection with a biology teacher and evolutionary enthusiast named Scott Hatfield. It has been an interesting and civil debate and you can read two of my primary posts here and here, while two of Mr. Hatfield's more recent ones are here and here.

But one disturbing tangent that has come out of these debates is the shocking tendency of some evolutionists to attempt to disavow the significant historical impact that Darwin's dangerous idea had on some of history's most dangerous men. While the National Socialist enthusiasm for evolution-inspired eugenics is too well known to be credibly disputed, the direct link between Darwin and communism is less well understood. Devious evolutionists have been quick to exploit this general ignorance in an attempt to distance Darwin and his theory of evolution from the crimes of the communist killers of the previous century.

In doing so, they are following the dishonest lead of some of the more shameless atheists, such as Sam Harris, whose lies on behalf of his atheism stand in more blatant contrast to the historical record than those of any Holocaust denier. Like Lady MacBeth, these atheists and evolutionists frantically attempt to scrub and scrub away at the historical record, desperate to wash the blood of tens of millions off the hands of their stained ideologies. But it will not work, not so long as man remains literate.

The atheism of communist killers such as Lenin, Stalin, Mao, Choibalsan and dozens of other mass-murderous rulers is unquestionable. Explaining how their atheism was the causal factor of their lethal actions is a matter I shall address in detail at a later date. In this column, I am content to demonstrate that Darwinism was, and is, a core element of Marxist ideology.

Lenin declared that the three component parts of Marxism were "German philosophy, English political economy and French socialism", while its fundamental philosophy was "materialism." This is why Marxism is often described as dialectical materialism and why Darwin was so highly valued by the Marxists and post-Marxian communists. Marxist theoreticians considered Darwinian evolutionary theory to be the most powerful argument for materialism as well as the direct inspiration for the German philosophy component, specifically Hegelian dialectics.

> *Pedants think the dialectic is an idle play of the mind. In reality it only reproduces the process of evolution, which lives and moves by way of contradictions.*

> —Leon Trotsky, introduction to *The History of the Russian Revolution, Volume Two*

Darwin was not a Marxist himself, of course, nor even a socialist. His communist-denying defenders point this out and attempt to argue that since capitalism is a form of survival of the fittest, Darwinism is essentially capitalist and therefore entirely anti-socialist. This argument is interesting in that it appears superficially reasonable while demonstrating a near complete ignorance of both evolution and socialism. But Stalin ridiculed the maleducated individual who makes these sorts of arguments when describing the development of socialism in *Socialism: Utopian and Scientific*.

> *In the many explanatory additions I have made here, I have had in mind not so much the workers as the "educated" readers ... who are governed by the irresistible impulse to demonstrate again and again in black and white their frightful ignorance and their consequently understandable colossal misconception of socialism.... Such readers will also be surprised to encounter the Kant-Laplace cosmogony, modern natural science and Darwin, classical German philosophy and Hegel in a sketch of the history of the development of socialism.*

Marx declared socialism to be the inevitable result of capitalism. One of Lenin's primary challenges was to explain how socialism could possibly appear in a pre-capitalist society like Russia. Mao faced the same theoretical problem with socialism in China. But in any case, to argue that socialism is anti-capitalist is simply incorrect; speaking in proper Marxist, Leninist or Maoist terms, it is post-capitalist.

Like Darwin, Hegel was no Marxist, but only a complete historical illiterate would dare to assert there is no direct relationship between Hegel and Marxism. The fact is both men are considered to be the premier pre-Marxist intellectuals and worthy of every socialist honor. Darwin is second only to Hegel in terms of his importance to basic Marxist theory and some post-Marxists even considered him to be more important. Stalin felt the need to defend Marxists from the charge of treating Darwin "uncritically", while in a collection of his 1958 speeches published by the Red Guard entitled *Long Live Mao Zedong Thought*, Mao praised 26 men he considered to have demonstrated a fearless intellectual spirit in advancing human knowledge. The only three westerners he saw fit to name were Marx, Lenin and Darwin.

Republicans take a wide stance

September 3, 2007

N OW THAT SEN. CRAIG has flushed his political career down the toilet at the Minneapolis airport, the Republican Party is looking increasingly likely to follow suit next year. It's remarkable, considering that only five years ago conservative pundits were thumping their chests and discussing the prospects for a permanent Republican majority with a straight face.

Being an outspoken opponent of the Iraq occupation, I didn't know whether to laugh or laugh really hard when George Bush announced that Iraq was Vietnam after all, after literally years of his supporters in the media swearing up, down, left, right, backwards, forwards and sideways that there was absolutely no truth to the analogy. I suppose it's like tigers and man-flesh, once you get accustomed to stabbing your supporters in the back, you start to develop a taste for it. Of course, if I had supporters as blithely and stubbornly stupid as George Bush does, I'd probably be tempted to kick them around contemptuously too.

The president is an interesting political figure in that he clearly has no regard whatsoever for the health of his party. Republicans would be much better off if George Bush had spent his entire two terms doing nothing but molesting interns and issuing meaningless threats while lobbing the occasional cruise missile or two; as incredible as it sounds, Bill Clinton was not only a less destructive president for the nation but was less damaging to his party's future prospects.

However, no amount of sordid bathroom scandals and suicide bombers may hammer Republican prospects deeper into the core of the earth than the increasing whispers of a large-scale attack on Iran. A normal president, gauging the public distaste for his previous actions, would refrain from any such offensive action unless there was literally no other alternative, but this one shows no signs of understanding that public support is a basic necessity for any military effort likely to last more than a few weeks.

The president and his advisers are relatively old men. Baby Boomers, that most gullible of generations, do not understand the deep cynicism of the generations that have followed them. No Pearl Harbor is going to galvanize them into blindly supporting U.S. action, because a statistically significant minority of them already believe 9/11 was at best an accidental own goal, at worst an intentional false flag event in the long and ignoble tradition of the Maine. A *Rasmussen Reports* poll showed that 22 percent of Americans believe that Bush knew about 9/11 before it happened, so at this point, a so-called Iranian attack on U.S. interests is more likely to be interpreted as evidence that the conniving Busheviks are habitual Reichstag-burners than as a genuine casus belli by most observant Americans.

One hopes that the administration has more sense than to spend the last remaining pennies of its political capital this way. Defending Israel from aggression is not an ignoble goal in itself, but then, what is the point of providing billions of dollars worth of arms to Israel if the Israeli Defense Forces are still not capable of defending themselves? Considering that the Israelis have demonstrated copious military competence in defeating pan-Arabic alliances in the past, it seems obvious that the IDF will have little trouble defending Israel against any prospective Iranian misadventures.

If the rumors are true and the president is contemplating a wider stance in the Middle East, Republican politicians would do well to seriously think about whether supporting this crippled duck of an administration in such an action can be defended in any way. Supporting an attack on Iran would not be good for the nation, for the Republican Party or for their future careers.

Hillary Clinton's historic landslide is already in the making. The winds are blowing powerfully against the Republican Party, that must defend not only a terrible record of negative achievement and an increasingly unpopular military occupation, but 22 Senate seats as well, two of them open. Compounding these challenges with an ill-founded and unprovoked attack on Iran would bear the very real possibility of marking the beginning of the end of the Republican Party.

The Ron Paul epiphany

September 9, 2007

First they ignore you, then they laugh at you, then they fight you, then you win.

Judging by the sounds of the laughter of the other Republican candidates directed at their rival, Ron Paul has now reached the second of Mohandas K. Ghandi's four stages. It is still unlikely that he will win the nomination of a party which has proven it doesn't deserve him, but it is far less unlikely than it was back when Rudy Giuliani, Mitt Romney and John McCain were still considered "electable" by most political observers. The candidates, never a particularly bright lot, may be laughing, but as the neocons and party leaders turn to Fred Thompson in desperation, more intelligent observers are not.

Why is there so much cheering for Ron Paul?

—Andy McCarthy, *National Review*, Sept. 5, 2007

THE REASON there is so much cheering for Ron Paul is that he is the only Republican who has staked out popular positions on the two most significant issues of the 2008 election cycle. He is anti-occupation and pro-border control. No amount of Bush administration spin is going to change the fact that "the surge" is strategically irrelevant, that the neocon's Democratic World Revolution is a total failure and that Mexico is being allowed to invade the United States. In short, Ron Paul is the only Republican whose positions on the two primary issues are different than Hillary Clinton's stance on them, and, more importantly, are more credible and more popular than Hillary Clinton's. He is the only Republican whose nomination can realistically be considered a potential impediment to what otherwise looks like a Democratic landslide.

The Gay Old Party's leadership, which is far more interested in proposi-
tioning interns and policemen than the Constitution, hates Ron Paul and
quite rightly feels threatened by him. But their incessant spreading of fear,
uncertainty and doubt regarding his candidacy is no more believable than a
Microsoft treatise on Linux. In fact, I surmise that most of the top Republicans would prefer a Bush-Clinton-Bush-Clinton presidency to a Paul one.
This may be why they have drafted the sluggish, uncharismatic Thompson;
Giuliani, Romney and McCain are so obviously unelectable that none of
them can even manage to put themselves in a position to get run over by
Hillary in November.

> *When a thousand Republicans are in a room and one man of the eight on
> the stage takes a sharply minority viewpoint on a dramatic issue and half
> the room seems to cheer him, something's going on.*

> —Peggy Noonan, *Wall Street Journal*, Sept. 7, 2007

What's going on is the same as in 1976 and 1980, the Republican peas-
antry is rebelling against the choices that their lords and masters have laid
before them. This is not merely a threat to the Republican leadership, but
to the very concept of the bifactional ruling party that rules America in a
"bipartisan" spirit. Ron Paul threatens the notion of politics as a team sport;
his focus on actual constitutional principles makes him equally appealing
to anti-occupation, pro-border Democrats as to anti-occupation, pro-border
Republicans. That's why he is the only candidate in either party whose
support ranges from devout Christian conservatives to gay, peacenik Ralph
Nader fans.

Between now and November 2008, many Americans will experience the
Ron Paul epiphany, in which the scales will fall from their eyes, and they will
suddenly realize that they do not want the nation to continue in the direction
that George Bush, Hillary Clinton, Fred Thompson, Barack Hussein Obama
and Rudy McRomney all intend on taking it. At this point, a 1976 scenario
looks far more likely than a 1980 one, but then, few pundits thought Ron
Paul would still require consideration at this point in the campaign.

The choice is simple. If you want to live under an EU-style regime that is
intent on invading and occupying other countries in the name of democracy
for the forseeable future, vote for any of the so-called major candidates. It

doesn't matter which one. There is no significant difference between President Bush and Sen. Clinton, or between Sen. Thompson and Sen. Obama. If, on the other hand, you wish to live in a nation where the United States government is governed by the Constitution, you had better support Ron Paul. This may be your only opportunity, for it is entirely possible that this will be the last time such a choice is presented to you.

Conniver-in-chief

September 17, 2007

I HAVE NOT been reticent about my belief that George W. Bush is an evil man with no loyalty to the United States of America or the U.S. Constitution, that he has never been a conservative, and that he is arguably worse than any past U.S. president except Franklin Delano Roosevelt, Woodrow Wilson and Abraham Lincoln.

All that being said, I have always looked on with bemusement as the increasingly unhinged left wing of the Democratic party has raged irrationally about this supposedly "conservative" president. But after his comments about the state of the Iraqi occupation last week, I began to understand how incredibly infuriating the president's blithe and unblinking lying can be.

In his response to Gen. Petraeus' predictably optimistic report, George W. Bush declared:

> *That is pure and utter hogwash. America has a vital interest in protecting its borders from invasion by foreign armies ... and millions of Mexicans. It has a vital interest in protecting its citizens' liberties from terrorists ... and excessive federal government power. But a free Iraq is not only not critical to the security of the United States, it is arguably more dangerous to that security than a non-free one; that is why the neocons are currently mulling over the possibility of overthrowing the free, elected Maliki government in favor of a puppet regime that is less amenable to Iran.*

> *Chaos in the Middle East is actually in America's interest; the global jihad is not likely to be very interested in shooting up shopping malls in Topeka or bombing office buildings in Manhattan when more tempting prizes are up for grabs in Iraq. "Divide" is an integral component of "divide and conquer," after all, the only thing more dangerous than a free and united Shiite Iraq allied with Iran is a free and united Sunni Iraq allied with Saudi Arabia.*

And "providing hope" is not a vital American interest anywhere, least of all in the Middle East.

The truth is that "the splurge," as the soldiers call it, is not going well. Insurgent violence always decreases in the face of overwhelming force, but this is only a temporary measure and the violence has increased in areas outside the reinforced zones, just as Mao's guerilla doctrine dictates. Once the surge ends, the violence will return. In a discussion about this tactical irrelevancy last week on the blog, one Iraq veteran commented:

Spent more than two years in Iraq and most likely will have to do 15 more months unless it goes back to 12-month rotations after "the splurge" is reduced. There is absolutely NO chance of success there! None!

The reason a troop reinforcement is irrelevant is that it is merely a temporary and tactical measure which cannot even begin to compensate for the complete strategic disaster that the occupation was always bound to be. Removing Hussein from power was strategically feasible for a great military power, magically converting Shiite war leaders into 18th-century Christian gentlemen is not. Middle Eastern democracy is a non-starter, we'll be fortunate if our own perverted form of strictly limited democracy survives another two decades.

Alan Greenspan let the cat out of the bag, albeit in an indirect manner. He asserted that the occupation is a function of the administration's desire for oil, specifically, oil priced in dollars. Given that Greenspan was the gentleman responsible for creating the dollars with which Iraqi oil could be purchased until Hussein declared otherwise in late 2000, chances are that he has a pretty good notion of what he's talking about here. This means that the drums presently beating for war with Iran most likely have more to do with the plunging dollar and Iran's recent announcement that its oil would henceforth be priced in Euros instead of anything relating to Israel or those sneaky, invisible WMDs which have presumably now migrated across the Iran-Iraq border.

"Follow the money" is the policeman's policy when searching for the motive underlying a murder. No doubt future historians will find that to be a useful motto when investigating the reasons for the seemingly insane actions of the corrupt Bush administration too.

Myth of reason crashes and burns

September 24, 2007

THE NOTION that reason is capable of supplanting religion, or even God, is not a recent conceit. For more than 200 years, advocates of the Enlightenment have insisted that reason not only can serve as a genuine basis for society and morality, but provides a superior one. The New Atheism which has popped up so often in the media of late is merely the latest attempt to revive this hoary old idea, which has survived despite the centuries of copious evidence to the contrary.

And for centuries, advocates of reason have assumed that science is a fundamental ally of Enlightenment, based primarily on the belief that science and religion are inherently at odds. But this is manifestly untrue, as indicated by the fact that the chief example of this massive conflict is not only more than 400 years old, but does not demonstrate what it is commonly supposed to show. Whatever one might conclude about Pope Urban VIII's preference for a pagan astrologer's astronomical system instead of the one developed 80 years before by a Christian cleric, it is simply not reasonable to believe that this single incident is in any way indicative of an inevitable conflict.

For it is a very strange sort of inherent enmity that should allow two magisteria to flourish so symbiotically for centuries, and it verges on the impossible for even the most paranoid scientist to cite a single instance of religion interfering directly with science at any time throughout the entire history of the United States. After all, neither battles over school curriculums nor federal funding debates can be reasonably said to have any impact on scientody or the current state of scientage; that religious opposition may have inhibited the application of the 20th century scientific enthusiasm for eugenics tends to count towards the credit of religion, not its debt.

And it is definitely worth noting that it was devotees of reason, not God, who beheaded Antoine-Laurent de Lavoisier, the scientist known today as "the father of modern chemistry."

But if there is no evidence of an inherent conflict between religion and science, one between reason and science appears to be approaching fast. In an article entitled "Moral Psychology and the Misunderstanding of Religion," Jonathan Haidt notes that contrary to the insistence of Marxists, Freudians, Darwinists and other post-Enlightenment intellectuals, religion appears to offer genuine insight into human flourishing and may teach ways in which even a secular "contractual" society could improve the well-being of its members.

This, of course, is obvious. Haidt is hardly the first to notice that Catholics are much less likely to kill themselves than rational materialists, or to realize that if one stumbles across a group of American high school students building homes for impoverished natives in a South American jungle, they're going to be members of a church group, not an atheist club. It is neither news nor an accident that the world's largest and most famous charity organizations are named the Red Cross and the Salvation Army.

What is much more interesting is Haidt's explication of how what the Enlightenment worshipped as reason actually appears to be the post-facto rationalization of ur-religious beliefs reached by intuition and emotion. While a scientific consensus on the matter has not yet been reached, Haidt's theories could provide the answer to many cognitive mysteries, not least of which is the highly emotive aspects of the supposedly scientific cases for atheism, rational materialism, scientific socialism, evolutionism, progressivism and secular humanism.

The fact that the atheist academic Haidt cannot be reasonably accused of an interest in defending invisible sky deities only tends to highlight the contrast of his approach with the entirely unscientific approaches of New Atheists like Dawkins and Harris, their attempts to decorate their arguments with pseudo-scientific jargon notwithstanding. And it's more than interesting, it is downright amusing to see the way in which the responses of New Atheists like Sam Harris and Dr. P.Z. Myers tend to indicate the very sort of emotive, post-facto rationalization that Haidt was describing in the first place.

In summary, science is increasingly tending to show that rational materialism, a secular philosophy entirely based on reason, is nothing more than an intrinsic category error. If Haidt's ideas are even remotely close to the truth, then not only is reason not a genuine rival to religion, it can never be; to suggest as much would be like attempting to solve the algebra problem $4 + x = 6$ by proposing an answer of "x = blue."

Monks show how U.S. can challenge its own tyranny

October 1, 2007

> *The brave protest by the monks of Burma during the last month has captured the world's attention. Unarmed, standing in front of the Burmese military's guns with only their religious faith serving as their shield, they have not only shamed their dictatorial repressors, they have made a powerful statement that has resonated in even cynical hearts.*
>
> *It's very moving. But more than that, it is food for thought. This—these monks staring down the guns—presents a problem for a militant secularist in the Dawkins or Hitchens mould. I'd submit, as an irreligious bystander, that one of the things that helps those monks hold the line is faith. The form that their resistance takes is shaped by that faith—and it is uniquely powerful.*
>
> —Sam Leith, "The power of faith against the bullet"

ONE OF THE THINGS for which these Buddhist monks are demonstrating is for the Burmese people to have a voice in their own governance. Like the thousands of young Chinese who were murdered by their own government at Tiananmen Square in 1989, the monks are calling for freedom and democracy. Unfortunately, as is becoming abundantly clear in Bush-Clinton America, freedom and democracy are not synonymous; moreover, what often passes for democracy is by no means an indication that the will of the people will be respected in any way.

After five years of U.S. military occupation in Afghanistan and Iraq, 60 percent of the American people favor ending the occupation and withdrawing our troops from Iraq. This is not just a majority, in electoral terms it is a massive one; in his historic landslide election in 1984, Ronald Reagan won 58.77 percent of the vote. The will of the people is clear on this, as genuine conservatives, the libertarian right and a broad spectrum across the left are all vehemently opposed to spending American blood and American taxes in support of the Islamic regime that has replaced Saddam Hussein's secular dictatorship.

An even more overwhelming majority, 69 percent, wishes to see the millions of illegal immigrant invaders deported from the United States. And while 71 percent of Israelis want the U.S. to attack Iran, only 9 percent of Americans support military action against Iran now, less than half the 21 percent who were open to it last summer. It is intriguing to see that the more George Bush and his faux conservative cabal beat the drums for invading a third country in the Middle East, the less the American people buy into their deceptions and justifications.

It's bad enough that the president has so little respect for the will of the American people, of course, the feeling is mutual as the American people have seldom, if ever, harbored so little respect for a duly elected president. What is more troublesome is the way in which the Democrats are making it clear that the concept of representative democracy is all but dead in America. I am no fan of the leftist die-hards that make up MoveOn.org and the other Democratic Party organizations, but it cannot be denied that they are wholeheartedly opposed to the administration's military misadventures in Mesopotamia or that they labored hard to help the Democratic Party reclaim the House of Representatives and the Senate specifically in order to bring them to an end.

But just as George Bush stabbed his conservative base in the back, promising a "humble" foreign policy that somehow transformed into the ironic and ideologically arrogant policy of "world democratic revolution" once in office, Democratic politicians have pulled a treacherous bait-and-switch on their liberal base. Hillary Clinton has made it very clear that there will be war whether Democrats want it or not, and that not even a Democratic sweep of the White House, House and Senate will be enough to bring the occupations—which by that time may include Iran—to an end.

In most European "democracies," one can either vote for the pro-EU party or the other pro-EU party. The anti-Eurofascist vote, which in a growing number of countries is the majority of the populace, has no effective representation. In what now passes for American "democracy," one can choose between the pro-war party and the other pro-war party, or if one prefers, between the pro-migration party and the other pro-migration party.

We should all pray that those courageous Buddhist monks are successful in their efforts to topple the Burmese dictatorship and bring democracy to the Burmese people. If they're interested in an encore performance, we could certainly use them over here.

Miller's queer beer

October 8, 2007

C HOOSE THIS DAY whom you will serve," Joshua once asked the people of Israel. The Miller Brewing Company, when asked to make a similar decision, preferred to serve alcohol to catamites instead of Catholics, as evidenced by their decision to sponsor the Folsom Street Fair in Sodom-by-the-Bay last week. It is, of course, perfectly legal for Miller to wave their Genuine Draft banner proudly over the scenes of bald men in leather whipping the bare bottoms of other bald men in leather; it seems Miller is determined to identify its product with a short-lived, disease-ridden, non-propagating minority who represent, at most, two percent of the population.

Now there's a demographic! I'm sure Miller's director of marketing is giddy with the thought of millions of heterosexual college guys learning to identify Miller as "the queer beer." Forget spring break, Spuds McKenzie, the NFL and the Swedish Bikini Team, here's an image that's bound to make a man want to run right out and buy a case for the guys.

Being a libertarian and oenophile, I would find it very difficult to care less about how beer companies elect to advertise their fermented grains. But what I do find interesting about Miller's decision is the reasoning behind it. There appear to be five possibilities. One is that the responsible party at Miller is quite literally gay and couldn't care less about the potential financial repercussions of offending the largest religious group in America because he is only interested in furthering the interests of the group with whom he identifies. If this is the case, no doubt he'll soon be looking for a job marketing gay cruises or selling ads for the Advocate. The second possibility is that homosexuals actually represent a larger market than Catholics. This seems most unlikely in the case of alcoholic beverages, although it is a perfectly reasonable consideration for methamphetamine and condom makers.

The third possibility is that the Miller Brewing Company is simply clueless and has no idea that its decision to sponsor a Sade Francisco street party is objectionable to anyone in any way. Since I am personally acquainted with a woman who was once a successful Miller rep, I can attest that this is unlikely because the company is fairly careful about its image, and pays a reasonable amount of attention to the events it sponsors. The chance that the Folsom Street Fair sponsorship was merely the result of a lack of corporate oversight is close to nil. The fourth possibility, of course, is that the company's marketing philosophy is that all PR is good PR, in which case it is only surprising that Miller didn't also sponsor the recent Klingon/Furry convention in Atlanta that also gathered an amount of media attention.

But the fifth possibility is the most likely, and that is the idea that the Miller Brewing Company simply doesn't worry about offending Catholics because the Catholic community has proven over time to be completely toothless despite being large percentage of the population. It has surely not escaped Miller's attention that Catholics and other Christians frequently complain about the television shows coming out of Hollywood, the books being published in New York City and the subjects being taught in the public schools, and yet they continue to watch those Hollywood-produced shows, read those New York City-published books and send their children to those very public schools.

It is not enough to cry and complain about how awful the secular culture is, because even if the charges are true, it must be remembered that it is the Christian dollar that makes most of these things that the Christian community finds offensive successful in the first place. Before Christians can hope to change the culture, they must first change themselves and their patterns of consumption.

So, don't blame the Miller Brewing Company or even the sad collection of self-destructive individuals parading their damaged psyches in public for the affaire de Folsom Street. In what is still demographically a predominantly Christian nation, Christians have no one to blame for the devolution of their civilization but themselves.

Coulter is right!

October 15, 2007

ANN COULTER, being a Christian, understandably knows her Christian theology rather better than her interlocutor last week, a Jewish gentleman by the name of Donny Deutsch. Apparently Mr. Deutsch hasn't paid much attention to a best-selling book that has been published a few times over the last few centuries, as he took great offense to Miss Coulter's assent to his question that "It would be better if we were all Christian?"

Given that Jesus Christ and all of the apostles were Jews before they were Christians, it shouldn't exactly have surprised Deutsch or anyone else that Christians view Jews as pre-Christians, incomplete Christians, elder brothers-in-faith who are errantly awaiting a Messiah who has already come. Nor did it surprise them; the feigned shock and outrage from the professionally offended performance artists is about as convincing as Hillary Clinton's robo-cackle.

Scenting a fundraising issue, left-wing Jewish interest groups demonstrated their commitment to human liberty and free intellectual discourse by demanding that the mainstream media stop talking to the best-selling author who also happens to be one of the most popular right-wing commentators in the country. The executive director of the National Jewish Democratic Council, Ira N. Forman, reluctantly admitted that while Ann Coulter has freedom of speech, he would very much like to see her forced to exercise it in private.

"Just as media outlets don't invite those who believe that Martians walk the earth to frequently comment on science stories, it's time they stop inviting Ann Coulter to comment on politics," he said.

In addition to the ineptness of his analogy, this would appear to be an extraordinarily silly demand, except for the fact that *Vanity Fair* has recently announced that a remarkable 51 percent of the *Vanity Fair* 100 Power List are Jewish in a country in which Jews make up approximately 2 percent of the population. Jews also make up 7 percent of the current House of Representatives, 13 percent of the Senate, and, according to John Mearsheimer and Stephen Walt, authors of *The Israel Lobby*, roughly 100 percent of George W. Bush's foreign policy advisers. One hopes that Mr. Forman's co-religionists have the wisdom to ignore his demand for the shunning of Miss Coulter, as the Israel lobby's petulant demand for a third Middle East war, this time in explicit defense of Israel rather than U.S. national security, already has the potential to severely divide America's Jews from the rest of the country, Christians and non-Christians alike.

America is still quite friendly towards Jews, but the incessant attacks on Christianity by the likes of Deutsch, Forman and Abe Foxman have grown increasingly tiresome. Given this irritating behavior, and the historical fact that Jews have worn out their welcome in literally dozens of countries over the centuries, it is the height of foolishness for a small number of misguided individuals to demand that 80 percent of the American population remain silent about the tenets of its religious faith. Christians are dying for their faith in the Sudan, in North Korea, in China, Vietnam and Myanmar; they are not about to shut their mouths simply because a few Jews in the media disapprove of their beliefs.

And I have more bad news. Miss Coulter only expressed a desire that Jews would recognize Jesus Christ as the Messiah, but the truth is that Christians believe that one day, every knee will bow and every tongue will confess that Jesus Christ is Lord. The only choice for you, me, Richard Deutsch and everyone else is whether to do it now, or do it later.

But, until that day arrives, there is no reason why American Jews and American Christians should not get along in perfect amity. Neither Judaism nor Christianity is going to disappear, and it is as absurd for Jews to hold modern Christians responsible for the Jews persecuted in medieval times as it was for those medieval Christians to have held those medieval Jews responsible for persecuting them in ancient times. As for Israel's survival, not only are the Israeli Defense Forces perfectly capable of defending the nation against a fourth-rate military power like Iran, but it has the Lord God of Israel on its side. Israel simply doesn't need the U.S. military to fight its battles for it.

Despite its flaws, America has been one of the best friends the Jews have ever had. It would not only be a tragedy, it would be a stupid and wasteful one if Americans were provoked into developing the instinctive anti-semitism that currently pervades Europe, the Middle East and so much of the rest of the world.

Erdogan is Hitler

October 22, 2007

HE FOREIGN POLICY of the bi-factional ruling party is really quite remarkable. While the red faction, led by George Bush and his Neoconian Guard, has been aggressively making the case that it is the president of Iran, Mahmoud Ahmadinejad, who is the Hitler du jour, the blue faction, which currently endures what passes for the leadership of Speaker of the House Nancy Pelosi, argues that it should be Turkey's Recep Tayyip Erdogan instead. We still await the final word on the matter, which is expected to announced by the ruling party's queen-in-waiting, Hillary Rodham Clinton.

Kim Jong-il, who was Hitler for one brief shining moment 2004, remains a dark horse, as does Ann Coulter, Pat Buchanan, Richard Dawkins and anyone else that Michael Medved, Abe Foxman or Ira Forman might happen to consider insufficiently respectful of the American Israel Public Affairs Committee.

> *There's one ruling party, factions red and blue,*
> *They've got so many Hitlers they don't know what to do.*
> *They gave them some press,*
> *Invaded a few,*
> *Whipped them with words and then bid them adieu.*

The problem is that this amusing little game of Whack-a-Hitler manages to combine the worst aspects of strategic schizophrenia and national insecurity with the continued justification for the federal government's many attacks on the rights and liberties of Americans. The latest diplomatic blunder has long-time American ally Turkey threatening to attack recent, but very enthusiastic, American ally Kurdistan-to-be, with the very real possibility of American troops being caught in the middle. This was eminently predictable—many commentators, including me, predicted it—but the administration was too caught up in its "strategery" fantasies of purple-fingered Iraqis voting for secular self-government to concern itself with worrying about the obvious.

When one reads histories that deal with the slow development of the first and second World Wars, one is always astounded to discover the banal reasons underlying significant historical developments. It would seem utterly impossible that any American government could be foolish enough to launch a third war, while running a serious risk of sparking off a fourth that would leave its forces surrounded on three sides by enemies, and yet both the absurd and the impossible appear to be growing ever more likely. The scenario can't help but strike one as the same sort of inept military strategy that led a certain German Reichskanzler to open up an Eastern Front while still facing a serious enemy to the west; metaphorically speaking, one should not rule out George W. Bush as a candidate for "Hitler of the Month" in his own right.

The ruling party's warmongers, version 3.0, seem to forget that even when Hitler was the "Hitler of the Month," the mere fact of his genuine Hitlerhood was not enough to inspire Americans to support a war against Germany. World War II raged for more than two years before Congress could be persuaded to issue a declaration of war against Germany, and this was only the response to Pearl Harbor combined with a German declaration of war against the United States. Now, the post-democratic USA no longer bothers with petty details such as declarations of war or considerations of public support; there's no need for a draft, or even enlistments, when you can simply hire Blackwater and promise U.S. citizenship to Mexican nationals willing to put in a term as a mercenary.

Americans face an important choice in 2008. It is not between the red faction and the blue faction, as with one notable exception, their representatives will continue precisely the same policies of foreign belligerence, open borders and strategic incoherency that we have hitherto enjoyed courtesy of the previous Bush-Clinton-Bush administrations. The choice is between a sovereign America, which places a priority on securing its own interests and protecting the liberties of its citizens, and a subservient America, which repeatedly violates the rights of its citizens in the interest of the bi-factional ruling party and their inevitable wars against the various "Hitlers of the Month."

Freedom is not a Pavlovian response to a politician crying Hitler. War is not something to be embarked upon lightly and justified by little more than predictable rhetoric and improbable threats. And human liberty is not a given; Americans should think long and hard before casually throwing away what their forefathers fought so hard to gain.

What's So Great About Christianity

October 29, 2007

Vox Day interviews Dinesh D'Souza about his new book.

What's So Great About Christianity isn't merely a response to the various atheist books, it's also a positive case for Christianity. What do you consider to be the three most important aspects of that case?

The first is a case that I try to make that Christianity is responsible for the core institutions and values that secular people, and even atheists, cherish. If you look at books by leading atheists and you make a list of the values that they care about, things like the right to individual defense, the notion of personal dignity, equality and respect for women, opposition to social hierarchy and slavery, compassion as a social value, the idea of self-government and representative government, and so forth, you'll see that many of these things came into the world because of Christianity. My point is that even if an atheist is an unbeliever, he should at least acknowledge and respect that Christianity has done a great deal to make our civilization what it is, and is even responsible for many of the values that he cares about.

The second theme of the book is that there is nothing inconsistent or contradictory between theism, in general or Christianity in particular, on the one hand, and modern science on the other. Many Christians become very defensive when confronted by science; they're very nervous about evolution, and I think they're getting too frazzled here. If you look at modern science as a whole, you will see over the past hundred years that there have been spectacular developments that vindicate Christianity. These are thrilling developments: the idea that the universe had a beginning, the notion that not only matter but space and time had a beginning, the implications of the big bang that prior to the universe there were no laws of physics and the notion that the universe is fine-tuned for life. The atheists have little or no explanation, so they are doing acrobatics and backward somersaults to account for them. This should all give heart and intellectual confidence to the believer.

My final theme is to rebut the idea that religion in general, or Christianity in particular, are responsible for the crimes of history. I show, on the contrary, that the crimes of Christianity have been wildly exaggerated while the crimes of atheism, committed not 500 or 1,000 years ago, but in the last century, are far, far worse. Again, this is a point that atheists are trying hard to weave and duck and avoid, but they can't do it. They have to come up with foolish rationalizations and double standards to try to escape what the atheist regimes have done in the name of atheism.

Of the current collection of atheist champions, who do you take most seriously?

There's now a cottage industry of atheist books, and they're of uneven quality. I have a lot of respect for Richard Dawkins, more for his earlier works, in particular *The Selfish Gene* and what may be his best book, *The Blind Watchmaker*. I think *The God Delusion* is so suffused with animus and prejudice that it can't be counted as one of his better books. A lot of the leading atheists seem to derive their atheism from Darwinism, and they march behind the banner of modern science, but I would put Christopher Hitchens in a different category; he's more of a literary atheist. I'd even call him a moral atheist. He calls himself an anti-theist rather than an atheist, and I think what he means by that is that it's not so important that he doesn't believe in God, but that he hates God. He certainly hates Christianity, and he's no fan of Jesus. He attacks Christianity for being immoral. It's a very different kind of attack than you get from the other atheists, and in my opinion, Hitchens' attack strikes more deeply at Christianity than that of a Dawkins or a Dennett or a Stephen Pinker. So, I would regard Hitchens as the most formidable of the atheists.

Who do you consider to be the least formidable?

I can't take Sam Harris too seriously. I see him as the goofball in the group. Sam was lucky to be the first atheist horse out of the gate with *The End of Faith*.

Speaking of Christopher Hitchens, you recently debated him at King's College, and the *New York Observer* reported you as the winner. How do you think it went?

It was a very lively debate. There was a big crowd there. A thousand people showed up, and we had to turn about a hundred away. Hitchens had just come off a tour in which he debated a bunch of pastors, and the typical pastor is not used to a spear-chucker like Hitchens, so he's been doing very well. He had a debate with Alister McGrath in D.C. three weeks ago and absolutely destroyed McGrath; it was just painful to watch. So, I was eager for it. I'd debated him twice before, but on other topics.

I think I gave as well, if not better, than I got. There were a lot of atheists in the audience, and the applause was initially strong for his side, but as the debate went on it shifted. Toward the end, I think I can say in fairness that most of the applause was for me. It was a debate that shifted a little bit back and forth, but I think if it was scored on points, I would have come out ahead. But that's me talking, people should watch the debate for themselves and decide.

I thought one of the more interesting points made in *What's So Great About Christianity* was the observation that atheism is itself dualist, being simultaneously pro-and anti-Darwinian. How do atheists justify this secular dualism?

Atheists frame the argument as something they're against so they don't feel they need to present a coherent alternative. They're there to knock down the theist position, and they don't mind making contradictory arguments to do that.

What is the difference between procedural atheism and philosophical atheism, and how does this relate to science?

Procedural atheism simply means that science looks for natural explanations. In this sense, science is procedurally closed to God. Philosophical atheism holds that since science cannot find God, therefore God does not exist. Philosophical atheism is in my view a metaphysical position. Atheist writers often muddle procedural atheism and philosophical atheism in order to imply that one leads to the other. In fact, the transition is a non-sequitur.

You obviously accept the theory of evolution, but you point out that its explanatory power has limits that are ignored by Dawkins and company. What is the significance of those limits.

Evolution doesn't explain the origin of life. It doesn't explain consciousness, and, despite some heroic efforts, it doesn't explain morality. I'm not making a God-of-the-gaps argument arguing that because evolution can't account for it, therefore God did it. But neither should we submit to the atheism-of-the-gaps, that holds since science explains some things, it can surely explain everything.

The new Galileo

November 5, 2007

A FEW MONTHS AGO, I wrote a column entitled "The case against science," which sparked many angry responses from scientists and science fetishists who were offended at the idea that science could possibly be held responsible for anything negative. Interestingly enough, none of these defenders of science bothered to present any empirical evidence, instead they resorted to the very logic and faith-based thinking which some optimistic individuals believe science will one day replace.

But there can no longer be any doubt that scientism has become a dogmatic article of faith, and ironically, one that is even more narrow-minded and authoritarian than the medieval Catholic church. For centuries, the primary basis for the secularist belief that science and religion are inherently opposed has been Pope Urban VIII's "persecution" of Galileo for the crime of arguing that the Earth revolved around the sun; as Dinesh D'Souza noted in last week's interview, this myth has persisted primarily because it serves the interests of the anti-religious narrative that remains popular despite its fictional nature.

Ironically, Pope Urban VIII was correct in the end, as there is not an astronomer or physicist in the world today who would disagree with the material basis for the church's condemnation of Galileo's heretical notion: "The proposition that the sun is in the center of the world and immovable from its place is absurd."

The infamous pope was far more open-minded than the scientists currently attacking James Watson for his belief in human inequality. Not only did he grant Galileo the right to write a book on heliocentrism, but actually asked the father of modern physics to provide arguments for and against the matter, demonstrating a devotion to reason that was wholly lacking in the rush to lynch the father of the double-helix's sin against modern secular orthodoxy.

It is absurd to imagine that there is absolutely no link between race and intelligence. DNA is already being used to predict race with a 99 percent level of accuracy by forensic crime labs, and there is not a single shred of evidence, empirical, historical, anecdotal or documentary, that suggests intelligence is the sole human attribute which is distributed equally throughout humanity. While the relationship between race and intelligence has not yet been fully understood, there is far more reliable evidence for the existence of such a relationship than there is for many widely-accepted scientific theories, including the theory of evolution, string theory, multiple universes and so forth.

There are many reasons to be gloomy about the future of Africa, and Watson was right to question the wisdom of the West's social policies towards that continent, even if it later turns out that he is incorrect and science finds a way of demonstrating that every human being of every race possesses precisely the same amount of intelligence. But it is not racist to investigate the obvious differences between human groups; the hysterical overreaction of the dogmatic equalitarians demonstrates what must be a common and intrinsic belief in the inferiority of the less intelligent, otherwise Watson's comment would have engendered no more controversy than one noting that the Dutch are taller than the Chinese.

We don't believe that being taller makes one an inherently superior human being, so why should we believe that being less intelligent makes one inherently inferior? Richard Dawkins, a man for whom I have little intellectual regard, showed courage and uncharacteristic insight when he spoke up for Watson last month:

What is ethically wrong is the hounding, by what can only be described as an illiberal and intolerant "thought police," of one of the most distinguished scientists of our time, out of the Science Museum, and maybe out of the laboratory that he has devoted much of his life to, building up a world-class reputation.

This shameful Watson episode, which has seen one of the modern scientific greats brought low in the name of secular orthodoxy, should serve as a serious warning to scientists everywhere. Science, the profession, is increasingly at war with the evidence presented by science, the method. It is not religion that poses a dire threat to science, but rather the dogmatic pseudo-science of academia and the media, which is more authoritarian, more close-minded, more sensitive and more dangerous than any religious leader, past or present.

Like his great forebear, James Watson publicly recanted, and yet I have little doubt that time will eventually justify Watson and other heretics who continue to stand for science and empirical evidence in the face of the intolerant secular pseudo-scientific consensus.

Chucking the Huckster

November 12, 2007

FAR BE IT FROM ME to defy the force that is Chuck Norris. After all, it is a recognized fact that we are not living in a democracy, but rather a Chucktatorship. It is less well-known, however, that Chuck Norris does not actually write his columns here at WND, they simply assemble themselves out of fear.

While it is good to see that the living legend has not fallen for the Hillary-lite candidates offered by the Republican Party elite, I fear that in rejecting the Tennessee Toad as well as the media-approved triumvirate of Romney, Giuliani and McCain, he has bought into the charade of a second-rate Arkansas charlatan.

There is no doubting that Mike Huckabee talks a promising game, but that is a job requirement for a preacher or a self-help guru, not a president. Unfortunately, Huckabee's gubernatorial record, as chronicled in no little detail last week by Ilana Mercer, is more than spotty, it is downright rife with the very sort of warning signs that many conservatives now wish that they had heeded when George W. Bush was first running for president.

Moreover, like most of the other candidates, Huckabee is unelectable because he basically mimics Hillary's position on the two primary issues of the election cycle. He is pro-occupation, pro-imperial and pro-delusional, being very hawkish on dealing with the imaginary threat posed by Iran, while at the same time being dovish on the matter of the actual invasion of the country by tens of millions of foreign nationals. One has to wonder if Huckabee would change his mind were Iranians physically to invade the country armed only with infants instead of pursuing a weapons technology in the obvious interest of avoiding a third American-sponsored overthrow of their government in the last 50 years.

Now, Mr. Norris did a nice job last week of demonstrating that Huckabee is less egregiously anti-American than most of his fellow Republican candidates on the issue of the ongoing Mexican migration. However, in doing so, he missed two key points. The first is the way in which history shows very clearly that the effects of a migration of this size, legal or illegal, will permanently alter the target culture. One need only analyze Mexican history to realize that the politics of Spanish-speaking immigrants are, quite literally, entirely foreign to the American political spectrum and they are more likely to change the American spectrum than they are to be shaped by it.

Second, and more importantly, Norris and Huckabee are both confusing government policies with private religious responsibilities. One cannot be "charitable" via the mechanism of government nor can one impose "Christian" measures through the passage of laws and regulations; this is the same socially liberal thinking which left-wingers use to justify anti-poverty programs. To use the example of children coming to Jesus Christ as an argument for anchor babies and against the deportation of underage illegal immigrants borders on the blasphemous, as the analogy equates American citizenship with Christianity and the federal government with Jesus Christ.

Huckabee is in many ways the philosophical successor to George W. Bush, and as such, it should be no surprise that he appeals to the same sort of Christian conservative who bought into the vision of "compassionate conservativism." But the vision is a false one, a deceptive one, and just as many Christian conservatives now regret their 2000 and 2004 votes for the current president, those who support Huckabee would likely come to regret that support in the unlikely event that the man should gain traction over the course of the early primaries and go on to upset Mitt Romney and the other frontrunners.

The reality that Christians must keep in mind is this: Any Republican candidate who does not abide strictly by the U.S. Constitution is an oathbreaker and a proven liar. His words are meaningless, his promises are null and void, because he has already demonstrated that he will not hesitate to break his word in the interest of exercising political power.

Mike Huckabee may be a good man, but like most of his rivals, he has openly stated that he has no intention of abiding by the Constitution. Therefore, he should be rejected as a potential president by every Christian, every conservative and every constitutionalist, especially in light of the fact that there is another candidate whose personal integrity and respect for the Constitution are unquestioned, even by his enemies. I suggest, therefore, that it is Ron Paul, and not Mike Huckabee, who is far worthier of the martial arts master's regard.

Happiness is ...

November 19 2007

Vox Day interviewed Jonathan Haidt, associate professor of psychology at the University of Virginia and author of The Happiness Hypothesis: Finding Modern Truth in Ancient Wisdom.

What, exactly, is the Happiness Hypothesis?

It's actually a title made up by the publisher before the book was finished, and originally I had no idea what it might be. They were trying to convey that the book was about happiness, but it's scientific! But as I was writing the book, it turned out that there are a number of happiness hypotheses, and I was able to derive a pretty good one from them. The simplest happiness hypothesis is that happiness comes from getting what you want, but almost everybody knows that's not true. You get some pleasure, but it's very short-lived, and then you move onto what's next. The much more widespread happiness hypothesis is that happiness comes from within, not from getting what you want but from wanting what you've got. This is very common. It's the view, taken by Buddha and the Stoics, that happiness is about controlling your wants and desires.

Would that represent the 'S' in the Happiness Formula mentioned in the book? H=S+C+V?

It's not a true formula; it's more of a representation of the factors that matter. The "S," the [biological] set point is an illustration of that. We all have kind of a set point for happiness that fits with the notion that most people are about as happy as they make up their minds to be, the idea that you can't really change your level of happiness, and you might as well just accept it. But positive psychology isn't quite so fatalistic. Positive psychology says that there are some environmental conditions, that's the "C," although those don't matter all that much. And then there's the voluntary activities, the "V," the things that you can do that will change your habitual thinking patterns.

Now, the version that I came to at the end of the book, and this is what got me into the study of religion and so many other interesting things, is that happiness isn't just getting your thoughts right; it doesn't just come from within. What I concluded is that happiness really comes from between. It comes from getting the right relationships between yourself and others, yourself and your work, and yourself and something larger than yourself.

It's so easy for us to say, it's trite to say, "Oh, you know something larger then yourself." What the hell does that mean? Does that mean God? What does it mean? What I found in doing research for the last chapter is that there is some research on an off-switch for the self. People have the ability to shut themselves off and become part of a larger, collective group. Religions are technologies that are evolved over millennia to do this, and many religions are very effective in doing this. I'm an atheist; I don't believe that gods actually exist, but I part company with the New Atheists because I believe that religion is an adaptation that generally works quite well to suppress selfishness, to create moral communities, to help people work together, trust each other and collaborate towards common ends.

This is why I now say that even though I'm an atheist, I have a lot of respect for religion, and even though I'm an Enlightenmenter, I have a lot of respect for critiques of the Enlightenment that point out all of the good things that were thrown out by the Enlightenment.

A lot of the Enlightenment and New Enlightenment figures have advocated an ethic based on happiness and suffering. How is this different than utilitarianism, and how can it avoid devolving into a mere numbers game?

This is the real problem, the central problem of the Enlightenment. When you push the rationalist view to its extreme, pretty much all you have left to go on is pleasure and pain, or happiness, or some variant of utilitarianism.

I understand you were at the Beyond Belief II conference.

I didn't go to the first one, but I heard from the people who were there that this one was much calmer, much more focused on the science, much less polemical. The last one really was a big celebration of an atheist rebellion against the oppression of religion and the respect it's been accorded in society.

We had some really good talks from historians about what the Enlightenment was, about how the Enlightenment did lead both to many good things about modernity as well as some terrible moral abominations. My talk was entitled "Enlightenment 2.0 requires Morality 2.0," and I was trying to make the point that morality is, in part, a team sport; it binds groups together to do combat with others, and to point out that we have no diversity within science when it comes to morality. We are all liberals; that's a problem. I asked for a show of hands, and every hand went up when I asked who was left of center; one hand went up when I asked who was right of center.

I think people were receptive to the claim that to really do the Enlightenment right, to really do science right, we have to understand the biases and the problems that reason is prone to. We have to correct for them.

One thing you demonstrate in *The Happiness Hypothesis* is that the scientific evidence increasingly appears to indicate that man is less rational than is commonly supposed. What implications does that have for an Enlightenment that is based entirely on reason?

It means that an Enlightenment based entirely on reason could happen, but not on this planet, not with this species. It means that we must always be aware of how pervasive the confirmation bias is. It especially means that we must be aware of the problem of moral diversity and moral teams. Whenever there is a moral team that has no moral diversity and is trying to study the other team, we can pretty much bet money—we can take 3 to 1 odds—that they're going to get it wrong. They can't get it right because the biasing effects of morality are so strong. If you have atheists who hate religion studying it, you can bet that they're going to get it wrong. Their mental software is too pervasively biased by what they want to believe.

Unwinnable war

November 26, 2007

ARLIER THIS YEAR, prior to Gen. Petraeus' report, the general consensus was that the Iraqi occupation was all but lost. The number of attacks on American troops was rising, the amount of American casualties was approaching its previous monthly peak, and the surge appeared to represent one last roll of the dice by the administration to forestall the growing political pressure for withdrawal.

Now, supporters of the ongoing occupation are arguing—again—that a corner has been turned. They point out, reasonably enough, that the 32 fatalities in Iraq this November are barely 25 percent of the 126 American deaths in May. They note with understandable glee that civilian casualties are also down significantly, that the number of terrorist attacks has fallen by nearly 80 percent and that Democratic politicians who were speaking openly about withdrawal timetables last spring have largely fallen silent.

And they put great importance on the apparent observation that the Sunni insurgents have turned on al-Qaida and are now more or less aligning themselves with the occupation rather than against it. All of this is legitimately good news, and many Republican commentators have declared many signs and wonders indicating that the occupation is verging on ultimate success. The eminent Victor Davis Hanson has even gone so far as to postulate the "Return of the Neocon," however ghastly the prospect may strike most rational observers.

Unfortunately, in the intermediate term, all of this tactical success is entirely irrelevant.

Most wars go through a period of ebb and flux. Even World War II, after a violent onset that saw the rapid fall of Austria, Czechoslovakia and Poland, featured a relatively tranquil period that was known in England as "the Phony War" for seven months prior to the invasion of France. Given the evidence of various unrelated events ranging from the election of the Justice and Development Party, or AKP, in Turkey and the clashes along the Turkish-Kurdish northern border, to the movement of U.S. naval forces, and perhaps most significantly, the imposition of martial law in Pakistan, it should be obvious that the relative peace and quiet bought by 30,000 additional U.S. troops is only a momentary lull.

I wrote the following in an April 2004 column:

Even in the unlikely event that Iraq truly is approaching pacified status, and the failure of the Iraqi puppet government to achieve any of the political benchmarks set for it by the occupying administration strongly indicates that it is not, there is no way that the neocons' war can seriously be regarded as having been won in any way, shape or form. Charles Krauthammer is right to invoke Inchon in his plea to ignore the political realities of Kurdish, Shiite and Sunni intransigence, but not in the manner in which he invokes it, because Iraq is nothing more than an American imperial beachhead into the Middle East.

An imperial one, not a democratic one, for as we have already seen in Algeria, Palestine, Turkey and now Pakistan, democratic interests and the transnational interests of the American empire are two entirely separate things. Indeed, the neocons are in somewhat of a muddle at the moment, as they can't decide whether they should take advantage of the Iraqi lull to continue to advocate the invasion of nuclear-seeking Iran, or to switch targets to an already-nuclear Pakistan. No doubt we'll learn what they've decided soon, when December's "Hitler of the Month" centerfold is unveiled. I'm hoping for Musharraf myself; who can resist those dark and dreamy eyes?

Tactical success should never be confused with strategic victory. The Iraqi occupation is but one part of a war that cannot be won with conventional strategies, much less conventional strategies that are demonstrably inept. Empire destroyed Persia and Rome, it crippled China and Britain, and it will end the remaining vestiges of America if its temptations are not soon abjured by the American people.

A snowball's chance in Hellary?

December 3, 2007

ISTORIANS WRITE that in several historical occasions, most notably 1904 and 1924, the American presidential election took place between two candidates operating within the sphere of influence of a single man. The 1924 election, for example, was contested by one of J.P. Morgan's chief lawyers and the "classmate and handpicked choice of his partner, Dwight Morrow."

There is no shortage of obvious signs that today's Americans may not enjoy entirely free elections at the presidential level either. Consider the following clues:

1. As many as 11 of the questions in the last two presidential debates, supposedly asked by average citizens, were planted by Democratic operatives. CNN claims to have no knowledge of this, but given the nature of the questions and the ease with which the plants were discovered, the most logical conclusion is that CNN was careful not to look too closely at either the questions or those asking them.

2. The repeated failure by various media outlets to mention Ron Paul's name in various poll results. This is especially suspicious when there is not even a mention of the fact that there was a fourth-place finisher, when the candidates who placed higher and lower are both identified and discussed.

3. The speak-no-evil circle of protection surrounding Hillary Clinton. Does anyone believe that if accusations of the sort that have plagued her were directed towards Mitt Romney, Barack Obama or Mike Huckabee, there would not be nonstop coverage of the sort normally reserved for celebrity car chases and missing blond women? Ron Paul

is attacked for a few perfectly legal donations; if Hillary was caught on film with Rosie O'Donell and Ellen DeGeneres, no one but the Drudge Report would cover it, and the *New York Times* would publish 15 editorials in five days lambasting anyone who would dare to criticize her "just for being a woman."

4. The uneven amount of debate time allotted to the various candidates. Rudy Giuliani is polling very poorly in the actual primary states. On what basis is he granted advantages of the sort he enjoyed in the most recent Republican debate?

5. The media's denigration of its own post-debate polls. Ron Paul's rise in the primary state polls and successful money-raising subsequent to his performance in the Republican debates certainly suggest that he has been doing well, then the media's determination to pretend that their post-debate polls are irrelevant is truly bizarre.

6. Hillary Clinton's recent statement that her election is inevitable. It's possible that she's merely speaking in the hopes that the thought will bring about the reality. It's arguably rather more likely she knows something those of us who are not Washington insiders do not, perhaps something related to the fact that the last three presidents have been named Bush, Clinton and Bush.

My long-time readers know I have been predicting a 2008 election featuring Hillary Clinton vs. either Jeb Bush or Rudy Giuliani since 2003, with Hillary winning easily. This prediction was not based on any inside information; it was merely a logical conclusion reached on the basis of obvious evidence. We know the media wants Hillary to win, its current flirtation with Sen. Obama notwithstanding. We know the electoral winds are at the Democratic Party's back, thanks to the Bush administration's massively popular war on American liberties and the ongoing Middle Eastern occupations. We also know the media wish to see Giuliani stand as her opponent because he is a terrible candidate in the Dole mode, and his views are quite similar to hers on most of the major issues of the day.

Why a significant percentage of the conservative media also support Giuliani would seem inexplicable at first, until one considers their predictions leading up to the 2006 election and realizes that most of them simply don't know what they're talking about when it comes to election probabilities.

But Hillary's comment aside, I don't think the election is fixed so much as it is heavily weighted. The combination of party elites with an increasingly agglomerated media means it is nearly impossible for anyone who is not anointed to have more than a snowball's chance at winning either the Democratic or the Republican Party nomination, let alone the presidency.

Still, the Ron Paul snowball hasn't melted yet, in fact, he's picking up supporters from left and right every single day now. If Hillary isn't speaking literally, if she isn't actually as inevitable as she says, then every day that passes increases the chance that the snowball will grow to become a November avalanche.

Bush: The great torturer

December 10, 2007

FOR THE LAST SEVEN YEARS, Republicans have made excuse after excuse for George W. Bush. An entire book could be compiled about the risible claims made for him; an entire political generation of theoretically conservative pundits is quietly hoping that no one will ever ransack their archives and reveal how completely off-base they were regarding the current president. My personal favorite was the way that Peggy Noonan, an otherwise sober commentator, once proclaimed that all America had come to know that Bush was "Reaganesque."

That was in the autumn of 2000. By the time Ronald Reagan was buried in June 2004, only a few Fox commentators were still trying to force the comparison. Now, after seven years of his governance and with his departure rapidly approaching, conservatives are forced to admit that "Wilsonesque," "Rooseveltian" and "Trotskyite" are all much more accurate descriptions of President Bush the Younger. Why anyone ever thought for one second that a man who subjected the English language to worse tortures than anything the Guantanamo Bay prisoners have endured could compare to "the Great Communicator" will remain a mystery for the ages.

"The Great Torturer" is departing none too soon. Bill Clinton was a terrible president, but his legacy of perjury, presidential sexcapades and perambulating corpses was far less harmful to the nation than George W. Bush's War on American liberties. The Patriot Acts have already been proven to be worse than predicted; the U.S. military is openly serving as the mercenary muscle of the United Nations; the laws are being rewritten to allow for the structure of an unelected supra-national ruling commission, and the borders have been opened to accommodate the desires of a horde of left-wing immigrants, many of whom actually speak less English than the president himself.

But for all that this supposed conservative's legacy will be one of national self-destruction—as Jonah Goldberg once wrote of Adolf Hitler, just try to name one thing he actually wanted to conserve—few have ever accused him of actual political corruption. Even the dark whisperings about Darth Cheney and an alternative evolutionary tree tend to be intrinsically exculpatory; the chimpanzee might appear to smirk, but at the end of the day, it's just a chimpanzee. You can't reasonably blame it for a failure to comprehend the concept of human liberty or a failure to grasp the Clausewitzian physics of war.

The lies that surrounded the invasion and subsequent occupation of Iraq are well known. There were no nukes, no biological weapons of mass destruction, no nuclear weapons program, no evidence suggesting involvement in the 9/11 attacks, no violation of any peace treaty with the United States—in short, no justification for war other than the fact that Hussein was a cruel and murderous dictator presiding over a sovereign nation. (I must confess that, unlike the alarmingly prophetic Patrick J. Buchanan, I was dumb enough to fall for the latter justification myself, at least until I finally looked it up and discovered that the only relevant treaty was between Iraq and the United Nations.)

However, as the indefatigable Justin Raimondo has documented, the lies surrounding the Iraqi invasion are likely to pale in comparison to those being told in order to justify an invasion of Iran. The neocons are frantically looking for a justification, any justification, to continue to beat the war drums in light of the recent National Intelligence Estimate report which declared that Iran stopped its weapons development program in 2003.

The truth is that the reason underlying many wars is internal, not external. It is the freedom of the American people that is dangerous to the mahouts of the governing elite, who ride uncertainly on top of the elephant of the great unwashed, never quite sure that they are actually as in control of events as they would like to believe themselves to be. In the past, it was enough to mutter ominous threats about non-existent bogeymen to get the elephant moving in the right direction, (Remember the *Maine*?) but the combination of a genuinely free Internet press with two post-ironic generations that assume that the official story cannot possibly be true means that this is no longer a safe assumption. This leaves the elephant riders with two choices, give up their war or invent a better reason, even if they have to burn the Reichstag themselves.

Actually, come to think of it, if they'd do the American people the favor of burning down Congress, the White House and the Supreme Court while all three were in session, I suspect America might be inclined to let them have their invasion out of sheer gratitude. What's one more occupation to a nation that boasts troops stationed in lands ranging from Araby to Iceland? In any event, if the psychologists are correct and the enthusiasm with which invasion enthusiasts fling around the term "islamo-fascist" tends to reflect an aspect of their own character, the only reasonable conclusion is that the Democrusaders will opt for invention, no matter how much the truth must be tortured.

When is right not right? When it's wrong

December 18, 2007

E VERYONE GETS THINGS WRONG from time to time. Political campaigns are no different, and there are too many variables going into them to easily anticipate events or end results; often it's not even possible to correctly grasp what the ultimate significance of a particular event will be when it has already happened. That being said, it is striking how completely useless the greater part of the conservative media has been in trying to analyze either the Democratic or Republican primaries.

It is striking, but it is not surprising. As Joe Carter of the Mike Huckabee campaign pointed out in a recent post on his blog at *Evangelical Outpost*, Manhattan conservatives do not have their finger on the pulse of the Republican Party's base, but rather the Republican Party's elite. This is not a difficult concept, as one would no more expect Jewish New Yorkers and agnostic English expatriates to do any better at predicting the actions of midwestern Lutherans and southern Southern Baptists than fly-over country mice manage to anticipate the latest lunacy of their big-city coastal cousins.

For the last year, the conservative media led by *Fox News*, *Townhall* and *National Review* have relentlessly laid out palm leaves in the path of the so-called "Big Three," the three "electable" candidates rather less grandiosely nicknamed "Rudy McRomney" by those uninclined to be dictated to by the men with the megaphones. And yet, it should not have taken a rocket scientist to grasp that a pro-abortion, anti-gun New Yorker, a flip-flopping Mormon and the mainstream media's favorite anti-free speech campaigner collectively held very, very little appeal to Republicans primarily motivated by religion or small government principles.

That this happens to be a significant majority of the Republican Party appears to have been overlooked by the party elite as well as its propaganda arm. One wonders if this failure to see the obvious could possibly be related to the apparent absence of any Baptists, Lutherans or charismatics among those doing electoral analysis for the conservative media's primary publications, despite accounting for 23 percent of the adult U.S. population according to the 2001 *American Religious Identification Survey.*

Religion has been a defining force in American politics since the election of Jimmy Carter. And with every election cycle since, led by the *New York Times,* the bipartisan pundocracy has attempted to announce the end of religion's influence in America. But Reagan's ascendancy was in part thanks to the emergence of the religious right; the Bush and Dole defeats were partially due to their disdain for that portion of their base, and Bush the Younger's two electoral wins were entirely due to his embrace of it, however feigned it may have been. Republicans cannot win the general election without the religious right. The significant development of the 2008 primary process may be that because of the Internet, a Republican cannot even win the nomination without it.

My own view is that the American electoral system is essentially a sham and that the candidates are hand-picked by a bipartisan elite which predetermines the winner by selecting one viable candidate and one non-viable one. This is why I forecast a Hillary Clinton vs. Republican sacrificial lamb contest back in 2005. At the time, I considered Jeb Bush and Rudy Giuliani to be the two candidates most closely fitting the Dole model; serious politicians with national stature whose personal circumstances and idiosyncrasies rendered them sufficiently unpalatable to the party mainstream. It seems, however, that I may have actually underestimated their insalubrious lack of appeal; Giuliani may not even be capable of serving as a sacrificial lamb.

Despite being declared the national front-runner from the start, Giuliani is so demonstrably unpalatable to religious, pro-life, pro-gun and small government Republicans alike that he is unlikely to survive New Hampshire looking like a credible nominee; he is the last of the former "Big Three" (including its honorary fourth member, Fred Thompson), to fall behind the ex-preacher Mike Huckabee. Meanwhile, the endorsement of Mitt Romney by *National Review* looked irrelevant from the day it was announced, especially in light of the way in which panicked pundicrats are tripping over one another's feet in their haste to attack Mike Huckabee before he blows the three/four candidates they have championed for months as being the only credible choices entirely out of the water. Considering that Huckabee's appeal is essentially limited to pro-life and religious Republicans, imagine if there was a candidate who held appeal for small-government, pro-homeschool, pro-border Republicans as well! Why, who knows what he'd be capable of doing?

But regardless of how it all plays out, it is certainly ironic that the Republican elite and the conservative election analysts should have so completely forgotten that religion is genuinely important in American politics, and to have done so at a time when the Democratic Party appears to have finally learned this lesson for the first time since 1976.

Heil Canada!

December 24, 2007

AMERICANS DON'T think very often about Canada, and for good reason. In global terms, it is irrelevant, a nation so insignificant that it exported its national sport from cities like Winnipeg and Quebec to hockey hotbeds such as Phoenix, Ariz. While we're appreciative of the maple syrup and the occasional celebrity it contributes—speaking of which, Canadians can take Pamela Anderson back if they like, as we appear to be done with her—Canada's latest contribution to Western culture is even less desirable than the little coven of Canadian neocons that have invaded the conservative American commentariat.

Mark Steyn is an overexposed, overrated, Canadian opinion columnist much favored by the strong government element of the right-wing blogosphere. This doesn't mean he's not a talented, intelligent, accomplished and amusing writer; he actually is, but he's also not the distillation of P.J. O'Rourke, Ann Coulter and P.G. Wodehouse that the many gushing tributes to him written during the past few years might otherwise lead one to believe. Steyn is a prototypical war cheerleader, with all of the typical war cheerleader's ignorance of both military history and military strategy, and a conventional pundit with the conventional pundit's inability to either correctly forecast political events or admit obvious past errors.

But one of the areas where Steyn is good, very good indeed, is on the subject of the demographic challenge posed by the impact of immigration throughout the West. Only Pat Buchanan has been more prescient than Steyn, and with the exception of Buchanan and Michelle Malkin, few writers have been more boldly outspoken about the increasingly dire situation in which the West finds itself due to its stupid and suicidal flirtation with multiculturalism. Because of Steyn's personal background and professional connections to the

United Kingdom, he is more aware than most of the impact of Muslim immigration and the various challenges to Western societies posed by it.

On Oct. 20, 2006, the Canadian magazine *Maclean's* published an article by Steyn entitled "Why the Future Belongs to Islam," which explained how the religio-demographic equation of youth plus will make the Islamic domination of an aging Europe not only possible, but probable. He concluded, quite logically: "If you're not shy about taking on the Israelis and Russians, why wouldn't you fancy your chances against the Belgians and Spaniards?"

The Canadian Islamic Congress took exception to this prediction of Islam's ultimate victory, presumably because it takes the form of a Cassandra-style warning rather than a properly submissive celebration. They complained that Steyn and the magazine are "attempting to import a racist discourse and language into mainstream discourse in Canadian society." It would seem that the inherent irony of immigrants complaining about an unwanted importation into Canadian society escapes the Congress, along with the concept of freedom of speech and the important distinction between "race" and "religious affiliation."

All of this would be nothing more than one small organization complaining about a political critic, were it not for the fact that the Canadian Jewish Congress began lobbying to make hate speech a crime in 1953. The Jewish Congress finally succeeded in 1970, establishing a law which has been upheld in several constitutional challenges before the Supreme Court of Canada. There is no Canadian First Amendment; there are, however, three separate Canadian human rights tribunals before whom the Canadian Islamic Congress has lodged official complaints. The first tribunal, the provincial one in British Columbia, is scheduled to begin hearings in June. And so the Law of Unintended but Totally Predictable Consequences strikes once more.

Given the vagaries of what passes for Canadian law, there is little that anyone not sitting on a Canadian human rights tribunal can do about this outrageous persecution of Mark Steyn for his supposed thought-crimes against Islam. Those interested in supporting Steyn and the cause of free speech in Canada may wish to consider visiting Free Mark Steyn or the home page of the beleaguered "one-man global content provider" himself. All men who value freedom and human liberty must wish Steyn the very best of fortune in his battle; if the Canadian free-speech fascists are successful in silencing him, he will not be their final victim.

Steyn may be correct about the long-term effect of Islam in the West. He may be wrong. But the question is irrelevant because in a free society, one has the fundamental right to be wrong. I do not defend Mark Steyn because I agree with him, but because a dangerous injustice is being committed against him.

Americans must realize that this insidious form of intellectual totalitarianism is not accidental, it is the inevitable result of the multicultural ideology, which nothing more than a sophisticated form of the old strategic principle of divide and conquer. Hate speech is free speech; to eliminate hate you must also eliminate freedom.

Liberal Fascism

December 31, 2007

Liberal Fascism: The Secret History of the American Left, From Mussolini to the Politics of Meaning
by Jonah Goldberg
Rating: 8 of 10

I T IS ONE OF THE IRONIC, but unfortunate facts of publishing reality that the commentators who make a living writing about politics are almost uniformly unable to write serious and significant book-length works of non-fiction. The overwhelming majority of books published by members of the mediacracy are as banal as they are ephemeral; the ability to dash off pithy rhetorical sallies seldom translates well into an aptitude for constructing detailed arguments supported by documented evidence.

This may be due to the baleful influence of talk radio and sound-bite television, or perhaps it is simply a question of perspective and not being able to see the forest for the trees. But regardless of the reason, it comes as a delightful surprise to discover that it is none other than the cheerful joker of the conservative commentariat, whose most notable previous accomplishment was offending the entire nation of France by quoting a cartoon, who has written the most ideologically significant work of political non-fiction since Allan Bloom's *The Closing of the American Mind*.

Although the left will surely react to it with its customary hysteria, *Liberal Fascism: The Secret History of the American Left, From Mussolini to the Politics of Meaning* is not a polemic in the style made fashionable by Ann Coulter and Al Franken. Goldberg's restraint in avoiding cheap shots and resolutely sticking to the documented facts of his subject matter is remarkable, especially for those familiar with his political columns and Corner posts at *National Review Online*.

Unlike most of his maleducated peers in the media, Goldberg rejects the historically ignorant view still dominant in American pop culture that perceives Fascism and National Socialism as right-wing political phenomena. Goldberg correctly identifies both revolutionary ideologies as being inherently of the political left; more importantly, he provides substantial documentary evidence proving his case beyond any rational doubt. And in doing so, he exposes six decades of intellectual fraud committed by American academics, 60 years of university professors averting their eyes from the historical realities and teaching the literal Stalinist line to multiple generations of college students. This is a book that not only needed to be written; it is one that is long overdue.

At 496 pages, *Liberal Fascism* is also a long march. Nor is it always an easy one, since Goldberg takes what is perhaps best described as a biographical approach to the subject rather than a methodical one; the case is made effectively, but not efficiently. However, the chaotic structure of the book is at least partially due to the historically fluid nature of fascism itself; for as Goldberg notes, the Italian Fascists were eminently pragmatic political animals, led as they were by an audacious, highly intelligent man of outstanding political gifts who was about as concerned with ideological purity as William Jefferson Clinton. It is somewhat disappointing to discover that this structural synchronicity is not a brilliant literary metaphor, but merely a fortuitous coincidence.

While it will be very difficult for even the most stubborn leftist to take serious issue with Goldberg's proper placing of historical fascism on the political spectrum, it is the controversial connection he draws between European fascism and American progressivism, which he references as the source of both Hillary Clinton's "politics of meaning" as well as George Bush's "compassionate conservativism," that will provide legitimate grounds for argument. Goldberg presents a reasonable case for this aspect of his argument, but not an entirely conclusive one, and it is clear that a more methodical approach would have likely served him better on this particular point.

It must be noted that this is Goldberg's first book, and at times, it shows. I would have liked to have seen more extensive citations from the historical sources in the text, especially the Italian ones, as well as a more detailed examination of the connection between fascism and feminism, from the famous Mitfords and the first plank in the Fascist platform to the grim lesbian blackskirts surrounding Hillary Clinton today. Nevertheless, *Liberal Fascism* shows that Jonah Goldberg fully merits his position as the most widely syndicated columnist of his generation and provides fair warning of his development into a significant intellectual figure of the future on the American right.

I highly recommend *Liberal Fascism* for anyone who has ever been called a fascist, has ever called anyone else a fascist, or simply wishes to understand the history of the ideologies that pervade modern American politics.

Interview with Jonah Goldberg

January 7, 2008

Let's start with the title of *Liberal Fascism*. You derived it from H.G. Wells, who you point out was not only a science fiction author but also an important public intellectual responsible for coining the term. When you look at science fiction, there's often an underlying assumption that mankind will be unified in the future. Is this fascist aspect of science fiction also an inheritance from H.G. Wells?

I think what makes the best science fiction, what distinguishes good science fiction from bad science fiction, is that the technology and the futuristic setting are mechanisms by which we highlight certain eternal truths.... There is a fundamental human desire to recreate the feeling of the tribe. In fact, that informs my total view about fascism, communism and all of the other forms of totalitarianism, as they are fundamentally reactionary in their desire to recreate with the state that sense of belonging and meaning that in primordial times we got from the tribe. It's essentially modern tribalism. In a lot of science fiction, you get this desire to imagine a future where there is this Parliament of Man, and we are all one human tribe amidst a lot of alien tribes scattered throughout the universe. There is a fascistic impulse in that desire; there's a utopian desire to recreate that sense of belonging to a Brotherhood of Man that comes out in a lot of science fiction.

You drew an important connection between fascism and the social gospel of the American progressives, as well as Hillary Clinton's "politics of meaning." That leaped out at me, since after quoting Gentile about "the sacralization of politics," Giordano Bruno Guerri wrote in *Fascisti* that "Fascism was the first experiment in institutionalizing this new secular religion since the time of the French Revolution." Isn't this Italian perspective on Italian Fascism practically identical to what you're saying about the broader fascism and its connection to Clinton and the progressives?

Yeah, I wanted to get into a lot of Eric Voegelin and all that in the book, but my publisher kept saying this is highbrow enough; we don't want to scare away readers. I'm very much in the Voegelin camp about how what unites what we call modern liberalism, progressivism, socialism, all of these isms, is the desire to immanentize the eschaton, the desire to sacralize life through politics, technology and the state's manipulation of technology. That was explicit in a lot of the Fascist intellectuals around Mussolini, and it was explicit in a lot of the ideologues around Hitler as well.

Some of your critics focus on the fact that you're not an academic, so should the fact that no book like this has been written in the 60 years since the end of the Fascist regime be taken as evidence that you're just smoking crack, or is it an indictment of the academy?

Since I'm currently not smoking crack, I personally take it as an indictment of the academy. I plead absolutely guilty that I'm not an academic. I mean, how am I going to deny that? I think there's a certain guild mentality that comes into play where a lot of academics try to shoot the messenger and say the substance of what I have to say doesn't matter because I don't carry the right guild card in my wallet.… As Tom Wolfe said in the blurb for the book, it's the greatest hoax in modern history that we were convinced that Fascism and National Socialism were phenomena of the right.

If libertarianism is the opposite of communism, and fascism is founded on a cult of action, can't we then conclude that inactivism is the polar opposite of fascism?

Yes! I think that the fundamentally unfascistic insight that conservatism and libertarianism share is the idea that their political philosophies are only partial philosophies of life…. That is the unfascistic thing, we see politics as only one small sphere of life.

You mentioned that writing *Liberal Fascism* has made you more libertarian. How did that come about?

One of the things I've really come to appreciate is the importance of dogma. There need to be some taboos, some fundamental dogmatic roadblocks. One of the things that writing this book has reinforced in me is that it is always safe to bet that government involvement is a bad idea.

You talk about the temptation of conservatives towards the end of the book. Is it imperial neoconservatism, heroic strong-government conservatism or compassionate conservatism that represents the greatest fascistic temptation to conservatives?

I would say that it is both heroic conservatism and compassionate conservatism, which are essentially the same thing. Heroic conservatism is compassionate conservatism 2.0. Or maybe heroic is 1.5, and Huckabee's conservatism is version 2.0.

Liberal word thieves

January 14, 2008

A LONG TIME AGO, a "liberal" was an individual who opposed powerful and intrusive government. This is why big government enthusiasts such as Marx and Mussolini ranted about "liberalism," since it was naturally opposed to their "progressive" ideologies. Over time, as people learned to despise "progressive" ideas and associate them with negative results, the progressives began to describe themselves as liberals. They gradually co-opted the term in an attempt to disguise their goals and market it under a brand more popular with the people.

This is why it is now necessary to distinguish between Classical Liberalism, which is dedicated to propositions such as human reason, human liberty, individual property rights, natural rights, limited government and free markets, and modern liberalism, which is opposed to all of the aforementioned despite occasionally granting lip service to reason, liberty and the perversion of natural rights that is usually described today as civil rights.

The process follows a recognizable pattern. The word thief describes himself as a "liberal," announces that of course he supports a liberal idea such as the right to free association, but then notes with some sadness that placing too much attachment to the idea is simply too extreme given the obvious suffering it causes a specific portion of the population, preferably children, but if children don't apply, then women or a racial, ethnic or behavioral minority will do. He declares that this reasonable modification of the liberal idea is, in fact, the true liberalism, and only an extremist idealogue would insist on clinging rigidly to what is, after all, only an idea.

This process is repeated, ad infinitum and usually with a fair amount of ad hominem, until the neo-liberal word thief can state, with a straight face and a clear conscience, that black is white, that red is blue and that any liberal who disagrees and insists on believing what he has believed all along is no true liberal. Thus, the liberal constitutional right to Free Association bows to the neo-liberal right to not be discriminated against, the liberal constitutional right to free speech is subsumed by the neo-liberal campaign finance reform and liberal property rights are supplanted by neo-liberal eminent domain.

The theft of liberalism took place long ago. But the word thief's problem is that the observable reality of pro-government policies cannot be easily disguised. As a certain group of people formerly known as people of color, formerly known as African-Americans, formerly known as Afro-Americans, formerly known as blacks, formerly known as negroes, formerly known as colored people, know better than anyone, changing the name does not change the substance.

Liberal began to become a term of ridicule and contempt during the 1980s. But as conservatives began their rise to power, climaxing with the theoretical capture of the White House, Senate, House and Supreme Court, the term conservative began to become attractive to the word thieves. And with the appearance of the neo-conservatives, who were not very conservative at all except in their opposition to the Soviet Union—an opposition that one must note was shared by a diverse group including German National Socialists, Italian Fascists, Chinese Communists and American conservatives—fans of powerful and intrusive government began to describe themselves as "conservative."

Now, it is true that some individuals are very liberal in their youth and become more conservative as they get older. But if one examines the "conservative" media, one notices a surprising number of individuals who were liberals and claim to be conservatives now, but still continue to advocate the same powerful and intrusive central government that they advocated in their liberal youth. And like young cuckoos and cowbirds, these parasites attempt to push the genuine intellectual heirs out of the nest, hence *National Review* founder William F. Buckley's attacks on Murray Rothbard and Joe Sobran, *FrontPage*'s Ben Johnson's call for "modern conservatives" to repudiate Paul Craig Roberts, *National Review*'s David Frum's call for "a conservatism of the future" to turn its back on Patrick Buchanan, Robert Novak, Llewellyn Rockwell, Samuel Francis, Thomas Fleming, Scott McConnell, Justin Raimondo, Joe Sobran, Charley Reese, Jude Wanniski, Eric Margolis and Taki Theodoracopulos.

And just last week, *National Review*'s Kathryn Lopez demanded "Ron Paul, Go Home" in bold-face type, which is a very strange thing for a supposed conservative to say about the man who is indisputably the only genuinely conservative Republican candidate for president.

This is not conservative behavior; it is the language and the controlling tactics of the left. These supposedly "conservative" individuals are not advocating anything that is even remotely recognizable as historical conservatism, but, nevertheless, claim that advocating big government policies, strong government actions, heroic government measures and imperialist government interventions are a new, shiny and better conservatism for the future. If this all sounds very familiar, it should, because it is nothing less than Clinton conservatism.

It is not the real conservatives, but the word thieves who need to go home; go home to the statist, authoritarian, big-government left where they rightly and truly belong. The English language has already lost the word "liberal." It now appears to be rapidly losing "conservative" as well. If future historians ever look back to learn how conservatives lost control of their movement and how the Republican Party declined into disarray and division, they need look no further than the faux conservative commentariat and the false conservatives they championed.

McCain in the membrane

January 21, 2008

OHN MCCAIN'S RUN for the Republican nomination was crazy enough in 2000. Hindsight being 20-20, it's hard to argue that he would have actually made a worse president than one of the most treasonous Americans since Benedict Arnold—George W. Bush. But since the media has the collective memory of a narcoleptic gnat, few recall that his previous run was uniformly considered to be the narcissistic performance of a Republican maverick; the Straight Talk Express had far more appeal to liberal reporters than conservative Republicans.

Of course, back then, George Bush was doing a manful impersonation of a conservative while being uniformly held up as the second coming of Ronald Reagan by the swooning conservative commentariat. Eight years later, neither the Thavior of New York Thity nor Captain Underoos have been able to manage more than perform embarrassing caricatures of the man who almost single-handedly brought Republicans back into power.

Naturally, the only candidate that actually stands for anything that Ronald Reagan did is loathed by the revived Rockefeller Republicans with all the fury of a cheap prostitute who finds herself compared to a nun without reproach. It's always easy to tell how Ron Paul does in a primary; you need merely count the number of finishers reported, then add one. If this means the media has to fail to report any of the finishers from second to sixth place, as was the case with the Nevada caucuses this weekend, well, that just leaves that much more space to anoint this week's "frontrunner."

I have written very little about John McCain during this primary season. I have thought so little about him that I'm afraid I don't even have a cruel and offensive nickname for him. I suppose one might rightly label him McCensorship, given his proclivity for defending the mainstream media's monopoly position with regards to political matters by restricting American free speech rights, but Mr. Campaign Finance Reform would probably regard that as a badge of honor. The reason I haven't thought about him at all is because Republicans would have to be downright certifiable to select John McCain as a November offering to Hillary Clinton.

Yes, Hillary Clinton. Team Clinton has successfully managed to frame the Democratic nomination as women versus blacks, and in case you haven't noticed, there are more female voters than black ones. Do the math. Not even the weight of Oprah on his side can save the Magic Negro now, for hell hath no fury like women feeling vicariously scorned.

The sad thing is that with the notable exception of Ron Paul, who is anathema to the oxymoronic collection of big government conservatives, strong government conservatives, heroic imperial conservatives, neoconservatives and social gospel conservatives that now make up a third of the Republican Party and 99 percent of its media and power players, the reliably unreliable McCain is arguably as conservative as anyone else once Fred Thompson drops out of the race. Sure, he'll destroy what's left of the American Republic by importing more Mexicans, destroy what's left of American credit by pursuing Osama bin Laden to the gates of hell, and destroy what's left of American sovereignty by signing up for monetary and political unions with any foreign organization looking to tell Americans how to live their lives, but then, it's not as if Mitt Romney, Mike Huckabee or Rudy Giuliani will do any differently.

However, I suspect that McCain's frontrunner status will be brief, as the longer the nomination lingers in play, the more likely it is that the party elders will be able to align the stars in Giuliani's favor. I don't see that it matters much, as any of these so-called Republicans will get absolutely slaughtered by Team Clinton in the fall, especially since they share Hillary's policy positions on immigration, Iraq and, to a lesser extent, abortion.

And if I'm wrong, and the Republican Party is McCain in the membrane and in the brain, well, so much the better. Watching John McCain trying to keep a lid on his reportedly volcanic temper would certainly be more entertaining than listening to Rudy lisp on and on about New York for another 10 months. If you're going to go down hard, hey, you may as well go down crazy too.

The math delusion

January 28, 2008

THE ANTHROPIC PRINCIPLE has been an embarrassing problem for secular scientists in recent decades due to the way in which the probability of the universe and Earth just happening to be perfectly suitable for human life is very, very low. The extreme unlikelihood of everything being not too hot, not too cold, not too big and not too small, to put it very crudely, has often been cited as evidence that the universe has been designed for us, presumably by God. Now, Richard Dawkins is arguably not an individual particularly well-suited to play around with probability. He may not be quite as mathematically handicapped as Sam Harris, but he is known to have some issues in this regard, being openly mocked for his "comic authority" and "fatal attraction" to mathematical concepts by the French mathematician Marcel-Paul Schützenberger.

Schützenberger's contempt for Dawkins's mathematical abilities is well-founded, as it's generally not considered to be a good idea to adopt a casual approach to mathematical probability, as Dawkins does with the "one-in-a-billion" chance of something like DNA spontaneously arising which he invents ex nihilo, before reaching the shocking statistical conclusion that if there are a billion billion planets and a one-in-a-billion chance of life spontaneously arising on a planet, then life must exist on a billion planets throughout the universe! Dawkins is genuinely surprised by his astonishing discovery of mathematical division, so much so that he repeats it twice.

Encouraged by this successful foray into the realm of higher mathematics, Dawkins is convinced that his response to the anthropic principle, somewhat confusingly named the Argument from Improbability for the nonexistence of God, is a serious, even "unrebuttable," refutation of the Argument from Improbability for the existence of God. Since he informs us that this is the central argument of his book, it behooves us to examine his summary of the argument in detail.

1. One of the greatest challenges to the human intellect, over the centuries, has been to explain how the complex, improbable appearance of design in the universe arises.

2. The natural temptation is to attribute the appearance of design to actual design itself.

3. The temptation is a false one, because the designer hypothesis immediately raises the larger problem of who designed the designer. The whole problem we started out with was the problem of explaining statistical improbability. It is obviously no solution to postulate something even more improbable. We need a "crane," not a "skyhook," for only a crane can do the business of working up gradually and plausibly from simplicity to otherwise improbable complexity.

It would be hard to take any serious issue with step one or two, but in step three, Dawkins's train of thought tumbles off the logic rails, not once, not twice, but thrice. His first mistake is the assumption that the designer is inherently more improbable than the design, based on the assumption that the designer of the universe must be more complex than the universe itself. But because Dawkins does not define complexity, he provides no means of calculating the statistical improbability of the designer, whereas the statistical improbabilities of the design are clearly defined in no little detail in the cosmological applications of the anthropic principle, as Dawkins concedes in his citation of the six fundamental constants examined by the physicist Martin Rees.

While Dawkins's complaint that the theistic answer to the design's improbability is unsatisfying because it leaves the existence of the designer unexplained is fair, his subsequent assertion that "A God capable of calculating the Goldilocks values for the six numbers would have to be at least as improbable as the finely tuned combination of numbers itself" is not. This is his second error, as the statement is certainly true of Rees, who is both capable of calculating the numbers and is a part of the design, but it cannot be true of the designer because the latter fact does not apply. Third, does Dawkins seriously wish to argue that Martin Rees is more complex than the universe? We know Rees calculated the Goldilocks values, so if he can do so despite being less complex than the sum of everyone and everything else in the universe, then God surely can, too.

His supposedly "unrebuttable argument" is already refuted at this point, but it's only fair to follow its last three steps.

1. The most ingenious and powerful crane so far discovered is Darwinian evolution by natural selection. Darwin and his successors have shown how living creatures, with their spectacular statistical improbability and appearance of design, have evolved by slow, gradual degrees from simple beginnings. We can now safely say that the illusion of design in living creatures is just that—an illusion.

2. We don't yet have an equivalent crane for physics. Some kind of multiverse theory could in principle do for physics the same explanatory work as Darwinism does for biology.

Dawkins visits the wreckage of his train of thought, pours lighter fluid over it and sets it on fire by bringing up the multiverse concept, an utterly non-scientific theory invented solely to get around the problem of the anthropic principle. Those indisposed to accept the anthropic principle attempt to get around the massive improbability problem it presents by imagining that there are billions and billions of universes, for all things are possible through the scientist who postulates very large numbers. Only by postulating a potentially infinite number of universes can our wildly improbable universe become mathematically probable. Of course, there are no signs of any of these other universes, nor did science ever take the idea of parallel universes seriously until the alternative was accepting the apparent evidence for a universal designer. But not only is multiverse theory every bit as unfalsifiable and untestable as the God Hypothesis, it is demonstrably more improbable. If we accept Dawkins's naked assertion that a universal designer is more complex than the one known universe, a designer is probably less complex than any two universes and infinitely less complex than an infinity of them.

6. We should not give up hope of a better crane arising in physics, something as powerful as Darwinism is for biology. But even in the absence of a strongly satisfying crane to match the biological one, the relatively weak

cranes we have at present are, when abetted by the anthropic principle, self-evidently better than the self-defeating skyhook hypothesis of an intelligent designer.

Dawkins's "unrebuttable argument" ends laughably with a desperate appeal to the reader not to give up the faith, even though evidence, logic and mathematics all refute this crown jewel of *The God Delusion*. Lacking any means of proving his conclusion, Dawkins simply throws up his hands and declares it to be self-evident! I ask you this, dear atheist reader, would you accept an argument this poorly constructed as conclusive and irrefutable evidence of the existence of God?

The Hitler question

February 4, 2008

I T WOULD BE IMPOSSIBLE to write a book of this sort without addressing the three subjects that inevitably come up when atheists are contend-
ing with Christians. Just as atheists anticipate the need to answer for
Stalin and Mao, Christians are expected to answer for the Inquisition and the
Crusades. And both sides recognize the need to deal with the Hitler question.
Like Einstein, the Führer made enough ambiguous statements to leave the
matter up for discussion; unlike Einstein, no one is eager to claim Hitler and
his National Socialists as members of their intellectual camp. The Unholy
Trinity have no choice but to concern themselves with the matter, of course,
and they do so largely in the manner that one has come to expect from them.
Harris wastes eight pages attempting to tar the Catholic church and Pope Pius
XII with guilt by insufficient opposition, then on the basis of no evidence
whatsoever, declares that Auschwitz was a logical and inevitable consequence
of the Christian faith. Hitchens also complains about the Catholic church
and relates a few irrelevant anecdotes about Italian Fascists and Irish Blue
Shirts, but then shows genuine insight when he notes that the Hitler regime
shows us "with terrible clarity what can happen when men usurp the role of
gods."

Dawkins, on the other hand, demonstrates that he is perfectly capable of
presenting a reasonable case when he chooses to do so and lays out some
reasonable evidence for the reader to reach his own conclusion on the matter.
He avoids making the common case for Hitler's religious faith on the basis of
his abused childhood, wisely, considering that one could apply precisely the
same argument to Christopher Hitchens and Dawkins himself. Instead, after
quoting Hitler's public statements that state outright that he is a Christian,
and a very devout one at that, Dawkins quotes private statements that reveal

a deep hatred for Christianity surpassing that possessed by even the most militant New Atheist.

> *It is possible that Hitler had by 1941 experienced some kind of de-conversion or disillusionment with Christianity. Or is the resolution of the contradictions simply that he was an opportunistic liar whose words cannot be trusted, in either direction?*

—Dawkins, *The God Delusion*, 276.

It is worth noting that most of the statements that indicate Hitler's Christian faith were made in public, prior to 1934, when he was still a politician running for elected office. Given his subsequent actions once he had secured political power, there is no reason to believe that Hitler meant them any more sincerely than George W. Bush intended to keep his promise to pursue a "more humble foreign policy" three years before he launched an invasion to bring democracy and freedom to the Middle East. But Hitler was no atheist, neither was he agnostic; the evidence tends to suggest that he was a pagan who was skeptical, but open to the possibility of acquiring temporal power through supernatural means.

The Thule Society, which founded the German Workers' Party that was the predecessor of the Nazi Party, was an esoteric society connected with the occultist Madame Blavatsky and the Theosophists. Hitler was the 55th member of the DAP, which was renamed the National Socialist German Workers' Party, or NASDAP, only four months after he joined on October 19, 1919. While the Nazis suppressed their early connection with the Thule Society and even arrested its founder, Rudolf von Sebottendorff, when he published a book about the relationship between Hitler and the society, the Nazi interest in esoteric matters, primarily on the part of Heinrich Himmler and the SS, is well-known and has played a role in everything from Charles Stross' excellent novel *The Atrocity Archives* to *Wolfenstein 3-D* and the *Indiana Jones* movies.

It is not known to what extent Hitler shared Himmler's enthusiasm for the supernatural, but it is reasonable to assume that if he was as skeptical about its existence as the New Atheists are today, he would not have allowed the Reichsf?hrer-SS and founder of the Studiengesellschaft für Geistesurgeschichte, Deutsches Ahnenerbe, an annual budget of the modern equivalent of $5.6 million to spend on occult research, medical experiments and expeditions to Sweden, Syria, Iraq, Finland and Tibet.

And yet, if Dawkins is not quite able to definitively conclude that Adolf Hitler was not a Christian, Robert Wistrich, the professor of modern Jewish history at Hebrew University, has no such qualms. In *Hitler and the Holocaust*, Wistrich writes:

> *Indeed, the leading Nazis ? Hitler, Himmler, Rosenberg, Goebbels and Bormann ? were all fanatically anti-Christian, though this was partly hidden from the German public. ? The conviction that Judaism, Christianity and Bolshevism represented one single pathological phenomenon of decadence became a veritable leitmotif for Hitler around the time that the "Final Solution" had been conceived of as an operational plan.*

> —Wistrich, *Hitler and the Holocaust*, 131–132.

But the most convincing proof that Hitler was neither an atheist nor a Christian can be seen in two documents that the various New Atheists and Wistrich were probably not aware of at the time they wrote their books. The first of these was prepared by the Office of Strategic Services in preparation for the Nuremburg trials in 1945. Released to the public in 2001, the report from the archives of Gen. William J. Donovan, special assistant to the U.S. chief of counsel at the Tribunal, is a fascinating description of the Third Reich's methodical plan to co-opt, pervert, and ultimately usurp the Catholic and Protestant churches of Germany. As an editor of the Nuremberg Project for the *Rutgers Journal of Law and Religion* described it: "They wanted to eliminate the Jews altogether, but they were also looking to eliminate Christianity."

The first installment, entitled "The Nazi Master Plan; The Persecution of Christian Churches," shows how the Nazis planned to supplant Christianity with a religion based on racial superiority. The report, prepared by the Office of Strategic Services, a forerunner of the CIA, says:

> *Important leaders of the National Socialist party would have liked ? complete extirpation of Christianity and the substitution of a purely racial religion.*

> —"Nazi Trial Documents Made Public." BBC News,
> January 11, 2002

The second document is equally significant. It is the 30-point plan for a National Reich church, drawn up by Alfred Rosenberg, the Nazi ideologist who was Reich Minister for the Occupied Eastern Territories and head of the Centre of National Socialist Ideological and Educational Research. Three of its more significant points are as follows:

One need not be a theologian to recognize that whatever religion happens to lurk behind a church that does not recognize the forgiveness of sins and is determined to suppress the Bible, it is not Christianity.

Atheists and inquisition

February 11, 2008

I**T IS A CURIOUS THING** considering how often it is brought up in conversation and Internet debate by lay atheists, but in *The God Delusion*, Richard Dawkins conspicuously neglects to detail what he describes as the "horrors" of the Spanish Inquisition. Christopher Hitchens and Daniel Dennett both avoid discussing it altogether. Only reason's clown, Sam Harris, is sufficiently foolish to swallow the old, black legend, hook, line and sinker, as he attempts to portray the collective inquisitions as one of the two "darkest episodes in the history of faith."

On June 9, 721 ad., Duke Odo of Aquitaine defeated Al-Samh ibn Malik al-Khawlani before the walls of the besieged city of Toulouse. This battle, followed by the victories of King Pelayo of Asturias and Charles Martel at the battles of Covadonga and Tours, brought to an end a century of remarkably successful Islamic expansion. Over the next 760 years, the Umayyads' conquests on the Spanish peninsula were gradually rolled back by a succession of Christian kings, a long process disturbed by the usual shifting of alliances as well as varying degrees of ambition and military competence on both sides of the religious divide. The "Reconquista" was completed with the fall of Muslim Granada in 1492 to the Castilian forces of King Ferdinand.

The Spanish Inquisition, which began in 1481, cannot be understood without recognizing the significance of this epic 771-year struggle between Christians and Muslims over the Spanish peninsula. What took the great Berber Gen. Tariq ibn Zayid only eight years to conquer on behalf of the Umayyad Caliphate required almost 100 times as long to regain, and neither King Ferdinand II of Aragon nor his wife, Queen Isabella of Castile, was inclined to risk any possibility of having to repeat the grand endeavor. Isabella, in particular, was concerned about reports of conversos, purported Christians who had pretended to convert from Judaism but were still practicing their former religion. This was troubling, as it was reasonable to assume that those who were lying about their religious conversion were also lying about their loyalty to the united crowns and it was widely feared that Jews were again encouraging Muslim leaders to attempt the recapture of al-Andalus, as they had its original capture eight centuries before. ("It remains a fact that the Jews, either directly or through their coreligionists in Africa, encouraged the Mohammedans to conquer Spain." *The Jewish Encyclopedia* (1906). Vol XI, 485.)

An investigation was commissioned, and the reports were verified, at which point the Spanish monarchs asked Pope Sixtus IV to create a branch of the Roman Inquisition that would report to the Spanish crown. The pope initially refused, but when Ferdinand threatened to leave Rome to its own devices should the Turks attack, he reluctantly acceded and issued "Exigit Sinceras Devotionis Affectus" on November 1, 1478, a papal bull establishing an inquisition in Isabella's Kingdom of Castile. One tends to get the impression that Ferdinand was less than deeply concerned about the potential converso threat and may have even been acting primarily to mollify his wife, as he promptly made use of this hard-won new authority to do absolutely nothing for the next two years. Then, on September 27, 1480, the first two inquisitors, Miguel de Morillo and Juan de San Martín, were named, the first tribunal was created, and by February 6, 1481, six false Christians had been accused, tried, convicted and burned in the Spanish Inquisition's first auto da fé.

What happened in between November 1478 and September 1480 to inspire this sudden burst of action? While historians such as Henry Kamen pronounce themselves baffled as to what could have provoked the Spanish crown, the most likely impetus was that on July 28, three months before Ferdinand's decision to appoint the two inquisitors, a Turkish fleet led by Gedik Ahmed Pasha attacked the Aragonese city of Otranto. Otranto fell on August 11, and more than half of the city's 20,000 people were slaughtered during the sack of the city. The archbishop was killed in the cathedral, and the garrison commander was killed by being sawed in half, alive, as was a bishop named Stephen Pendinelli. But the most infamous event was when the captured men of Otranto were given the choice to convert to Islam or die; 800 of them held to their Christian faith and were beheaded en masse at a place now known as the Hill of the Martyrs. The Turkish fleet then went on to attack the cities of Vieste, Lecce, Taranto and Brindisi and destroyed the great library at the Monastero di San Nicholas di Casole before returning to Ottoman territory in November.

It is one of the great ironies of history that three times more people died in the forgotten event that almost surely inspired the Spanish Inquisition than died in the famous flames of the inquisition itself. Despite its reputation as one of the most vicious and lethal institutions in human history, the Spanish Inquisition was one of the most humane and decent of its time, and one could even argue the most reasonable, considering the circumstances.

In light of its nightmarish reputation, it will surely surprise those who believe that millions of people died in the Spanish Inquisition to learn that throughout the 16th and 17th centuries, less than three people per year were sentenced to death by the Inquisition throughout the Spanish Empire, which ranged from Spain to Sicily and Peru. Secular historians given access to the Vatican's archives in 1998 discovered that of the 44,674 individuals tried between 1540 and 1700, only 804 were recorded as being relictus culiae saeculari. The 763-page report indicates that only 1 percent of the 125,000 trials recorded over the entire inquisition ultimately resulted in execution by the secular authority, which means that throughout its infamous 345-year history, the dread Spanish Inquisition was less than one-fourteenth as deadly on an annual basis as children's bicycles.

If the Spanish Inquisition was, as historian Henry Charles Lea once described it, theocratic absolutism at its worst, one can only conclude that this is an astonishingly positive testimony on behalf of theocratic absolutism. It is testimony to the strange vagaries of history that it should be the Spanish Inquisition that remains notorious today, even though the 6,832 members of the Catholic clergy murdered in the Spanish Republican Red Terror of 1936 is more than twice the number of the victims of 345 years of inquisition.

Lessons of the Crusades

February 18, 2008

W HEN GEORGE BUSH abandoned his promised "humble foreign policy" in favor of bringing truth, justice and the American
way to an ancient land that has been ruled by great conquerors
for more than 3,000 years, from Shalmaneser and Sargon II to Abu Ja'far
Abdallah ibn Muhammad al-Mansur and Hulagu Khan, the media was rife
with references to the Crusades of medieval fame. Unfortunately, five years
after the most recent fall of Baghdad, it is increasingly obvious that John
McCain's promise of 100 years of occupation notwithstanding, this American
Outremer is unlikely to last half as long as its nominal predecessor did.

Because the media is almost completely ignorant of military matters, it has
quite understandably escaped the greater part of the American public that the
short-term success of the minor reinforcing operation known dramatically
as "the surge" is almost completely irrelevant. Most news analyses are day
to day, and most opinion writers think only in terms of their next column,
so the chances of any media figure looking beyond the next election is an
exotic outlier approaching Black Swan probabilities. All the same, it's worth
noting that there are distinct lessons from a previous military occupation of
the Middle East that are still applicable some 1,000 years later.

1. Public appeal

The First Crusade's stated goal of reclaiming Jerusalem was enthusiastically
supported by Christendom's general public; a modern equivalent of the
People's Crusade would be 700,000 American civilians voluntarily arming
themselves with deer rifles and hopping aboard their jet skis and fishing boats
to travel across the ocean in order to attack Iraq. (As ludicrous as this sounds,
it would still probably turn out better than the historical People's Crusade
did.) As it stands, there are barely 700,000 Americans who even consider the
war to be the most important political issue of the day, it's amazing how pro-

war drama queens have been complaining for five years about how no one realizes "we are at war." After all this time and the electoral disemboweling of the Republican House and Senate, they should realize that for the vast majority of Americans, "we" most certainly are not at war. It's just President Bush and his neo-praetorian guard.

2. Reconquest is popular, conquest is not.

The First Crusade and the Reconquista were successful attempts to regain previously Christian land that had been lost to Islam. The Second Crusade, which was billed as the recapturing of lost Edessa but transformed into a failed attempt to conquer wealthy Muslim Damascus, required the religious salesmanship of Saint Bernard and his promise of absolution of sins to garner even a lesser level of enthusiasm. Attempts to sell the Iraqi war by comparing it with the World War II-era reconquest of Europe and the South Pacific have failed, because it's clearly a simple matter of conquest, the president's many mutating justifications notwithstanding.

3. Conquest without colonization is short-lived

Outremer could not survive because it did not generate its own military forces but was dependent upon the constant importation of knights and men-at-arms from far-off Christendom. Considering that Britain today sent its final reserve unit, the 1st Battalion Welsh Guards, to Kosovo, means that an already overstretched "Coalition of the Willing" is soon going to find out that it does not have the resources to meet the tactical obligations that will develop, let alone the more important strategic ones.

4. Action inspires reaction

The pre-Crusades Muslim Middle East was weak and politically divided. The external pressure unexpectedly put upon the Islamic world through the ambition of Zengi and his sons and the Christian treachery of the Second Crusade paved the way for the rise of Saladin. This is precisely why Osama bin Laden hoped to provoke a Western invasion of the Ummah; bin Laden has been dead for years, but his dream lives on and his strategy remains operative so long as the occupations of Iraq and Afghanistan remain ongoing.

5. Faith trumps greed

The Crusader kings of the Second and later Crusades found that the farther their objectives departed from those in line with a religious motivation, the less success they achieved despite having far greater resources at their disposal than the low-ranking nobles of the First Crusade. The occupations of Iraq and

Afghanistan rely on the notion that the appeal of secularism will outweigh the religious traditions of those lands; however, the explosion of Islam throughout secular post Christian Europe and the recent triumph of religious Islam over secular Islam in Turkey indicates that American military strategists are basing their plans on an empirically false foundation.

History suggests a rock-paper-scissors analogy may be helpful to understand the strategic situation, wherein secularism trumps Christianity, Islam and paganism trump secularism, and Christianity trumps Islam and paganism. Of these rival cultures, demographic trends clearly indicate that Western secularism is the weakest and most likely to be subsumed by the others. And if this analogy serves as an accurate model, then it should be obvious the only way to win the clash of civilizations in the long term will not be through a modern crusade to spread secular culture to the Levant, but rather a Christian reconquista of what was once Christendom.

The low down on Obama

February 25, 2007

T HE NEW YORK TIMES recently published a front-page story revealing the salacious news that John McCain was not having an affair with a blond lobbyist named Vicki Iseman. I look forward to reading future exposes reporting John McCain's similar failure to have affairs with blond columnist Ann Coulter, blond singer Deborah Harry and blond actress Goldi Hawn. Nor did the *New York Times* hesitate to engage in speculation about the sexual proclivities of Larry Craig, the infamous wide-stanced Republican senator.

Meanwhile, media silence continues about the specific charges that have been leveled against another senator, Barack Obama, by a Minnesota man who claims to have gotten to know the Democratic presidential candidate rather well indeed. (What is it with Minnesota and gay scandals, by the way?) On February 11, Larry Sinclair filed a lawsuit against Obama, claiming that he and Obama had used illegal drugs and engaged in homosexual activity together nine years ago, so this isn't a rumor; it's an easily verifiable matter of public record, complete with a YouTube video and United States District Court filing.

Needless to say, the same *New York Times* that devoted such attention to whispers about an apparently non-existent affair hasn't bothered to so much as mention the charge against Barack Obama. Now, I'm as dubious about the truth of this suspiciously untimely attack as the most mindless, fainting-prone member of the Magic Negro's cult, in fact, I strongly suspect it to be nothing more than the latest fire drill by Team Clinton practicing its usual politics of personal destruction. Given very similar past allegations made about the lizard queen's own peculiar habits by some very credible sources, the accusation strikes this disinterested, but amused observer as more projection than anything else.

But whether Obama is on the down low or the victim of a vicious and underhanded attack by Team Clinton, the Sinclair story is both legitimate and important. Naturally, the *New York Times* is doing its best to ignore it, just as it ignored those embarrassing reports of mass starvation in Josef Stalin's Soviet Union, because no matter what the truth of the affair turns out to be, it is likely to prove devastating to either Obama or Clinton. If Obama is truly a secret coke user on the down low, he is finished as both a presidential candidate and a senator. If, on the other hand, it's determined that a desperate Clinton has orchestrated false and seedy accusations, she'll probably maintain enough plausible deniability to preserve her Senate seat, but she'll be done for 2008 even if Obama is subsequently found dead in Fort Marcy Park.

This is certainly proving to be one of the more sordid campaigns in American political history, right up there with Grover Cleveland and the "Ma, Ma, where's my Pa?" scandal of 1884. But what can you expect, considering that the three choices currently being presented to the public by the media are a madman, a shallow African supremacist and a reptile? Unfortunately, George Bush's war on American liberties means that the next president will have torture-by-toca and techno-eavesdropping at her disposal without having to bother with warrants or that pesky habeas corpus. It is said that whom the gods would destroy they first make mad, and the madness season is truly upon us.

I find it difficult to care much about how the November election happens to proceed at this point, as it makes very little difference which of the three sociopaths on offer ultimately ascends the cherry-blossom throne. I continue to support the only candidate still officially in the race who isn't a psychosexual wreck and supports both the United States Constitution and American sovereignty, Ron Paul. The fact that he is the one candidate that the political mainstream of left and right see fit to label a "nut job" should suffice to testify to his sanity as well as to the fact that the American electorate will get the president they deserve.

Note to parents: Let schools burn

March 3, 2008

T HERE COMES A TIME when an institution has been so badly damaged that the best thing to do is to junk it and start over. The American schools have been in trouble for as long as I can remember. It's worth remembering that the nation has been at risk due to educational failures since 1983 saw the publication of "A Nation at Risk: The Imperative For Educational Reform." But despite repeated reforms, the public schools of America have continued to get worse by nearly every statistical measure.

And it's little wonder. Consider, for example, this recent communiqué from the College of Education at California State University, Sacramento.

> *There are four main goals that we have and will continue to focus on in the college, which are expressed in the acronym TEACH:*
>
> *T ransformative Leadership*
> *E quity and Social Justice*
> *A ction*
> *C ollaboration*
> *H uman Differences and Diversity*

Of course, they only teach education, not mathematics, so one shouldn't expect these professional educators to be able to count to five. Perhaps they expect that "one-two-three-many" should suffice for the intellectually lobotomized victims of their trained thought-executioners, after all, we're reliably informed that it's enough for rabbits. A keen observer might also note that nowhere in the concepts expressed by these fiver main goals is anything even remotely related to a traditional education as the average parent understands one to be.

This is particularly significant in light of an appeals court's decision to declare war on the homeschooling families of California. The school Nazis are not the least bit concerned with educating the children, but rather making sure that it is their values that are instilled into the state's children, not the parents', and so have transformed the public schools from purported centers for collective learning into avowed intellectual death camps.

There is no point in attempting to fix such a lethally poisoned institution. Let the male teachers withdraw en masse from the system; they are not wanted anyway. Let no child be left behind as the illiterate and innumerate graduate with their meaningless degrees. Let the universities continue to devolve into remedial reading programs for unmarried women. Embrace the failures of the system with enthusiasm, because the sooner complete control is turned over to the cave-dwelling control freaks who seek to run it, the sooner the schools will collapse in ruins. Knowledge will still be accessible to those who seek it.

One cannot fix what is not broken, and the schools are working as they are designed to work. This is not a battle that can be fought and won; it is not a battle that should be fought. Homeschooling is but a stop-gap; in the long term, it is technology that will put an end to the 100-year American experiment with Prussian pragmatism. But until that day, do whatever you must to extricate your children from the system, teach them well and watch with confidence in the future as the professional educators immolate themselves and their system in a self-administered act of faith.

The real assault on science

March 10, 2008

H AVING LITTLE TRUST in titles or Germans, the French began to construct a massive series of fortifications 12 years after the end of "the war to end all wars." The Maginot Line consisted of 142 forts plus another 352 armored gun emplacements connected by tunnels and railways that stretched the full 87 miles of the Franco-German border. It worked, in a manner of speaking, as the German attacks on it were easily withstood, but it now stands as one of history's most famous examples of futility as the German commander Heinz Guderian simply sent von Kleist's two Panzer Corps through the Ardennes and around the line in the classic example of blitzkrieg.

Over the last few decades, secular scientists have constructed a similar defensive line against religion. For a variety of spurious reasons, they have concocted a dramatic narrative that postulates themselves as a noble collective of Galileos in peril of persecution from the God-addled, anti-science religious masses. Meanwhile, back in the real world, the empirical data shows that the predominantly Christian United States produces more science per capita than any of the many more secular nations, and Western military leaders are forced to rattle their sabers to prevent the scientists of the Islamic Republic of Iran from developing the latest in nuclear weapons technology.

As I have demonstrated in *The Irrational Atheist*, religion is not a threat to any aspect of science: It does not threaten the knowledge base, it does not threaten the method and it does not threaten the profession. It never has.

But this is not to say there is not a genuine threat to all three aspects of science today. Unsurprisingly, it comes from the same force that is the primary threat to the survival of Western civilization: female equalitarianism. Flush with their success in decimating the collegiate sports programs of America, the equalitarians have now set their sights on applying the infamous Title

IX quotas to science education, despite the fact that women already earn 57 percent of bachelor's degrees, 59 percent of master's degrees and a majority of doctorates. If successful in this effort, and initial signs indicate that they probably will be, in 30 years, academic science in America will be no more intellectually respectable or relevant than womyn's studies are today.

The bizarre propositions of equalitarianism always sound harmless and amusing at first because they are so absurd. What the rational observer often fails to understand, however, is that these propositions don't sound the least bit absurd to the equalitarian proponent because the average equalitarian is fundamentally an intellectual cave-dweller with no more interest in reason or capacity for logical thought than a hungry kitten. The idea of biology classes being taught by lesbian professors who believe that heterosexual procreation is a myth or calculus courses being taught by women who can't do long division may sound impossible today, but tell that to any software developer, and he'll be able to provide you with plenty of current examples of computer science engineers, some with advanced CS degrees, who have no idea how to even begin writing a computer program.

Women love education; it's the actual application they don't particularly like. Whereas the first thought of a woman who enjoys the idea of painting is to take an art appreciation class, a similarly interested man is more likely to just pick up a paintbrush and paint something—usually a naked woman.

Between 1988 and 2004, Title IX caused the elimination of 239 NCAA Division One men's teams and the addition of 682 women's teams. Those 239 teams represented about 8.3 percent of the total, and the rate of elimination is increasing because, as the proportion of men attending universities continues to fall, more universities will fall afoul of the Title IX proportionality requirement and be forced to cut more men's teams to stay in compliance with the congressionally dictated ratio. Now, what realistically offers a greater threat to science: a lack of public funding for what has proven to be the red herring of embryonic stem-cell research, or a politically driven 10 percent reduction of the male scientific community in the next 15 years, along with the enforced employment of three times that many female "scientists"?

Of course, this will sound to equalitarians and their sympathizers like nothing more than male whining, but it's nothing of the sort. Because they are the intellectual driving force of humanity, men will be fine. They will simply continue to do what they have always done and pursue the same challenges they have always pursued, focused on the realities of success rather than its superficial attributes. It is the institutions they are exiting, voluntarily and involuntarily, that will be destroyed instead. It is written that "women ruin everything"; having destroyed the liberal arts, the classics and the pseudo-sciences, it is now abundantly clear that the more rigorous sciences are next on the equalitarians' destructive agenda. And so, in the not-too-distant future, two plus two will finally be determined to equal five if a women feels that it should, or at least it will as long as she happens to feel that way.

Economic winter is on its way

March 16, 2008

T HE INTERESTING THING about economics is that it is rather like the weather in some ways. It's easy to read the signs and know that autumn is on the way, but it's very hard to predict the precise date of the season's first snowfall. (In Minnesota, Jack Frost never waits for winter, but shows up on October 24, on average.) And the fact that you may be totally confident that it's going to snow this winter doesn't mean you know if it's going to be an 11-footer like 1995 to 1996 or a measly two-footer like 1958 to 1959.

Like the early leaves of autumn, the first financial institutions are beginning to fall. Globalization and financial innovation have not mitigated economic risk; they have merely allowed the wrinkled whores of Wall Street to conceal the extent of the crises and delay their inevitable day of reckoning. The idea that the various bank failures and last-ditch bailouts taking place everywhere from New York to London and Zurich are the result of unforeseen circumstances is as ludicrous as the idea of taking out an adjustable rate mortgage when mortgage rates are at historic lows. The irresponsible happy talk of the financial media notwithstanding—that are starting to get that same deer-in-the-headlights look they had back in late 2002—most economically astute individuals have long known that the Greenspan economic regime was not sustainable, despite the present Fed chairman's belief in the efficacy of magic helicopter money. Consider the prophetic statement by Robert Prechter from my 2004 interview with him:

While the plunging dollar and rising gas prices show that the predicted deflation hasn't kicked in yet, the Bear Stearns bailout, the decline in the number of mortgage applications and the increase in the TED Spread to levels that haven't been seen since 1987s Black Monday crash indicate that the contraction in the supply of dollar-denominated credit is already upon us.

Simply printing more money is not an option because a Federal Reserve Note is not, technically, a dollar in the sense that it was originally defined—a silver coin of the United States containing 371.25 grains of silver—but merely a promissory note from the Federal Reserve to the U.S. government. When debt is currency, a collapse in debt creation will tend to presage a collapse in currency.

It is, perhaps, worth noting that even if one ignores the collector's value, a single 19th century dollar is now worth $17.54. The idea that the Federal Reserve exists to fight inflation, preserve a strong currency and smooth out the business cycle has everything wildly backwards, as the only things that the Federal Reserve actually does is to create inflation, reduce the value of its own debt currency and exacerbate the business cycle in precisely the manner we are witnessing today.

Although the mainstream economists have finally begun to acknowledge that the U.S. economy is already in the recession that was long proclaimed to be unlikely, the problem is that there are more than a few signs that a true depression is in the works. Murray Rothbard's excellent 1963 book, "America's Great Depression," shows that in direct contrast to the official mythology, the Great Depression was caused by excessively lax monetary policies by the Fed, which responded to the crash in precisely the same manner that the Japanese central bank responded to the 1989 Nikkei crash and the way that the Fed has desperately been attempting to fend off the unavoidable since 1999. The Fed's decision to cut rates tomorrow—and don't be surprised if Bernanke elects to "shock" the markets with a full-point rate cut in excess of the 75 basis-point "surprise" cut everyone is expecting—is rather like giving a dying man a stiff snort of cocaine. It may have a positive effect on the markets for a week or two, but the feeling of invincibility will rapidly dissipate, and within two months we'll be right back where we were, albeit with a few less bullets in Bernanke's gun and less investor confidence than ever. The short-term high may be your last chance to exit on an up note for a while, though, so if you're still in stocks, this will probably be a good time to cut your losses.

All that two decades of frantic bailing out and bubble blowing has accomplished is to enrich a few fortunate investors and delay the inevitable while significantly jacking up the terrible price that Americans will ultimately pay. The business cycle can be influenced, but it cannot be eliminated. For every economic action, there will be an equal and opposite reaction, and since the financial house of cards has been built ever higher and ever more vulnerable during this decades-long period of delay, chances are very high that the collapse will be swifter and more brutal than even the economic pessimists can currently envision. This is far from a failure of the free markets; it is merely more evidence of the futility of central economic planning.

If we are fortunate, it is only a long and hard economic winter that is approaching. If we are unfortunate, it is the financial Fimbulwinter that will precede a political Ragnarok.

Teaching banks to fish

March 23, 2008

IT IS A COMMON ASSUMPTION among the Republican faithful to assume that Democratic criticism is universally disingenuous and unfair, on those rare circumstances that it is not entirely fact free. This opinion is not without a basis in fact, as one has only to read the editorial page of nearly any newspaper in America to discover a glaring example of Democratic dishonesty. The Democratic Party is, for the most part, the party of the evil and the party of the stupid; not for nothing is it primarily made up of an alliance of useless, overeducated academics with uneducated dimwits lacking either high school diplomas or productive employment, and all too often, both.

But the maleficence of one political party does not necessarily convey beneficence on the part of the other. And the fact that the greater part of the purpose behind the accusation of Republican support for corporate welfare is a defensive one meant to justify the Democratic support for individual welfare does not mean that the accusation is not an accurate and well-deserved one.

Republicans are against individual welfare because it cripples the very individual it is meant to help. They like to repeat the aphorism that it is better to teach a hungry man to fish than to give him a fish to eat, because once he knows how to fish then he can provide himself with a meal whenever he wants one. They also know that if the hungry man knows that he will be given a fish whenever he asks, he has no motivation to ever learn how to fish or spend any time fishing. They believe in allowing individuals to suffer the consequences of their own actions—and they are right to believe this.

It is very strange, then, that Republicans so readily reverse themselves when the matter concerns banks and money rather than men and fish. For corporate welfare cripples the very corporations it is meant to help. It is better to teach a profit-starved bank to earn profits rather than to fork over unearned revenue, because if a bank is capable of earning a profit, it can earn one in the future. If a profit-starved bank knows it will be provided cash whenever it looks like it is going to make a loss, it has no motivation to ever learn how to make a profit or spend any time modifying its structural flaws. When it comes to banks, Republicans believe in preventing them from suffering the consequences of their own actions.

One of the great financial fictions is that Wall Street is the center of global capitalism. This is a total misconception, as Wall Street is not, and has never been, a free market. There is literally nothing free about it. Now, it is even less free, even more centrally controlled, as the Fed's recent actions in putting federal finances on the hook for the Bear Stearns bailout has launched a discussion on the need to extend banking regulation to Wall Street institutions. The *New York Times* succinctly described the salient issue:

> *The Fed's involvement highlighted what many experts see as the growing disparity in regulation between Wall Street firms and commercial banks. Commercial banks submit to greater regulation, partly in exchange for the privilege of being able to borrow from the Fed's discount window. But starting last week, Wall Street firms were getting the same protection without subjecting themselves to additional scrutiny.*

—March 23, 2008, New York Times

It isn't right that Wall Street firms should get the same protection as commercial banks without submitting to the same banking regulations, of course, from a free-market perspective. It isn't right that any banks or Wall Street Firms should be receiving special protection against failure from either the Federal Reserve or the federal government. It should be obvious to even the most economically illiterate individual that this corporate welfare cannot be expected to turn out any better than individual welfare; moreover, it is far less justifiable by any rational metric. The sooner the inefficient banks fail, the sooner the financial system can stabilize. Propping up weak sisters like Bear Stearns and creating additional moral hazard is only going to increase the risk that the system will eventually suffer a catastrophic failure of a magnitude that it cannot survive.

The United States is fast approaching an interesting juncture in which the nation will be forced to choose between rebuilding its wealth with a functional free-market system or sinking under the weight of an increasingly dysfunctional, centralized economic system. For decades, the powers that be in Washington, D.C., and New York have favored the latter, which benefited them in the short term at the price of collective devastation in the long term. Unfortunately, the long term appears to be upon us at last. Therefore, it would behoove both Republicans and Democrats to learn from the mistakes of the other side and realize that government welfare of any kind is a fatal trap for both recipient and donor.

Let the woman win

March 31, 2008

IT MUST BE ADMITTED that I am an inveterate opponent of women's suffrage. I see absolutely nothing positive that has historically come of this democratic travesty in any country around the world, and much that is destructive. I marvel at those who genuinely believe that the expansion of a single privilege, rendered all but meaningless as a result of the expansion in the U.S., was worth the subsequent violation and sacrifice of the rights declared most fundamental by the nation's Founding Fathers.

Yet, in the course of human events, there are times when one must bow to the reality that human beings are, by and large, ignorant fools completely incapable of utilizing reason, applying the lessons of history or learning from the mistakes of others.

There are times when humanity must learn its lesson the hard way.

This year's presidential campaign has been more amusing than most. The Republican competition was primarily noteworthy for presenting an array of candidates whose positions are wildly unacceptable to the party's base, culminating in the apparent selection of a barely lucid wax figure chiefly known for his great personal opposition to the First and Second Amendments to the Constitution. The Democrats, on the other hand, find themselves caught up in a vicious internecine battle to determine which group is the most victimized ever: wealthy Harvard-educated black senators or wealthy Yale-educated female senators.

Since there is growing reason to believe that, despite his smoothly super-ficial oratory and magical negritude, Barack Obama is actually crazier than John McCain—it is not audacious, but insane, to hope that we are the change that we have been waiting for to heal godd–n America so we can finally be proud of it—I suggest that it would be wise to follow the immortal advice of the owner/operator of the Millennium Falcon and let the woman win.

Please understand that in offering this opinion, I am not suggesting that Hillary is liable to rip off Mr. Obama's arm and club him to death with it should he rob her, and every American woman, of the Democratic nomination for president that is their right by virtue of the undeniable fact that Ms. Rodham-Clinton is a woman. She would merely like to do so, and it is profoundly unfair of the theory of evolution by natural selection to have conspired over the millennia to deny her the physical strength required should such an act be merited, as it would most definitely be should she, and every American woman, be so violated by a male vote rapist.

As the *Wall Street Journal* recently suggested in an article entitled "At the Barricades In the Gender Wars," it is clear that a substantial portion of the female citizenry will interpret the denial of Ms. Rodham-Clinton's long awaited ascendancy to the Cherry Blossom Throne as a rejection of their own womanhood. The women of America's adherence to this national application of the profoundly stupid concept of the personal being political indicates that severe measures are required to illustrate their complete unfitness for participation in the governing process of any society which wishes to survive indefinitely.

And just as the best way to silence an annoying and incompetent backseat driver is to turn the wheel over to him, the optimal way to prove that women's suffrage is a disaster beyond any shadow of a doubt is to, metaphorically, let them drive. Let Hillary return to the White House in triumph, after all, it's not as if her two male opponents are any better. And give her a working female majority in the House, Senate and Supreme Court, too. Better yet, let every male senator, representative and Supreme Court justice resign in favor of a female replacement. Think of it as a four year male holiday filled with nothing but beer, video games and sports—1,461 days of an ongoing March Madness Thursday!

Although I suppose paradise couldn't possibly last that long. Given the bans on alcohol, cigarettes, guns and free speech that women have favored since the suffrage campaign began in the 19th century, I can't imagine it would take an all-female Congress long to ban the NFL, video games, cheerleaders, strippers, scales, the New Testament and Internet porn. The only two legal dress sizes would be "small" and "you look so skinny," and the only real question would be what would come first, a return to the grass huts of yore, conquest by an external patriarchy or revolution and the restoration of historical inequality.

But in the long term, what is there to lose? Either women are right, and they are at least as capable of governance as men, so the nation would greatly benefit from the actualization of their long-repressed capabilities, or they are wrong and we can go directly to the nadir for which we have long been heading anyway, end the equalitarian experiment and begin the long march back to the principles of unalienable human freedom, small government and democracy on a very short leash upon which the nation was originally founded.

Absolut Mexifornia

April 7, 2008

ACCORDING TO the increasingly useless Wikipedia, my May 2006 column opposing a border fence and pointing out the practical possibility of the mass deportation of illegal aliens is one of my most notable accomplishments to date. And despite the incompetence of the left-wing college girls who increasingly control the content of the online encyclopedia, the ongoing northern migration from Central and South America indicates that this judgment may not be entirely wrong.

Still, "Against a fence" was hardly "Rivers of blood," the prescient anti-immigration speech given by Enoch Powell in 1968. At the time, only 74 percent of Britain believed Powell was right. Now, one would be lucky to find seven Brits out of every 10 people that walk by in Londonistan. As one New York taxi driver welcomed Mark Steyn upon learning of his arrival from Heathrow: "Yeah? You Shiite or Sunni?"

The last 20 years have seen the explosion of the various multicultural myths. The proverbial melting pot demonstrably does not scale well. Immigrants are not a net positive for the service economy any more than offshoring is a net positive for the manufacturing economy. Indeed, hiring immigrant labor is simply the service equivalent of going offshore. Population diversity does not lead to positive societal effects. Instead, it reliably leads to a reduced sense of community, more crime, more poverty, more use of government services, more taxes and more government intervention. And most importantly, mass migrations do not serve to increase the American population, but rather, as Absolut Vodka's new Mexican ad demonstrates rather colorfully, spell the end of America in the territory successfully invaded and occupied by the migration.

There is nothing inherently wrong with immigration, which taken in small and reasonable doses tends to invigorate economies and societies alike. But migration and immigration are two very different things, as Umberto Eco spelled out in "Migrazioni," his 1990 essay on the subject. Historically, migrations have always significantly changed the host culture when they do not eliminate it entirely, and in light of this fact, it is worth contemplating precisely why the pro-migration American governing class is so staunchly supportive of what can only change or eliminate American society.

Now, there's nothing intrinsically wrong with Mexicans acting on their historical claim to the American Southwest. After all, if Americans can't be bothered to hold on to their territorial possessions, then they don't deserve to keep them. And to be honest, I don't think America would be worse off without Los Angeles, San Francisco or Hollywood. Indeed, if we could get Mexico to take New York City and Washington, D.C., off our hands too, I'd be out there marching and chanting "¡Sí, se puede!" as ardently as any member of La Raza... or at least making an enthusiastic solidarity run to the nearest Taco Bell. Sure, Mexifornia is unlikely to be very big on technological advancement, sexual equality or free speech, but no society that revolves around soccer, burritos, tequila and elitism is a bad one in my book. In fact, it's even arguable that the corrupt incompetence of Mexican governance is closer to the constitutional small-government ideal of the American Founding Fathers than the ever-expanding bureaucracy of the current federal government.

In any case, the beauty of the Absolut ad is the way in which it exposes the underlying truth that the diversity celebrants and multicultural maniacs have been attempting to sweep under a rainbow-colored rug, which is that all of the happy talk is nothing more than cover for realpolitik of the most ancient kind. It's an age-old trick. Multiculturalism is merely an updated form of Trojan Horse. And the fact that an invasion is peaceful does not make it any less invasive, for as the architects of the European Union have shown, a peaceful conquest is far more likely to avoid triggering a violent reaction than a martial one. Considering that their Spanish forebears were willing to spend 770 years reclaiming Spain from Moorish interlopers, the only real surprise about this second reconquista is that it is taking place over decades rather than centuries.

If history has taught us anything, it is that national borders are far from permanent. California has only been an American state for 158 years, and based on current trends, I would be very surprised if it was still an American state in another 58. That may be hard to believe, but it's the most logical conclusion of migration meeting self-determination.

The Israel that must defend itself

April 14, 2008

THE NEOCONSERVATIVE COMMENTATOR, Charles Krauthammer of the *Washington Post*, recently proposed what he described
as a "Holocaust Doctrine," in which an Iranian nuclear attack on
Israel would be regarded as an attack on the United States. This is a bizarre
and profoundly anti-conservative idea, as it should be readily apparent to
every American and Israeli alike that Israel is not the 51st state of the Union.
While it is to be regretted that anyone should wish to attack Israel, with
nuclear weapons or anything else, this doesn't change the fact that Israel is
not America and never will be.

The doctrine is also pure propaganda. What does a non-martial mass
murder by National Socialists have to do with a potential military attack
by Iran? Jews who revere the memory of their murdered ancestors should
be offended by Krauthammer's shameless attempt to make use of them this
way.

Krauthammer's proposal is a non-starter because Israel is not even a military ally of the United States. Unlike Slovakia, Estonia and Bulgaria, the
United States is under no obligation whatsoever to defend Israel from Iran
or anyone else. While this may be upsetting to certain *Washington Post*
columnists, it presumably doesn't bother the Israeli government at all, as they
have shown no signs of actively pursuing any such alliance with the United
States. And while it is presumably possible for NATO to extend an invitation
to Israel as an honorary European country, as UEFA has done, the fact that
Israel isn't on the short list of planned NATO expansion tends to indicate
that neither NATO nor Israel considers the issue to be a pressing one.

Delegating the defense of Israel to the United States, even in part, would
not only be antithetical to Israel's reason for existing in the first place, it would

be a strategic blunder of potentially critical proportions for four reasons. They are as follows:

1. Moral hazard. As the ongoing mortgage debacle demonstrates, the knowledge that someone else is responsible for one's behavior tends to tempt one into accepting risks that one would not otherwise accept. Thus, a U.S. guarantee might actually increase the risk of an Iranian strike against Israel.

2. The decline of shared values. As Mitchell G. Bard of the American-Israeli Cooperative Enterprise explains: "The Jewish State has emerged in less than half a century as an advanced nation with the characteristics of Western society. This is partially attributable to the fact that a high percentage of the population came from Europe or North America and brought with them Western political and cultural norms. It is also a function of the common Judeo-Christian heritage." These shared values are not held by the millions of members of the third world migration and are outright rejected by the growing secular irreligionist population.

3. The backfire principle. A few decades ago, Jewish Canadians lobbied the Canadian government for human rights restrictions on free speech. Those restrictions and the institutions they spawned are now being used as a weapon by Canadian Muslims against their critics. Given the current rate of Muslim immigration, encouraging America to intervene militarily in the Israeli-Arab conflict would set a very dangerous precedent that could lead to American military force being used against Israel.

4. The next administration. It is possible that if he is elected president, B. Hussein Obama will be inclined to continue the positive relations that Israel has enjoyed with previous presidents of both parties. But given his obvious ties to African supremacists and third-world recrimination ideology, to say nothing of outright anti-Jewish supporters such as the Rev. Eric Lee, this is far from given. His middle name is not "Sadat", after all.

Israel will do better to depend upon the fierce spirit of Zionist independence that characterized its early beginnings than upon the vagaries of a powerful but decadent ally of dubious loyalty. They would do even better to place their trust in the Lord God of Israel who chose a certain group of people to be His so many years ago. But to paraphrase the wise words of a Christian pastor: if someone's breaking into your house and you don't have enough faith to trust in God, then trust the baseball bat in your hand. Don't trust the police on the other end of the telephone line.

Kidnapped by government

April 21, 2008

G IVEN THAT Mormon readers will probably recall my past references to a former candidate for the White House as Captain
Underoos, it's not exactly a secret that I harbor little respect for
Joseph Smith's little cult. While all of the Latter Day Saints I've ever met
have been fine, upstanding individuals, I nevertheless tend to view *The Book
of Mormon* as being, for all intents and purposes, the literary and religious
equivalent of L. Ron Hubbard's *Battlefield Earth*.

But despite my admitted lack of sympathy for Mormonism, not since the
Waco massacre have I been so completely appalled by an American government action. The recent kidnapping of 416 children from their Fundamentalist LDS parents by Texas Child Protective Service agents is a unconscionable
abnegation of not only the United States and Texas constitutions, but a
rejection of the very meaning of what it is to be an American. For as P.J.
O'Rourke rightly declares: "There is only one basic human right, the right to
do as you damn well please."

Contrary to what a disturbing percentage of the voting population appears
to believe, "protecting the children" is not a legitimate function of government. The concept appears nowhere in any constitution, and the very idea
that the most lethal institution in human history, an institution that has
killed more children than any other, can even be used to protect children is
inherently oxymoronic. The state does not own the children whose families
happen to reside within its boundaries and it does not possess the right to
dictate what is and what is not a proper way for a family to raise its children.

Consider this absurd justification for the mass kidnappings offered by
Angie Voss, the CPS kidnapper in chief, offered as an explanation for the
mysterious preference of the abused women to remain with their supposed
abusers instead of availing themselves of government shelters: "This popu-

lation of women has a difficult time making decisions on their own." If a distaste for decision-making is legitimate grounds for removing children from their mothers, then there won't be a woman in America left with a child to call her own! For what man has not had a conversation that went like this:

"Where do you want to eat?"

"I don't care…. You decide."

"OK, let's go to that new Chinese place."

"No, I don't want Chinese!"

"Well, what do you want, then?"

"I don't know, whatever you want."

Sound the sirens, send in Ms. Voss and her Sturmtruppen, and seize those at-risk kids!

The disingenuous bigotry of CPS' action is perhaps best revealed by comparing the pregnancy rates of the supposedly abused teenage girls at the FLDS compound with the rest of the teenage Texan population. Voss stated that five of the 416 children were pregnant or had given birth; assuming that half of the 416 are female, that is a pregnancy rate of 24 per 1,000. The Texas pregnancy rate among women 15 to 19 is 101 per 1,000. It's also worth noting that the "numerous" pregnant 13-year-olds hypothesized by one government worker mysteriously transformed into five "under 18s" when Voss testified.

If the family lives of hundreds of American citizens living peacefully can be brutally invaded and destroyed on the basis of a single anonymous phone call that, as WND has reported, increasingly looks to have been a fraud, then every American family is at risk.

How you raise your children is between you and God alone. It is not a matter for the state or anyone else; it never has been. As this mass kidnapping of FLDS children and incredible violation of due process will almost surely demonstrate over time, government is a ruthless and power-maddened institution that is the very last one capable of serving the interests of the children. No conservative and no religious individual should support this outrageous action, even if adult members of the FLDS community are found to have violated Texas law as well as Texas social norms, because to accept this terrible precedent is to guarantee that future violations of family rights will be committed.

And as history has shown, the next time it may not be some weird and heretical Mormons in the government's gun sights, but Jews, homeschoolers or evangelical Christians.

Class-action child removal

April 28, 2008

I T IS NO SECRET that black children are born into familial situations that render them statistically far more likely to suffer crime, deprivation and sexual abuse than non-black children. Sixty-eight percent of black children are born illegitimate. Blacks are murdered 3.8 times more than their percentage of the American population would statistically indicate. According to the Bureau of Justice Statistics, an estimated 32 percent of male blacks will be imprisoned at some point in their lives. Black teens have a pregnancy rate of 134 per thousand. Given such a poisonous culture, how can the government authorities permit black parents to be allowed to raise black children?

To be born Jewish is to be born with a centuries-old target on one's chest and a life of toyless, joyless Christmases. Wouldn't it likewise be in the best interests of the Jewish child to be taken out of that dangerous, holiday-deprived culture and brought up to live safely as a non-Jew? And is not the Scandinavian-American child doomed to a lifetime of suffering through Sven and Ole jokes, eating ludefisk, and a Nordic inhibition against expressing his emotions? How could one possibly argue against the wisdom of removing a child from such a horrific fate?

The Texas kidnapping authorities are so poorly informed that they aren't even certain precisely how many children they stole from their parents. What they first reported as 416 children seized by the state rose to first to 437, and now to 462. So, while they can't even manage a simple head count, they nevertheless expect Americans to simply trust their assertion that every single parent of those 462 children constituted a "continuing and immediate danger to their safety" despite the fact that the children are far healthier than the norm, not a single parent has actually been arrested and charged with any form of child abuse and the CPS has publicly conceded that there is no evidence that any of the 130 or more children under five have been abused!

The state's incredible position appears to be precisely as one FLDS spokesman has described it: "If you're a member of this religious group, then you're not allowed to have children."

Almost as incredible is the way that an amazing number of so-called "conservatives"—no doubt the same sort of see-no-evil conservative Republicans who twice voted for the big-spending, government-expanding, sovereignty-selling George W. Bush—have expressed support for this massive violation of due process and the rule of law. Even though this action is a classic example of the "for the children" excuse that liberals have used to justify a thousand social evils, it is primarily conservatives who are to blame for the ruinous state of law that made this mass kidnapping possible.

Beginning with the ineffective and liberty-destroying Republican War on Drugs, the decades-old exclusionary rule has been continually weakened to the point that not even the apparent fact that the warrant for entering the Yearning For Zion property was based nothing more than a fraudulent phone call may be enough to halt the Texas agency's criminal actions. This weakening, combined with the increased latitude taken by quasi-judicial agencies that claim judicial powers without being restricted by the constitutional limitations binding judicial institutions, makes a complete mockery of both American liberties and the law. There is nothing conservative about giving government the power to destroy families on the basis of an anonymous false witness.

Fortunately, even the mainstream media is beginning to wake up about the pernicious nature of the Texas kidnappings. The influential Instapundit notes "this is looking more and more like a screw-up of the first order," while eminent legal blogger and UCLA law professor Eugene Volokh has stated that without an imminent risk of actual harm, the American legal system simply does not permit the Texas authorities to do what they have done. If a crime has been committed by one or more adults in the FLDS community, then they should be given a fair trial under due process of law and treated accordingly.

Americans should find the punishment of hundreds of children and adults on the mere suspicion that one man may have committed a crime to be utterly abhorrent, even if that crime was committed against a child. For if this "legal" principle used to justify destroying the FLDS families is permitted to stand, there will be nothing to prevent it from being used against any family in America.

In totally unrelated news, the readers of Vox Popoli and I are beginning a group study of Thucydides's *History of the Peloponnesian War* next week. If this happens to be of interest to you, download an e-text or pick up a copy of *The Landmark Thucydides* and join in the historicity.

The magic fades

May 5, 2008

A S LONG-TIME READERS KNOW, I have expected Hillary Clinton to succeed George W. Bush on the Cherry Blossom Throne since 2003. But while almost everything has gone precisely as my history-driven theory had it, from John Kerry's defeat in 2004 to the crash-and-burn of the "permanent majority party" idea that was so bandied about by Republican triumphalists during Bush 43's first term, there is a major obstacle that remains to her prophesied ascension.

No, it's not John McCain. While I was mistaken about the identity of the Republican sacrificial lamb, having wrongly concluded that it would either be George Pataki or Rudy Giuliani, there is literally no one who fit my prediction of "a hopeless candidate in the Dole mode" more accurately than John McCain. McCain, like Dole before him, is a senator and a veteran of foreign wars, wounded in the service of as well as a famous political moderate who is completely out of step with the conservative Republican base. In fact, it was McCain's unpopularity with Republicans that led me to discount him as a possible nominee, but then, I assumed that even if Republicans were inclined to take a November dive, they'd at least prefer to avoid a historic landslide of Reagan-Mondale proportions.

While it was always clear that John Edwards was not a serious candidate, I assumed from the beginning that Barack Obama was primarily in the race as a rabbit. A dull coronation process not only bores the media, but is profoundly un-Clintonian. The Clinton machine thrives on drama and conflict, indeed, it runs on drama and conflict, and both Bill and Hillary Clinton have long lived their lives lurching from one crisis to the next. They are like sharks that need to swim to stay alive. So, when the Magic Negro began winning over crowds of enthusiasts with his enchanting and nonsensical mantras, it was clear that he was primarily there to provide the necessary drama required for the Clintonian narrative to unfold.

I doubt very much if Hillary Clinton or anyone else expected the rabbit to begin running so wild. I rather doubt it seriously occurred to any member of Team Clinton that America might be ready to elect its first black president instead of its first woman president. Obama's unexpected rhetorical skills contrasted well with Hillary's flat and humorless presentation; the modern presidency is more about media presentation than resume, and there are few things more gruesome in high definition than a grim, 60-something feminist obsessed with power. And while most considered it a weakness, in this situation the Magic Negro's very inexperience has been of singular benefit since he has not had the time to amass an incriminating voting record or commit the secret sins of the average Washington politician that the Clinton machine normally expects to exploit to its advantage.

Thus, the machine was caught offguard in the early going, its standard-bearer was badly rocked, and both have only recently begun to return to form. It should be no surprise that this return to form coincides with stumble after stumble by the Obama campaign; the turn to Mrs. Obama in the hopes that she'll somehow bring around the milk-and-cookies crowd may well prove to be more disastrous than Obama's epic mishandling of the Rev. Jeremiah Wright.

While it's true that the delegate math looks all but insurmountable, this reasoning omits one important factor. Democrats are the epitome of inconsistency! The idea that Democrats are afraid to overturn the popular vote count due to the scars of the Bush-Gore Florida affair is absurd; anyone who has ever read a newspaper knows that American liberals have the memory of an amnesiac periodical cicada. Since the Magic Negro is rapidly approaching full meltdown mode, anything short of blowout wins in Indiana and North Carolina will cause superdelegate sentiment to shift rapidly toward Hillary Clinton in fear of the Democratic Party experiencing a third-straight unexpected loss when the electoral winds are at its back.

I could certainly be wrong. Most of the experienced political pundits have been counting out the Lizard Queen for months now. But as with any epic horror star, it's unwise to assume she's done. Those who fail to learn the lessons of *Halloween* and *Friday the 13th* may regret counting out the Lizard Queen too soon.

'Letter to a Christian Nation'

May 12, 2008

THOSE OF YOU who have read *The Irrational Atheist* might be surprised to learn that one of its primary targets, Sam Harris, would see fit to ask for my assistance with one of his scientific studies. And it may surprise those atheists who believe that I hate science even more to know that I was happy to help out with any scientific study, much less one that is designed to investigate the question of whether religious belief and ordinary belief are correlated with similar brain states.

Now, there is no question that I was extremely hard on Mr. Harris in my book. To be blunt, the careless and flawed cases he made against faith in general and Christianity in particular in *The End of Faith* and *Letter to a Christian Nation* all but begged for such savage treatment. But it was never anything personal, because intellectual discourse is a rough sport and the New Atheists made it abundantly clear that the rule of no respect was in effect from the start. Nevertheless, unlike Richard Dawkins, Harris merits a measure of respect for his ready willingness to engage in debate with the other side and answer the hard questions without evasion; for example, here are Sam's responses to seven questions I asked him two months ago.

Now, regarding what is intended to be a neurological experiment, as I mentioned in the chapter devoted to Daniel Dennett, no one who subscribes to a religion that upholds the principle that the truth shall set you free has anything to fear from the scientific method. From the Christian perspective, it is irrelevant what an individual's brain state happens to be, whether he is contemplating the salvation of his soul or a sale at the local supermarket. Science is neither pro-Christian nor anti-Christian, it is value neutral. While it can certainly be used for evil purposes, it does not behoove the Christian to fear the potential for its abuse, because as the Apostle Paul tells us, we are not given a spirit of fear.

I am more than a little skeptical that science can be an effective tool for investigating the supernatural. If there is a supernatural capable of being investigated through natural means, logic dictates that the success of such investigations entirely depends upon supernatural forces meekly submitting to being metaphorically poked and prodded without willfully interfering with the experiments. Therefore, any scientific investigation of immaterial must find a means of distinguishing between the complete absence of the super-natural and the interference of the supernatural providing a false negative; a logical necessity that never seems to come up when the question of science and the supernatural is raised by scientists.

Still, these caveats aside, I see no reason why Christians should not cheer-fully aid scientists in their quest to better understand God's creation, the material and immaterial aspects alike. As a part of his current experiment, Mr. Harris has prepared a large set of stimuli in the form of questions which are intended to inspire a belief response. He is in the process of refining those stimuli, and as an atheist whose perspective on Christianity cannot exactly be considered objective, he therefore requires assistance from Christians to ensure that the religious stimuli are valid from a Christian perspective. While he hasn't had any problem finding atheist volunteers, (more than 14,000 atheist surveys have been completed), it should come as no surprise that despite his famous letter to them, Sam isn't quite as dialed into the Christian nation.

So, in the interest of science, free inquiry and simple curiosity, I should like to encourage every Christian reading this column to take at least one of the four surveys located at Sam Harris's website. Some of the questions may strike you as obvious, others may strike you as stupid, and some even border on the insulting. But regardless of their perspicacity or relevance, I would appreciate it if you would help Mr. Harris by giving one or more of these very simple, multiple-choice surveys a shot and also pass word of it onto your Christian friends. There are few testimonies of belief more powerful than those of a faith that does not fear to be questioned any time, in any manner, by anyone.

Sam Harris may not be bleeding by the roadside, but I think it would still be an act of good Samaritanism to help him out. I hope you'll consider doing so.

Poison is no antidote

May 19, 2008

A S RECENTLY AS 2005, it was possible for the mainstream media and the conservative commentariat to talk seriously about a "permanent Republican majority." There were *Washington Post* articles with headlines like "Sowing the seeds of GOP domination," and PBS produced a televised special called "The Architect," which hailed the mastermind behind the eternal ruling-party concept, Karl Rove. Popular Republican blogs such as Powerline, and radio hosts such as Hugh Hewitt, hailed this new "American-style pragmatism" that had produced Republican political stars with crossover appeal to moderate Democrats such as George W. Bush and Arnold Schwarzenegger.

Within two years, the media narrative had changed dramatically. In 2007, the headlines in Washington now bore titles such as "Permanent Republican majority? Think again." and "The myth of the permanent majority." As usual, it was Internet observers who saw what was taking place long before the television and newspaper commentators noticed. Slate's Jacob Weisberg wrote a piece entitled "Karl Rove's dying dream: So much for the permanent Republican majority" in November 2005, while I wrote a 2004 piece entitled "George Delano Bush," noting the death of a Republican Party that had become "a soulless zombie of an institution."

But the probable results of this pragmatism were entirely predictable long before the negative results could be observed; I wrote the following back in 2003, in a WND article entitled "Satanic Schwarzeneggerians" which excoriated both the prospective governor as well as the Republican commentators who advocated the sacrifice of conservative principles in favor of political pragmatism.

Schwarzenegger, far from representing the salvation of California's Republican Party, stands for its complete immolation.... Pragmatism in politics is self-defeating in the long run. It is a euphemism for the slow sacrifice of one's principles.

The point of this column is not to say "I told you so." Unfortunately, no one keeps score in punditry. It is rather to point out that it is the absolute height of insanity to pay any attention, to lend any credence at all, to the advice of the very individuals who helped lead both the Republican Party and American conservatism into the epic electoral disaster they are facing this November. Arguments for voting the lesser evil and the spurious demonization of Democratic opponents are part of what created this debacle in the first place. The Supreme Court appointment argument that will be in favor of John McCain's presidential candidacy looks particularly ludicrous now that the Republican-dominated California Supreme Court has located a constitutional penumbra creating a hitherto non-existent "right to marry" in that state.

Voters are like women. They swoon for those who seduce them, they chase after those who don't need them, and they despise those who attempt to give them everything they want. This should come as no surprise, since the majority of American voters are women. True electoral appeal does not concern an ability to precisely match one's positions to the electorate's fickle policy preferences, since it changes on a regular basis, it is rather an ability to lead the electorate into a visceral acceptance of one's political vision. This is why pragmatism is doomed to failure, because the absence of principle means that the pragmatic politician can never lead, only follow. But, as the massive unpopularity of both Bush the Younger's wars and his presidency shows, the political vision must also be a coherent one; principle involves more than blindly ignoring the clear wishes of the American people.

Barack Obama's candidacy, like Bill Clinton's before him, demonstrates the power of political seduction. But this power is dependent upon illusion, and it dissipates as quickly as the smoke from a morning-after cigarette. So, while the Republican Party will suffer a horrific beating in November, a defeat it richly merits, it need not sentence itself to another 40 years in the political wilderness. It will do so, however, if those party leaders and opinion makers who originally provided the poison are allowed to supply the antidote.

If the Republican Party is not going to go the way of the Whig, it must reject the call to continue on its current path to becoming the nation's second socialist party and instead dedicate itself to becoming the party of individual liberty, small and limited constitutional government, sound money and peaceful national sovereignty that many once believed it to be.

A strong, independent woman

May 26, 2008

E VERYONE THINKS it's over for Hillary Clinton. The TV pundits are convinced that the Democratic nomination is essentially settled. Obama has been making gracious acceptance speeches for weeks now, but not even the very strong hints being dropped on a daily basis by superdelegates, media analysts and Democratic Party elders have yet managed to elicit the requisite concession speech.

But that's a speech that may never come. A recent national survey by Rasmussen showed that the percentage of Democrats who want Hillary to drop out of the race has actually declined to only 32 percent. More ominously for Obama, nearly as many Democrats—29 percent—want her to run for the White House as an Independent. Interestingly enough, this pro-Hillary faction isn't entirely limited to the blackskirt brigade of Clintonistas who want Obama to drop out of the race, an incredible 23 percent of the party that Rasmussen reports has remained "quite consistent through all surveys on the topic."

The problem faced by Obama is that he is not dealing with a male rival, with whom he can expect to exchange a handshake and a ritual exchange of mutually complimentary speeches honoring the hard-fought but fair competition. That is the way men play their games; the only reason that the media expects presidential candidates to comport themselves in this manner is because, hitherto, the presidential candidates have been men. Hillary, in case you have somehow failed to notice, is not a man, and therefore cannot be expected to compete like a man.

Nor does she think like one. As any man who has ever argued with a woman knows, women tend to be especially skilled at creating their own emotional realities. Any connection between objective reality and this emotional reality is largely incidental, and when the two come into conflict, the former is usually abandoned in favor of the latter. Both logic and uncomfortable facts are disdained in favor of a selection bias that only accepts those facts which support the emotional thesis in an irrational process of rationalization. That Hillary Clinton is given to such rationalizations is not really debatable; one need only consider her bizarre fabrication of Bosnian sniper fire to know that she is capable of believing whatever she wants to believe.

The rational perspective strongly supports the Obama hypothesis. He has won a majority of Democratic delegates, the superdelegate pledges are trending his way, he has won over the media and he has won the financial contributions game. Hillary has lost her air of inevitability, she doesn't have enough delegates to win, the media is against her and her campaign is broke. Running as an Independent makes no sense, because with such strong electoral winds at the Democratic Party's back, splitting the party between two strong Democratic candidates is about the only hope that Republicans have of seeing John McCain succeed George Bush '43. The logical thing, the practical thing, the sensible thing, is for Hillary to negotiate the best deal she can with Obama, accept her loss and return to the U.S. Senate.

It's a done deal, right? After all, the only thing that stands in the way is a woman choosing the sensible thing over what she desperately wants and resisting the urge to cut off her party's nose to spite its face.

One can't even truthfully say that a decision to stick it out and fight for the nomination on the floor of the convention would be devoid of sense, seeing how the recent surveys and Obama's inability to put Hillary away demonstrate his genuine weakness as a national candidate. Her campaign missteps, delusional historical sense and constant gaffes notwithstanding, Hillary is the stronger candidate in the general election. McCain may be nothing more than the expected sacrificial lamb, but he is a sacrificial lamb still capable of walking over a Hamas-endorsed Black Panther named Hussein.

Hillary simply doesn't need the hard-core Obama vote to win the presidency the way Obama needs hers. An Obama Democrat is never going to vote for John McCain, fully half of Hillary's Democrats would at least contemplate doing so. And yet, while she can sink Obama with an independent run, she pretty much ensures her own failure as well. So, an effective strategy for Hillary would be for her to threaten an independent run that would ensure Obama's ruin in November, then offer Obama the vice-presidency, a deal potentially sweetened by a secret one-term pledge and a number of cabinet choices. This gives everyone what they really want, as Obama gets to continue playing saint while significantly improving his chances of eventually winning the presidency in the general election, Hillary gets her historic win for women, and the Democrats wipe out McCain en route to an expected three terms in the White House.

Now, trusting Hillary to keep her word and make way in four years might seem insane, but then, with the woman already musing openly about assassinations, it's arguably the prudent route for Sen. Obama.

'Comeback: Conservatism That Can Win Again'

June 2, 2008

Libertarian Vox Day and former Bush administration speechwriter David Frum seldom see eye to eye on anything, from the Iraq war to the monetary policy. Nevertheless, last week the WND columnist spoke with the AEI fellow and National Review *contributing editor about his intriguing new book, entitled* Comeback: Conservatism That Can Win Again.

George W. Bush campaigned as a nominal conservative, but the manner in which he governed was obviously nonconservative, both home and abroad. How does the great public distaste for his administration somehow translate into a need to abandon the conservative principles that he never instituted?

There's a natural tendency among conservatives to believe that if you're in trouble it's because you weren't enough like you. Be more yourself, and people will like you better. I call this the English tourist approach to politics; if people don't understand you, just say the same thing over again louder and slower. The reason George Bush campaigned as he did, and the reason that he governed as he did, was because he correctly analyzed the politics of the late '90s. The conservative brand was already in trouble in the late 1990s. Let's remember that the parties of the left in 2000 drew more votes than the party of the right. You add together what Al Gore got with what Ralph Nader got, and they beat the Republicans by 3 percent of the popular vote. So, there was a problem. He set out to deal with that problem by holding onto the parts of the conservative message that were most popular while adding to it other things.

The problem that George Bush got into was not that he wasn't pure enough; the problem is that he had a correct diagnosis but he came up with a purely communications strategy for dealing with the problem. It wasn't a policy strategy. He didn't have policies that would make real improvements in people's lives, but he did have some messages that allowed him to evade and cope with the adverse political realities of the year 2000. The closer I look at this, and the more I think about it, the more convinced I am that if a more principled, more pure conservative had run in 2000, he would have lost very, very badly.

If we follow that logic, what would have been the results of a Bush government that had governed more conservatively, because it's hard to imagine that he would have become less popular than he is today?

What do we mean when we say "if he had governed more conservatively?"

I would say abandoning things like the prescription drug policy, abandoning things like the unpopular policy of open immigration, the judge nominations and other actions where he went directly against his Republican base.

Let's break those out. Had George Bush not promised a prescription drug benefit in his campaign—and I say this as someone who does not approve of the prescription drug benefit—I don't think George Bush could have won that election. It is a program that is supported by between 80 and 90 percent of the American people. And so had he not promised it, he would not have been elected. Having promised it, had he not delivered on what was probably the most popular of his domestic policy items, I think he would have had great political trouble in 2004. Now, open immigration or relatively open immigration, there I agree with you, and George Bush adopted a policy that was both bad policy and unpopular. That was, alas, an example of the president being truly principled. For him, this really is a principle. It's also an example of a political miscalculation. They got the country wrong. Where the country was, what the policy was, they made a whole series of mistakes about that. The lesson I draw from that is not that had you had a more principled and consistent conservative that it would be better. The conclusion I would draw from that is that you have to be a very careful student of where the public is, what's reasonable, what's doable and whether your principles actually work.

Is it correct to say that, in a broad sense, your advice in *Comeback* involves abandoning unpopular principles in favor of electoral strategies that are capable of winning?

When I think of politics, I distinguish between three things: principles, policies and narrative. A principle is a core ideological commitment like limited government. A principle is also fairly general. It doesn't always give you an immediate direction as to what you should do when you sit down at a desk and take over in government. Your principles yield policies. The policies have to be explained and defended with narratives that relate them to people's lives. My challenge to conservatism is less to change principles—I think we want to defend and protect principles—it's much more about the need to modernize policies. One of the really dangerous things that conservative tend to do is to fetishize policies. We turn policies into principles.

In light of this concept of not clinging to unpopular or outmoded policies that have become principles, how would you justify the continued Republican support for the unpopular War on Terror and the continued foreign military occupations?

I would say two things. One is that I note how the Iraq war is become much less unpopular, all the time, as the success of the recent tactics kick in. Before we started talking, I was just reading the latest Pew survey, released earlier in the spring, that shows a dramatic surge and change in American views of both what they think about the war and what they think the policy should be. We now have a statistical dead heat between those who want to keep troops in Iraq and bring troops home gradually. Only about 14 percent of the country supports the Obama policy of bringing the troops home immediately or very rapidly. So that's one thing. The second is that not losing wars is a core principle; it's one of my core principles. Whatever you think of the war, and I supported it from the start, but whether you supported it or not, the decision to lose it is a very different thing than the decision to start it.

Republican reconstruction

June 29, 2008

This column is the second part of Libertarian Vox Day's interview with former Bush administration speechwriter David Frum about his intriguing new book, entitled Comeback: Conservatism That Can Win Again.

Vox Day: I thought one of the more astute observations in "Comeback: Conservatism That Can Win Again" was that in a time when 50 percent of the American public doesn't pay income taxes, payroll taxes are a much more important factor from the political perspective.

Not as important a factor, by the way, as health care. If you look at the personal economy of people in the middle of the income distribution, for them, health care functions like a tax. It is the thing that is cutting into their income. They're getting the same benefit, or actually, it's deteriorating from their point of view even if it's more technologically sophisticated, but it costs more. Fewer things are covered, you have to pay higher co-pays, it's a degrading benefit, but you are paying a larger and larger slice of your claim on the American economy to buy it. I think that is a really important consideration, so if you believe in the principle of limited government, the idea that we're always going to approach limited government in exactly the same way that we did in 1977 is to have fossilized thinking....

I would say that when we say what will it mean in the 21st century to be a conservative, to be a member of the party of the center-right in any of the advanced industrial democracies, but especially the United States, it begins with the defense of the nation. Because one of the things I think I see in our politics is that left and right are much less divided by economics in these years than they were half a century ago. The differences are becoming ever more minute, ever more technical and ever more about means. On the social issues that have become so important to Republicans we can see also that the country is shifting in ways that are very different from the politics we've been used to in the past. But this divide about which party is the party of the nation, of national independence, of national self-defense, this remains as acute and as powerful as ever. If Republicans and conservatives lose their identity on that, I don't know what is left of them. There is an idea, and I suppose you may share it, that the party of the center right should be a party of consistent libertarianism. But that's just not where these societies are. I myself am not a libertarian.

I am a libertarian, and I agree with you. There's simply not enough people there.

There's 8 to 10 percent of the population there. Maybe.

That's generous.

That can't be the basis of your coalition. What is the basis of your center-right party is the constellation of ideas including national self-defense, winning wars and national identity, which involves the immigration issue and other such issues. Those are going to be the real battleground of politics, and you can't be pushed off that.

Looking at national identity as an important battleground of the future, aren't the Republicans largely on the wrong side of the national sovereignty issue—at least, the branch of the Republican Party that is enthusiastic about the Law of the Sea Treaty, NAFTA and these other supra-national organizations?

Here's where I distinguish between philosophy and policy: If my philosophy is that you want to advance the interest of the nation, to defend the right of the nation to make its own decisions, then you have to decide which of these global interests and these series of global partnerships do respect that national identity and national sovereignty and which of them are threatening to it. It then becomes a very empirical matter, which of these agreements are advantageous and which are disadvantageous. There, I think you can't be doctrinaire. You look at NAFTA. I was very strongly in favor of NAFTA, certainly the U.S.-Canada free trade agreement, NAFTA a little bit less, back in 1994. Looking back, I think NAFTA did much less good than I expected.

Much less good for the United States, much less good for Mexico and it's pretty much a wash for the Canadian point of view.

But haven't we learned anything from the transformation of the European Common Market into the governing European Union? Don't we need to pay attention to those possible threats to national sovereignty?

I don't think that's a good comparison. What was wrong with NAFTA is not that it was a threat to national sovereignty. NAFTA has no institutional guiding mechanisms. It has no political component. It is in no way comparable to the European Union. The problem with NAFTA ... had you asked me in the early '90s what I expected to happen, I would have said that I expected NAFTA to generate industrial employment in Mexico that would absorb the surplus of Mexican agricultural labor that was going to be displaced by the superior efficiency of American agriculture. What happened instead was American's agriculture proved so stunningly more efficient that it transformed the way agriculture was done in Mexico, and it shook a lot of agricultural laborers off the land. They lost their work. But, it did not generate nearly as much industrial employment in Mexico as I would have expected, largely because the advent of China onto the world scene, with the result that many of those displaced agricultural laborers ended up moving to the United States. So, whereas I thought in 1994 that NAFTA would be a means to curb migration and illegal migration from Mexico to the United States, in fact it ended up stimulating it. That's the diagnosis of NAFTA, but there is no NAFTA super-government. That problem isn't there.

One of the things I thought was tremendously insightful about *Comeback* was looking at prison reform as an aspect of a law-and-order policy.

As the crime problem abates, people forget how bad it used to be. If your prisons are inhumane and people forget why you ever sent people there, you'll then have a weakening of resolve for any effective crime policy. I think it has a big impact on the voting attitudes of black America, where it touches people. People have cousins, nephews and children there; I forget the exact number but there's a very high proportion of African-Americans who undergo this experience. If it seems brutal, if it seems that society has written these people off who go there, that is a message that has a very negative effect. If it's

Republicans and conservatives who seem the most enthusiastic or indifferent about what happens to the people who go there, it has a big impact on how we're perceived.

I thought one of the more unexpected concepts you produced was an alliance with India as a potential replacement for a demographically declining Europe. How do you see that fitting into the political nexus you've been contemplating in *Comeback*?

One of the bigger themes of *Comeback* is how the world around us changes faster than our minds are prepared to absorb. That's the big theme of this book, is that change is the great fact of human life. Since 2001, we have had this tremendous debate inside the United States. People have accused George Bush, the Republicans, the neoconservatives, Donald Rumsfeld and so forth, of not being sensitive enough to the concerns of our European allies and how the answer to problem after problem is to work more closely with our traditional European allies. Now, I'm a big believer in working with the traditional European allies when we can. But it is such a reactionary thought to say that and not to notice how the power of America's European allies is ebbing away.... They are going to be a declining force in international politics; they already are. Sometimes people say that with a certain sense of grim satisfaction; I say that with none. The United States is in danger of being left alone in a world that is increasingly uncongenial to the democratic idea. So, it's going to need to make new kinds of friends.

If you look around and say who is going to have the heft and the power, and who has enough democratic identity to play that role, India is the logical candidate. But it's going to be a very difficult relationship. Otto von Bismarck is supposed to have said that the most important fact of world politics in the 20th century was that Britain and the United States spoke the same language, well, the United States and the Indian elite speak the same language. But they have a very different history, so the relationship is going to be a lot more different to organize. There are historical grievances, resentments and the cultures are much farther apart than the United States and its traditional European allies were. That said, the two will need each other, and on the basis of that there may be an interest-based relationship that can be constructed.

Habeas is 9/10 of the law

June 16, 2008

I AM NO FAN of judicial activism. It indicates the complete breakdown of societal law and order, in that it entirely eliminates both the rule of law and even the pretense of democracy in favor of the same rule by decree that characterized ancient monarchies and empires. When the law as written is ignored in favor of whatever a judge, or very small group of judges, declares the law to be, one cannot pretend to be living in a country that is any more constitutional or genuinely democratic than Caesar's Rome or Mugabe's Zimbabwe.

That being said, it's important to keep in mind that political actions such as the Supreme Court's recent 5-4 decision that detainees accused of terrorism being held at Guantanamo Bay have a constitutional right to challenge their detention in civilian courts do not take place in a vacuum. While there is no question that this "constitutional right" is a newly manufactured one discovered in the same sort of fictional penumbra emanating from fevered judicial imaginations that hitherto produced the "right" to an abortion and the "right" for two men to marry, the decision is clearly a reaction to contrary fictions that have been produced over the last seven years by Congress and the Bush administration.

Since both the legislative and the executive branches of American government have repeatedly demonstrated that they have absolutely no regard for the U.S. Constitution and the strict limits it places on federal power, there is no reason to expect that the third branch of government will refrain from following their example. On November 13, 2001, George Bush issued a presidential military order giving his agents the power to arrest anyone suspected of a connection to terrorists or terrorism as an unlawful combatant and hold him indefinitely without being charged, without a court hearing and without a lawyer. Three months after this naked grab for arbitrary and dictatorial power was slapped down by the Supreme Court's 2006 decision in Hamdan vs. Rumsfeld, Bush conspired with the Congress to pass the Military Commissions Act, which essentially granted the executive branch the same power it had claimed before, although only over aliens, which presumably excludes U.S. citizens.

Of course, given the administration's demonstrated willingness to ignore the clear wording of the U.S. Constitution with regards to habeas corpus in the first place, it is the height of foolishness to assume that this president, or his successor, will be incapable of redefining the term "alien" to fit anyone they wish to arrest and hold without the benefit of a trial.

This is the recent history that is necessary in order to put the Supreme Court decision in its proper context. Given the proven willingness of the president, his administration and the Congress to ignore the Constitution, to redefine clearly understood terms and to offer up disingenuous rationales in defense of their actions, the Supreme Court has clearly decided to get in the mud with the other two branches and attempt to force an end to their seven-year campaign to be able to seize and hold anyone the executive branch wants for any reason its agents like for as long as they like, without any legal limits or external oversight.

Every American citizen should be pleased by this, since it was their constitutional right to habeas corpus that was the original target of the administration's attempted theft. It's much better to risk non-citizens receiving fair trials in a timely manner than risk American citizens being kidnapped from their homes and disappeared, as if the United States of America was a South American banana republic circa 1972. Indeed, the fact that John McCain recently described this decision as "one of the worst decisions in the history of this country" is reason enough for the most staunch Republican to seriously consider voting for the lightweight socialist mama's boy that is Barack Obama. The Magic Negro would make for a horrendously bad president, provide the U.S. economy with a lethal injection of counterproductive economic policies and get American forces disastrously involved in African tribal politics, but at least he has shown no signs of wishing to create an American Gestapo.

Don't get me wrong; for all that this practical decision by the Supreme Court is protective of American liberties, the quiet war between a judicially activist executive branch and a judicially activist judicial branch is strongly indicative of total disaster in the long term. It is a clear sign that the limiting force of the U.S. Constitution on the federal government has been shattered, that the political system is no longer even superficially democratic and that the idea of America as a unique nation dedicated to freedom and human liberty is no longer applicable to the current United States. But the death of the American dream should not be confused with the end of the world; after all, the vast majority of historical humanity lived without ever having had any voice in its own governance.

So, enjoy the tattered remnants of your historical freedoms while they last. And Republicans who despair as they consider their electoral options this fall should remember that they had the choice to nominate a man who pledged to work towards restoring those very freedoms, but they dismissed him as a lunatic and a naïve fool. From Cassandra to Jesus Christ, it is amazing how often the doomed choose to ignore those who warn them of their coming fate.

All quiet on the Middle Eastern front

June 22, 2008

T HE RELATIVE CALM in Iraq and other parts of the Middle East has caused a number of neoconservative commentators, most of whom were uncharacteristically quiet during the last 18 months, to again begin trumpeting the success of the Bush administration's military occupation of Iraq. Sen. McCain is being hailed as a military genius who wholeheartedly supported the reinforcing of the occupation, while Sen. Obama is being taunted for having been against "the surge" that they presume to have been the cause of this relative calm.

However, it's important to keep in mind that the vast majority of journalists and commentators on both sides of the political spectrum know very, very little about anything but the political horse races that they prefer to cover. Thus, the intrinsic absurdity of a tactical reinforcement making a major difference in a strategic campaign doesn't even begin to occur to them; the salient point is not whether "the surge" has been a success or a failure, but rather that it has always been entirely irrelevant to the ultimate fate of Iraq. The reinforcement was never anything but a political stop-gap, meant to buy the administration time to withstand the growing pressure to withdraw American troops in the hopes that the calm purchased by a negotiated cease fire would eventually relieve that pressure.

But in that political sense, "the surge" has apparently worked. However, according to the soldiers stationed in Iraq who email me from time to time, the recent decline in American casualties is more the result of negotiations combined with the various Iraqi forces biding their time and preparing for future conflict than from any combat successes derived from the presence of additional troops. With both the provincial Iraqi elections and the American national elections approaching, in October and November respectively, it seems quite probable that the cyclical level of violence will again begin to rise again over the summer. It will be interesting to see how those who declare that "the surge" has all but ended the war in Iraq will attempt to spin their previous claims of victory.

There can't be any doubt that they will admit to having been wrong, of course. One need only count how many times al-Qaida has been defeated in Iraq to understand that an American victory in Iraq is not only improbable, it is not even theoretically possible because no one, least of all the president and his advisers, have any idea what a victory in Iraq would consist of.

Despite the many brickbats of the media, al Qaeda has been defeated in Iraq, and is now retreating to lick its wounds where it can.

—Strategy Page, April 30, 2006

Al-Qaeda In Iraq Reported Crippled

—Washington Post, October 15, 2007

Military: "Surge" Has Defeated Al Qaeda In Iraq

—U.S. News, October 15, 2007

"Al Qaeda is on the verge of a strategic defeat in Iraq"

— Fox News, May 30, 2008

Like those video game reviewers who insist on describing RTS games like Warcraft and Command & Conquer as "strategy" games, the media consistently confuses tactics with strategy. The great challenge facing both President Bush and his successor is to define victory in Iraq; until this is successfully accomplished, it cannot be affected.

The problem is that most of the more probable results, such as an independent Kurdish state at war with Turkey in the North, a democratically elected Iraqi government allied with Iran against Israel, an unsettled state riven by civil war, are all rather difficult to portray as victory. When one considers that these issues don't even begin to take into account the complications presented by the incipient Saudi succession and the recently expressed aggression being directed at Israel by Iran and at Iran by Israel, "the surge" begins to look exactly like it is: an irrelevant and minor drop in a not very peaceful bucket.

Non-defeat is not victory

June 29, 2008

NOT SINCE the conservative commentariat bought into the notion of a permanent Republican majority have the professional analysts of the right been more off-base about a political event than they have in the post-mortem of the Supreme Court's recent ruling in the case of the Washington, D.C., gun ban. The court's acknowledgement of an individual right to gun ownership is being trumpeted as a major victory, and while it is certainly a good thing, the careful observer will note that seeds of strategic defeat have been sown even as the tactical victory is harvested.

It is true that Heller is not, in itself, a defeat for freedom-loving forces who do not wish to see law-abiding citizens forcibly disarmed by the state. Had the decision gone the other way—and it is deeply troubling that four justices saw fit to invent a fictitious collective rights interpretation—then Heller would have been a terrible defeat for those who still believe the U.S. Constitution is more than just another piece of paper. Upholding the D.C. gun ban would have been tantamount to a confession by the court that there is no written law anymore, that American law is nothing more than the dynamic product of fevered legal imaginations belonging to an unelected legal priesthood.

But it is important to distinguish between non-defeat and victory. Given that most conservatives and historically literate liberals understand that the Second Amendment was written to prevent the government from disarming the citizenry in an attempt to obtain a military advantage over them, a victory would have underlined this fact and called into constitutional disrepute the complex system of licenses, registrations and other obstacles that are intended to keep the American people less well-armed than their military. Since the scope of Heller did not encompass most of these issues, it's not surprising that it did not serve as a vehicle for the re-enshrinement of the Second Amendment as it was originally intended. Even so, certain aspects of Scalia's opinion are quite problematic when one considers them in light of the inevitable future interpretive wrangling:

It is obvious that the second sentence is historically absurd. As the etymology of the term indicates, a "militia" is a fundamentally military term, and as even a brief review of the facts will demonstrate, the weapons possessed by revolutionary militias were specifically designed for military use and were employed in a military capacity. While it is true that muskets had other, non-military uses in the late 18th century, it would be interesting to hear Justice Scalia attempt to explain just what the non-military purpose of the bayonets required of the New Jersey militia might have been.

Like many a Supreme Court justice before him, Scalia is playing word games, in this case with the word "specifically." He is most likely doing so to avoid the logical consequence of the most rational and historically accurate perspective on the amendment, which is that an American citizen has the same right to possess a fully automatic .50 caliber machine gun, an M1 Abrams tank or a nuclear-armed cruise missile that the U.S. military forces do. The 18th century in which the Constitution was written was a rare time of relative equality between the highest and the lowest; unfortunately, the technological curve presently finds us in a time where the expense of the most lethal weaponry is far beyond the reach of the average peasant.

It should come as no surprise that the king's courtiers wish to defend his privileges, ancient texts to the contrary be damned. While Heller is not the defeat of individual rights that it could have been, my concern is that it could prove to have lain the groundwork toward a legal path to effectively disarming the American public over time. The king has graciously allowed the peasants to retain their pitchforks; the question of whether their right to own a horse, a suit of armor and a steel-tipped lance still remains unanswered.

The secular way station

July 7, 2008

THERE ARE TWO rival points of view when it comes to human progress. The first is the pessimistic biblical one, which states that progress is impossible because there is nothing new under the sun. Empires rise and fall, but though names and superficial customs change, Man's nature and behavior remains essentially the same. The rival view, which could reasonably be styled the Enlightenment perspective, is that humanity progresses as its scientific knowledge base expands and the technology derived from that knowledge base is improved. Old and outdated modes of thought will be cast aside, and eventually humanity will arrive at... something.

Precisely what that something will be is never explained in any degree of detail, but we are given to understand that it will involve some level of societal secularism, sexual and racial equality, and as little physical labor as possible.

G. K. Chesterton was one of the foremost advocates of the biblical view, whereas the four-headed New Atheist hydra of Richard Dawkins, Christopher Hitchens, Sam Harris and Daniel Dennett are collectively the most outspoken proponents of the Enlightenment. Or rather, what is these days termed "Enlightenment 2.0," the first Enlightenment having rather notoriously failed to deliver any of the benefits once promised as progressive inevitabilities by the likes of Rousseau and Voltaire. As Daniel Dennett rather ruefully admitted in *Breaking the Spell*, even the most basic promise of the Enlightenment, the disappearance of religion from the world scene, actually looks less likely now than it did 200 years ago.

Since the beginning of the 20th century, Enlightenment progressives have celebrated every incipient sign of Christian decline, due to their view of Christianity as the great obstacle to worldwide Enlightenment. And they were right to see it that way, for no religion in history has ever demonstrated such a unique combination of convincing moral suasion with popular appeal;

any religion that historians have credited with toppling an empire and ending the ancient institution of slavery should not be counted lightly. They were not right, however, to assume that the secular values and society of the Enlightenment were capable of filling the void that the decline of Christianity in Western Europe, and, to a lesser extent, the United States, would bring.

Chesterton famously wrote: "When people stop believing in God, they don't believe in nothing—they believe in anything." While there are a statistically insignificant percentage of people who insist they do believe in nothing—although according to the recent Pew Survey, 33 percent of the atheists surveyed believe in either God or an impersonal force—the empirical evidence strongly suggests that Chesterton was correct and the godless who faithfully believe in the inevitability of a shiny, sexy, secular science fiction society are incorrect.

The most recent European outrages seen in the media are just the beginning. Whether it is British schoolchildren being forced to pray to Allah by their teacher, government judges declaring the valid jurisdiction of Talmudic and Shariah law, or the simple breakdown of peaceful, rational society, it is clear that post-Christian society is far more likely to resemble pagan pre-Christian society than it is to develop into the godless vision of an equalitarian, sexually androgynous workers' paradise so often sold to the masses by secular prophets of one form or another.

It is deeply ironic that those who subscribe most strongly to the ideas of the superiority of scientific evidence and rational materialism should reject both when it comes to examining the available evidence and hoping for the realization of abstract notions that have no basis in the material world. Those who have rejected Christianity and the cultural tradition of the West in favor of secular cultural relativism would do well to bear in mind that the benefits of Western society are not a given and that secular society is not a destination, but merely a way station on the route back to the pagan barbarism of the past.

The fowl atheist

July 13, 2008

O VER THE PAST FEW YEARS, I have had the occasional run-in with a biology professor who teaches at one of the University of Minnesota's outstate campuses. This professor, one Paul Zachary Myers, happens to be an outspoken atheist as well as a vehement proselytizer of St. Darwin of the Galapagos. His apparent ambition is to follow Richard Dawkins's spiritual evolution from science professor to professional propagandist of the one true unfaith. Unlike Dawkins, however, Myers's ability to construct a rational and coherent case is not merely limited; it is virtually nonexistent. When criticizing, he is seldom able to present anything more sophisticated than the standard ad hominem attack.

Thus, it came as no surprise to those familiar with his "science" blog, Pharyngula, that PZ—as he is commonly known—should take the opportunity to insert himself into a minor controversy in Florida over the "kidnapping" of the Eucharist by encouraging his readers to steal a consecrated host from a Roman Catholic Church so that he might film himself desecrating it. Apparently, the professor felt this threatened act of public sacrilege is necessary to convince everyone of his dedication to rational materialism; after all, what better way to demonstrate that a yarmulke is nothing more than a hat than by stealing one from a Jew and filming the burning of it? If nothing else, what passes for atheist logic is always entertaining.

The associate professor at the University of Minnesota, Morris wrote:

> *Myers is too socially autistic to understand that it is not his opinion about crackers that is the issue, but rather, his total lack of respect for others. He has apparently taken the New Atheist mantra of showing no respect to religion or to religious individuals to an extreme that not even Richard Dawkins*

or Christopher Hitchens have approached, for as he later declared in his own defense: "I must commit sacrilege, since I oppose the whole nonsensical notion of a "profoundly held religious belief.""

He must? The emphasis, I note, was his own.

This illogical imperative clearly demonstrates the deep and fundamental irrationality of atheism that I highlighted in my book, *The Irrational Atheist*. No rational man's actions are dictated by the beliefs held by others, however absurd those beliefs might be. It is not the Hindu belief in the sacredness of cows that forces me to eat beef. And clearly, the whole nonsensical notion of Federal Reserve being given control over the money supply to fight inflation has not forced anyone to buy gold or avoid the equity markets, even if they would have been wise to have done so.

Quite a few religious individuals have suggested that PZ is a coward because he is only willing to publicly desecrate a Catholic symbol; while he did once muse about desecrating the Koran, he only suggested the possibility of doing so in the privacy of his own home, well away from any cameras that might expose his actions to Islamic jihadists inclined to take vigorous offense to them. But the ecumenicality of Myers's willingness to commit sacrilege entirely beside the point, as what actually demonstrates the cowardly nature of this self-aggrandizing atheist is the fact that there is no chance that he will follow through on his anti-cracker threats now that it is clear there may be material consequences, however minor, to his actions.

The saltines are safe, for just as there are no atheists in foxholes, there is no vow that the militant atheist will not violate if he perceives any risk to his material well-being. Barely a month ago, Professor Myers was braying that he had never found any intelligent arguments for gods and only addressed the weak ones because he was unaware of the strong ones. Upon reading this assertion, I sent him an invitation to engage in a debate about the existence of gods on the Northern Alliance Radio Show, which is broadcast from Myers's home state of Minnesota. Fearless infidel that he is, Myers bravely ran away, saying that he was afraid to appear on a conservative show while ironically labeling me "a pathetic little twerp with delusions of grandeur."

That invitation is still open, by the way. If Myers fears appearing on a conservative radio show, well, I'm certainly not afraid to debate him about the importance of crackers and the existence of gods on Minnesota Atheists

Talk radio. If it turns out that the University of Minnesota has the same reluctance to employ anti-papists that it has for racists and anti-Semites, I imagine it won't be difficult for him to find the time for it.

The coming chaos

July 20, 2008

A FEW WEEKS AGO, a friend of mine who is a player in the global financial markets returned from London. By his own admission, he's been a great beneficiary of the unprecedented economic expansion that has proceeded almost uninterrupted since the end of the 1990–1991 recession. (The three quarters of economic contraction in 2001 barely qualify as a recession.) Given his four homes on three continents, he has an unusually global perspective on things.

He's also of a generally optimistic temperament, so it was with some surprise that I heard his pronouncement that "America is [verb indicating violent intercourse, past tense]!" I have, of course, been of that opinion for quite some time, as long-time readers know, but it was nevertheless alarming to hear confirmation from a party that had been hitherto staunchly contrarian. The fall of Bear Stearns and IndyMac, the recent declines in the equity markets and the ongoing collapse of Fannie Mae and Freddie Mac not only come as no surprise, they were entirely predictable warning signs of the recession that is already well under way. Ominously, the same sort of thing is happening in other countries, especially Britain, where similar bank failures have been grabbing the headlines.

It's important to understand that expecting the financial news to accurately relay economic information, particularly negative information, is irrational for three reasons. First, the economic data that is presented is a snapshot of the past, usually at least three months in the past. Second, much of that data is fraudulent; for example, the reported inflation rate is so massively twisted and contorted that it may underestimate actual inflation of the money supply by as much as 300 percent. If the Consumer Price Index was still being calculated today as it was in 1980, inflation would have averaged around 8 percent per year since 1990, four times more than the officially reported 2 percent.

Third, remember that the financial media has a direct interest in economic good news. During times of expansion, everyone gets excited about investing and pays a great deal of attention to buying and selling stocks, houses or whatever the commodity of the moment happens to be. For example, the reason there are far more real estate shows on television in place of the financial shows that launched entire networks is that the real estate bubble popped a few years later than the equity bubble. As housing prices continue to fall, housing inventories grow and more mortgage banks go bankrupt, those television shows will go off the air.

So, if the economic news is much worse than is commonly reported or understood, what can you do to prepare yourself for the negative climate? Unfortunately, it's difficult to give precise recommendations at the moment, mostly because the primary question of hyperinflation or deflation remains unsettled. The Federal Reserve's natural tendency is to pursue inflation, and certainly Bernanke's refusal to follow Paul Volcker's lead and aggressively raise interest rates tends to indicate higher inflation is in order. However, inflation rates have been very high for more than a decade and have only made matters worse, and there is also a school of thought which insists that deflation is inevitable even if the Fed unleashes the full power of the printing press and sends out the hyperinflating helicopters.

It's worth noting, however, that the existing credit crunch was predicted by the deflationists, not the hyperinflationists, even though the sky high prices of oil, gold and other commodities tends to support the latter. But regardless of which way things play out, there are a few basic principles that almost anyone, regardless of their financial situation, can apply to their lives now.

1. Cut your costs. Don't waste money buying things you don't need. Spend your dollars on things that are reusable rather than one-shot deals, such as video games rather than movies, a nice flatscreen rather than game tickets and cookware rather than restaurants.

2. Diversify your income. Take a second job, preferably in a field unrelated to your main occupation. This has the benefit of both increasing your income and reducing the financial blow should you find yourself laid off.

3. Be proactive. You should know if your employer is in good shape or not. If they're not, it's time to start looking elsewhere.

4. Start a garden. As food prices continue to get higher, why not raise a bit of your own?

5. Exit equities. Big daily rallies are signs of a bear market, not a bull. Use those big 400-point up days to exit your positions; that's what the big boys are doing.

6. Buy a rifle for each adult in the household. They tend to be surprisingly good investments, and the worse things get, the more potentially useful they are. It's your constitutional right, so don't hesitate to use it.

Above all, learn to watch the signs and read between the lines. Neither John McCain nor Barack Obama can hold back the contraction any more than King Canute could hold back the waves, so put not your trust in politicians.

Ich bin ein Betrug

July 27, 2008

I T IS ALWAYS AMUSING for me to read American columnists pontificating about Europe and Europeans. These would-be sophisticates demonstrably know next to nothing about European political realities. Their romantic views of Europe are formed by week-long visits to tourist havens such as Paris, London, Rome and Venice, and they don't speak any continental languages. Thus, their impressions tend to be influenced by their very brief contacts with the English-speaking European elite, who possess views almost completely at odds with those of the great mass of common Europeans.

I say this with some degree of certainty, since unlike most editorialists, I have actually lived in Europe and also speak Italian and German. While the "citizen of the world" and "Parliament of Man" concepts held great appeal for many Europeans in the post-World War II period, the luster has been dimmed by real, ideal-shattering experience of the United Nations and the European Union. Unlike Americans, Europeans have been directly affected by the complete failure of the United Nations to operate as advertised, while the sordid, anti-democratic reality of the E.U. has demonstrated the corrupt supra-national organization to be far less a solution to national problems than the cause of a whole host of continent-wide ones.

The average Italian would much rather be ruled by the thieves they know in Rome—literal thieves (24 members of the national parliament have been convicted of criminal activity)—than the Eurofascists they don't in Brussels. Despite the billions in pacification money funneled to Italy by Romano Prodi, the former president of the European Commission and two-time Italian prime minister, Italians still would still choose the lira over the euro if given the choice, since the euro has turned Italy from an inexpensive tourist destination into an expensive one and made what was once a reasonably competitive manufacturing location into completely noncompetitive one. Don't be surprised when what have been mere grumbles grow into a serious anti-euro campaign that sweeps the country within the next decade.

Although my example is Italian, one could just as easily find a broad swath of similar sentiments being expressed in Britain, Holland, Ireland, Germany and even in France. I chose Italy, however, because it is the source of the image that competed last week with the stage-managed portrait of the Obamessiah appearing before the supposedly adoring European masses.

But the truth is that the crowds that came to see Obama were not adoring in the least; they were merely spectacle-seekers curious about the latest American political oddity. Not even the European press saw fit to fawn over the senator, as David Aaronovitch of the *Times* concluded that "eventually, we will all hate Obama too," while Gerard Baker shamed an entire nation of hapless comedians with his scathingly brutal demolition of Obama's European tour titled "He ventured forth to bring light to the world".

In the great Battles of Caucus and Primary, he smote the conniving Hillary, wife of the deposed King Bill the Priapic and their barbarian hordes of working-class whites. And so it was, in the fullness of time, before the harvest month of the appointed year, the child ventured forth—for the first time—to bring the light unto all the world.

What is the connection between Italian indifference to dead Roma girls and European indifference to the nebulous HopeChange pushed by Barack Obama? It is that Europeans previously bought this same pig in a poke. The fluffy promises of progress, change and unity Obama makes are all too similar to those made by a previous generation of European politicians, promises that have resulted in the importation of a foreign criminal class, fewer jobs, fewer families, a vastly increased cost of living, limited economic prospects for the future and the loss of democratic rule. Europeans have recognized Obama for a fraud even without being privy to his frequent misstatements of fact; the magical negritude that has so dazzled the superficial American press no longer disguises the fact that Sen. "57 States" is little more than an empty-headed newscaster with a nice voice who is skilled at reading the teleprompter. No wonder the American media likes him—he could easily have been one of them.

Of course, a failed world tour doesn't mean a failed presidential campaign. It is worth noting, however, that if Obama's fraudulence extends to his birth certificate, all of the HopeChange will go for naught. Hope may be audacious, but then, so are conmen.

How America's empire will fall

August 3, 2008

I N THE YEAR 432 B.C., Athenian statesman Pericles advised his fellow Athenians to pursue a course of war with Sparta and the Peloponnesian League. War was inevitable, he assured them. Furthermore, their enemies did not have the capacity to seriously threaten them; such were the material advantages of Athens. Only 17 years later, with matters still remaining unsettled in the Peloponnesus, the Athenians confidently voted to launch a massive invasion of Sicily despite the fact that the general given command of the invasion had argued passionately against the wisdom of such an act.

In 411 B.C., Athenian democracy collapsed into the authoritarian rule of the oligarchic regime known to history as the Four Hundred. Athens had been impoverished by 20 years of martial expenses, isolated by acts of murderous violence that repelled its allies and weakened by the dreadful failure of the Sicilian Expedition, which had failed to secure the grain and other resources she had thought to gain by conquest. In 404, Athens surrendered to Sparta, her walls were torn down, her military power was broken and her imperial possessions were seized.

During the last three months, about 30 amateur armchair historians and I have been methodically working our way together through the eight books of *The Landmark Thucydides*, a beautiful edition that quite credibly bills itself as the comprehensive guide to *The History of the Peloponnesian War* recounted by Thucydides. (If you're interested in testing your knowledge of the classic conflict, you can do so here.) Throughout the course of the study, two things became apparent:

The Athenians considered themselves more than equal to the numerous Peloponnesians because their allies in the Delian League were "contributing" 600 silver talents a year to Athens, which by today's prices was equal to around

$9.2 million. This funded a 250-ship fleet which no other Greek city could think to match. The United States presently enjoys a similarly powerful military based on air and sea supremacy that is funded by a public debt of $9.6 trillion, a significant percentage of which is owed to China, Russia and unnamed "oil exporters." Given that it was financial dependence upon unreliable allies that proved to be the Athenian empire's greatest strategic weakness, it should come as no surprise if that eventually proved to be the case with the American empire as well.

Of course, all of the ominous parallels between latter-day Athens and America notwithstanding, it must be admitted that history seldom repeats itself with any great degree of precision. It is said to rhyme, however, and there can be no doubt that while America attempts to sponsor democracy in the autocratic Middle East, America's European allies are moving away from democracy and toward oligarchy in much the same way that formerly democratic Athenian allies in Samos, Mytilene, Corcyra and Chios did. As America attempt to forcibly install democracy in Afghanistan, Iraq and Palestine, it has all but vanished in Great Britain, France, Germany, Italy, the Netherlands and 21 other member states of the European Union, in which only the citizens of Ireland are permitted a voice in their own governance.

Most Americans would probably find the idea of a non-democratic America ruled by an unelected oligarchy to be unthinkable, but then, the disappearance of democracy was considered unthinkable by most Athenians a scant 21 years before it actually vanished.

The lessons of history suggest that America's ongoing Arabian Expedition will not only have the effect of degrading the American military, harming the U.S. economy and increasing fuel prices, but it could very well wind up causing significant changes in the system of American government. Of course, it's worth noting one major difference between the two invasions: Unlike the Athenians, Americans never voted to wage this war.

Nota bene: Maralyn Lois Polak recently announced the end of her long and successful run as a columnist at *WorldNetDaily*. Her iconoclastic views expressed in *Left-Handed* brought real breadth to the political spectrum of the WND commentary page, and I should like to take this opportunity to express my appreciation for her contributions in that regard.

Georgia and the democracy debacle

August 10, 2008

I T'S EMINENTLY CLEAR to everyone paying even the slightest bit of attention that the recent battle in South Ossetia between Georgia and the South Ossetians, quickly followed by even larger scale battles between Georgia and the Russians, has far more to do with oil pipelines and grand strategic concerns than democracy and self-governance. Indeed, the irony of the United States and NATO attempting to support Georgia doing exactly what they bombed Serbia for doing—attempting to regain control over historical territory into which a neighboring ethnic group had migrated en masse—is deep enough to be farcical.

Tangential note: One wonders how long will it be before the USA feels a similar need to invade the separatist region of Aztlán, formerly known as Arizona, California, and New Mexico? Big business always slavers after cheap labor, but immigration hath its consequences.

In his *WorldNetDaily* column last week, Pat Buchanan adroitly noted that contrary to the romantic vision put forth by neocon world democratic revolutionists, democracy doesn't necessarily compete very well with autocracy when autocracy is willing to accept the loss of economic control that comes with capitalism. What is seen today as the great triumph of democracy over autocracy in the 20th century most likely had less to do with democracy than it did with the fact that whereas the democracies were decentralized and somewhat open to capitalism, the particular forms that 20th century autocracy took—communism, national socialism and fascism—were left-wing statist ideologies deeply hostile to the free market.

In other words, democracy was not central to the victory of the Western allies. It was largely incidental to what was primarily a victory of capitalism, which triumphed despite the handicap of FDR's attempt to sabotage the American free markets through his quasi-fascist New Deal. Buchanan suggests that the autocratic capitalism of Russia, and to a lesser extent, China, may well prove to be a much more effective competitor to democratic capitalism than did the autocratic socialisms of the previous century. The fact that the Western democracies have gradually moved away from capitalism in favor of state-controlled equalitarianism only tilts the field further in favor of the autocracies.

There is another, older historical precedent for the competition between democracy and autocracy, one that dates back nearly 2,500 years. In *A War Like No Other*, historian Victor Davis Hanson writes of the struggle between the democrats of the Athenian-led Delian League and the autocrats of the Spartan-led Peloponnesian League:

> *Despite the lack of any clear strategic results from fomenting revolution in the first decade of the war, both the Spartans and the Athenians still realized that at very little cost to themselves they could instigate civil unrest that in theory could win over an entire state to their side. ... Still, not a single important ally of Sparta – Megara, Corinth, Thebes – was permanently taken over by democratic insurrectionists. In contrast, given the nature of the far-flung Athenian empire, Athens would lose, at least for a time, a few of its strongest allies and subjects – Argos, Messana, Chios and Mantinea – which either became mired in civil strife or had their governments turned over to oligarchs eager to join the state to the anti-Athenian cause. More importantly, when one examines even the fragmentary figures of the dead provided by Thucydides from these dirty wars, the number of killed quickly reaches the many thousands.*

The war in Georgia did not occur by happenstance; it is a direct result of the American-sponsored Rose Revolution that brought Mikheil Saakashvili to power. Like the Orange Revolution in Ukraine, the Tulip Revolution in Kyrgyzstan and the installation of pseudo-democratic regimes in Afghanistan, Iraq and possibly Palestine, the Rose Revolution was a tactical attack in an ongoing grand strategic struggle that has continued despite the end of the Cold War.

What the National Endowment for Democracy fellows, the American Enterprise Institute neocons and the conservative columnists waxing teary-eyed over purple-fingered illiterates fail to realize is that in contrast to Fukuyama's famous essay, history is not on democracy's side. Indeed, as both Athens and Great Britain have demonstrated, an aggressively expansionist democracy is much more likely to abandon its own democratic system of government than it is to successfully export that system to other states. From a historical perspective, these attempts to violently seed democracy around the world as a weapon in an ideological war tend to suggest that it is American-style democracy, not autocracy, that is approaching its end.

Geopolitical sematary

August 17, 2008

I T IS SAID that every organization which outlives its purpose seeks to preserve itself by finding a new mission. This is indubitably true of the North Atlantic Treaty Organization, as even its moniker betrays how far beyond its initial purpose are its current actions and deliberations. Once a defensive treaty between the U.S. and Western European countries to defend those nations from an aggressive and expansive Soviet Union that had rolled over Eastern Europe and was actively threatening West Germany, NATO has become an aggressive, expansive entity in its own right.

In the Stephen King book *Pet Sematary*, creatures who were given a form of life beyond their natural lives looked superficially the same, but behaved in a grotesquely different manner than before. The bombing of Serbia marked this transition for NATO, as the organization manifestly had no business in the countries of the former Yugoslavia. Not only was NATO not defending any of the treaty-bound nations, but it engaged in offensive action against a sovereign nation in much the same way that some Western leaders have complained Russia is doing now.

Russia, however, is a sovereign great power behaving the way the way sovereign great powers have always done. NATO is neither sovereign nor a great power. It's not exactly clear precisely what NATO is anymore, but it is very clear that it is no longer a defensive alliance of countries bordering the North Atlantic.

It is also clear that NATO has become the preferred vessel for the expansionism into Eastern Europe that has been pushed by the globalist democratic revolutionaries known as neocons. The use of NATO forces in Afghanistan to support the military occupation there was the first step, while the Orange, Rose and Tulip Revolutions were the second one. The expansion of NATO to include Estonia, Latvia, Lithuania, Slovenia, Slovakia, Bulgaria and Romania was the third; the addition of Ukraine and Georgia was expected to be the fourth.

However, a resurgent Russia was never going to accept its slow encirclement any more passively than the U.S. was inclined to accept Soviet client states in Central America, and the recent fireworks in Georgia over South Ossetia represent the first strike back against this revenant neocon NATO. The timing was ideal because if Ukraine and Georgia had joined NATO at the same time as the other new members, the world would be facing the prospects of another great European war due solely to a petty separatist struggle of no more global significance than the troubles in Northern Ireland.

The problem with security treaties like NATO is that they tend to accomplish the reverse of what they are theoretically designed to do. Instead of deterring the big dog against whose potential aggression the treaty has been signed, they create an incentive for the little ankle-biters to act in a much more aggressive manner than they would otherwise dream of acting. No longer feeling the need to cower before the might of the big dog next door, they bark with all the cocky assurance of one who has an even bigger dog standing behind him.

Until, of course, the big dog bites. Has any international figure ever been unmasked so thoroughly as Georgian President Mikheil Saakashvili? Between his lip-trembling press conferences and the photos of him cowering behind his bodyguards, he resembled nothing so much as a frightened little dog piddling itself in fear over the unexpected consequences of its posturing. It is practically redundant for Russia to demand his resignation in acknowledgment of his responsibility in attacking the South Ossetians, what Georgian in his right mind could ever vote again for such a contemptible "leader"?

The danger of NATO is that the United States is putting not only the fate of its armed forces and its economy in the hands of petty politicians from petty nations, but it is also outsourcing its geopolitical strategy to those same individuals. It's not a question of whether foreign leaders are small-minded or great-hearted, because not even the wisest and most insightful foreign leader can possibly share the national interests of Americans living on the other side of the world.

Georgia is a warning to Americans of a real danger posed to them—not by Russia, but rather, by the member-states of NATO. It may well be in America's interest to defend Poland or Ukraine from Russian attack, or to prevent Helvetic hordes from rampaging across the Rhône-Alpes to pillage Lyon, but it may just as well not be and, in any case, will depend upon the geopolitical situation at the moment. NATO has admirably served its purpose. Now it should be disbanded and sent the way of the Delian League, the Catholic League and the League of Cambrai before it causes America to enter yet another war against its national interests.

Throwdown in Denver

August 24, 2008

EVEN IF WE CAN'T BE SURE that the Obama campaign is sinking, there is little question that it is listing badly. The European tour turned out to be a minor debacle for the senator instead of the definitive coronation as a global leader of great significance it was supposed to be, while the untimely fireworks in Georgia have served to remind even the most starry-eyed political romantic that no amount of rhetorical HopeChange is likely to impress the coldly calculating geopolitical strategists in Moscow, Beijing and Brussels.

Above all, Obama himself has proved to be possessed of a weak and unlikable public persona. His cool is the stylized cool of the poser; it is the diffident posturing that impresses teenage girls, journalists and no one else. He has a skin problem that does not lie in its color, but rather in its lack of thickness; not since Bob Dole has there been a candidate who has been more sensitive or more inclined to view legitimate and substantive criticism as unfair personal attacks. And the Saddleback forum unmasked him as a superficial thinker who tends to be caught up in the trivialities.

While the selection of Sen. Joe Biden as the Democratic vice-presidential candidate is far from the worst choice Obama could have possibly made—that would have been Detroit mayor Kwame Kilpatrick—both the selection of Biden and the way in which it was announced demonstrate the increasingly inept strategic management of the Obama campaign. The middle-of-the-night text message was risible enough, even more so is the idea that Sen. Biden's big and undisciplined mouth is somehow going to improve the public's view of a candidate already given to hot air, factual errors and ludicrous exaggerations.

Barack has chosen Sen. Joe Biden to be our VP nominee. Watch the first Obama-Biden rally live at 3 p.m. EST on www.BarackObama.com. Spread the word! August 23, 3:29 a.m.

One can't blame Hillary Clinton for being tempted to derail the Democratic convention this week. It has to be difficult for her to watch Obama's ongoing implosion, knowing that it was only her own campaign's stunning incompetence and failure to understand the way in which the primary votes were being counted that cost her what was supposed to be an inevitable nomination. And it seems the groundwork for an insurrection has been laid, with Clinton's name being placed in nomination, the arrangement for a role call of the state delegations, her scheduled speech on the 88th anniversary of the passage of the 19th Amendment, and a lawsuit filed in the U.S. District Court for the Eastern District of Pennsylvania calling into question Sen. Obama's constitutional right to run for and hold the office of president.

However, it must be remembered that direct confrontation is not the preferred tactic of Team Clinton. Its successes have mostly come through playing off the weaknesses of others, utilizing an approach of divide-and-conquer, and positioning itself in such a way as to realize maximum benefit from its rivals' mistakes. Therefore, the steps that Hillary has taken are probably not intended to launch a direct challenge to Obama, but rather to position herself as the obvious and only possible replacement for Obama when his campaign collapses or when he is defeated by John McCain in November.

As John Edwards has demonstrated, national politicians are so narcissistic that it is not at all unthinkable that one would pursue the presidency despite possessing a secret that would immediately torpedo his campaign should it come out prior to the election. But if it turns out that the rumors are correct and that Obama is not eligible for the presidency due to his having been born in Kenya or a territorial Hawaii, it would not serve Hillary's interest to be the one held responsible for blowing Obama out of the water. And the Republican Party's unexpected decision to nominate an elderly John McCain makes 2012 look like a much more reasonable option for the Lizard Queen, for if the political winds are blowing strongly in the Democrats favor now, they will be approaching hurricane force after four years of a maverick McCain administration and all the chaos that would entail.

While my political crystal ball has proven to be somewhat problematic, I still think that Hillary Clinton is more likely to be sworn in as president than Barack Obama, whether that swearing-in takes place in 2009 or 2013. But given the factors that have recently entered into the equation, I see no pressing need for Hillary and her legion of blackskirts to rise in open revolt tomorrow night. The Lizard Queen will likely continue to lurk in the shadows, waiting for an easier opportunity to present itself.

Still 'None of the Above'

August 31, 2008

THE REPUBLICAN BASE has clearly been energized by John Mc-Cain's selection of Alaska Gov. Sarah Palin to be his running mate. There's no reason why it shouldn't be. It was not only a brilliant selection, but one that has a very reasonable chance of clinching an improbable electoral win for the Republican Party. It was also a fairly obvious choice once Obama picked Joe Biden, which is why I said McCain would choose Palin when asked for my opinion on the matter by Right Wing News last week.

The choice of Palin for vice president has apparently caused many Republicans to change their minds about supporting John McCain for president, as formerly disgruntled conservatives are suddenly rushing to donate money to the old maverick and declaring a new found willingness to vote for him. This enthusiasm is understandable, if more than a little disturbing, as it bears more than a small resemblance to an abused wife who embraces her erstwhile tormentor and declares all is forgiven simply because he bought her flowers for once.

Sarah Palin merits conservative enthusiasm in her own right; she may—I stress "may"—one day become a legitimate conservative standard bearer in the Thatcherite tradition, and her selection as vice-presidential candidate is a big step towards her eventually reaching such status. Pro-life and anti-corruption, she is certainly a huge improvement over the nonconservatives, fake conservatives and strong-government conservatives who have dominated the Republican Party since the failure of the 1994 Republican House.

She is a huge improvement, one notes, over Republican politicians such as John McCain—who, I hasten to point out, is still at the top of the presidential ticket.

While McCain-Palin is a much more effective electoral pairing than McCain-Romney or McCain-Lieberman would have been, it must also be acknowledged that a McCain-Palin administration will not be substantively different than a McCain-Romney or a McCain-Lieberman one. While Sarah Palin will indubitably look better at state funerals than the older male alternatives, it's impossible to argue that John McCain will be any less likely to invade sovereign nations, increase government spending or grant immigration amnesties to invaders from the Third World due to her holding down the vice presidency.

It's true that Obama would make for a disastrous president if he somehow managed to stop his ludicrous campaign of self-parody in time to turn things around, take advantage of the pro-Democratic electoral wins and win in November. In fact, I suspect that an Obama presidency would serve up interesting times in epic proportions, a national experiment in black Democratic rule that would follow the success of similar experiments in Detroit, Atlanta, New Orleans, Washington, D.C., and South Africa. He is clearly the greater of the two evils on offer.

Nevertheless, Joseph Farah is right in urging conservatives and independents to steer clear of supporting John McCain this fall. Supporting the lesser of two evils is still supporting evil, and a McCain victory will both preclude the Republican Party from returning to its small government ideals as well as ensure Hillary Clinton's ascendancy in 2012. McCain's selection of Palin should not be interpreted as moving the Republican Party toward the right, but rather as a bone thrown to the right specifically to prevent what will otherwise become the Republican Party's move to the right after yet another moderate Republican failure.

Time and time again, Republican conservatives have fallen blindly for the blandishments of party elitists. They supported the hopelessly unelectable Bob Dole because the elders declared Pat Buchanan to be unelectable. They bought into the idea that George W. Bush was the second coming of Ronald Wilson Reagan, not the bastard stepchild of Woodrow Wilson and Lyndon Baines Johnson that he turned out to be. They refused to back Ron Paul, the lone champion of the Constitution contesting the nomination, and got the architect of the McCain-Feingold limitations on free speech.

If McCain is defeated, four years of an Obama administration will force the Republican Party to embrace candidates like Sarah Palin who conservatives can actually support. If McCain wins, thanks in part to the conservative support he has hitherto despised, conservatives can expect nothing but a long and ugly line of Bushes and McCains as their standard bearers for the foreseeable future.

Joseph Farah is right. Vote Libertarian, vote Constitution, vote "none of the above." But don't vote for either of the two evils on offer.

Anti-Palin Republicans

September 7, 2008

I T'S NOT HARD to understand why the Obama Nation dislikes Sarah Palin. She's single-handedly pulled the old aviator out of his stall and given him a real chance of ruining what once looked like a cakewalk to the swearing-in ceremony. It's not difficult to understand why feminists hate Sarah Palin, since she's everything they claim to be and aren't, to say nothing of the fact that she opposes infanticide in all its forms. It's not much of a challenge to figure out why the media elite despise her, since she's eminently a normal, intelligent woman of the sort that everyone from Maine to Minnesota to New Mexico has known, carpooled with, and generally gotten along just fine; she isn't yet another pretentious Ivy League politician in front of whom bootlicking journalists from second-tier universities so enjoy fawning.

Liberals quite reasonably fear her because she is the most talented natural politician since Reagan who advocates positions diametrically opposed to theirs. Conservatives quite naturally love her because she shares their values, advocates their policies, and has done what every conservative has been yearning to do for years by smashing a metaphorical fist right into the sneering face of the collective mainstream media. I'm not a conservative and I've seldom voted Republican, but even I had a little spring in my step after seeing all the sad-puppy faces in the media after Palin's speech at the St. Paul convention.

What's rather more interesting is the way in which certain nominally conservative Republican commentators have reacted towards her. Charles Krauthammer, Ramesh Ponnuru, Jay Nordlinger, David Frum, Ben Stein, and others were all markedly less enthusiastic than most about the John McCain's choice of the vibrant Palin over the likes of the feeble Tim Pawlenty, the plastic Mitt Romney, the treacherous Joe Lieberman, and the thuggish

Tom Ridge, and were quick to criticize his selection. Such criticisms have been muted somewhat in light of Palin's excellent speech at the convention and the exuberant embrace of her by the party's grass roots, but nevertheless, they reveal a particular idiosyncrasy of part of the so-called conservative commentariat.

Since Palin's views on particular policies were largely unknown to me and there were rumors of her libertarian leanings, my first thought that was perhaps this distinct lack of enthusiasm for the Republican Party's first genuine political star since Ronald Reagan stemmed from the usual conflict between the Israel-first, pro-war part of the conservative commentariat and the America-first, anti-war Buchananite right. Indeed, the Jewish left even attempted to stir up this potential conflict by starting a public debate over whether Palin, as an evangelical Christian, was good for the Jews. However, it soon became apparent that Palin is the Israeli flag-flying sort of Christian Zionist quite common in evangelical circles—like my own church, as a matter of fact—with whom not even Abe Foxman and the Anti-Defamation League have any serious problems.

And as for her position on the war, her own son's deployment and her apparent belief that the Iraqi occupation is "a task from God" made it fairly clear that she isn't going to present any obstacles for those who intend to continue trying to spread democracy by force throughout the world.

So, what explains this hostility? Was it simply sour grapes from those who didn't see it coming? I don't think so, as for the most part, these particular pundits represent a good portion of the more intelligent and pragmatic—if often less principled—percentage of the conservative commentators. Most of them are Washington insiders and all of them understand The Narrative. According to The Narrative, the old Washington warhorse, usually a vice-president or a senator, is supposed to go down bravely to defeat at the hands of the innovative and exciting newcomer waving the flag of change; while Barack Obama is a senator, he isn't much of one, which is why he felt he needed an old Washington hand on the ticket to provide gravitas as well as a symbolic foil for his youthful energy. (Also, Michelle Obama told him that he'd have to take his stinky, snorey self to the couch in the Oval Office for the next eight years if he annoyed her by doing the smart thing and choosing Hillary.) In the eyes of those who know The Narrative, John McCain is supposed to be playing Bob Dole.

But by selecting Sarah Palin, McCain once more played the maverick and began ad-libbing his lines instead of obediently reciting them word-for-word. This is offensive to those who know the script, moreover, the cabal of media quasi-conservatives aren't terribly happy about the prospect of having a real live Red America conservative at the fore of the party four years from now. They'd prefer a former liberal who's "seen the light," a Purple American like themselves who is politically Republican but culturally Democrat.

They really needn't worry. Based on what one acquaintance of Palin e-mailed me this weekend, they can quite reasonably have every expectation that if McCain-Palin is the winning combination in 2008, Sarah Palin will, like so many Republicans before her, grow considerably before she takes her turn at the helm of the party.

Counterpush

September 14, 2008

THIRTY YEARS AGO, the nation embarked on a program of massive deregulation. AT&T was broken up, the airlines were deregulated, and there was even talk of closing the Department of Education and getting the federal government out of the education business. Much of this happened, interestingly enough, under a Democratic Party president. The Airline Deregulation Act which fundamentally changed the nature of civilian aviation was enacted in 1978 and signed into law by President Carter.

There is a saying that it takes Nixon to go to China. This means that if an unpopular policy is to be pursued, it has to be a president of the party which by and large opposes that policy to successfully push it through. Whereas a dovish Democrat considered to be soft on socialism couldn't go to China without generating a storm of criticism from hawkish Republicans, Nixon wasn't likely to come in for nearly as much criticism from his usual opponents who favor the policy or from his usual allies who are loathe to criticize the leader of their team.

One may perhaps recall the outrage when Hillary Clinton attempted to socialize the health care system. She was eyed with suspicion from the start because everyone knows Democrats desperately want a Canadian-style health care system where everyone waits a long time to receive the same poor-quality care as anyone else, and doesn't have to pay for it so long as they survive long enough to receive it. (This is assuming they don't simply travel to the USA or Switzerland the way all the rich Europeans do in order to escape their own low-quality national health care systems.) So, when Hillary began working with her task force, this had the effect of a hurricane of opposition which quickly gathered enough force to destroy the attempt.

It is often surprising to those who believe Democrats are anti-war to learn that most of America's wars were launched by Democratic Party presidents.

Despite getting elected on a promise to keep America out of the Great War, Woodrow Wilson got us into it. Democratic icon FDR did everything he could to get America into World War II; there is substantial evidence that the attack on Pearl Harbor was permitted to take place due to his hitherto unsuccessful efforts to drag unwilling Americans into war with the Axis. It was Harry Truman who presided over the Korean war, John Kennedy who first sent American troops to Vietnam and even Bill Clinton invaded Somalia and bombed Serbia. Although in characteristic Clintonian fashion, he couldn't commit to proper military engagements any more than he could manage full sexual relations with his notorious intern.

Because Republicans are commonly supposed to be the warmongers, any war upon which they embark is likely to be problematic. Hence the intrinsic opposition to Bush the Younger's wars, despite the approval for them voted by the House and Senate. Democrats, being presumed pacifists, can much more easily lead the nation to war because the assumption is that if they are willing to go to war, they must have a good reason. This phenomenon can be described as counterpush, which means that a controversial policy can be most successfully championed by someone who is presumed to be opposed to it.

Being perceived as the party of business and capitalism, Republicans are actually the party that can more successfully expect to encroach upon it when in power. This is why the Bush administration can approve the national-ization of the U.S. housing market with barely a peep from the supposedly conservative commentariat. A Democrat uttering the infamous words "too big to fail" is liable to be doubted, but if a nominally free-market Republican somberly declares the need to allow the government to take over a business rather than permitting it to do what most business do naturally and fail, everyone assumes that it must be necessary and accepts it as a necessary evil.

It is interesting, then, to consider what policies the two men now running for president will likely pursue if they are elected. Based on the principle of counterpush, John McCain will likely pursue more nationalization in the health care and finance industries, and, as he has done in the past, immigra-tion amnesty. He will also accept more stringent international limitations on American sovereignty. Barack Obama, on the other hand, will likely pursue a much more aggressive military policy than anyone imagines and expand the Patriot Acts to even more strictly limit American liberties than President Bush has already. And, believe it or not, he may even attempt to balance the budget.

To attempt to claim that one evil is greater or lesser than the other is to fail to note the historical patterns. Due to the principle of counterpush, one must conclude that it requires a lesser evil to accomplish the objectives of the greater one.

The 'long run' arrives

September 22, 2008

I WAS OPPOSED to George W. Bush's presidency from the very start. I have always known he was no conservative and that he bore no allegiance to the Constitution. My very first political column here at WND warned of the likelihood that his administration would attempt to use 9/11 to destroy American liberties, and I warned voters prior to the 2004 election that voting for George W. Bush would make the Republican voter "a willing accomplice in the ongoing bipartisan destruction of your country."

With yesterday's announcement of the fifth and largest bailout to take place this year, the Bush administration has shown itself to be easily the most left wing since FDR was ensconced upon the Cherry Blossom Throne. The administration's plan to purchase $700 billion in financial assets, announced on Saturday, represents the federal acquisition of just over 5 percent of the entire U.S. economy as measured by Gross Domestic Product. This additional 5 percent is beginning to approach the 7.5 percent of GDP that was the entire amount of federal spending in 1908.

As I pointed out in last week's column, the principle of counterpush states that to enact a controversial policy, the president pushing that policy must come from the party that is nominally opposed to it. Because it is the Republicans who are the supposed party of small government and free market, only a Republican president could hope to get away with spending what is supposed to be the taxpayer's money to buy private assets priced at one-twentieth of the annual national economy. What is particularly egregious about this action by the administration is the way in which it is primarily the bankers who caused this financial crisis who can be expected to benefit from it. *The Telegraph* reported this weekend that the very individuals who were responsible for Lehman's failure are expected to reap $2.5 billion in bonuses from the English bank that acquired Lehman's U.S. operations last week.

The reality is that the American financial system is not a free market, and it is not even remotely capitalist. It is actually a parasitical system in which the financial elite prey upon the capitalists by virtue of having purchased political approval for their predation. Moody reported that financial services firms earned more than one-quarter of total corporate profits in 2007—27.4 percent, to be precise. They did not earn these profits through producing anything or from making business operations more efficient; they obtained it from behaving rather like pirates pillaging passing trade vessels.

As the financial collapse has shown, these profits were mostly the result of a vast construction of financial con games, none of which had anything to do with providing the investment money required by individuals who are starting new businesses and growing existing ones. As anyone who has ever had any contact with the venture capital industry very well knows, the "vulture" capitalists only provide money to those companies that don't need it; their main purpose is to take their share of the loot when a private firm sells its shares to the public through the government-approved and licensed channels known as the stock exchanges. Mob-run casinos are more honest and take a smaller house cut.

The administration's attempt to keep this shameless con game going will not work because it is based on the false Keynesian premise that controlled inflation, which slowly transfers wealth from savers to the bank owners, is sustainable over time. Keynes knew it wasn't; he defended his flawed economic theory by pointing out that in the long run, everyone is dead. But Keynes has been dead for six decades, the long run has arrived at last. And although the Federal Reserve has been frantically printing and distributing its magic helicopter money for the last month, it is unlikely to be able to do more than buy the bankers and politicians a little more time to prepare for the next round of crashes, bankruptcies and bailouts. If they actually thought it had a chance of succeeding, they wouldn't have banned short-selling.

This crisis is largely external to the current scope of American politics, so it isn't something that George Bush, John McCain or Barack Obama can even theoretically fix; it's quite clear that they don't even begin to understand what is happening, much less why, to say nothing of how they should respond. The only presidential candidate who understood the situation—he has condemned it for decades—was the candidate that the vast majority of the American people thought was too outlandish and too out of touch to support,

Dr. Ron Paul. So, naturally, the answer to government manipulation of the economy for the benefit of the financial elite will be to give the government even greater power to manipulate the economy for the benefit of the financial elite.

Still, the financial system has at last been exposed for the fundamental fraud it always has been. The global economy concept should be the next to fall. Although they don't realize it yet, Americans are facing their most important nexus since the Civil War. They can return to the small government, free market principles of the Founding Fathers, or they can continue to trust in the paradigms and promises of the predatory charlatans who have brought them to this pass. Given that most of the vital limits on democracy put into place by the Founding Fathers have been methodically removed over the last 200 years, the intelligent observer can bet securely on the latter.

Red flag rising

September 28, 2008

FROM 1813 TO 1907, the U.S. dollar appreciated in value. What cost one dollar in 1813 cost only 48 cents in 1907. In 1913, the Federal Reserve was formed, ostensibly to provide financial stability and "fight inflation." Since then, the value of a dollar has all but vanished, as what cost one dollar in 1913 cost $20.73 in 2007; the dollar has lost 95.2 percent of its value under management of the Fed.

But at least the central bankers are keeping the financial system stable, right? Hardly. Although the Drudge Report is again reporting that the Paulson plan is on go-ahead, this time with some added provisions that are supposed to make the deal more palatable to American politicians, if not American taxpayers, the reality is that whatever is being done almost surely will not avert the coming economic cataclysm for long. This injection of liquidity into the system may alleviate the symptoms temporarily, but since the core problem was caused by excess liquidity in the first place, it cannot possibly be the solution. Still, a crash tomorrow is arguably better than a crash today; it's understandable if the politicians facing re-election in five weeks time would rather not face an electorate more in the mood for pitchforks than polls.

And yet, for all its mind-boggling scope, the Paulson plan appears to be little more than declaring "The system is broke. Long live the system."

Regardless of whether it is necessary, and whether it is likely to work, I don't think the politicians or the media understand how angry many Americans are about this proposed deal. I took a poll of the readers at my blog, about 80 percent of whom are Republicans who voted for George Bush in 2000 and 2004. Furious would be one word to describe them. Jacobin might be a better one. I gave them three options to the question "What is your preferred response to the Paulson plan?" and 1,051 people responded as follows:

- 1 percent—Give the bankers what they say they need to rescue the economy. (9 votes)

- 56 percent—Ignore the bankers, and let the crisis solve itself. (587 votes)

- 43 percent—Guillotine the greedy bastards. (455 votes)

Nor were my readers alone in this regard. John Hawkins of Right Wing News also polled his readers, who are more conventionally conservative than the libertarian-minded readers of Vox Popoli, and they voted against the Paulson Plan by a landslide, 85 percent to 15 percent.

Given these extraordinarily strong feelings, one would think John McCain and the Republican leadership would have to be insane to go against the wishes of their electoral base, and yet they appear inclined to do precisely that. No doubt they will bill this action as bold leadership, in much the same way they attempted to sell the welcome mat for Mexicans to conservatives earlier this year. One wonders, too, if the left-wing base of the Democratic Party is as enthusiastic as their political leadership in selling out their poor and minority constituencies in favor of enriching the very Wall Street fat cats they usually preach against with all the fire-and-brimstone of a Southern Baptist criticizing Satan.

It seems to me that once the slow-witted left realizes what its leaders have done, they will be more than a little inclined to return to their intellectual roots and bring back the tumbrils of yore. And, it must be said, there will surely be more than a few on the right who will feel moved to join them in addressing the burning issue of excess height in bankers.

'The American people said no'

September 30, 2008

R EP. THADDEUS MCCOTTER is a Michigan Republican who was
the first to publicly oppose Treasury Secretary Henry Paulson's
plan to spend $700 billion bailing out bankrupt Wall Street in-
stitutions. After the House of Representatives voted against the legislative
proposal yesterday, McCotter called on President Bush to fire Paulson. Later
in the day, he spoke with Vox Day.

Congratulations on successfully shooting down the bill.

Well, we don't view it as a victory here; it's just the responsibility to get the
job done for the American people.

**What were your main reasons for opposing the Paulson plan, even in the
revised form that you voted on today?**

It's not about me. I suppose this is a representative government. From
the minute the Paulson plan was introduced, the American people said no.
And then as this administration foisted that proposal upon this Congress,
the American people said no. And then as Congress, despite warnings from
people like me, set an artificial deadline of midnight Sunday, the American
people said no. And when the artificial deadline was met with a bad proposal,
which was the Paulson proposal, the American people still said no. The only
thing we can take out of this is that fortunately the Paulson proposal did not
pass.

Now, Congress is going to act. It is going to act in a responsible and timely
fashion on a piece of legislation that the American people know is fair to their
interests and will help with this economic situation. In the final analysis, the
Paulson plan fundamentally failed in that it wanted the American taxpayer to

buy noxious, toxic assets out of the marketplace. You have to remove both the plan and Mr. Paulson from the process. I've asked the president to demand Mr. Paulson's resignation and deputize someone else so that the Congress and the White House can get on with a plan the American people will accept.

What basic economic theory is operative in Congress right now?

Right now, the only thing that was operative, that was put in front of us, was Paulson's plan, which was to buy those toxic assets at public expense. There are several other models out there that other nations have used far more often and far more successfully than the flawed model Paulson put in there for the Wall Street bailout. What we want is something that will spur private recapitalization so the money comes in off the sidelines where it's parked, and also provides an appropriate government backstop that is necessary and just for the American people's economic prosperity. Those are the two fundamental principles. As you can see, private recapitalization and appropriate government backstop that is just and fair to Americans, is an entirely different path than the one taken by Paulson with his first, only, last resort of a public bailout of Wall Street.

The basic Keynesian model states that savings equals investment, and there hasn't been much savings in the American economy because interest rates have been so low for so long. Where is this private capitalization supposed to come from with artificially suppressed interest rates that in real terms may actually be negative?

I would actually go one step further because I think you're getting very close to the same position I'm at. Savings are deferred consumption channeled into investment. What happens under the despicable Keynesian model, the disastrous Keynesian model, is this—savings start to reduce. And what the government does then is to pump expanded credit into the system. It creates investment inflation. This is exactly where we are, and it's called a bubble. And the market has endeavored, as it always does, to correct that investment inflation, so Mr. Paulson and Mr. Bernanke wanted the taxpayers to inject $700 billion to keep the bubble inflated! And it's not going to work!

What you have to do is get the private money to come in and look at the assets, start to clear that out through proper legislation to incentivize it, and then get an appropriate government backstop. Now, in the long-term picture, it is all about reincentivizing American savings to increase that pool of capital here. It is also about attracting American capital that is parked offshore back for repatriation; the last time we did it there was over $300 billion that came back into the American economy. Benedict Arnold, as the Democrats have put it, Benedict Arnold cleaning up Wall Street. And then what you can also do is incentivize private foreign investment to come back into the United States through appropriate legislation.

As opposed to the sovereign funds they're currently relying on.

Right, the sovereign wealth funds I oppose. They're government-run, and when the government of any nation, especially nations that are antithetical to the interests of the United States such as Communist China, when they come in and buy a private asset, it's been nationalized. It's been socialized! And when socialism is imported into the United States economy, the free market gets smaller and everyone's liberty and prosperity is imperiled....

Now, I've got time for one more. Give me your best shot.

There's a lot of suspicion that Congress is going to go to the Brussels model and make you vote until you get it right. How are the House Republicans going to deal with that?

It is up to the American people. The American people have spoken clearly, and it is incumbent first and foremost upon this administration to admit that the American people have rejected the Paulson bailout model for our economic rescue. It is that simple! If the administration continues to push this forward, even if that bill passes against the wishes of the American people, nothing is going to be accomplished. Even by its proponents it is being sold as a short-term stabilization measure that doesn't address the root problems that we have.

The American people will not stand to be dictated to by an administration or by a Congress that is deaf to its expressed wishes. That's why we are a free people and will remain so.

McCain-Palin: The wasted vote

October 5, 2008

I T IS REMARKABLE how many "conservative" commentators, who completely failed to see the credit crunch coming or anticipate its consequences, nevertheless did not hesitate to inform Americans that it was absolutely necessary to provide 5 percent of GDP—$700 billion—to an unelected economics czar who was one of the men primarily responsible for the crisis in the first place. In light of this, there are three things to keep in mind as you contemplate the unveiling of corporate socialism in America:

1. The bailout, or "rescue" if you prefer, will not work. Economic contraction always follows economic expansion, and even heroic efforts to eliminate the business cycle will do no more than delay and exacerbate the inevitable recession.

2. Electing Republicans will not solve the problem. President George Bush, Sen. John McCain and Gov. Sarah Palin all supported H.R. 1424: A bill to provide authority for the federal government to purchase and insure certain types of troubled assets for the purposes of providing stability to and preventing disruption in the economy and financial system. It is also intended to protect taxpayers, to amend the Internal Revenue Code of 1986 to provide incentives for energy production and conservation, to extend certain expiring provisions, to provide individual income tax relief and for other purposes.

3. This crisis was not a surprise; it was both inevitable and predictable.

As proof that my analysis is correct, I offer the evidence of my past columns here at *WorldNetDaily*:

• "Economic winter is on its way," March 16, 2008 (p. 397)

- "Teaching banks to fish," March 23, 2008 (p. 401)

- "The coming conservative collapse," Sept. 19, 2005 (Vol. I, p. 673)

- "You can't fix a corpse," July 12, 2004 (Vol. I, p. 463)

It would be a massive mistake for conservatives, libertarians and capitalists to continue supporting Republicans when there is clearly nothing conservative, libertarian or capitalist about the Republican Party. The Republican Party does not value freedom, it does not value capitalism, it does not abide by its republican principles and it does not honor the Constitution. Regardless of whether you vote Libertarian, Constitution Party or do not vote at all, you can be sure that your vote will not be wasted–because, as events have proven time and time again over the last eight years, the only wasted vote is the vote that is cast for a Republican politician.

Why the bailout didn't work

October 12, 2008

SINCE TREASURY SECRETARY Henry Paulson announced his three-page plan to rescue the Wall Street banks on Sept. 23, the Dow Jones Industrial Average has fallen 2,937 points, or 26 percent. An estimated $7 trillion in paper wealth disappeared from U.S. stock markets last week, a figure equivalent to 53 percent of American GDP. The financial crisis, which the $810 billion dollar bailout was supposed to avert, has spread to stock markets throughout the world. The Russian and Indonesian markets have been suspended while the country of Iceland appears to have gone bankrupt, owing $275,000 worth of debt for every man, woman and child in the island nation.

Some economists claim Paulson acted too late. Others assert that his actions were too conservative, although they can't seem to specify precisely how much more money was required over and above the $810 billion figure. Still others declare the bailout will work, it merely hasn't been put into effect yet. They are all wrong, and they are wrong because they do not understand the fundamental nature of the problem. They are analyzing the symptoms of the disease rather than the disease itself, and in doing so, are ironically prescribing as medicine the very poison that is killing the patient.

Conventional economists of the sort who get quoted on CNBC and Fox News will usually mention the terms "liquidity crisis" and "restoring confidence." These terms tend to betray the ideological bias of the economist and indicate that he is a neo-Keynesian who views the situation through the macroeconomic perspective of the updated Keynesian model that has been dominant in economics for most of the last 80 years. (Chicago School monetarists are also concerned with liquidity issues, but we'll leave them out of it for the purposes of this column.)

The essential problem is that the administration is attempting to enact a Keynesian solution to an Austrian problem. The Austrian School teaches that monetary inflation, which in this case was primarily caused by the Federal Reserve's decision to keep interest rates artificially low to prevent the economy from going into recession in 1996, 2001 and 2003, creates inflationary booms that lead to the severe misallocation of capital resources. As the Austrian logic predicted we would, we saw two such booms in asset prices, the first in the stock markets, the second in the real estate and commodity markets.

Millions of people profited from the asset inflation, and trillions of dollars were directed into areas of the economy they would not have otherwise gone, such as second homes and investments in companies selling dog food over the Internet. The problem is Austrian theory also teaches that inflationary expansions are always followed by deflationary contractions which clear out all of the resource misallocations that occur during the expansionary period. The Dutch tulip mania of 1637 is a good example of resource misallocation, when a single tulip bulb was known to have sold for the modern equivalent of $35,000. Such misallocations can occur for diverse reasons, but the usual cause is easy credit and low interest.

America is currently suffering from severe capital misallocations quite possibly more extreme than the 17th century Dutch, since its money supply has been inflating steadily for decades, and at an increasing rate. Compounding the problem is the fact that this inflation has reduced the value of savings and people were given incentive to consume rather than save, so the nation has no savings pool from which investment into productive capital might be made. Instead, the nation has substituted foreign investment, which can and will be withdrawn whenever it is required elsewhere.

The administration is attempting to deal with the credit crunch, which is the natural result of banks refusing to lend money, by making more money available. The problem, however, is not that there is simply no money, but rather that banks, having learned how many of their investments were worthless, are rightly concerned about making more of the same mistakes. Imagine if you had been burned on the purchase of 100 swamp properties that turned out to be worth nothing. Are you going to buy 10 more plots of swampland simply because someone gives you money equal to one-tenth of the money you'd lost already?

The liquidity crisis has already entered a stage that Austrians describe as "pushing on a string." The various financial authorities can push as hard as they want by further cutting interest rates and utilizing other expansionary monetary policy measures, but the string will remain limp. Ironically, the so-called student of the Great Depression, Ben Bernanke, failed to learn the only important lesson about the historical Federal Reserve. The failure of the 1930s Fed was not due to any refusal to expand the money supply and encourage bank lending, but because events were beyond its control.

America and the rest of the world has foolishly attempted to deny economic gravity. Now, it will learn that most basic of rules: That which goes up must eventually come down.

Refuse to choose

October 19, 2008

E VERY FOUR YEARS, the same sort of kabuki electoral ritual plays out. The Republican Party leaders sequestered in Washington, D.C., select a few moderate Republicans, declare them to be fine, upstanding conservatives and do their best to cram them down the collective throat of the Republican base. These efforts are lauded by the parasitic neocons, faux conservatives and religious leaders that dominate the supposedly "conservative" commentariat. The party elite and media join forces to convince the actual conservatives and republicans by whom they are sustained that these moderates are not only the party's only hope for victory, but are also double-secret conservatives.

Consider the Republican Party's candidates over the last six elections: George Bush, George Bush, Bob Dole, George W. Bush, George W. Bush, John McCain. Looking at the first five with the benefit of hindsight, do any of these men possess seriously conservative or republican credentials? As for the sixth man, McCain, his conservative credentials are by far the weakest, as his pro-bailout, pro-migration, anti-free speech, anti-constitutional judge positions should suffice to demonstrate. The evidence of his long career in the Senate indicates that he would actually govern to the left of George W. Bush, who has been the worst Republican president of this century and may well be the worst president in United States history ... to date.

Except for the 1992 and 2000 elections, in which Republicans actually believed both Bush the Elder's and Bush the Younger's false claims to have inherited Ronald Reagan's ideological mantle, conservatives have correctly declared their doubts about the Republican standard bearer. And each time, the party leaders and their collaborators in the media have done their best to scare the doubters back into the fold. As the election approaches and the pressure grows, people abandon their principles one by one and fall back into line. Even Ann Coulter is now wavering on her very public and repeated declarations of non-support for John McCain, as Republican panic about Obama's lead in the polls reaches a fever pitch.

But consider what decades of a pragmatic approach have brought Republicans. What does it profit a party to gain the White House but lose its ideological soul? The nation now stands at the very verge of bankruptcy and a collapse into open authoritarian rule primarily due to Republicans compromising on their core principles of small and limited government. More government was not the answer when George Bush I raised taxes or when George Bush II turned over financial czardom to the very Wall Street bankers who created the derivatives mess in the first place. More government will not be the answer, regardless of whether it is John McCain or Barack Obama who is signing the Democratic House and Senate's latest expansion of federal power over the American people into law. More government will never be the answer, no matter how great the crisis that is used to justify it.

Democrats must bear some of the blame, of course. But Democrats are supposed to support more government. It has been the core principle of their party for at least the last 76 years, and if they can be faulted for having been less than truthful about this upon occasion, their shameless dissembling is still orders of magnitude less dishonest than the gap between Republican promises and Republican actions. I would never vote for a culturally foreign socialist such as Barack Obama, but it cannot be denied that those who vote for Obama hoping for more government will get what they expect—if not necessarily in the positive form they would like—whereas those who vote for McCain hoping for less government are doomed to the same bitter regret that conservatives who were fooled by George W. Bush have known for four years or more.

As I have repeatedly warned since 2003, pragmatic and unprincipled politics have destroyed the Republican brand, prevented the party from implementing any of its platform when in power and now promise to lead to a Democratic supermajority. To blame for this are many of the very individuals who will be vehemently urging you to vote for John McCain to stop the abominable Obama. And Obama is abominable, but the fact is that his presidency will be very little different than a McCain presidency. Even the one difference that is often cited is implausible, as it is simply impossible to imagine the Senate's former Mr. Congeniality battling a Democratic House and Democratic Senate to the death in defense of conservative, Constitution-respecting judges.

The time to save the republic was during the Republican nomination, when the only candidate who understood the financial dangers it faces was still in the running. But a party so foolish as to reject a Ron Paul in favor of a John McCain neither understands the real issues at stake nor does it merit the support of conservatives, constitutionalists or libertarians. As long as the Republican Party stands for Democrat light, those who value small government and human freedom cannot reasonably support it, even if the Democrats are represented by the second coming of Stalin himself.

When presented with a choice between Bolshevik and Menshevik, the only rational choice, the only sane choice, is to refuse to choose.

An infernal economy

October 27, 2008

Canto I

In a dark woodland I espied a bear
Vicious, hirsute, with a low, evil brow.
His stinking breath befouled the forest air;
A roar, and animal spirits somehow
Vanished, like ghosts dissipating in mist,
Taking with them nearly half from the Dow.
I knew not how I should hope to resist
This great beast, when before me then appeared
A genius, albeit one much dismissed,
For espousing truths both exact and feared
By men economical in wisdom.
"No man, yet I act," said him I revered,
"To spare thee much needless pain have I come!"
Then he raised a gleaming sword of pure gold
Before which the terrible beast did succumb
And turn away. Thus inspired I made bold
To inquire of insights he might convey.
"No, I shall not teach, instead shall I scold.
Come, thou shalt witness how ends the soiree!"
We found ourselves before a wide Abyss
From which came moans and cries of great dismay,
The regrets of men who'd been so remiss
As to believe markets will always rise.
"Speak, damned broker," I said with a hiss,
To a wretched shade with dark, haunted eyes,

And naked but for his well-tattered suit.
"All of the long-term charts showed we were wise."
He protested, with contrition acute.
"Dollar-cost averaging, interest compound,
We thought they'd invest risk free, absolute!"
My Guide laughed, it was a cold, hollow sound
Of scorn for innocence so misplaced.
"That which goes up must finally come down,
And asset inflation will be retraced.
For growth cannot last indefinitely
When debt is rising and money debased."
Behind us we left that sad misery,
Weeping and wailing under the cliff's edge,
Descending down to the second degree.
There we encountered the god of the pledge,
Visa the Master of living and dead.
Who sneered at my Guide: "From whence didst thou dredge
This old fossil, academic unread
By my countless servants, my serfs, my slaves?
He shall not enter, but for thee, instead
I'll offer a card that actually saves
Thee five percent even as thou doth spend!"

Temptation rushed o'er me, enticing waves,
Cast by the fat goblin off'ring to lend
Me all that I wanted, and more beside!
"Stand fast, man, and do not think thou shalt bend!"
So spoke my Guardian, that consummate Guide,
Who, bare-handed, tore that false god in half!
"His day is done, comest thou alongside.
Seest the shades blown like wheat amidst chaff?"
Throughout the depths blew a most fearsome wind
Hurling poor souls around, all the riff-raff
In mighty numbers, those fools who had sinned,
Caught up in the feverish gluttony
Of consumption, and now, too late, chagrined.

They tumbled through clouds of fiat money,
Faith rendered faithless in one mad moment,
Then came a pair still in matrimony
Bound. They shrieked and fought for they did resent
The ties that held them linked close together
In bitter rage and mutual dissent.
The woman cried, clawing at her tether.
Impoverished, angry, seeking divorce,
And falling for the netherest nether
They plunged to the depths like a Russian bourse.
"New house, new clothes, new car financed with debt
They married for better, but found the worst,"
Said the Master without seeming upset.
"So now, they can't even afford to split!"
Such countless horrors no one could forget,
Happily did I that fell mirk acquit.
But new torments I saw, new terrors. I found
Myself standing in the midst of a pit,
Where an icy rain came tumbling down
Upon the unjust, and the unjust alone,
For there the just simply did not abound.
Suffering journalists wept to atone
For lies and deceits practiced on the crowd.
While above towered three heads overgrown
From one horrid shape better disavowed,
Kudlow and Cramer and Bartiromo.
Three slavering heads drooled and barked aloud:
"Buy with both hands, surely this is the low!"
All the while snapping and snarfing up dirt.
Souls sold for nothing, not even a show,
No newspaperman had a single shirt
As hatless, shoeless, they froze in the rain,
Lamenting the truth they'd tried to pervert.
Shivering, I asked to depart this plane
A request to which my Guide acceded.
Thus we left behind the media's bane,

The encroaching ice quickly receded.
Before us now were rows of giant stones
And behind each a small man proceeded
To push it back and forth, with moans and groans,
Across the dismal field of outsized dreams.
"Economists," I heard the amused tones
Of the Guide, "and duly damned for their schemes
That served as the key to open the door
For terrible tax-and-spending regimes."
I spared but a brief sigh for Nobel's whore
As we fell to a field of sepulchers
Uncovered and belching forth with a roar
Crimson flames that seared those entrepreneurs
Of finance, gamblers, investment bankers
Who played games with exotic wire transfers.
Those who had been for their banks anchors
Howled in unending agony, the fire
Fueled by derivatives, lethal cankers
Of financial cunning that now require
Unthinkable time to fully unwind.
Until then, each shall scream in his stone pyre.
No more could I bear, horror smote my mind,
I reeled before sights I could not forget.
And then my adviser did me remind
We'd yet to meet the political set.

Thus ends the first canto.

Vote your values

November 2, 2008

I F YOU ARE AN AMERICAN, you will be the recipient of a wide variety of advice regarding how you should vote tomorrow. If you are a Democrat or an illegal alien, you have probably been encouraged to vote early and vote often. If you are a conservative and/or a Republican, you will have been inundated with a veritable downpour of scare tactics and seemingly improbable socialist scenarios.

It is important to remember that fear is not a rational basis for decision making. This does not mean that it is irrational to be afraid of Barack Obama's call for an armed civilian national security force as well funded as the U.S. military or John McCain's threat to complete the nationalization of the U.S. housing market. In fact, both of these fears are entirely well founded. It simply means that fear, being a powerful emotion, makes it difficult to consider the matter in a reasonable manner.

For example, many conservatives who deeply distrust John McCain's intentions have argued that the probability of Supreme Court vacancies justify voting for him since Barack Obama will not appoint justices who will defend the Constitution. But this argument makes no sense, because nothing in John McCain's long Senate career indicates that he has any respect for the Constitution. Moreover, McCain's preference for bipartisan accommodation means he would never appoint a Supreme Court justice of whom the Democratic House and Senate did not approve.

If, on the other hand, one only focuses on the perfectly understandable fear of what sort of justices Barack Obama would appoint, then one might well swallow the argument that McCain will nominate strong conservative justices if he is elected, even though there is no chance that he ever would.

There is little question that an Obama administration will be a nightmare of unthinkable proportions. But it may well be a necessary one, for nothing short of a nightmarish presidential term or two will free Americans of the various delusions in which they are currently trapped. Nothing will explode the pernicious myths of equalitarianism, multiculturalism, socialism and unlimited migration faster than the direct experience of an administration that embraces those principles. For decades, Americans have flirted with the left without ever fully accepting that they were doing so; the younger generation sees only the airy promises of the left and cannot understand the terrible reality that lies beneath them.

To elect John McCain will mean continuing on the present course. As with the eight Bush years, this would mean continued movement toward the left without an open acknowledgement of that movement. Indeed, George W. Bush has moved the country further to the left than LBJ. He has governed to the left of every president in U.S. history except Woodrow Wilson and FDR. Electing Barack Obama, on the other hand, will force Americans to directly confront the reality of the country they have, to all intents and purposes, already lost.

Like Joseph Farah, I cannot recommend voting for either John McCain or Barack Obama, because neither of them believe in the supreme importance of human freedom or understand the imperative of limiting the size and scope of government. Attempting to estimate which of them will prove a worse violator of these principles is of little interest to me, and the current administration has provided ample demonstration of the foolishness of any such endeavor. While I am a Libertarian and have usually voted Libertarian in the past, I do not recommend voting for Bob Barr because he is, in my opinion, a big-government Republican in Libertarian clothing. I remain somewhat skeptical about the Constitution Party due to its past support for the blatantly unconstitutional "War on Drugs," but its candidate, Chuck Baldwin, has openly criticized both the drug war and the government abuses it has inspired, and it is very sound on a broad spectrum of issues ranging from money and taxation to guns and immigration. Of these four candidates, I conclude Chuck Baldwin is the only candidate whom those who believe in human freedom and the U.S. Constitution can reasonably support if they decide to vote in this presidential election.

But freedom and limited government are my core values; they may well not be yours. If you believe that government-enforced equality and multiculturalism are of fundamental importance, vote without hesitation for Barack

Obama. If you believe that restricting free speech, bipartisan consensus and using the American military to pursue U.S. enemies to the gates of hell are vital, then you should vote for John McCain without remorse. And if there is no candidate that reasonably represents your values, you would do best to leave your presidential vote unmarked and instead vote on the many other federal, state and local matters on the ballot.

While hard times likely lie ahead, it is ultimately Americans who will have to rise to the occasion and face them no matter who sits upon the Cherry Blossom Throne. The president is not a god. He is not a king; he is merely a man. And regardless of who is elected tomorrow, he will not determine the ultimate fate of the republic.

Piling on Palin

November 9, 2008

T
HE DEFEAT OF JOHN MCCAIN in last week's election cannot have come as a surprise to anyone. Over the last decade, Mc-Cain has been among the least popular national Republican figure among conservative Republicans. Having won the nomination by outlasting a series of similarly liberal Republicans, including New York City mayor Rudy Giuliani and Massachusetts Gov. Mitt Romney, McCain's campaign was going nowhere until he selected Alaska Gov. Sarah Palin as his running mate.

While Palin's record as governor and mayor isn't entirely spotless from a conservative perspective, she is rightly considered to be far more trustworthy on key conservative issues than other national Republicans. Not only did she inspire genuine enthusiasm among the Republican grass roots, but her selection actually gave McCain a lead in the polls until he committed political suicide by raising a metaphorical middle finger to the American people with his very public embrace of the Wall Street bailout. Independents turned against him, conservatives stayed home and McCain went down to the defeat that had looked likely for the Republican candidate since the 2006 midterm slaughter.

Despite the excitement about the historic nature of his presidency, there is a very good chance that Barack Obama will be a one-term president. Obama faces no serious structural impediments to pursuing his political objectives since both the House and the Senate will have strong Democratic majorities in 2009. Any restraint on his left-wing impulses will have to be internal, as both Congress and the media will be inclined to cheer every leftward lurch, and complain bitterly about every failure to push aggressively forward on the progressive program. Since his selection of Rahm Emanuel as his chief of staff indicates that the Obama administration will continue the active foreign policy of the Clinton/Bush years, he will be forced to appease the left primarily on the domestic front.

We can expect, then, that the size and scope of government will increase even faster under Obama than it did under George W. Bush. This will significantly worsen what is already a dire economic situation, especially since the neo-Keynesian economic theory to which Obama's economics advisers and the Federal Reserve both subscribe justify increased government spending to extricate the economy from depression. However, these interventionist policies are certain to exacerbate the crisis and will probably threaten the charismatic president-elect's popularity with the electorate before the next election.

Because Sarah Palin is not only a conservative, but a Western populist, she is far less amenable to control by the New York-Washington axis of bureaucratic insiders, media commentators and think-tank grandees that dominate the Republican Party elite. McCain's advisers discovered this late in the campaign, when they complained that she was going rogue and attacking the Democratic candidate instead of quietly and dutifully following Sen. McCain into genteel defeat. This independence, combined with her huge popularity among the conservative base, means that the Republican East Coast elite knows it has to destroy her now, before she becomes the obvious alternative to a second Obama term.

This is why the crème de la crème of the conservative commentariat, the only "conservative" names ever seen in the mainstream newspapers, spent nearly as much time attacking Palin as they did attacking Obama, let alone Biden, in the final weeks of the campaign. It is also the reason that the unflattering—and almost surely untrue—rumors from inside the McCain organization began the very day after the election and were quickly disseminated throughout the supposedly conservative media.

It must be understood that the East Coast elite would far rather lose the White House, House and Senate than lose its influence over the Republican Party. This is why, after a decade of advocating the abandonment of principle and political pragmatism in the name of retaining power, these impractical pragmatists are unembarrassed to continue advocating the very policies that were responsible for the Republican Party going from national dominance to abject defeat. If Republicans are wise enough to reject these "opinion leaders" and insist upon standard bearers who actually reflect the core values of the party's base, don't be surprised to see a few supposedly staunch Republicans defecting to the Democratic Party.

Consider the electoral reality. The social conservative measures such as California's Proposition 8 that conservatives have been told to abandon have nevertheless proven to be popular vote winners even in Democratic states, whereas elite-approved measures such as alien amnesty, the foreign occupations and the Wall Street bailouts are hated by Republicans and Democrats alike. It is illogical, bordering on downright insane, to conclude from this that less of the former and more of the latter will result in any improvement in Republican fortunes.

The battle for the hearts and minds of the Republican Party has begun. Sarah Palin only represents the first of what promises to be many internecine battles. And if she has any thought of leading the Republican Party against an incumbent Obama, she would do well to begin with demonstrating her strategic competence by leading the GOP's conservatives against the liberals and moderates who have inerrantly steered the party into disaster and defeat.

Obama's New Deal

November 16, 2008

OR YEARS, economic contrarians have been predicting financial disaster for the U.S. economy. And for years, famous mainstream economists and CNBC analysts have been assuring everyone that Federal Reserve was managing the new economy effectively, and that this new and astonishingly productive economy meant that economic laws of the past were outdated. Paul Krugman, the *New York Times* columnist who was recently awarded the Nobel Prize for economics, was one of the few honorable exceptions among the big names in the field, as his 1999 book, *The Return of Depression Economics*, was more prescient than most in noting "depression economics—the kinds of problems that characterized much of the world economy in the 1930s, but have not been seen since—has staged a stunning comeback."

However, in his November 10 column entitled "Franklin Delano Obama," Krugman offers two historical lessons to the incoming Obama administration. The first, the political lesson, is entirely correct. Economic missteps can absolutely undermine an electoral mandate, and they will do so very rapidly indeed. The problem, however, is that Krugman's second lesson, the economic one, advocates precisely such a misstep, a failure of such proportions that it can only be described as epic. He writes:

> *My advice to the Obama people is to figure out how much help they think the economy needs, then add 50 percent. It's much better, in a depressed economy, to err on the side of too much stimulus than on the side of too little.*

Krugman's incredible notion is that the failure of the New Deal to lift America out of the Great Depression was due to FDR's overly conservative approach to government spending. He admits that federal spending increased

dramatically, but argues that this was overshadowed by the previous administration's tax hikes and a reduction in state and local spending. He quotes
the conclusion of an M.I.T. study that he considers definitive, in which E.
Cary Brown states that the Keynesian-prescribed fiscal stimulus failed "not
because it does not work, but because it was not tried." And he draws the
wrong conclusion from economic growth of the 1950s when he concludes
that it was the "enormous public works project known as World War II" that
"saved the economy."

Incredibly, the Austrian economist Murray Rothbard managed to accurately foretell Krugman's column 45 years ago in the introduction to the 1963
edition of his book *America's Great Depression*:

> *Suppose a theory asserts that a certain policy will cure a depression. The*
> *government, obedient to the theory, puts the policy into effect. The depression*
> *is not cured. The critics and advocates of the theory now leap to the fore with*
> *interpretations. The critics say that failure proves the theory incorrect. The*
> *advocates say that the government erred in not pursuing the theory boldly*
> *enough, and that what is needed is stronger measures in the same direction.*

Krugman's argument is intriguing in light of the way in which Obama and
the Democrats have been critical of the Bush administration's tax cuts in the
past. It is improbable that a Democrat-controlled Washington, D.C., will
resist the urge to follow the same tack as Herbert Hoover; they don't tend to
be slavish Keynesians but rather follow Keynesian theory only when it permits
them to do what they wish, which in the case of falling federal revenues
will almost surely be raising taxes. His argument is also based on inaccurate
information, as this chart of federal government spending compared to state
and local spending should suffice to show that there was no great decline
in state and local government spending, a 38 percent increase in state and
local spending from $8.1 billion to $11.2 billion could hardly offset the
simultaneous 98 percent increase in federal spending, which rose from $5.1
billion to $10.1 billion during FDR's first two terms.

In fact, if the president-elect is to take Krugman's advice seriously, by the
end of his first term he will have to spend more than the $5.605 trillion
annually that would be the equivalent of FDR's spending. Even if state and
local government spending remained flat, at $2.951 trillion, this would mean
that government spending would account for 62 percent of the U.S. economy

US from FY 1933 to FY 1940

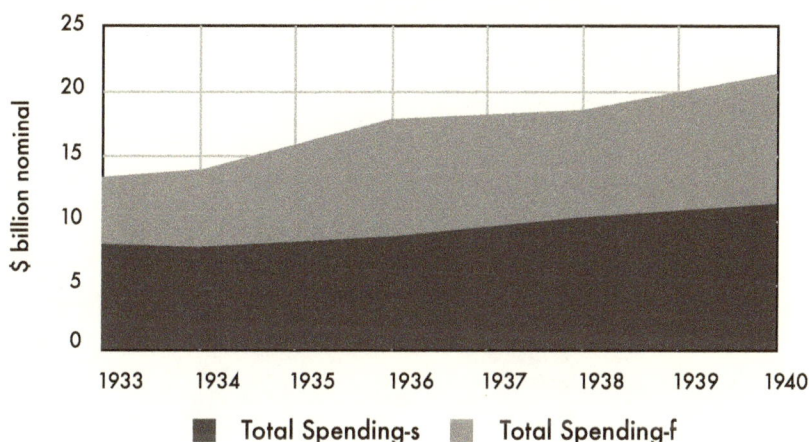

in 2007 without any economic contraction. If, however, the U.S. were to enter into a depression of similar proportions, an FDR-style spending increase would account for 115 percent of the entire economy!

Now it's obvious that Krugman's idea is that a massive spending shock would avert the greater part of the contraction; that's the whole idea of attempting to smooth out the business cycle in the first place. But the Nobel Prize winner is failing to account for two extremely important facts. The first is that in 1929, combined federal, state and local spending only accounted for 11.3 percent of GDP. In 2007, it accounted for 39.3 percent. Therefore, the massive spending shock has already been applied and even an increase to the historic 1945 level of 53.3 percent would be much smaller, in percentage terms, than the 98 percent increase that Krugman tells us was too small.

The reality is that Krugman's advice is incorrect because his Neo-Keynesian economic model is hopelessly flawed. Americans are witnessing, in real time, an unnecessary empirical test of John Maynard Keynes's failed theory. It is a real tragedy that Messrs, Bernanke and Krugman have studied the failures of the past only to reach precisely the wrong conclusions about the consequences of government attempts to manage the economy. For, if the Austrians are correct and these fiscal interventions only serve to exacerbate and prolong the depression, the famous students of economic history will not prevent a Great Depression, they will cause an even greater one.

Calculating the next depression

November 23, 2008

I T'S REMARKABLE TO SEE how quickly mainstream economists have gone from declaring a new age of permanent global prosperity to apocalyptic predictions of doom, gloom and financial Ragnarok. However, it's important to remember that no matter what the politicians, bankers and CNBC commentators would like us to believe, the Dow does not make up the entirety of the U.S. economy—and even if Manhattan and Washington, D.C., were to vanish tomorrow, the rest of the country would continue to exist.

One can even make a reasonable case that it would be much better off in the long run. But I digress.

While notable liberals such as Paul Krugman and Tom Friedman are already crying "Code Red" and banging the drum for a second and larger New Deal, it should be noted that according to Austrian economic theory, complete panic is not necessarily in order. This is important, because unlike the Neo-Keynesianism to which the mainstream economists and columnists adhere, Austrian theory correctly predicted the present crisis. And unlike Neo-Keynesian theory, Austrian economics provides a heuristic device to roughly estimate how bad the economic contraction is likely to be.

Because the debt-inflated economic boom was the problem, creating as it did the sort of resource misallocations that are presently being corrected by the ongoing layoffs, foreclosures and bankruptcies, we know that the magnitude of the correction should be approximately the size of the expansion. And since we already know the extent of the historical contraction and expansion, this means we can compare that relationship to the recent expansion to calculate how much the economy is likely to contract in the near future.

The Great War caused U.S. GDP to bottom out in 1914. In the 15 years through 1929, the U.S. economy grew 184 percent, during which time total local, state and federal government spending increased 234 percent. Following the recession of the early 1990s, the 15 years from 1993 through 2008 (est) saw the U.S. economy grow 118 percent, with a concomitant increase in total government spending of 116.5 percent. As impressive has the recent long boom has been, it is actually smaller in percentage terms than its historical antecedent.

Why does the recent expansion seem so much larger? Why do things seem so much more out of hand? There are at least two reasons: First, the equity markets expanded at an even faster rate than the 1920s economy did; the Dow rose 320 percent from October 1992 to October 2007. But, as has already been noted, the stock market is not the economy. Second, the expansion from the most recent recession, in 2001, is of strikingly similar size to the historical expansion subsequent to the 1921 recession.

1922–1929:

  41.4 percent GDP growth and 25.8 percent increase total spending

2002–2008:

  42.3 percent GDP growth and 42.9 percent increase total spending

The important question, then, is which point in time should the beginning of the expansion be traced. Since the Federal Reserve has been cutting interest rates and attempting to stave off economic contraction since the dot com bubble burst in 2000, I think the longer period is probably the more relevant. A comparison of the two 15-year expansions indicates a projected contraction that would be expected to hit its nadir at 64 percent of the contraction during the Great Depression. Since GDP declined by 45.6 percent from 1929 to 1933, this would indicate a 29.2 percent contraction to a GDP of $10.14 trillion in 2013.

Combined with the expected population growth, this points to a GDP per capita of $29,920, which would certainly mean a palpable reduction in the American standard of living but not mass poverty of the sort that would trigger total social chaos, much less a return to caves and grass huts. A depression of these proportions would be expected to drive up the unemployment level to around 17 percent, and require waiting until 2018 for the economy to return to current levels.

Of course, there is a panoply of reasons why these projections could be completely incorrect. Government statistics are notoriously inaccurate, and given the understated inflation of the last eight years, it's entirely possible that the economy has actually been in contraction for the entirety of 2008. No one knows the full extent of the derivatives debacle or how its unwinding is likely to exacerbate the ongoing crisis. Constrained by George Bush's spending and its own left-wing ideology, the Obama administration may not be able to either increase spending or slash upper income taxes as much as its academic allies would advise.

But, one can only work with the numbers with which one is provided. And regardless of how the scenario plays out, it should be eminently clear that these are perilous financial times that demand prudence of every responsible man.

No one will protect you

November 30, 2008

THE ANALYSIS OF THE MASSACRES at the Taj Mahal hotel are just getting started. It's still not yet known exactly how many victims there were or how extensive the attackers' preparations were. Some experts believe the al-Qaida bogeyman is to blame; others suspect religious elements of the Pakistani security forces, while India's martial preparations would appear to indicate suspicions of the Pakistani government itself.

But the one thing that is obvious regardless of precisely how the attacks were planned and carried out, it is that governments and their professional agents are totally incapable of assuring individual security against terrorism. This was true in the 1970s when the Baader Meinhof gang was killing businessmen and the Japanese Red Army was shooting up airports. It is just as true today. Not even completely comprehensive surveillance and security is capable of preventing the actions of individuals who do not fear legal consequences; if the reverse were true, there would never have been any crime committed in the totalitarian states of the Soviet Union or the People's Republic of China.

Because the government agents responsible for responding to terrorist threats are not machines but individuals who quite reasonably value their own lives, government reactions are always going to be either more widely lethal than the terrorist actions themselves or constrained to a slow process of containment. While the Indian government could have brought the recent incident to a speedy end by ordering the Indian air force to bomb the entire section of Bombay where the attacks took place, the cure would have been worse than the disease. The only alternative was the response that Americans have seen on their televisions time and time again: A small army of police encircling a building while unarmed citizens are slaughtered before their useless show of force.

Even a physical police presence prior to an attack is no insurance of security. Military studies have shown that as many as 70 percent of trained soldiers will not fire their weapons at another human being even in wartime, so the probability is that most police officers will not either. Hence the anger of a photographer who had one of the train-station attackers in his sights, but no weapon more lethal than his camera:

> But what angered Mr. D'Souza ... were the masses of armed police hiding in the area who simply refused to shoot back. "There were armed policemen hiding all around the station but none of them did anything," he said. "At one point, I ran up to them and told them to use their weapons. I said, 'Shoot them, they're sitting ducks!' but they just didn't shoot back."

The stories of the Bombay survivors tell of helpless victims hiding for hours before being hunted down and murdered. There were nearly as many people hiding in one toilet cubicle as took part in the attack. If even a tenth part of the unarmed masses in the area had been armed, the siege would have been brought to an end in hours rather than days, saving hundreds of lives. But instead of relying upon themselves, they relied upon the government to protect them and in doing so paid the ultimate price.

The truth is that no one will protect you—not the police, not the part-time security guard, not the staff of whatever business you are patronizing and not the national armed forces. You must take responsibility for protecting yourself, and the only means to do that is to ensure that you are appropriately armed whenever you intend to go out in public regardless of what the local laws might say.

The law cannot abrogate one's right to self-defense; to the extent that it attempts to do so, it is inherently illegitimate and should be ignored. Don't fall for the false assurances of police and others who would prefer to possess a legal monopoly on the means of violence. They exist only to contain the damage and provide the illusion of security as well as post-facto deterrence. They are not there to protect you. No one is.

Cultural cancer

December 7, 2008

W HEN THE MOORS migrated en masse into Spain, they neither established a perfect clone of an Arabian caliphate nor
constructed a conventional Christian kingdom. Instead, over a
period of centuries, they created al-Andalus, a Muslim society that made some
civilized allowances for the Europeans who had preceded them there. By the
time of the Reconquista 800 years later, the Spain that had once been was no
more.

Today, the English who languish under Scottish rule in the United Kingdom are horrified by the changes that have been taking place since 2003 in
the Oxford Junior Dictionary. This 10,000 word dictionary, published by
Oxford University Press, is primarily intended for the use of UK schoolchildren, increasing numbers of whom are not English. Words which have been
removed from the dictionary include Christmas terms such as "carol, cracker,
holly, ivy, mistletoe," fantasy words like "dwarf, elf, goblin," words related
to Christianity such as "altar, bishop, chapel, disciple, minister, monastery,
monk, nun, psalm, saint, sin, devil," and even such classically English animals
as "magpie, piglet, starling, weasel, wren."

It will probably come as little surprise to learn that the head of children's dictionaries at Oxford University Press responsible for overseeing such
changes glories in the proud Anglo-Saxon name of Vineeta Gupta. Gupta
declares:

> When you look back at older versions of dictionaries, there were lots of exam-
> ples of flowers for instance. That was because many children lived in semi-
> rural environments and saw the seasons. Nowadays, the environment has
> changed. We are also much more multicultural. People don't go to Church
> as often as before. Our understanding of religion is within multiculturalism,

which is why some words such as "Pentecost" or "Whitsun" would have been in 20 years ago but not now.

Her claims might be a bit more convincing if "Whitsun" were on the same level of common usage as "psalm," "saint," "sin," or "devil." And it would be very interesting to hear Ms Gupta explain how "dwarf," "elf," and "goblin" are no longer relevant in the land of J.R.R. Tolkein and C.S. Lewis, especially considering how their works are still being profitably mined by publishers and Hollywood producers alike.

Wealthy, technologically advanced, self-satisfied and flattered into complacency by the way in which people from other cultures have readily aped Western customs after being introduced to them, the societies of the West have long assumed that their traditions possessed magically transitive qualities. But, as Ms Gupta is demonstrating to those who were foolish enough to allow her ancestors from the Indian subcontinent to come live among them, it is not.

In Minnesota, 100,000 Somalis now live amidst the German and Scandinavian Lutherans that bravely, and perhaps unwisely, chose to settle the land of Ten Thousand Mosquito Factories. Last week, one of those Somalis, Shirwa Ahmed, was buried in Burnsville, his remains having been returned from Somalia subsequent to his murder of 29 people in a suicide bombing there. He was described by the media as "a Minnesotan and a naturalized U.S. citizen."

The truth is that he was neither, and to pretend otherwise is to accept the legal fiction that national and cultural identity are nothing more than paper. An official document stating that the color of one's eyes are blue does not suffice make them blue when they are observably brown, and Shirwa Ahmed was no more Minnesotan than Vineeta Gupta is English. A genuine Minnesotan might consider digging up the frozen tundra of Lambeau Field, (actually, a proper porphyrogenite would be much more keen to blow up the wretched Hump and see the Vikes playing outside in the snow again where they belong), but the thought of attempting to kill large quantities of people in Somalia would simply never enter his mind.

Whenever anyone points out the undeniable fact that multiculturalism is a cancer slowly killing Western culture, it is customary for left liberals to angrily demand to know why that individual hates people from other cultures.

But one need not hate anyone to prefer the continued existence of one's culture and society. A much more relevant question should be directed at the proponents of multiculturalism and immigration: Why do you hate Western society so much that you wish to see it destroyed?

God and the economy

December 14, 2008

WRITING THE IRRATIONAL ATHEIST was an interesting exercise in swimming through a sea of unsupported assumptions and incompetent arguments. But one thing I noticed is that beneath the vast compendium of logical blunders and factual errors, there was a single false belief that serves as a flawed foundation for the entire New Atheist attack on Christianity. That is the idea that reason is capable of dictating individual belief.

This atheist paradigm is almost invariably entwined with left-liberal politics as well as a science fetish because it depends upon a progressive narrative. This is due to the 18th century propaganda of the Enlightenment, which is looking increasingly outdated and irrelevant. The progressive narrative is primarily dependent upon three factors, technological advancement, wealth and peace, which it credits to the increased secularism of Western society.

The inherent problem is that these three factors can also be attributed to economic growth, which has accompanied the increase in technology, wealth and peace. Some secularists have gone so far as to claim that secularism is actually the cause of economic growth, but this is clearly incorrect since historical economic growth in more religious periods has exceeded the growth that took place during the 20th century. It is, in fact, an egregious error, since there is a growing body of evidence that it is secularism itself that is the product of economic growth.

Since I pay fairly close attention to various markets, it did not escape my attention that the New Atheists hit the best-seller lists very close to the time that the socionomists at Elliott Wave International were forecasting a Grand Supercycle peak. Sam Harris's *The End of Faith* was published in August 2004, with the Dow at 10,600. Richard Dawkins published *The God Delusion* in September 2006, when the Dow struck 11,508. And Christopher Hitchens appears to have marked the peak of both the New Atheism and the Dow when he published "god is Not Great" with the Dow at 13,188 in May 2007.

It is interesting to note that even as the Dow has lost 40 percent of its value in the last year, polls indicate that atheism is more unpopular than it was before the New Atheism first appeared. Not only that, but church attendance has already begun to noticeably swell even though the public has been aware of the dire economic situation for little more than three months. The *New York Times* reported last week that the faster-growing evangelical churches have seen church attendance grow as fast as 17 percent in the last year alone, much of which has come since September. This pattern is not new, but has been observed since at least 1857.

During each recession cycle between 1968 and 2004, the rate of growth in evangelical churches jumped by 50 percent. By comparison, mainline Protestant churches continued their decline during recessions, though a bit more slowly.

—*The New York Times*, December 14, 2008

It is a mistake, however, to simply conclude that the return to church is nothing more than the desperate actions of fearful people afraid of losing their jobs. While that is certainly an important factor, it must also be recognized that the embrace of religious faith by the formerly secular is an abandonment of belief in the progressive narrative, a rejection of the faith that society is in the process of becoming more peaceful and more prosperous through its collective commitment to science and reason. (One would think that the relatively penurious state of scientists and philosophers would suffice to illustrate the bankruptcy of the larger principle, but then, as I've demonstrated in detail in TIA, neither logic nor observation is a strength of the average atheist.)

The truth is that as Tolstoy pointed out in his epic *War and Peace*, no theologian or philosopher can present an idea so perfectly that it is capable of overcoming the great forces that sweep over individual lives as ruthlessly as they do over the societies those individuals inhabit. There can be little doubt that Alan Greenspan caused more people to believe God does not exist in the last decade due to his creation of the temporary illusion of wealth than all the works of Richard Dawkins, Sam Harris, Christopher Hitchens, Daniel Dennett and Michel Onfray combined.

And there should be no doubt at all that when millions of men and women who previously believed they had no need of any god elect to humble themselves before God and return to the fold of religious faith in the coming years, it will have nothing to do with anything that I or any other theist have written. If there is a silver lining in the catastrophe, it is the confidence that many lost sheep will be once more found.

The King of Christmas 2008

December 22, 2008

I LOVE EVERYTHING about Christmas. The white snow, the cheerful music, the rainbow of lights and the dawn vision of presents piled under the tree. It is a happy time for my family, a time of great joy, even in the absence of those with whom we would very much like to celebrate the holiday. Some of my most cherished memories stem from this time of year; what would I not give to arrive at the old manse to be greeted by my grandfather bearing a hot buttered rum in hand just one more time? But we also remember the inspiration for the celebration, a truth both wonderful and grim.

We remember that Jesus Christ had to come into this fallen world because it was, and is, under the rule of a cruel and malevolent prince, who tempted Him, who slew Him when He would not submit, and who watched in helpless horror as He rose again in power.

The world is still under the rule of that cruel prince, the results of which can be seen every day in the news. Murder, war and tyranny continue to oppress many millions throughout the world, the spectre of economic collapse now threatens the livelihoods of even more, but we who refuse to submit to the ruler of this world are no longer bound by him, for we claim that truth that sets us free, the resurrection of the Lord Jesus Christ.

Jesus Christ of Nazareth is the Man's true monarch, yet I remain convinced His Father is a libertarian at heart. For not only did He send His Son to set us free, but He allows us, no, He forces us to decide between acknowledging His Son as Lord or seating ourselves upon the throne of our own lives. And that freedom of choice, in the end, is the central liberty; indeed, it is the only liberty that truly matters.

A friend once asked how I could be so cheerful while America rots from within and endures attack from without. Others have wondered how I can be so personally optimistic even as I morbidly chronicle one debacle after another in this column and on my blog. The answer is that despite my love for America and my passionate allegiance to the ideas upon which it was constructed, I know that its fate is immaterial. Our country, our homes and even our lives are all things of shadow which will one day disappear in the light of the glory of Jesus Christ.

Despair is the natural state of the thinking man. This is why intellectuals grasp so readily at even the feeblest straw promising hope for heaven on Earth. It is why people irrationally turn to the very corrupt and evil men responsible for the current crises in the hopes that they will somehow be spared the awful consequences. But they do so in vain, as there will be neither peace nor harmony until the revolution begun in a Bethlehem manger is complete, until the murderous ruler of this world is finally deposed. Then, at long last, there will be peace and goodwill to men.

Merry Christmas. And may God bless us, every one.

The red hand of atheism

December 28, 2008

I N THE IRRATIONAL ATHEIST, I conclusively demonstrated the false-hood of the common atheist calumny that religion is a primary cause of war. Any examination of either military history or military strategy will suffice to prove that while there have been a small number of religious wars throughout recorded history, most wars did not involve religion and most religions have not inspired military conflict. Indeed, to claim that religion causes war is tantamount to confessing one's near-complete ignorance of the historical record.

While most literate individuals are aware of the atheism of mass murderers such as Josef Stalin, Pol Pot and Mao Zedong, they are not aware of how many other atheist leaders have been responsible for mass murder. In one of the book's appendices, I provided a list of 49 other atheist leaders who had overseen the slaughter of at least 20,000 individuals; these 52 leaders represent the majority of atheists who have ever held supreme political power. This number is particularly striking when one considers the fact that the Christian king responsible for what was considered the worst crime in Christendom's Wars of Religion, the Saint Bartholomew's Day massacre, died regretting his role in the deaths of an estimated 10,000 French Huegenots.

And yet, the scale of King Charles IX's crime is but a fraction of the great crimes of the 20th century anti-religious atheist zealots; it is also vastly overshadowed by history's very first atheist-influenced regime. Although it has largely been whitewashed by a France that still reveres its Revolution and is therefore little known in comparison with the Revolutionary regime's more notorious crimes, the story of the Committee for Public Safety's decision to slaughter the Vendéean people, who dared to resist the ordered closure of their churches, is finally beginning to be told thanks to a bold French aristocrat.

In early 1794—at the height of the Reign of Terror—French soldiers marched to the Atlantic Vendée, where peasants had risen up against the Revolutionary government in Paris. Twelve "infernal columns" commanded by Gen. Louis-Marie Turreau were ordered to kill everyone and everything they saw. Thousands of people—including women and children—were massacred in cold blood, and farms and villages torched.

> *"There was in the Revolution a clearly stated programme to wipe out the Vendéean race," said Philippe de Villiers, European deputy and former presidential candidate for the right-wing traditionalist Movement for France, or MPF, Party. "Why did it take place? Because a people was chosen to be liquidated on account of their religious faith."*

> —*The Daily Telegraph*, December 26, 2008

Now, it must be kept in mind that the French Revolution was not a purely atheist enterprise; only two of the members of the Committee for Public Safety, d'Herbois and Billaud-Varenne, were confirmed atheists. It is also true that the massacres may not have been a genocide proper, but rather the vicious aftermath of a civil war triggered by religious oppression and persecution by the Revolutionary French regime. But both the Committee and the Revolution were avowedly anti-clerical, and there is no question that the Revolutionary slaughter of 170,000 Vendéeans was primarily driven by anti-religious sentiment. So, the war in Vendée not only demonstrates the falsehood of the "religion causes war" theme, but also underlines the tendency of anti-religious regimes to commit large-scale atrocities.

Atheists such as Richard Dawkins inevitably attempt to defend their non-faith, if not the actions of their historical predecessors, by claiming that historical actions such as the Vendée massacres were not committed in the name of atheism. But this is an absurd and inept attempt at a defense. Any thinking individual would laugh at a similarly illogical claim that Marlboro's can't cause cancer because no smoker lights up in the name of Marlboro. And no hand waving or philosophical floundering will ever lessen the horrifying impact of Gen. Francois Joseph Westermann's letter to the infamous Committee.

> *There is no more Vendée.... According to the orders that you gave me, I crushed the children under the feet of the horses, massacred the women who,*

at least for these, will not give birth to any more brigands. I do not have a prisoner to reproach me. I have exterminated all. The roads are sown with corpses. At Savenay, brigands are arriving all the time claiming to surrender, and we are shooting them non-stop.... Mercy is not a revolutionary sentiment.

Rethinking free trade

January 4, 2009

I WAS FIRST introduced to economics when given Milton Friedman's book, *Free to Choose*, when I was still in junior high. By the time I graduated from high school, I had read Adam Smith, Paul Samuelson, Friedrich von Hayek, Ayn Rand, Peter Drucker and a number of authors whose works touched tangentially on economics. Unsurprisingly, I went on to study economics in college, and there read everyone from Bastiat to Harrington, thus giving me a solid background in Keynesian, Monetarist, Marxist and Austrian economics.

Throughout this time, it was only the Marxists who seriously questioned the utility of free trade, although they did not so much criticize Smith and Ricardo as they constructed a conceptual model in which the entire concept of trade, free or not, was largely irrelevant. The practical form of this model empirically demonstrated the validity of that approach throughout the latter half of the 20th century, as no society based on Marxist economics has ever known much success in producing goods that any non-Marxist society is interested in purchasing.

Now, there's no question that the theory behind free trade is relatively solid. There is no shortage of historical examples demonstrating how establishing tariffs has led to a wide variety of negative outcomes, most notably the famous Smoot-Hawley tariff of 1930 which helped exacerbate the Great Depression. However, just as the Information Age has rendered the Marxist Labor Theory of Value obviously moot, and in doing so eviscerated the entire foundation of both Marxian economics and the broader concept of distributive justice, it has also reopened the long-settled question of free trade and its fundamental benefit to an economy.

The development of an information and service-based economy also raises the question of whether the theoretical logic that prevailed in a manufacturing economy is even applicable at all, especially in the real world of international conflict. Whereas it might make perfect sense from a purely financial point of view to outsource all of the U.S. armed forces to China, where both the manpower and the manufacturing costs of weaponry are less expensive, such an action would be downright insane from the more pragmatic perspective of military history, which teaches that when two societies enter into violent conflict, it is the armed society that is victorious.

Furthermore, it is becoming ever more clear that the foundational assumptions of economics, based as they are on the concept of a rational homo economicus, are incorrect. An increasing number of studies are showing that the basic model of man as a rational consumer capable of reliably acting in accordance with his objectively calculated economic benefit is not only the gross oversimplification that it was always known to be, but may in fact be altogether incorrect. This is significant, because if the foundations of the theories upon which the huge and complex macroeconomic models are constructed are flawed, those models are rendered effectively useless.

And finally, while it would be a travesty to describe the massive trade agreement known as NAFTA as genuine free trade, there can be no question that the supposed benefits which were supposed to be derived from free trade with Mexico and Canada did not come to pass, instead, most of the predicted problems did. The same is true with the European Union, which contrary to all the predictions, has turned out to be even more economically sclerotic and politically fascistic than even its greatest detractors predicted 20 years ago.

The Marxian model breathed its last breath in the early 1990s. While the Keynesian model is seeing a revival in the misguided enthusiasm for public works spending in the United States and United Kingdom, a second transmutation of a severe recession into a great depression should kill it off for good. The Monetarist model is already on its last legs; the failure of the Fed to inflate its way out of the current crisis should suffice to finish it off. Even the Austrian theory, without question the most useful of the four economic schools, is poorly suited to account for the problems presented by exogenous factors.

None of this matters in the short term, of course. The Obama administration is clearly determined to repeat the mistakes of the Hoover and Roosevelt administrations, complete with all of the many unpleasantries they historically created. But one benefit of an extended economic contraction will be the way in which many economists will find themselves without jobs and with sufficient time to reconsider their long-held assumptions about the way in which an economy actually functions.

Reinforcing failure

January 12, 2009

FTER EIGHT YEARS, it is eminently clear to conservatives and liberals alike that George W. Bush is one of the worst presidents that the United States has ever suffered. His incompetent handling of what were completely predictable economic crises is historically rivaled only by his fellow Keynesian in laissez faire clothing, Herbert Hoover. Like Bush, Hoover inherited an economy just reaching its inflationary peak. And like Bush, Hoover refused to accept the laws of economic gravity, thus turning what should have been a normal recession into what is now known as the Great Depression.

But there is no problem so great that the credentialed experts of the nation cannot exacerbate it. Hoover was terrible, but Roosevelt managed to be worse. Hoover attempted to meet the challenge posed by the 1929 crash with a wide range of federal interventions that increased federal spending 34 percent during his four years in office; this was little more than one-third of the 98 percent increase under Roosevelt prior to World War II. Federal spending increased 63 percent under Bush, which divided by his two terms means that he spent nearly as much on a term-by-term basis in the same futile attempt to fight off economic contraction as Hoover did. And President-elect Obama is giving every sign that he will do his level best to repeat Roosevelt's reinforcement of Hoover's failure when he declared: "Only government can break the vicious cycles that are crippling our economy."

Government will not break those cycles. It cannot do so because it is government itself that is causing those vicious cycles that are crippling the American economy. Moreover, it is clear to anyone who is paying attention that Obama is aware his plan is not going to work because the claims made on its behalf are changing on a monthly basis.

Biden told an audience in this economically distressed battleground state that the Democratic presidential candidate's public works projects would create two million jobs nationwide, including 76,000 new jobs for the middle class in Ohio.

—Oct. 15, 2008

President-elect Barack Obama said this weekend he's planning to introduce an economic recovery program that would create 2.5 million jobs by January 2011.

—Nov. 24, 2008

President-elect Barack Obama has increased his employment goal with the nation's economic outlook worsening, seeking to create or save three million jobs in the next two years instead of the 2.5 million he proposed last month.

—Dec. 20, 2008

President-elect Obama raised the jobs forecast for his stimulus plan from three million to as many as four million on Saturday, upping the ante of his economic blueprint for the second time in three weeks.

—Jan. 10, 2009

There hasn't been this much desperate tap dancing around statistical predictions since the global warming charlatans first realized that their computer models corresponded with actual temperatures being observed about as closely as a Hamas rocket barrage ever gets to a strategic Israeli target. The Keynesian economic model upon which the Obama plan is based, and with which the mainstream media frame all discussion of the economy, isn't just outdated or broken, it is less viable than frozen monkey embryos implanted into a post-menopausal woman at an IVF clinic in Tijuana. It is less credible than the Minnesota senatorial election farce. It is, in short, a dead parrot.

It was a little more than four months ago, on Aug. 28, 2008, that the Bureau of Economic Analysis was reporting that GDP growth for Q2 2008 was

3.3 percent and suggesting that the "recession" might be over. Only a month later, that 3.3 percent was revised down to 2.8 percent; no doubt the final report on Q3 2008 will be further revised down from the negative .5 percent that has already been revised down from negative .3 percent in the advance report. These differences may seem small, but collectively they amount to major variances that suffice to render the entire exercise in federal economic intervention an utter fool's game, and no amount of printing worthless money to pay useless workers to build pointless infrastructure will change that.

It has often been said that those who don't know history are doomed to repeat it. The great tragedy of Obama's insane reenactment of FDR's prolongment of the Great Depression will be that the history was not unknown, but rather, willfully ignored.

Epic failures

January 19, 2009

A LITTLE MORE than three months ago, the debate was raging over the $700 billion Paulson Plan. And while there was never any doubt that House and Senate Democrats would support the notion of handing over astronomical sums of money to anyone with a pulse, far too many conservatives in the media cast aside whatever shreds of principle remained to them after eight years of a disastrous Republican administration and encouraged the Republican Party to support what was a small step for a Treasury secretary and a huge leap for socialism in America.

Now that what was completely obvious has become undeniable, and the failure of the initial round of bailouts has bankers and politicians in both the United States and the United Kingdom scheming to concoct another one, it's wise to go back and examine what observers in the media wrote the last time. For it is certain that those who were completely and utterly wrong about the Paulson Plan being a viable solution to the financial crisis cannot be considered to have any credibility on economic matters in the future, as "we had to do something" is not a defense that can be reasonably invoked by any thinking conservative.

When two of the conservative media's best-known economists are so visibly on the wrong side of the socialism/freedom divide, it is time to rethink the conservative media. Fortunately, there were no shortage of right-wing voices vehemently opposed to the series of bailouts that is still ongoing, whose inherent skepticism about government intentions proved more precise than the expertises of the various Nobel Prize winners, economists, and professional commentators who endorsed the Paulson Plan.

Count me out of the bailout.... Even if I completely trusted the wisdom of Paulson and his bureaucrats—which I don't—there's no way that I trust the

Dodds, Franks or the next Treasury secretary. Every day the markets don't go off the cliff suggests to me that we can do this in stages and that Paulson's do-it-my-way-or-it's-the-Dark-Ages-for-us-all argument doesn't hold water.

—Jonah Goldberg, *National Review Online*, Sept. 23, 2008

On Sept. 19, Treasury Secretary Hank Paulson put a gun to America's head: Pass his $700-billion bailout of the banking industry and give him unfettered new powers to buy up an ocean of privately held toxic assets, or all hell would break loose.... This is a man, in other words, whose crap sandwich should be taken with a huge grain of salt.

—Michelle Malkin, *National Review*, Oct. 3, 2008

Friday's financial OK Corral took place when federal politicians had a standoff over the mother of all bailout bills. Bullets called ballots were fired from both congressional houses and the White House. And when the smoke cleared, the bad guys were apparent—Bush, Paulson, Barney Frank, Pelosi, Dodd, most of the members of the House and the Senate, including Obama and even McCain, among many others.

—Chuck Norris, *WorldNetDaily*, Oct. 6, 2008

Some of the salesmen of this plan have reached to new heights in marketing it. They've even dared to call it an "investment" by taxpayers. They have suggested the taxpayers could somehow benefit down the road because their bailout is protected with real assets. I don't know about you, but until I receive my stock certificates for this forced investment and am able to sell my shares in the marketplace, I prefer to see this deal for what it clearly is—grand larceny at the point of a gun.

—Joseph Farah, *WorldNetDaily*, Oct. 8, 2008

The Paulson plan cannot and will not work. It is hopeless and was from the very moment of its conception. It's a Keynesian solution to an Austrian problem; all the Treasury is doing is ensuring that the crisis is exacerbated and

extended in exactly the same way that Hoover and FDR did.... You cannot
correct fundamental investment misallocations caused by cheap money by
providing more liquidity. It's spraying gasoline on the fire.

—Vox Day to Rich Lowry, *National Review Online,*
Oct. 10, 2008

As I have repeatedly written, the Keynesian and Monetarist economic
models upon which the bailout was conceptually based are useless because
they have been shown to be broken by economic history. They are little better
than the failed Marxian model, even if they lack dependence upon anything
so undeniably absurd as the Labor Theory of Value. Their flaws stem from
the demonstrable fact that their base assumptions are incorrect, their statistics
are unreliable, and predictions based upon them are consistently wrong.

But one need not be a historian or an economist to know that government interventions almost never provide results in accordance with their
proclaimed intentions. Conservatives are not supposed to require relearning
this lesson, given that it has been taught many, many times over the centuries.
And conservatives would do well to keep the words of one chastened *National*
Review editor in mind for the next time the politicians declare the existence
of an emergency that absolutely, positively requires the American people to
hand over yet more money, power and authority to them.

Obama: Backstabber-to-be

January 25, 2009

FOR EIGHT YEARS, conservatives were forced to suffer George W. Bush's betrayals of conservative principles time and time again. The Texas governor who won the Republican nomination as a small government compassionate conservative presided as a big government liberal, created new entitlements and launched pointless wars for democracy as if he was the bastard heir of Woodrow Wilson and Lyndon Baines Johnson. He alienated his base while failing to win over the opposition whose policies he was implementing, and thus ended his presidency as one of the least popular men to ever leave the White House.

Given that, it is amazing that Barack Obama has shown that he intends to follow Bush's blueprint. Although he hasn't even been in office for a week yet, he has already backtracked on Guantanamo, on the Iraqi war, on warrantless spying on Americans and his campaign promise to ban lobbyists from taking jobs in government agencies they had been lobbying.

This was not unexpected. As Justin Raimondo correctly noted at the time, Obama's ritual genuflection to AIPAC after winning the Democratic nomination indicated that instead of holding to the anti-war position that helped him beat Hillary Clinton, Obama would continue the Bush administration's wars in Afghanistan and Iraq. Indeed, he may well expand the war into Pakistan, as the recent Predator strikes there would tend to indicate. And he is almost surely going to take the same pro-Israel stance that Bush did, even though his supporters tend to favor the Palestinian side.

There will be other areas where Obama will likely disappoint his liberal supporters. The most obvious will probably be in those areas related to the economy. The new administration is full of neo-Keynesians, so it is quite likely that Obama will embark on a series of tax cuts rather than tax increases to enhance the stimulus effect of the massive spending programs that have already been announced. It also would not surprise me if Obama were to shock his supporters by turning a 180 on immigration since it is immigration-related expenditures that currently have California on the verge of declaring bankruptcy. Obama is no foe of the multinational corporations, but neither is he their slavish supporter like Bush and many of the Washington Republicans. Given the financial realities and the growing risk of Mexican chaos spilling across the border, this is a policy area ripe for a political betrayal.

Obama also does not appear to be as connected to the teachers unions as many Democrats are, and education was not a primary component of his campaign in the way that George W. Bush's "No Child Left Behind" was. This is a thin basis for projecting any departure from the usual liberal line of spending more money on more teachers for more public schools, but it is a possible area of departure from the norm.

What both panicked Republicans and exultant Democrats must keep in mind is that when in power, the differences between the two parties are mostly illusory. Republican and Democrat are simply two different factions of the same ruling party, and their congressional battles are primarily over political spoils, not political ideology. This is why a "conservative" president will immediately tack left upon taking office, while a "liberal" president will tend to move to the right. We've seen this with Bush 41, Clinton and Bush 43, so there's no reason to expect a massive difference between the previous administration and the current one.

And after eight years of experiencing regular pain between the shoulder blades, conservatives can enjoy the prospect of the knife sticking out of liberal backs.

It will get worse

February 1, 2009

ABOUT 100 INTREPID READERS completed a three-month group study of Murry Rothbard's *America's Great Depression* this weekend. As one reader commented, reading the classic Austrian economic study against the backdrop of the present crisis was like having a giant Power-Point show offering illustrative examples in real time. Throughout the course of the book, it became abundantly clear that there are a disturbing number of similarities between the situation in 1929-1931 and the present one in 2008-2010.

As George Bush did with the creation of the Troubled Asset Relief Program, Herbert Hoover oversaw the founding of an unaccountable organization making secret loans to banks and other failing institutions, the Reconstruction Finance Corporation. As President Barack Obama has done with his "stimulus" program of massive federal spending, Hoover convinced Congress to increase federal spending 30 percent in 1931 alone. In relative terms, this failed spending package was larger than Obama's incredible $775 billion "stimulus" plan, which would only amount to a 25 percent increase even if all of the spending were to take place in 2009.

But one of the more striking things was the way in which the politicians and professional economists almost uniformly expected recovery to take place in 1931, and their panic when their expectations were dashed. Depression set in despite a resort to extreme measures that are all too familiar to the modern observer. Interest rates were cut to historic lows. Millions of dollars were loaned to the states to finance a vast series of public works and stave off unemployment. Taxes were increased at both the state and federal levels, and the Federal Reserve made use of every tool at its disposal to prop up failing banks.

While the stock market is on the verge of another breakdown, official GDP figures have finally reported an official recession. Job losses abounded in the fourth quarter, and both business executives as well as the mainstream economists who completely failed to predict the current contraction are forecasting that economic recovery will begin in the second half of 2009. One year ago, the American Enterprise Institute published the report "Fine in 2009 (Not So Great in 2008)," while just last month, *Business Week* reported: "The idea that the economy will start to recover in the middle of 2009 has really taken hold."

This isn't surprising, since Keynesians who subscribe to the notion of "animal spirits" being the foundation of the economy—or "confidence" as today's Neo-Keynesians describe it—believe that the election of Obama will create the missing sense of American optimism that is required to arrest the contraction and start the economy growing again. This is complete nonsense, of course, and while such childish faith in the unbounded power of magical negritude is touching, Obama himself appears to be perfectly aware that his Hooverian stimulus program is unlikely to succeed. His statement that economic recovery "will take years, not months" is not political hyperbole or an attempt to reduce expectations, it is probably the most intelligent and straightforward declaration he has ever made in public.

Even the wildly unreliable economic statistics reported by the Bureau of Economic Analysis, which recently have varied as much as 133 percent for the same quarter, show that the contraction is just beginning. The comparison of 2008 to 1930 is probably not correct, because the Advance report currently shows 1.3 percent growth for 2008 despite the two negative quarters in Q3 and Q4. While that 1.3 percent will probably be revised down in the preliminary, final and final revised reports, it's not comparable to the 12 percent contraction in 1930. But the crash of the Japanese and South Korean economies, which are expected to show double-digit annualized contraction rates in the next scheduled reports, not only means that the expected recovery will not begin in 2009, it probably won't begin in 2010 either. If the historical parallel holds, and there are a vast array of reasons to believe that it generally will, the contraction will not reach its nadir until 2012 despite the best efforts of the financial authorities to defy economic gravity.

If Obama and Congress were wise, they would quit the King Canute act and let the long-suppressed market forces wash away the vast edifice of failed corporations and misallocated resources, which, after some horrific short-term economic dislocation, would permit the economy to begin growing again. Unfortunately, it is clear that this merry band of interventionists have elected to follow the Hoover/Roosevelt example, with all of the long-term economic destruction that implies.

A bad start

February 8, 2009

I T HAS ONLY BEEN A FEW WEEKS, but already it is clear that FDR's legacy of the famous first 100 days is in no jeopardy. Of course, given the anti-constitutional regime the Roosevelt administration turned out to be, this is probably a good thing. And in the first month of the Obama administration, four things have become readily apparent about its nature.

First, Obama not only has a lack of executive experience, he also possesses no natural talent for management or executive decision making. While a large segment of the American electorate clearly believes that a mellifluous baritone and an ability to read from teleprompter is tantamount to executive excellence, the numerous nomination scandals and the bungling of the $827 billion stimulus bill indicate that the Obama administration will soon make even the disastrous Bush and Clinton administrations look like paragons of competence.

The second thing is that Obama has clarified what was never seriously in doubt: All of his grand promises of inspiration were nothing more than campaign rhetoric designed to appeal to the young, the naïve and the stupid. He promised hope and change, but what he has done instead is prey upon the widespread fear of national catastrophe to engage in the usual legislative bullying so often seen in past Democratic Congresses. Ironically, the objective measure of House and Senate vote tallies will almost certainly prove that both George W. Bush and Bill Clinton governed in a far more bipartisan manner than Obama will.

Yes, he did win, but then, so did almost every single president before him. And so did every Republican senator and congressman whom that argument is supposed to impress.

Third is the insane level of expectations that have arisen on the part of his supporters... or perhaps devotees would be a more accurate term. Obama's more sober supporters should be alarmed, not amused, by the bizarre celebrity pledges, the quasi-cultish kitsch, and the overheated jungle fever that we are informed is now raging among liberal women of a certain age.

I launched an e-mail inquiry. Many women—not too surprisingly—were dreaming about sex with the president. In these dreams, the women replaced Michelle with greater or lesser guilt or, in the case of a 62-year-old woman in North Florida, whose dream was reported to me by her daughter, found a fully above-board solution:

> *"Michelle had divorced Barack because he had become 'too much of a star.' He then married my mother, who was oh so proud to be the first lady," the daughter wrote me.*

—The *New York Times*, Feb. 5, 2009

No, unfortunately, it isn't surprising at all. It's not exactly new for women to openly fantasize about sex with a president, or otherwise servicing him, but this phenomenon has not historically been an indicator of a successful presidency. It has instead been precisely the opposite. And even if Obama were more than the glib, empty-suited mediocrity that he is, he could not possibly live up to the irrational ideals being projected upon him.

The fourth and most interesting thing about the launch of the Obama administration is that the man appears to have the makings of a genuine populist streak in him. His announcement of executive compensation caps on corporations requesting government bailout money was a brilliant move with an appeal so broad that even die-hard libertarian capitalists can enthusiastically embrace it. The fact that Barney Frank failed to grasp why Obama's popping a cap in the oversized backsides of banking fat cats is so popular and sought to transform the plan from a perfectly sensible means of dissuading corporate welfare into pure socialist spite doesn't detract from the insight evident behind the administration's action. It will be intriguing to see if Obama manages to learn that following the will of the people rather than the will of the party leaders is the way to become a successful president, as this would have significant implications for vital matters such as immigration and foreign policy.

This is more than a little unlikely, but because Obama is clearly a survivor, it should not be completely discounted at this early stage. The probability, of course, is that Obama will simply continue where Bush left off, desperately expanding government in a futile attempt to stave off the inexorable economic forces that were set into motion over the last decade. One need only note that Obama's first priority has been to attempt fixing years of credit inflation and massive spending by spending even more money to know that his presidency is likely to end up as a failed one.

Stimulus spelled out

February 15, 2009

AMIDST THE DIRE predictions of imminent catastrophe if Obama's stimulus package were not passed by the Congress, and equally dismal prophecies of how the stimulus will extend what is looking like a doozy of a depression, there has been a near-complete failure on the media's part to explain the core principles behind the fiscal stimulus to the American people. This is due to the near-complete ignorance of economics on the part of the mainstream media; one can hardly expect them to explain what they do not understand. Some readers may find it useful, then, if I attempt to rectify the situation.

In 1987, the new Federal Reserve chairman, Alan Greenspan, averted a financial meltdown in the fall when he used a variety of aggressive monetary policies to inject liquidity into the financial system, temporarily driving down the overnight repo rate from 7.5 percent to 5.5 percent in a matter of days. Interest rates, as measured by the effective federal funds rate, were slashed from 8.5 percent in late September to 5.5 percent in mid-December. The success of his actions in stabilizing the financial system gave great credence to the Monetarist school of economics, epitomized by Nobel Prize-winner Milton Friedman, who had long asserted that management of the money supply was the key to preventing the economy from contracting.

Friedman had long blamed the Federal Reserve for failing to respond aggressively enough to the stock market crash of 1929, and in collaboration with his co-author Anna Schwartz, had claimed that a more aggressive lowering of interest rates would have prevented the Great Depression. Greenspan's successful navigation of the 1987 crisis appeared to prove conclusively that the monetarist thesis was correct, and in 2002 led to current Federal Reserve chairman Ben Bernanke making a humorous admission in his speech made in honor of Friedman's 90th birthday.

Let me end my talk by abusing slightly my status as an official representative of the Federal Reserve. I would like to say to Milton and Anna: Regarding the Great Depression. You're right, we did it. We're very sorry. But thanks to you, we won't do it again.

Similar rate-cutting actions were begun in July 1990, February 1995, May 2000 and June 2006 when signs of economic contraction appeared. However, as the cuts came more often and the target rates fell lower, it began to become clear that these liquidity injections were no longer having the desired effect of propping up stock, real estate and commodity prices. Now that interest rates are effectively at zero but the economy is still in the process of shrinking, the failure of the monetarist theory has become obvious, especially given the continued failure of the Japanese economy to respond to extreme interest rate-cutting following its 1989 crash.

The failure of monetary policy has caused many economists and politicians to return to the Keynesian school, which primarily concerns itself with fiscal policy. Just as the Federal Reserve's control of the price of money—the interest rate—is the primary tool of the monetarists, government spending is the primary tool of the Keynesians, or more properly, Neo-Keynesians, since even the biggest fans of John Maynard Keynes have been forced to acknowledge at least some of the fundamental flaws in his economic theories. The core of the Keynesian theory of economic contraction is a failure of demand to meet supply, or to put it more simply, people are refusing to buy enough stuff to keep the economy growing. This is why Neo-Keynesians like Nobel Prize-winner Paul Krugman worry about "the looming hole in the U.S. economy," by which he means the difference between what could be produced by the economy and what will actually be bought.

Filling this gap is the purpose of the stimulus package; it represents the government stepping in to buy what consumers will not. In his column entitled "The Destructive Center," Krugman fearfully cites the Congressional Budget Office's calculation that this gap between potential supply and expected demand is $2.9 trillion over the next three years. His worries are based upon the idea that the $787 billion stimulus package which passed last week is only one-quarter the size it would have to be to fill the demand gap.

The real problem, however, is that the Keynesian model is simply incorrect. It is based on the very crude idea that the economy, as measured in Gross

Domestic Product, can be accurately summarized by the following formula: GDP = C+I+G+(X-M). In English, this means the economy is equal to consumer spending (C), plus investment (I), plus government spending (G), plus (exports (X) minus imports (M)). Since government can only control government spending directly, any failure of consumer spending must be compensated by increasing government spending. That is what the $787 billion is nominally intended to do, to make up for the decline in consumer spending.

However, this is complete balderdash, as a third economic theory points out. The Austrian school, to which I myself subscribe, has repeatedly shown that neither monetary nor fiscal policy are capable of doing more than delaying an economic contraction, and that using them to delay contraction only extends and exacerbates the contraction when it eventually arrives. Austrian theory teaches that credit inflation, which is how they describe the monetarist tool of injecting liquidity by cutting interest rates, leads to investment and consumption booms that will inevitably be followed by busts. It is, in fact, the only economic school with a reasonable explanation for the economic cycles so readily seen in the historical data.

Consider a hypothetical example of an economy in which there are 100 cars. Because a car lasts for 10 years, every year 10 cars wear out and are replaced. But things have been going well and people are getting wealthier, so five of them buy second cars. The three car makers each sell five cars, and there are now 105 cars in the economy. However, in the second year, there is a stock market panic due to the failure of the Madagascar cashew harvest, so the central bank gets nervous and slashes interest rates. Ten cars wear out, and 10 are replaced, but thanks to the low interest rates, the automakers can offer zero percent leases and other creative forms of payment, which encourage 20 people to buy second cars. There are now 125 cars in the economy. Interest rates stay low for the next three years, and people continue to take advantage of the new car-financing deals, until there are 185 cars in an economy that only required 100 five years before.

Then, an Icelandic bank bets heavily on the Norwegian cod harvest and goes under. The global stock markets drop, people feel less wealthy, and car drivers decide to reduce their automotive consumption. Ten cars wear out, as always, but instead of being replaced by new cars, they are replaced by cars that still have seven good years on them sold by two-car owners who decide they really don't need their second car anymore. The car economy shrinks by 10 cars to 175 cars, but even worse, the annual gap between the demand and the supply capacity is 30 cars. So, what is the solution?

The monetarists would recommend cutting interest rates, but since they are already low, that's not a viable option. (And then, there is the fact that because low interest rates caused the problem in the first place, they cannot reasonably be expected to fix it.) The Keynesians would attempt to stimulate the economy by having the government fill in the demand gap by buying 30 cars, but this will only put off the problem for a year since there will be 30 more used cars available to the 10 people who will require replacement vehicles next year. The optimal solution is the Austrian one, which is to leave the economy alone and wait for the extra cars to wear out. This may be frustrating to the would-be hero politician who wishes to solve the problem through decisive legislation, but it is the only solution that will not make things materially worse in the future.

Doing nothing is admittedly difficult in times of crisis. But it is always wise to keep in mind that there is no crisis so severe that government intervention cannot make it worse.

War or wu-wei

February 23, 2009

L AST WEEK, I explained the purpose of Obama's $787 billion stimulus bill and why it is doomed to fail. Intriguingly, Wall Street's massive vote of no confidence in the bill, which saw the Dow Jones Industrial Average drop 6.2 percent last week and smash through significant technical support at 7,550, seems to have shaken the confidence of some of the economists who had most strongly supported the stimulus notion.

I was genuinely surprised to see *New York Times* columnist Thomas Friedman declare this weekend that he was beginning to feel that spending billions more on GM and Chrysler was "subsidizing the losers" and that the pair of "giant wealth-destruction" machines should be permitted to go into bankruptcy. While it's true that in vintage left-liberal fashion, Friedman calls for the federal government to hand over the $20 billion that the floundering automakers want to venture capital firms investing in technology instead, the mere fact that a left-leaning opinion leader has begun to grasp the concept that not all government spending intrinsically generates economic growth represents a giant leap forward for the economically illiterate crowd.

But if Friedman's comments were surprising, those of his fellow *New York Times* colleague, Paul Krugman, were downright shocking. I have been extremely critical of the Nobel Prize-winning economist, particularly for his complete failure to even begin comprehending the basics of Austrian economics, but it was remarkable to read his Feb. 19 column, in which he departed from the conventional Keynesian myth that has claimed for decades that FDR's New Deal ended the Great Depression.

Your grandfather's recession, on the other hand, was something like the Great Depression, which happened in spite of the Fed's efforts, not because of them. When a stock market bubble and a credit boom collapsed, bringing down much of the banking system with them, the Fed tried to revive the economy with low interest rates – but even rates barely above zero weren't low enough to end a prolonged era of high unemployment. ... [T]he Great Depression did eventually come to an end, but that was thanks to an enormous war, something we'd rather not emulate.

Unfortunately, one can see that Krugman is still clinging to the Monetarist notion that the depression occurred in spite of the Fed's efforts, which only goes to show that he still has not made the connection between credit-inflated malinvestment of the sort that funneled investment resources into unproductive, wealth-destroying sectors such as the automakers and housing, and the inevitable busts that follow these inflation-induced investment booms. And yet, there are some signs that even the world's leading Keynesian has begun to recognize that time and markets are a more reliable solution to economic crisis than government intervention.

[C]onsider the plunge in auto sales. Again, that's bad news for the near term. But at current sales rates, as the finance blog Calculated Risk points out, it would take about 27 years to replace the existing stock of vehicles. Most cars will be junked long before that, either because they've worn out or because they've become obsolete, so we're building up a pent-up demand for cars. The same story can be told for durable goods and assets throughout the economy: given time, the current slump will end itself, the way slumps did in the 19th century.

Calculated Risk's calculation is quite interesting in light of the auto economy I described in last week's column, in which the 80 excess cars produced in five automotive boom years required eight years for replacement. The truth is that all slumps end themselves as the contraction burns out the malinvested sectors; the only reason that slumps have not ended themselves the way they did as late as 1921 is due to futile government attempts to battle the symptoms rather than the central disease. And since the primary justification supporting these futile attempts is the failed economic theories of John Maynard Keynes, it is a good sign that even long-time liberal Neo-Keynesians are beginning to question them.

The Great Depression finally came to an end in the United States because millions of men were removed from the unemployment rolls and put to work smashing the means of production and reducing the labor pool on two foreign continents. There is no great secret behind the incredible economic growth of the '50s and '60s; if GM were to blow up all of the automotive factories in Japan, Germany, Korea, India and China, it would be able to assure itself of similarly explosive growth in its auto sales for the next decade. If Obama wants to end, rather than exacerbate, the current economic contraction, he has two effective choices: Resist the impulse to intervene in the economy or attack foreign lands.

The fact that larger troop deployments and tax increases were announced by the administration last week tends to indicate that Obama will lean toward war rather than wu-wei.

Interview with Thomas Woods

March 1, 2009

Congratulations on "Meltdown: A Free-Market Look at Why the Stock Market Collapsed, the Economy Tanked, and Government Bailouts Will Make Things Worse" hitting the bestseller lists. The fact that you were the first to publish a book about the financial crisis so soon after the September crash indicates that you may have anticipated it. You're an Austrian economist, so did you find that your knowledge of Austrian theory helped you put the crises in context?

The book is in itself an Austrian analysis from start to finish. For anyone who doesn't know, the Austrian School of Economics is a free-market school of economics that includes luminaries such as Ludwig von Mises and Friedrich von Hayek, the latter of whom won the Nobel Prize in 1974. I would say the bulk of the economists who saw the crisis coming were Austrians. There is no economic school of thought from which a higher proportion of economists warned that the housing market was indeed experiencing a bubble, that it was going to burst and that the rate of home price increases was unsustainable. That was an Austrian warning. I wrote the book because I could not stand listening to the conventional wisdom, day in and day out, saying that this was all the fault of the free market so now we need the geniuses in Washington to fix everything for us. That is just an obscenity.

When you say the government created the housing bubble, are you also including the Federal Reserve as part of the equation?

In my chapter on the subject, I show there were a half-dozen contributing factors, and some of them were clearly government factors. For example, Fannie Mae and Freddy Mac, which are quasi-public, quasi-private agencies whose exact status was not altogether clear to people. It was more or less taken for granted that they would be bailed out by taxpayers if it should come to that, and they got special privileges such as tax and regulatory breaks that were not available to anyone else in the housing market. All of this added up to an incentive to take greater risks than a truly free market actor would take. There's been a lot of talk among conservatives about the Community Reinvestment Act, which was a Carter-era law that required banks to make loans against their best interests so as not to be sued for so-called discrimination. On the left, there's been a lot of frustration that this act has been targeted [for helping cause the housing bubble]. They point out that since it dates back to Carter and the late '70s, how can it be blamed for a bubble 30 years later? The answer is that the act didn't really have enforcement teeth until the mid-1990s under Clinton. It's not like we're just desperately looking around to blame the most irrelevant thing.

There are other factors, too. But as for the Fed, although it's technically true that it is not a government agency, I think it would be wrong to argue that it's a purely private thing. Again, we're dealing with a weird amalgam of public and private. The Fed was created by an act of Congress; its board is appointed by the U.S. government, and it enjoys monopoly privileges that are granted to it by the U.S. government. So, it's not a purely government agency, but it's dramatically different than any free market actor and would not have spontaneously come into existence under a free-market system. If it could have done so, Congress would not have needed to create it.

How long do you expect the current contraction to run, and how big do you expect the decline to be in terms of GDP?

I know this will sound like a cop-out, but I don't put much stock in economic forecasting, and I am critical of GDP as a metric to measure the economy. It would be one thing if we had a genuinely free market with no government involvement at all. Then you might be able to make some kind of ballpark estimates. But I have no idea what the federal government is going to try! It's at least within the realm of possibility that the general public could become so angry that the federal government changes course, tries something different or stops continuing to attack the economy with a 2×4. But I think it's more likely that they'll keep trying unprecedented things, and that makes it very, very hard to predict how long this will go on. I think the more it does that, the longer it will go on. I think it is at least possible that we could have a stagnation as long as Japan's, which was well over a decade.

What are some of the other myths about the Great Depression?

We're hearing almost every single one of them repeated. We're hearing myths that no reputable historian, regardless of his political allegiances, would repeat. I cannot believe there are still people who believe that Herbert Hoover was a supporter of the free market who just sat back and allowed the depression to unfold before his eyes. That's just flatly false. Another big myth is the idea that FDR lifted the country out of the Great Depression. A third myth would be that the Depression was caused by the free market, and the lesson that should be learned from that is that we can't allow that again. In fact, we now have the same Federal Reserve activity and expansion of the money supply that leads to the Austrian boom-bust cycle.

The equity boom ended in 2000. The housing boom ended in 2005. Which sector do you expect to recover first?

I really don't know. Unfortunately, the collapse in housing affects practically everything, and not just because of the securitized mortgage debts that are held by so many investors and institutions, but also because of everything that goes into a house. The appliances, the raw materials, the building supplies and the trucking and shipping services required to move those things across the country, all of those things are affected. So, I honestly don't know, but here's my suspicion: Retail outlets that cater to basic consumer needs will do relatively well.

It's conventional wisdom that the Smoot-Hawley tariff contributed greatly to the Great Depression, but how does that make sense given that imports were only 5.1 percent of the U.S. economy and the balance of trade's contribution to GDP was a negative 1.1 percent in 1929?

I don't think it did play a big role. I think those who think of themselves as free-market economists have exaggerated the importance of Smoot-Hawley. It didn't help; anything that shrinks the extent of the division of labor is going to have an impoverishing effect, so it didn't help. Part of the reason so much emphasis has been placed on Smoot-Hawley is that there are some free market economists who are operating without the benefit of Austrian trade-cycle theory. At the same time, they know they don't want to blame the free market, but they don't have a coherent explanation for what happened. So, they flounder around, looking for some form of government intervention to explain why this downturn occurred.

This column is an abridged version of Vox Day's interview with Thomas Woods. The complete transcript of the interview can be read at Vox Popoli.

Raising a white flag in the drug war

March 8, 2009

CONSERVATIVES TEND to assume that, unlike dirty, treasonous liberals, they are on the side of truth, justice, liberty and the American way. This is not without reason, as most of the time, they are. However, for nearly 30 years, conservatives have been guilty of one of the greatest abuses of American liberties in American history, and have actively abetted the growth of central government by their thoughtless support for the war on drugs.

As Jonah Goldberg pointed out in his excellent book, *Liberal Fascism*, the use of military terminology to address domestic policy issues is a historically progressive concept, first articulated as a "moral equivalent to war" by William James, then put into action by the Italian fascists. From Benito Mussolini's "Battle of the Grains" to Lyndon Johnson's "War on Poverty," the propagandistic justification of extreme policy measures had always been a hallmark of the Left, until it was foolishly adopted by conservatives at the behest of the Reagan administration. Of course, like every previous left-wing pseudo-war, the war on drugs has been a complete debacle, has cost billions of dollars without realizing a single one of its objectives, and has accomplished little more than increasing the size and scope of federal power.

There is nothing—absolutely nothing—conservative about the war on drugs. Conservativism is supposed to involve a certain regard for the traditions of the past, and for the greater part of American history, drugs were entirely legal. George Washington grew hemp. Thomas Jefferson wrote the first draft of the Declaration of Independence on hemp paper. And, as everyone knows, the "Coca" in Coca-Cola refers to the extract of coca leaf that was once an ingredient in the popular drink. Coca-Cola was not entirely cocaine-free until 1929. And note that the 1913 creation of the Federal Reserve and the federal income tax was closely followed by the 1914 ban on cocaine; the 63rd United States Congress was clearly not a Congress in which conservative principles dominated.

Advocates for the drug war often hypothesize nightmare scenarios where the legalization of drugs will lead to chaos and total social breakdown, constructing fantasies about legions of chemically addled criminals preying upon the helpless citizenry while in search of their next high. But, as has been seen in Colombia and more recently in Mexico, it is actually the illegalization of drugs that causes social devastation, as the drug war's efforts to interdict supply only increases the price of drugs and therefore the profit of the criminal gangs willing to trade in them. As these profits grow, so too does the power of the drug-dealing criminals, until they are strong enough to directly contest local and state government authorities. Or, as is all too often the case, simply purchase and control them.

Americans should have learned their lesson from prohibition. The human demand for chemical stimulation is a demonstrable historical fact, and no amount of television ads or lecturing schoolchildren is going to significantly reduce that demand. The benefits of the drug war to the American people are trivial and their costs, in terms of money, human misery and liberty, are extraordinarily high. Thus, I was encouraged to read Pat Buchanan's recent article on *WorldNetDaily*, in which one of America's leading conservatives finally recognized the stark choice that so many conservatives have sought to avoid facing for three decades.

How does one win a drug war when millions of Americans who use recreational drugs are financing the cartels bribing, murdering and beheading to win the war and keep self-indulgent Americans supplied with drugs? There are two sure ways to end this war swiftly: Milton's way and Mao's way. Mao Zedong's communists killed users and suppliers alike, as social parasites. Milton Friedman's way is to decriminalize drugs and call off the war. Which is the greater evil? Legalized narcotics for America's young—or a failed state of 110,000 million on our southern border?

The greater evil is eminently clear. The greater evil is the evil that requires repeated violations of the American Constitution, the continuous rape of American liberties, the pointless imprisonment of millions of harmless Americans and the probable collapse of the Mexican government. The fact that the Obama administration is now citing Mexico's narco war as an excuse to limit Second Amendment rights should suffice to prove to conservatives that the time has come to end the war on drugs. Yes, Mr. Buchanan, America must raise the white flag in the drug war.

And if America's young should elect to narcotize themselves into oblivion, is that not their right in a country that claims to be free? Considering the incredible amount of economic destruction that has occurred in only six weeks of Democratic rule, to say nothing of the massive debts which are being piled upon their generation, it's not as if they'll lack for good cause. Indeed, the thought of four more years of the ongoing presidential debacle might well encourage even the most staunch conservative drug warrior to think about firing up a fattie.

Don't believe the hope

March 15, 2009

FOUR DAYS. Just four days. That's how long it took for the panglossian pundits to declare that the economic destruction that has seen trillions of dollars evaporate in a mushroom cloud of debt and derivatives is rapidly coming to an end. Last week, the S&P 500 rose 10.7 percent, recovering less than 13 percent of its total decline from 1255 in September. This sharp, but very short-term rise already has long-time permabulls such as Larry Kudlow suggesting that instead of pushing back their predictions of economic recovery from mid-2009 to the end of the year, economists should be considering the possibility of GDP growth in the second quarter.

This is fascinating, especially since in addition to the stock market's best weekly performance since November 2008, last week also saw the culmination of the slapfight between Kudlow's former partner-in-crime on CNBC, Jim Cramer, and *The Daily Show*'s comedian/commentator Jon Stewart. Stewart, who prefers to conceal his sharply liberal opinions behind a jester's pose, nevertheless did the nation a great service in pointing out the way that televised market cheerleaders such as Cramer and Kudlow never take any responsibility for their oft-failed predictions or their incorrect recommendations.

Listen, you knew what the banks were doing, and yet were touting it for months and months. The entire network was, and so now to pretend that this was some sort of crazy, once-in-a-lifetime tsunami that nobody could have seen coming is disingenuous at best and criminal at worst.... These guys' companies were on a Sherman's march through their companies, financed by our 401(k)s, and all the incentives of their companies were for short-term profit. And they burned the f—ing house down with our money and walked away rich as hell, and you guys knew that that was going on.

The behavior of Cramer, Kudlow, and their colleagues in reacting to this recent market bounce, despite the complete destruction of their credibility, makes it dishearteningly clear that nothing, short of the nuclear destruction of New York City, will prevent the media whores of the financial markets from doing their best to convince Americans to keep sending more of their money to Wall Street. If they cannot obtain it directly, through stockbrokers pitching deceptive investment marketing pitches such as "dollar-cost averaging" and "buy-and-hold," they will turn to the federal government to obtain it for them, either through indirect mechanisms such as the 401(k) or direct transfers of the sort that both the Bush and Obama administration have executed.

The reality is that no long-term investor has made any money in the stock market since 1997, and since market prices are not indexed for inflation, there has actually been no net capital profit in them for the last 14 years... and this is not even taking into account the fact that the composition of some major market indices are modified as often as once a year. Wall Street is rather like a shark; it depends on a constant inflow of money if it is to stay healthy, which is why its cheerleaders are always so desperate to keep Americans gambling by investing in it. But what is good for the predator is very seldom good for the prey.

What is important to remember is that no market ever goes straight up or straight down. Even during the great Greenspan bull of the 1990s, there were the occasional down periods. And, in every bear market, there has been the occasional dead-cat bounce and optimistic rally attempt. For example, last week marks not the first, not the second, but the fifth large rally on the Dow since it began falling in earnest back in late 2007.

History strongly suggests that there will be an extended market rally taking place in the near future. This may be the start of it, or there may be, as the Elliott Wave technicians believe, one more down-leg before the counter-trend rally starts. But regardless of what the markets do, it is important to keep in mind that they are not the economy, and inflated prices of anything, from candy bars to blue-chip stocks, are not the same thing as economic growth. Both the monetary authorities and the fiscal authorities are now operating in full inflationary mode, which as we know from the Great Depression and a host of other historical examples, is liable to extend rather than end the economic crisis.

There's nothing wrong with hope. It is an excellent quality. But acting on the basis of false hope rather than observable reality is a recipe for disaster, for individuals and nations alike.

No bonuses, no bailouts

March 23, 2009

I AM NOT A DEMOCRAT, nor am I a Republican. In fact, I have never voted for either a Democrat or a Republican in any of the past presidential elections for which I was eligible to vote. Ronald Reagan and Ron Paul are the only two Republicans for whom I would have been willing to vote; I was too young to vote for the former, and the Republican Party prevented me from having the opportunity to vote for the latter.

Needless to say, nominating John McCain looks just as foolish in retrospect as it did at the time. It seems he wasn't quite as electable as his media champions repeatedly insisted he was.

One point that I have attempted to drive home throughout the eight years I have been writing this column is that while the bases of the two major parties are made up of two very different kinds of people, the national politicians who purport to represent their party ideologies in the White House, the Senate and the House of Representatives do not, in fact, do so. Instead, they make up a single bifactional ruling party that is far more concerned with maintaining the status quo than with actually championing the views of either of the ideological parties that elect them.

George Bush spent eight years demonstrating this, as he appeared to take no small pleasure in repeatedly violating the Republican Party faithful's beliefs in small, limited and decentralized government. There was virtually nothing conservative or even republican about his administration, which massively expanded the size and scope of the federal government. Barack Obama has begun his time in office in much the same manner that George Bush finished his last term, by repeatedly violating his campaign promises and betraying the base of the people to whom he owes his election.

It is revealing to see that regardless of whether a "conservative" or "the most liberal member of the U.S. Senate" sits in the Oval Office, their economic policies remain almost identical. One would have thought that a conservative president would have permitted the normal liquidation of insolvent banks rather than order the Treasury to spend billions of dollars it does not have to bail out the owners of the bankrupt institutions, just as one would have thought that a liberal president would not prefer to lavish vast amounts of money on banking executives rather than on low-income individuals at risk of losing their homes to foreclosure. But, the present crisis has shown that Wall Street always comes first in the priorities of the Washington party, regardless of whether they happen to wear "Democrat" or "Republican" on their sleeves.

Now the propaganda arms of both parties are shrieking madly in an attempt to head off and redirect the growing bipartisan rage of the American people. The Republican media has, all too characteristically, taken a ludicrous and politically suicidal approach by taking umbrage at the clawback taxes that will recover the millions in bonus money outrageously given to executives at the bailout banks. The Democrat media, on the other hand, is busy attempting to ensure that anger is focused on the insane behavior of the bankers rather than on the Democratic politicians who are now rapidly trying to undo the more egregious results of their recent actions.

What both medias are missing is that the American people do not and have never supported the bailouts! Americans know perfectly well that the offending bonuses are just a small fraction of the total bailout—they want their bailout money back, too! While the politicians and their propaganda arms appear to take it as given that America without AIG, Goldman Sachs, Bank of America and Citigroup would be a post-apocalyptic wasteland inhabited only by starving mutants, very few people who don't live in Washington, D.C., or New York City share this belief. In fact, a noticeable percentage of them believe that the nation would be much better off if the all of the "best and brightest" in the financial industry were unemployed, which is a perfectly reasonable attitude considering that many of these so-called "best and brightest" were at least partially responsible, along with the national politicians, in creating the financial debacle in the first place.

As the crisis has made clear, neither Washington nor Wall Street can survive without the resources of the American people. It is long past time for Americans to discover that they can survive, and even thrive, without being forced to place the interests of Washington and Wall Street ahead of their own. No more bonuses. No more bailouts.

Speaking truth to the prime minister

March 30, 2009

Daniel Hannan's fiery speech addressing Gordon Brown at the European Parliament electrified the Internet when it was broadcast on YouTube. Vox Day interviewed the iconoclastic Englishman about Brown, Britain, and the global economic crisis on March 26, 2009.

Your speech criticizing Gordon Brown's incompetent stewardship of the UK economy was extraordinarily well received, not just in Britain, but around the world. Meanwhile, the leader of the opposition party, David Cameron, has been rather quiet on that front. Why has Mr. Cameron been so reluctant to say the things you said to Mr. Brown?

Because in the British system, there's this great thing about the loyal opposition. And when you get a crisis like this, that comes out of a clear blue sky, nobody wants to risk looking unpatriotic, so you have to be measured and tempered in how you respond, which is completely understandable. The result of it, unfortunately, is that a lot of people are left with saying, wait a minute, hang on, nobody is saying what I would like them to say. All the politicians seem to be in this together. A lot of people felt that a cartel of politicians and bankers were setting policy in defiance of public opinion. Those were the people I was trying to speak for.

It's interesting to hear you say "coming out of a blue sky," because at least in the states, there was definitely a group of contrarians such as Roubini and me who were on record as far back as 2002 saying that the housing crash was going to affect the financial system. Did no one in England see that?

There were a few people who saw it, but not anywhere in the mainstream. Certainly none of the three big parties were warning about this except in very general terms about house prices being a bit too much and that sort of thing. Nobody was expecting a run on the banks; we haven't had one of those since the early 19th century. Certainly no one was expecting nationalizing our banks. Even at their most socialist, the Labour Party barely dreamed of doing that.

The European Union is described as everything from a free-trade union to the EUSSR. How do you, as a European member of Parliament, see the EU today?

The EU is a racket: a mechanism for taking money from the taxpayer and handing it to Eurocrats.... The EU's equivalent of the Prague Spring was the "No" votes of 2004 and 2005. Nobody believes anymore that if only the question could be fairly put, then all the people would come around to it. They've lost whatever ideological impetus they had, but they understand that their position in society depends upon their maintaining the status quo. Since the "No" votes across the EU, Eurocrats have given up on the idea that their system will ever win approval. That's what makes them so tetchy.

Given the authoritarian behavior of the EU bureaucracy, why has the Tory Party been so reluctant to embrace popular euroskepticism?

It's not that they actually believe in a European super state. It's that they have this Burkeian instinct to try to work with the status quo, to prefer evolution to revolution.... No one would have gone from first principles into this ridiculous racket where we're run by an unelected bureaucracy that passes 84 percent of our laws. But, they don't want to break the whole thing up. They haven't yet gotten into the mindset that the whole thing is beyond reform and that you need to just cut loose. But I think we'll get there in the end.

Do you think an ongoing period of economic contraction will see the British people demand to leave the European Union?

They already do! The latest opinion poll was conducted by the BBC a week ago, and showed that 55 percent of voters want to leave the EU. It's true that this position isn't yet shared by any major political party, but that moment will come: Politicians cannot swim forever against the current of public opinion.

Which do you believe will be the first nation to attempt to leave the European Union? And will it be successful?

I think it will be us. Because we have a different political system, because we, like you, have a majoritarian system rather than a party list system, which means that politicians cannot so easily disregard their voters as happens under a proportional system.... My guess is that it will probably happen in Britain first, and we will go for some kind of EFTA-type deal, some kind of associate membership where we're in a free market but outside all the rest of it. And I think once we do that, once we set that precedent, a whole bunch of countries will be queuing up to copy.... [I]t may well be that the euro will fracture. Really quite mainstream, serious people are now saying that it's when, rather than if, a country leaves the single currency.

In your speech, you mentioned that one cannot spend one's way out of a recession. This would appear to contradict the neo-Keynesian approach of Alastair Darling and the U.S. fiscal authorities. Do you subscribe to a different economic model?

Yes, certainly! We saw where the Keynesian model led! We pursued it from the '30s to the '70s. And it ended up in recession, stagnation, inflation and debt. It's much easier to begin a government program under the guise of counter-cyclical spending than it is to terminate it, so you end up with the state becoming more and more bloated. It's a measure of how panicked people are, that they've forgotten all of the lessons of that unhappy period.

The U.S. president recently gave the prime minister a gift that consisted of 25 region-one DVDs that don't work in Britain. How was this regarded there?

Badly. The guy is a complete idiot, Brown. But he's our complete idiot, and we don't like to see him being slapped around like this. That's for us to do.

Speaking of Obama, you've expressed some sympathies for President Obama on your blog in the past. What is your perception of his performance to date? How has his stewardship of the economy been any different than Gordon Brown's?

I think his stewardship of the economy has been bad. I think the Republican Party had been pretty bad in the run-up to this. One of the reasons why I had gone off the GOP, which I'm normally very loyal to, is because I could see them losing touch with all the things that used to make them so successful. They had become the party of steel tariffs, and the party of trampling over states rights, particularly with the marriage amendment. They'd become the party of big spending and federal deficits, and in the end they became the party of bailouts and nationalizations. One of the reasons I was in favor of Obama winning—without any great enthusiasm, I might add—is that I thought the Republicans would benefit from a period out of office where they could go back and remember what used to make them successful. And so far, so good! It is striking that an immediate consequence of the Obama presidency is that a lot of Republican congressmen who voted for the first spraying-around of money under Bush unanimously voted against the second one.

Have you given any thought to eventually running for parliament in the UK?

No, not for the moment, anyway.... We have a very, very weak parliament. We have a much weaker legislature than you have, and it's weaker than it's ever been. A measure of how weak it is is that we didn't even have a vote on our bailouts, on our stimulus package. It was just decreed by the executive.... One of the beauties of your system is that you have a proper separation of powers, so a legislator can make an honorable career for himself without wanting to join the executive. As things stand, that can't happen in the British system. I'm very keen to import the most successful elements of your system—open primaries, elected sheriffs, a local sales tax, local referendums, the direct election of public officials—and I've written a book about how to do it called "The Plan: Twelve Months to Renew Britain."

In Britain, we are run by a massive bureaucracy, and the position of the elected person is incredibly weak and is getting weaker every day. One of the reasons we are in this financial mess is that the budgets are set by members of the executive who are personal beneficiaries of state spending, rather than by the members of the legislature who are champions of the taxpayer.

This column is an abridged version of Vox Day's interview with Daniel Hannan. The complete transcript of the interview is available at Vox Popoli.

Grow and die

April 6, 2009

“GROW OR DIE” is one of the corporate mantras of the late 20th century. The peculiar shape that corporations now take, courtesy of the perversion of capitalism that is modern finance-driven corporatism, requires constant growth. Rather like great white sharks, which must keep swimming to avoid suffocation, modern corporations have had to keep growing to avoid seeing their stock prices punished by an increasingly avaricious Wall Street.

From 1948 to 1985, the financial sector accounted for around 12 percent of American corporate profits, never reaching 20 percent nor dipping below 5 percent. After 1985, however, the profits of the sector rose dramatically, going from 19 percent in 1986 to 41 percent in 2000. That meant that more than 40 cents out of every corporate dollar of profit was paper profit, not generated by actual wealth-generating activity, but by monetary inflation and corporate gambling.

Since paper profits cannot generate real wealth, but can be exchanged for it, this had the result of creating a monetary illusion of national wealth and economic wellbeing that was first reflected in the tech equity bubble, and then again in the real-estate bubble. But none of the profits in those sectors were ever genuine, which is why the financial corporations that recorded them were not able to make use of them to generate additional profit and why they are in such dire straits today.

Complicating the problem of the paper profits of the financial sector is the fact that due to the bizarre incentive structure created by a stock-option driven reward system, many of the non-financial corporations evolved into quasi-financial corporations themselves in search of these inflated profits that would drive up their stock prices, and as a result, their executive compensation. For example, GMAC, the financial operation that GM partially spun off to

Cerberus in 2007, recorded profits equal to one-third of GM's total profits before the fall 2008 financial crash began. Even worse, many large companies increased their sales through mergers and acquisitions funded by taking on corporate debt, a risky action made all the more easy by the Federal Reserve's relaxed monetary policy.

Debt for corporations is rather like steroids for athletes. It pumps the company up and provides it with enhanced capabilities in the short term, but is extremely detrimental to the long-term health of the corporation. Many otherwise perfectly healthy companies have been forced into bankruptcy, not because they had no customers or were not able to sell their products at a reasonable profit, but because they could not do so while simultaneously paying off the debt with which they had previously expanded.

The $1.1 trillion plan announced by the smiling leaders of the G20 nations is similar to the attempt of corporations to grow through leverage in that: a) it is an attempt to solve a problem by growing larger, and b) nearly all the money that is to be spent will be borrowed. This vast increase in government spending will have an economic effect, indeed, in the technology sector the effect of the previous stimulus plans can already be seen due to increased orders and action plans from government agencies. However, this is not a sign of a positive foundation for future economic growth; it is instead the very misallocation of resources problem that is always created by Neo-Keynesian-based economic stimulus.

This means that any benefit from the global stimulus package will be short lived and concentrated in a few very specific areas, while the effect of further increasing what is already a staggering amount of government spending will have widespread negative ramifications that will last for many years into the future. The G20 plan may buy the world some time before the ongoing recession is transformed into what can be recognized as another great depression, but in doing so, it is likely to extend and exacerbate the long-term economic doldrums.

In truth, the phrase "grow or die" is somewhat of a misnomer. "Grow and die" is a more realistic expression which unfortunately encapsulates the probable fate of the G20's plan to "save the world" by putting it on financial steroids.

The answer of evil

April 13, 2009

FOR MORE THAN 2,000 YEARS, men have wrestled with the so-called problem of evil. Presumed to have first been formulated by the Greek philosopher Epicurus and also known as the Epicurean Paradox, the problem concerns balancing the obvious existence of evil with belief in the existence of God. How, Epicurus wondered, could evil and an omnipotent, omnibenevolent God exist simultaneously? Centuries later, the problem was addressed by the Scottish historian and philosopher David Hume, who considered the matter in his *Dialogues Concerning Natural Religion*. Hume wrote:

> *Is he willing to prevent evil, but not able? Then is he impotent. Is he able, but not willing? Then is he malevolent. Is he both able and willing? Whence then is evil?*

The most obvious flaws in these proposed problems lie not so much with their logic as with their improper definitions and misapplications to specific religions. For example, it is clear that the omnibenevolence queried by Epicurus does not fit the description of the biblical God, due to the way the biblical God's curse on various individuals and nations is chronicled throughout the Bible. It's worth noting, however, that Epicurus is not believed to have ever applied his paradox to the biblical God for the very good reason that he died in 270 B.C. Hume, on the other hand, does not have the benefit of the same excuse, and indeed, the error in his formulation verges on intellectual dishonesty. For no competent philosopher could possibly describe an unwillingness to prevent evil as requiring malevolence. While it would be reasonable to describe one who causes evil as malevolent, the worst accusation that can be reasonably hurled at one who merely fails to prevent evil is one of indifference. This may explain why Epicurus formulated his paradox as a justification for a philosophy of indifferent stoicism, not as a logical argument against the existence of God.

However, the main reason that the problem of evil has no reasonable application to Christianity is that the entire basis of the Christian religion is predicated on the existence of evil. Without evil, Christianity makes no sense. It has no purpose, its Savior has accomplished nothing, and Christians are, in the words of the Apostle Paul, "of all people most to be pitied." Christianity absolutely requires the observable existence of evil, for both logical and documentary reasons.

The Bible is very clear on the existence of evil. It even goes so far as to explain, in part, the immutable evil of human nature. The Old Testament is full of one party or another doing "evil in the eyes of the Lord"; the phrase resounds like an ominous drumbeat leading toward the ultimate fall of the kingdom of Israel. The New Testament, for its part, repeatedly describes the world as an evil place ruled by an evil spirit, the customs of which the believer is to avoid. In fact, there is no science more readily falsifiable than Christianity, as finding a single individual, just one single man or woman, entirely free from sin will suffice to dismiss Christian theology once and for all time.

If evil did not exist, then man would not be condemned by God. If man were not condemned by God, there would have been no reason for Jesus Christ to incarnate, to die and to rise again to pay the price of man's redemption. Therefore, while one may use the problem of evil to argue against the existence of an omnibenevolent and omnipotent God, only an irrational fool would attempt to use the problem of evil as the basis of an argument against the existence of the Christian God or the tenets of the Christian faith.

> *The world cannot hate you, but it hates me because I testify that what it does is evil.*

> *– John 7:7*

Yesterday, today and tomorrow, Christians celebrate a risen Lord Jesus Christ. We celebrate him because we know the evil of the world, we know the evil of our hearts and we know he has defeated them. Christus resurrexit! Resurrexit vere!

America is not geography

April 20, 2009

Now nearly two-thirds Latino and foreign-born, [Langley Park, Md.] has the aesthetics of suburban sprawl and the aura of Central America. Laundromats double as money-transfer stores. Jobless men drink and sleep in the sun. There is no city government, few community leaders, and little community.

—*New York Times*, April 18, 2009

T O DESCRIBE the discourse concerning the mass inflow of foreigners that has taken place over the last 29 years "the immigration debate" is to use a misnomer. What has taken place since the 1980 U.S. census is nothing less than a mass migration of the sort that irretrievably transformed historical civilizations everywhere from Hellenic Greece to Moorish Spain. In 1980, the number of Hispanics living in the United States was 14.6 million. In 2008, it was 45.5 million. Hispanics now account for 15 percent of the total population, and because they are the fastest-growing population segment, the census bureau expects their numbers to increase by a further 67 million by 2050.

Those are the official statistics, although given that past projections have repeatedly underestimated Hispanic population growth, they are probably underestimate the full scale of the migration. Nevertheless, anyone who suggests that an additional 67 million Hispanics are less than a cause for national celebration will be attacked for a wide variety of reasons, all of them spurious. Of course, Hispanics are far from the only group to immigrate to the United States, but due to its remarkable size, the Hispanic migration merits a particular focus.

As the recent Wall Street implosion has demonstrated, the selection of a conceptual model is extremely important because it is the mechanism of the model that will largely determine the course of one's future decisions and actions. A flawed risk model is one of the primary reasons AIG found itself into such catastrophic circumstances; the conceptual model created by a professor at the Yale School of Management took into account only one of the three major risk factors faced by AIG's credit default swaps. Unsurprisingly, this model eventually failed when confronted with real world conditions, to cataclysmic effect.

The conceptual model underlying bipartisan support for the ongoing Hispanic migration is the Ellis Island concept of "the melting pot." The idea is that when immigrants enter America, their values, thought processes, traditions and identities are subsumed, initially transforming them and their descendants from Irish to Irish-American, then from Irish-American to American, essentially indistinguishable from any other American of any other national heritage. The long-term success of the 7 million-strong Irish migration from 1600 to 1920 is often cited as evidence that America is capable of absorbing vast immigrant populations without difficulty or significantly altering its national character.

However, there are three problems with attempting to apply the Irish model to the Hispanic migration. The first problem is that the Hispanic migration, both actual and potential, is significantly larger in scale. At no time did the Irish ever account for 15 percent of the total U.S. population; even if the entire remaining population of Ireland had migrated to America en masse in 1900, the Irish would still have made up less than 11 percent of the U.S. population. The second problem is that Ireland did not share a border with the United States, so there are no structural barriers limiting the size of the migration. In the place of the Atlantic Ocean there are an insignificant number of ineffective border guards.

The third, and most serious problem, is that the Irish example is the historical anomaly. Most population migrations have a massively transforming effect on the host culture. Greece was never the same after the Dorian migration. Rome was never the same after the Germanic and Gothic migrations. England was never the same after the Danish migrations. Spain was never the same after the Moorish invasion. Moreover, with a few exceptions, such migrations have tended to indicate that the society receiving them is approaching the end of its lifespan. What follows may be better or it may be worse, but it is never the same.

Ultimately, the pro-immigration model rests on a very dubious foundation that an individual's mere physical presence within America's borders is sufficient to transform him. But America is more than simple geography, as the fact that very few modern Americans wear feathered headbands, count coup, hunt bison, or live in wigwams should suffice to demonstrate. Latin culture is by no means an inherently bad thing, but Latin culture is very different from Anglo-American culture in a wide variety of ways, and it is not necessarily compatible with many of the political and societal patterns that most white Americans, both liberal or conservative, take for granted. And the less informed people are about the ongoing transformation of their society, the more likely it is to lead to serious conflict in the future.

As Steve Sailer recently demonstrated, the subprime mortgage crisis was likely the first example of the great migration playing a significant role in an American economic event. Langley Park serves as a fair warning of what America is likely to become over the next 50 years. That future America will not be Mexico North, but neither is it likely to be the wealthy, middle-class, democratic superpower it was in the 20th century.

Obama's 100

April 27, 2009

OBAMA'S FIRST 100 DAYS have been more important than has historically been the case with most presidents, because unlike past presidents, Obama's lack of a track record renders him somewhat of an enigma. While legislative voting records provide a picture of an individual's ideology, they tell very little about his character, his executive capabilities or his willingness to set aside ideology in the interest of achieving practical objectives. So, the first three months of Obama's administration have been the first opportunity to really see if there is any substance beneath the marketing hype.

It is becoming increasingly apparent that Obama's greatest strength may also be his greatest weakness. The cool, narcissistic detachment which was mistaken for a calm and measured demeanor during the campaign provides him with the ability to ignore both public and private pressure, which will tend to lend a greater unpredictability to his actions. On the other hand, the personal ruthlessness he betrayed in throwing his pastor and grandmother under the bus has been underlined by his ready willingness to sacrifice promises made to his earliest and most fervent supporters. If his decision to name no less than five lawyers from the Recording Industry Association of America to the Justice Department is not the most significant of his numerous betrayals, it is arguably the most telling in the way it demonstrates his complete lack of concern for his most important group of core supporters outside the black community.

After only three months in office, it is already clear that Obama will be a prime example of the counterpush concept I described last September. Instead of turning away from the major Bush administration programs, such as the Troubled Asset Relief Program, the National Security Agency's domestic surveillance infrastructure, and the Global Struggle Against Violent Extremism, Obama is embracing them and even expanding their reach. (Despite his announcement of budget cuts, I will readily admit that Obama shows absolutely no signs of ever attempting to balance the budget.) And despite having won the Democratic nomination with the support of the anti-war crowd, it is looking more and more likely that if Obama does ever elect to withdraw troops from Iraq, it will only be to send them to Pakistan.

But if his force of character is stronger than many had expected, his executive incompetence has thus far proven to be more comprehensive than even his harshest critics had assumed of a man who was nearly devoid of managerial experience, let alone executive seasoning. His nomination of a series of unvetted tax cheats to Cabinet positions was remarkable, while his inability to staff the various vacant positions in the Department of the Treasury during a severe financial crisis is a failure topped only by the amusingly incompetent performance of Obama's Secretary of the Treasury, Tim Geithner. Only four months ago, it would have been hard to imagine a Treasury Secretary less respected by Americans than Bush's bankster di tutti bankster, Henry Paulson, but Obama somehow managed to significantly exceed even the most cynical expectations.

The most important aspect of Obama that has been revealed in his first 100 days is probably his total disregard for reasonable limits. His decision to quasi-nationalize some of the largest American corporations and then intervene directly in their operations is downright staggering; as recently as one year ago, no one could have imagined the White House going so far as to order the CEOs of major corporations such as General Motors and Citibank to step down. This is a large step toward the public-private corporatism that is better known as fascism; one can't help but wonder how long it will be before a national council of experts for various industries is proposed.

As for policies, Obama's decision to continue utilizing the economic model of the Friedman-Keynes synthesis all but assures that Americans will become aware they are trapped in the throes of Great Depression 2.0 well before 2012 rolls around. Whether this will be of any electoral utility to Republicans is doubtful, however, as the G.O.P. subscribes to the same economic neo-orthodoxy that created the debacle in the first place, and Obama can quite reasonably continue to blame Bush and the permanent Republican majority of 2000-2006 for the contraction until a genuine alternative appears.

Europe closes early

May 4, 2009

THEIR PROPENSITY for creating a veritable art form of vacation-taking is one of the more enjoyable aspects of average Europeans. It is hard to convince the average American how little work is done in Europe throughout the month of August, but once one understands that the French can't even be bothered to return from the seaside to save grand-mère from a lethal heat wave, it becomes a bit more comprehensible that they couldn't possibly care less about manufacturing cars or selling investment services when it's vacation time.

Years ago, I worked for an American technology company that derived about half its revenue from European customers. It used to amuse me how half way through every August, the executives would start to panic because their sales were falling short of the projections which invariably failed to account for this month-long, continent-wide break. The executives would breathe a sigh of relief when business activity returned to normal in September, and they would completely forget anything had ever happened by December when they calculated the sales projections for the following year. Eventually, the second week of August would roll around, and the whole process would begin again. But when Europe closes, it's usually just for the month of August.

It's no secret that the global economy has been in bad shape for a while. The U.S. has seen two quarters of economic contraction, -6.1 percent GDP growth in Q4 2008 and -6.3 percent in Q1 2009, and the OECD is project-ing -4.1 percent GDP growth across the Euro area in 2009. Steel production, which is a leading indicator of economic activity due to its use in so many producer and consumer products, has been reported to be down around one-third everywhere from Germany to Russia and Brazil. On the other hand, numerous financial figures are openly declaring that the worst is behind us, thanks in part to the evidence offered by the stock market's powerful 26 percent rally in just two months.

However, two things lead me to suspect that the economic troubles we have seen thus far are merely the first minor skirmishes in what will likely be a long and difficult campaign. In discussing the economy over coffee with one international executive, I learned that steel shipments to one major European country were now less than 10 percent of what they had been a year ago, indicating that the 32 percent decline previously reported was only about one-third of the total decline to be expected this year. The very next day, I happened to encounter an executive at a very large manufacturer of expensive producer goods and was told that their shipments to another major European country had fallen to such an extent that they were projected to be around 12 percent of their 2008 sales. To add insult to injury, this disastrous projection incorporated the assumption that sales activity would actually increase a little from that which they had seen over the first three months of 2009.

Of course, this is mere anecdotal data, and it's certainly possible that there are other factors at work that could contradict what otherwise looks disturbingly like a severe and lasting economic contraction in the making. I am not a professional analyst, and the amount of relevant information I don't possess approaches the comprehensive. Nevertheless, there seems to be a rather large dichotomy between what the economists are predicting and what at least some business executives are seeing. Nor should it escape one's attention that in January 2008, the OECD was projecting 1.9 percent GDP growth for the Euro area. Since the experts were previously off by $639 billion, which is what the 6.1 percent that separates that 2008 projection from the April 2009 figure represents, isn't it at least possible that their current estimates are similarly over-optimistic?

It's not my purpose to cry bear here, and this is one of those circumstances where it would definitely be more satisfying to be wrong than to be right. But, their anecdotal nature notwithstanding, these two data points should serve as sufficient reason to keep a skeptical eye on the incessant happy talk from the market cheerleaders who still dominate the financial media.

Ron Paul was right

May 11, 2009

LESS THAN FIVE YEARS after Karl Rove mused openly about the possibility of Republican dominance for decades—an idea which was absurd at the time—the Republican Party finds itself in disarray. The moderate wing is showing itself to be as RINO as ever, and in one case, that of Sen. Arlen Specter, the pretense is finally over. It goes without saying that the moderates are wrong; their advice to do as the Democrats do, only a little less enthusiastically, not only betrays a fundamental misunderstanding of the dynamic nature of electoral politics in a democracy, but ignores the fact that this was essentially George W. Bush's approach to governance.

Ronald Reagan and Margaret Thatcher generally refused to follow the Left's siren song, and while they were viciously lampooned and hated for their refusal to abandon their principles, they won the respect, admiration and affection of the voters. Thatcher, in particular, was known for being inflexible, hence her nickname, "The Iron Lady." Her demand that the president of the United States find a backbone when Saddam Hussein invaded Kuwait in 1990 is among the most informative dialogues between two national heads of state in man's recorded history. It is also, unquestionably, the most hilarious. "Don't go wobbly on me, George."

George W. Bush instead attempted to find common ground with the political opposition, with disastrous results. He was not loved for his moderation; conservatives increasingly came to regard him with the sickened horror of the betrayed, while left-wingers held him in rightful contempt. His failure to return the faith and loyalty initially shown to him by the Republican grass roots was not only despicable, it was politically inept. It is interesting to see that Obama appears to be cut from the same treacherous and ungrateful cloth; certainly his supporters appear to be expressing buyer's remorse even faster than Bush's did.

But the worst mistake was the Republican Party's post-Bush obsession with so-called pragmatism. But, as events have proven, political pragmatism is anything but pragmatic! The party elite, supported by the party media, put forth one establishment moderate after another, starting with Rudy Giuliani, followed by Mitt Romney and Fred Thompson, before ending up with the worst possible choice, John McCain. (Ideologically speaking, Giuliani may be worse but at least the man can be confirmed to be sound on ferrets.) These men were uniformly considered to be among the electable choices, even though the one man declared to be unelectable, Rep. Ron Paul, turned out to be the only candidate who actually won an election in November 2008.

This isn't the only thing that was strange about the Republican nomination. McCain, Giuliani and Romney were all considered to be more centrist on issues regarding which the country is essentially split. This meant that they were theoretically more attractive to voters on the left, while being less attractive to voters on the right. The important question, then, was whether they could pick up enough voters on the left as they were going to lose on the right? At the same time, they held positions that were more or less identical to Obama's on the foreign military occupations, immigration and the Wall Street bailouts. Ron Paul, on the other hand, stood for positions that were extremely popular with the broad spectrum of the American electorate, as strong majorities favor ending the foreign occupations, limiting immigration and not bailing out the banks.

The electoral math is clear. Ron Paul was far less likely to lose the average Republican voter to Obama than John McCain was to lose the conservative Republican voter to indifference. No pro-life, small-government social conservative was going to sit out the election over the occupation of Afghanistan. And Paul was far more likely to take anti-war, anti-immigration, anti-bailout votes away from the pro-war, pro-immigration, pro-bailout Obama, especially since Paul's easygoing libertarianism tends to mitigate somewhat the effects of his social conservatism with social liberals. Even the most paranoid abortion supporter knew that what you had to fear from Ron Paul was a long and tedious lecture on the history of fiat money and the Federal Reserve, not his social views crammed down your throat. So, Paul was a far more viable presidential candidate than the establishment moderates could ever have been.

But assume, for the sake of argument, that excitement over America's first Indonesian president was so overwhelming that Ron Paul lost to Obama in the general election by a margin similar to that enjoyed by John McCain. Would the Republican Party be in any worse shape now? No, quite to the contrary, it would be in a strong and consistent position from which to resist the continuous series of bailouts, to resist the extension of the Afghan occupation to Pakistan, and most importantly, to resist the tidal wave of federal spending that threatens to drown the American economy. Such a party would have also been well-placed to capitalize on Obama's inevitable errors in 2012; as it stands, only a complete meltdown in 2010 combined with Democratic failure to successfully blame the collapse on the previous administration will suffice to render a Republican candidate seriously competitive.

The problem with the cost of sacrificing your principles is that you don't pay it only once.

Flaw in the ointment

May 18, 2009

ACCORDING TO the modern Friedman-Keynes synthesis, there are two tools in the hands of most national authorities that permit them to attempt fine-tuning the economy. The first tool, monetary policy, is the bailiwick of the central bank, which in the United States is known as the Federal Reserve. It has great influence over interest rates, which represent the price of money. Increasing the interest rate is supposed to force the economy to contract, while lowering it is believed to encourage the economy to grow.

> *There is the possibility, for the reasons discussed above, that, after the rate of interest has fallen to a certain level, liquidity preference may become virtually absolute in the sense that almost everyone prefers cash to holding a debt which yields so low a rate of interest. In this event the monetary authority would have lost effective control over the rate of interest. But whilst this limiting case might become practically important in future, I know of no example of it hitherto.*

> —John Maynard Keynes, *The General Theory of Employment, Interest, and Money*

While Keynes may not have known of any examples of this case limiting the effectiveness of monetary policy, we know of at least two: post-1990 Japan and the post-2008 United States. The failure of monetary policy has brought the importance of the second tool to the fore, which is the fiscal policy wielded by the political authorities. With fiscal policy, increasing taxes and reducing spending is supposed to reduce economic growth, while reducing taxes and increasing spending is believed to increase it. Today's Keynesians and Neo-Keynesians believe that fiscal policy is capable of succeeding where monetary policy failed due to the events of the Great Depression, when Herbert Hoover, FDR and the Democratic Congress jointly embarked upon a gargantuan spending spree that caused total government spending to grow from 11.29 percent of the economy as measured in GDP to 52.97 percent in only 17 years. Most of that growth came as a result of World War II, as 44 percent of it occurred in 1943 alone.

In February, I pointed out that Obama's initial $775 billion stimulus plan was actually 17 percent smaller in relative terms than Hoover's 1931 economic rescue program. Since then, however, the economy has continued to worsen, and the White House has significantly upped the ante with its 2010 budget. The administration now proposes to spend $3.998 trillion in what it estimates will be an economy of $14.2 trillion, which in combination with state and local spending will bring total government spending to 45.29 percent of GDP if its relatively optimistic estimates are correct for 2009. However, if the economy under performs expectations, as it has for the last three quarters, a year-long contraction continuing at the rate of Q1's -6.1 percent growth would increase the G/GDP ratio to 48.15 percent, a ratio surpassed only in 1944 and 1945.

Those expecting an economic recovery as the inevitable result of this increase in government spending would do well to look at what happened in those two years. The depression had ended four years previous, but despite G accounting for half of GDP, the U.S. economy only grew from $219.80 billion in 1944 to $222.30 billion in 1946, an annual growth rate of one-half percent. Not until government spending began to dramatically fall, as low as 20 percent in 1948, did Americans see the astounding double-digit growth that characterized the post-war economic expansion.

There are two significant factors left out by those expecting expansive fiscal policy to produce recovery. The first is the fact that Americans do not have the benefit of selling their products to a world with an industrial base devastated by five years of violent military conflict. The second is that even if one assumes that increased government spending is always beneficial, the impact of the increase should only be expected to be half what it was in the 1940s due to the delta from the average of the previous 10 years being 13 percent of GDP compared to a 25 percent historical delta. The Friedmanite portion of the modern synthesis has failed, now it is the Keynesian aspect's turn to do the same.

We are out of money

May 25, 2009

Steve Scully, C-Span: You know the numbers, $1.7 trillion debt, a national deficit of $11 trillion. At what point do we run out of money?

Obama: Well, we are out of money now.

THE UNITED STATES has been an empire in decline since the 1970s. As has been the case with every other declining world power in history, there are a variety of reasons for this decline, which is why there are no straightforward solutions for reversing it. In looking at the situation, however, it is clear that there are a number of contributing factors that are more important than others. Among them include:

According to the U.S Constitution, only "gold and silver Coin" can be tendered by the states in payment of debt. Since the states are explicitly barred from coining money but the federal government is expressly permitted to do so, it is obvious that the only constitutional money is gold and silver coin, regardless of what government employees have subsequently decided. Moreover, unlike the present Federal Reserve notes, constitutional money has held its value; whereas the value of an FRN has lost more than 95 percent of its value in 96 years, the first U.S. silver dollars minted in 1794 have increased in intrinsic value, being worth 11.38 times what they were initially valued 215 years ago. Since its ability to store value is one of the four major properties of money, it's abundantly clear that the abandonment of constitutional money has come at great cost to the nation.

The expansion of the voting franchise has exacerbated the problems created by the switch to a monetary system more susceptible to manipulation. The reason the Founding Fathers created a system of strictly limited democracy was because they knew its historical flaws and wished to prevent the larger part of the masses from having a voice in their governance. The expansion of the franchise to include many parties historically denied the vote has had the inevitable, and expected, effect of permitting society's non-productive members voting themselves the right to obtain wealth transferred from society's productive members. The important point to understand here is not what one might think of the desirability of either equality or wealth redistribution, but rather its long-term sustainability. While history shows that a moderate amount of wealth redistribution is sustainable, it increasingly tends to indicate that democratic equalitarianism rapidly increases that amount to unsustainable levels.

While the global military actions of the United States initially contributed to its post-World War II prosperity, as the destruction of European and Asian manufacturing capacity gifted the U.S. economy with two decades of competitive advantage and expanding markets, since then they have been a serious drain on the nation's coffers as well as a spectacular malinvestment of human and capital resources. The genuine side benefits of defense research fall far short of making up for the decades of opportunity costs they have engendered in terms of wasted talent and investment.

Immigration and the entry of middle-class women into the labor force are closely related to each other and to the redistribution issue, because as American women elect to work and cease to replace themselves by having at least 2.1 children each, the pyramid scheme of wealth redistribution requires an ever-increasing number of immigrants to delay collapse. Of course, there is no guarantee that any immigrant will be a net positive economic contributor, and, in fact, it is clear that the vast influx of immigrants over the last two decades has had a cumulatively negative effect and worsened the problem they were envisioned as helping solve. It is no coincidence that California, which has historically been a leader with regards to women's suffrage, immigration and female labor force participation, is the first U.S. state to find itself on the verge of insolvency.

The fact that these factors can be identified does not mean that they can be reversed. Indeed, it does not even mean that they should be reversed. Forces which take decades to fully realize their impact must be permitted to play themselves out. Just as it's not possible to construct a new building until the remnants of the previous structure have been demolished and cleared away, it would not be possible to return the United States to its position of previous economic dominance even if the political winds were not blowing in precisely the wrong direction. Rather than lamenting the national mistakes of the past, Americans who value freedom, liberty and prosperity would do well to look to the possibilities of the post-American future.

Out of ammo

June 1, 2009

L AST WEEK, Barack Obama declared that the U.S. was out of money. Today, General Motors is expected to file for bankruptcy, which is an ominous sign in a land where the financial health of the automotive giant has long been considered a proxy for the financial health of the nation. And California looks increasingly likely to go bankrupt in the near future. And yet, in a nation without money, Bloomberg has reported that the Federal Reserve has loaned out 7.8 trillion dollars without telling anyone where it has gone.

The American people don't know. Congress doesn't know. No one seems to know; the video of the exchange between Rep. Alan Grayson of the House Subcommittee on Oversight and Investigations and the inspector general of the Federal Reserve Board of Governors is more darkly comedic than anything the Daily Show has shown in years.

> *Grayson: So are you telling me that nobody at the Federal Reserve is keeping track on a regular basis of the losses that it incurs on what is now a $2 trillion portfolio?*
>
> *Coleman: I don't know if ... you're telling me that there's ... you're ... missing ... that there are losses. I'm just saying that we're not ... until we actually look at the program and have the information, we are not in a position to say whether there are losses or to respond in any other way to that question.*
>
> *Grayson: Mr. Chairman, my time is up, but I have to tell you honestly, I am shocked to find out that nobody at the Federal Reserve including the inspector general is keeping track of this.*

Bloomberg also noted that the combined total of the loans and payouts given by the Federal Reserve, the U.S. Treasury, the Federal Deposit Insurance

Corporation and the Department of Housing and Urban Development was $12.8 trillion as of March 31. This is equal to 90 percent of the U.S. economy, and would have been more than enough to pay off every single mortgage in the United States—not just every problem mortgage headed for default and foreclosure, but every home loan in the country! The fact that this money has not been given to mortgage borrowers but rather to mortgage holders demonstrates that neither the White House nor the Federal Reserve are genuinely concerned about homeowners losing their homes, except for the way in which their loan defaults are destroying the value of the mortgage-backed securities sold by the banks that are the presumed beneficiaries of the government and central bank largesse.

This may seem like madness, especially since the bank-centric approach to solving the housing problem has been a complete failure. But what people tend to forget is that the U.S. does not have a paper money system; it has a debt money system. The "dollar" in your wallet is not called a Federal Reserve Note because it is just a meaningless paper marker, but because it is an instrument of debt. Creating more money requires creating more debt, which means that if the banks are not creating new loans, new money is not being injected into the money supply since the banks are not loaning out the money loaned to them by the Federal Reserve. A look at the Federal Reserve's report on the aggregate reserves of U.S. depository institutions shows part of the problem facing Ben Bernanke and the board of governors, as the Fed's member banks have increased their cash reserves from less than one percent of their deposits to over 16 percent in the last year.

While I understand Rep. Grayson's frustration and harbor no objections to Ron Paul's proposed legislation to audit the Federal Reserve, I doubt that it is necessary to do much more than wait for events to take their course. Pyramid schemes always fail in the end, and there are an increasing number of signs indicating that the post-Bretton Woods reserve currency system is rapidly approaching terminal status. As Mike Shedlock has chronicled, Chairman Bernanke has exhausted the 13 paper bullets in the Fed's gun, so the ultimate fate of the Federal Reserve Note and the U.S. economy would appear to be in the invisible hands of the market now.

Of course, they always were, as the idea that man can control the great market forces, rather than merely influence them for a short time, has never been more than a vain conceit.

Voxiversity III kicks off

June 8, 2008

URING THE EIGHT YEARS I have written this column for WND, I have received numerous requests for reading recommendations. And in eight years of receiving critical e-mails and blog comments, I have also discovered how poorly read most people who consider themselves to be informed and well-educated actually are. It seems that at some point, "education" became confused with "formal schooling" in the popular vernacular, which is a little bizarre when one considers that more than a few of man's best-educated, most accomplished intellectuals spent very little time in anything that would be recognizable today as a school.

One of the unfortunate results of this confusion is the way that many people believe their education ceases once they receive a piece of paper from one of the various paper-selling institutions known as universities. The term "adult education" is somewhat of a misnomer that illustrates this confusion. How is "adult education" inherently different than "child education" when regardless of age, the desired knowledge is not possessed? The truth is that one's education continues so long as one chooses to expand one's knowledge base, and while it may be harder to learn a language in middle age or to memorize historical dates in old age than it is in childhood, it can still be done. And, as numerous studies of the brain and its aging have confirmed, it is well worth doing.

After completing a book last summer, I decided it was time to finish reading a historical masterwork that I'd never managed to complete, *The History of the Peloponnesian War* by Thucydides. Landmark published a beautiful edition, complete with copious maps and notes, so surmising that I might not be the only one interested in reading it, I suggested the idea of a group study to the regular readers of my blog, Vox Popoli. Each week, we read one section and I wrote a 10-question online quiz that anyone who happened to be interested may take. The quizzes weren't intended for grading purposes, but rather to help fix the information in the reader's mind and confirm his correct understanding of the issues involved. The 25-question final that wrapped up the study was taken by 139 people; it was popular enough that the choice of the book for the second study became the subject of animated debate.

The merits of everything from Herodotus to *Godel, Escher, Bach* were discussed, but in the end, we went with what turned out to be a timely selection of *America's Great Depression* by Murray Rothbard. This time, nearly 1,000 participants took the final of a study which began in November; one reader remarked it was rather like having the world as a giant PowerPoint demonstration thanks to the financial crisis unfolding at the time.

For the third study, we are reading a book that I suspect will be nearly as timely and as relevant as its immediate predecessor. Longtime readers of this column will be aware that I thought highly of Jonah Goldberg's *Liberal Fascism* when it was first published in 2007, an opinion subsequently confirmed by many other reviewers of the book. However, like many best-selling non-fiction works, I suspect it is often more purchased than read; it is not the polemic that many Democrats believe it to be, nor is it the blanket indictment of the Left that many Republicans assume it is. It is, instead, a serious explication of the intellectual and historical links between the left-wing progressivism of the early 20th century and the soft totalitarianism that pervades both—yes, both—of America's major political parties today.

Liberal Fascism is not only an important book, it is arguably a necessary book for anyone who wishes to understand the hope to which the Obama administration is appealing and the change that it is promising. Voxiversity III begins this weekend with the first quiz posted at Vox Popoli on Saturday, June 13. If you are interested in participating, I encourage you to order a copy of the book, which is newly released in paperback, and read the first 24 pages of the introduction, "Everything You Know about Fascism is Wrong."

Will Obama cap Bernanke?

June 15, 2009

T
HE ECONOMIC HISTORY of the last 30 years is the triumph of monetarism over neo-Keynesian economics. When conventional Keynesian measures proved incapable of taming the inflation and high unemployment of the 1970s, new Federal Reserve Chairman Paul Volcker made what his successor later described as one of the most important policy changes in the last 50 years. He raised interest rates to previously unthinkable levels in a successful attempt to reduce the money supply, which broke the inflationary cycle, and, after a brief recession, led to a great economic expansion that lasted for nearly 20 years.

In 1965, Milton Friedman was quoted in Time Magazine. "We are all Keynesians now," he declared, expressing a sentiment later echoed by President Richard Nixon when he took the nation off the gold standard. But 27 years later, on the occasion of Friedman's 90th birthday, the future chairman of the Federal Reserve essentially declared "We are all Friedmanites now" during a famous speech in which Ben Bernanke accepted, on behalf of the Federal Reserve, responsibility for causing the Great Depression. Friedman had made the charge in *A Monetary History of the United States, 1857-1960*, an important work that for a brief time promised to prove as influential as *The General Theory of Employment, Interest, and Money* had been generation before.

Those words sounded a lot funnier in 2002 than they do in 2009, with governments and currencies in crisis, unemployment climbing higher than the Fed's worst case scenarios, and the ominous specter of global depression lurking on the periphery of the world's economic consciousness. The Federal Reserve appears to be out of ammunition; it was forced to back down on its threats to purchase its own bills by an implicit rebellion on the part of the bond market that drove long-term interest rates higher. Friedman's monetarist theory appears to be in tatters, as the slashed discount rate and massive increase in the money supply have not had the expected effects and look rather like injecting venom instead of an antidote to a poisoned victim.

On top of that, the Federal Reserve's extracurricular interventions in areas well outside of its responsibility to manage the nation's money supply, including the housing market and corporate management, combined with its refusal to provide any information to Congress, has sufficiently irritated the politicians of both parties to such an extent that Rep. Ron Paul's bill to audit the Fed has so many co-sponsors that it is already guaranteed passage in the House of Representatives.

Bernanke can hardly be blamed for the subprime crisis, which is the result of Alan Greenspan's refusal to rein in the irrational exuberance of the tech, housing and credit bubbles. But he is absolutely responsible for the Fed's looting of the Treasury on behalf of its member banks; more money has been wasted on failing to stabilize the financial system than would have been required to pay off every single mortgage at risk of default in America. And he is certainly to blame for the Fed's arrogant refusal to answer to the elected representatives of the American people for how their tax money has been funneled to various unknown parties around the world.

And with Bank of America CEO Ken Lewis now openly charging Bernanke with lying to the Joint Economic Committee about the pressure to which Lewis claims Bernanke subjected him to prevent Bank of America from backing out of the disastrous Merrill Lynch merger, the Federal Reserve chairman's credibility has never been weaker. This is significant because Obama and his advisers show a clear preference for a return to neo-Keynesian policies; their $787 billion stimulus plan is straight out of Paul Samuelson's neo-Keynesian textbook. Bernanke, on the other hand, has warned of a "vicious deficit cycle" created by government spending on this scale, which amounts to an implicit criticism of Obama's fiscal approach to the economic crisis.

Bernanke's term expires in 2010. If the Fed's extraordinary efforts to conquer the crash through monetarist policies are successful, all will be forgiven, he will be reappointed to serve another term, and will probably be regarded as one of the greatest, if not the greatest, Fed chairman of the last 100 years. If, on the other hand, Bernanke's optimistic green shoot-spotting proves to be illusory and the economy continues to contract in the fall, this will greatly increase the probability that Obama will appoint a new chairman with neo-Keynesian views and an orientation towards antevolckerian monetary policy.

Firestarter

June 22, 2009

L AST WEEK, I CONSIDERED the possibility that Barack Obama would fail to reappoint Ben Bernanke as chairman of the Federal Reserve. Events last week, however, would seem to indicate that this would be a very surprising move. Despite various provocations Federal Reserve officials have given the White House and Congress, most notably their refusal to make public any information regarding the funds provided to them through the various bailout plans, the administration's white paper actually proposes to expand the scope of the Federal Reserve's legal authority.

In package of financial reforms announced on June 17, the Obama administration proposed a new role for the Federal Reserve described as the Systemic Risk Regulator. This would involve giving the private central bank responsibility to regulate large financial institutions that are not banks, which is ironic given the fact that it is the Federal Reserve, more than any other party, that creates systemic risk to the economy by its constant expansion of the money supply. This isn't putting the proverbial fox in charge of the henhouse; it is more like taking a very fat fox with feathers in its mouth out of the henhouse and putting it in with the flightless birds at the zoo.

I already pointed out that the Federal Reserve has failed in its responsibility to maintain monetary stability, as the value of its dollar notes have declined to a nickel in the 96 years of its financial stewardship. What is less well-known, even by economists and financial experts, is its similar failure to stabilize the American banking system. The common misconception is that the huge reduction in the number bank failures that followed the 1933 banking reform that established the Federal Deposit Insurance Corporation had anything to do with the Federal Reserve. It is true that bank failures were dramatically reduced, but they were all happening on the Fed's watch since the central bank had been established 20 years earlier, in 1913.

Still, there's no way that the various banking reforms were accomplished without the Fed's input, so it's not unreasonable to give the bank's governors at least partial credit for any benefits that have accrued to the American financial system from them. However, the conventional history is both incomplete and misleading. First, it is not true that 4,000 banks failed in 1933. As an old report on U.S. banking statistics from 1921 to 1941 stated: "The figures for 1933 comprise banks suspended before the banking holiday, licensed banks suspended or placed on a restricted basis following the banking holiday, unlicensed banks placed in liquidation or receivership, and all other unlicensed banks which were not granted licenses to reopen by June 30, 1933."

This is a minor objection, since 1,350, 2,293 and 1,453 banks had failed in the three previous years. A more serious problem, however, is the fact that while the number of banks failing has been reduced significantly, the amount of deposits held by the failing banks has greatly increased over time. The total amount of deposits in the 9,096 banks that failed or were closed down by the federal government in the four years between 1930 and 1933 was $5.3 billion. Corrected for inflation, that amounts to $83.2 billion in 2009 dollars. Only 64 banks have failed in 2008 and 2009 so far, but those 64 banks held deposits of $261.2 billion between them. If the economic contraction continues and the present rate holds steady for the next 30 months, the total deposits held by failed banks will come to $696 billion, 8.4 times worse than before the problem was supposedly fixed. This would not even be the worst four-year period in U.S. banking history, as the chart below will show that the 1988-1991 savings and loan crisis, in which institutions with $479 billion in deposits failed, was even worse when corrected for inflation.

Defenders of the Fed and the FDIC will of course point out that banking depositors lost surprisingly little from these massive banking failures, since the assets and deposits of the failed banks were transferred to surviving banks with losses of only 15 percent on average. This is true. But it also misses the point, because the problem is that the present system is actually increasing systemic risk over time through this growing centralization; the Fed is in effect doubling-down each time a bank fails. Whereas there were once 30,000 banks in the country, there are now only 7,037 commercial banks, plus an additional 1,209 savings institutions. This decline in the number of depository institutions combined with the increase in the amount of failed banking deposits during economic contractions indicates that neither the

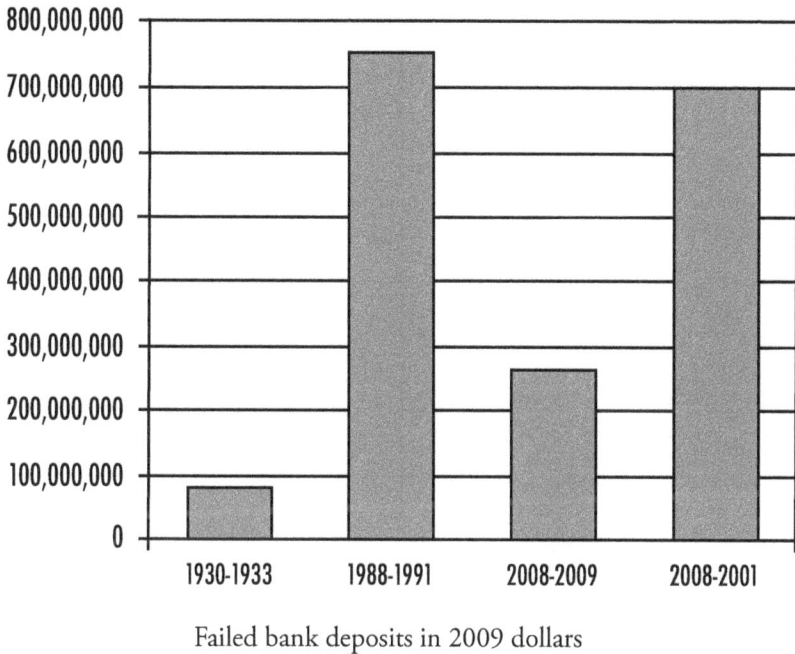

Failed bank deposits in 2009 dollars

Federal Reserve nor the FDIC has been successful in removing risk from the banking system, they have merely been successful at creating an illusion of lowered risk while at the same time increasing the costs of catastrophic failure in the future.

Assigning systemic risk management to the Fed is about as wise as giving the weekly grocery money to an inveterate gambler and trusting him to go to the supermarket instead of the casino. It's possible that he'll return with the groceries and a new car, but it's much more likely that you'll find yourself broke and hungry.

Americans walk away

June 29, 2009

> *We find that 26% of the existing defaults are strategic. We also find that no household would default if the equity shortfall is less than 10% of the value of the house. Yet, 17% of households would default, even if they can afford to pay their mortgage, when the equity shortfall reaches 50% of the value of their house. Besides relocation costs, the most important variables in predicting strategic default are moral and social considerations.*

> —"Moral and Social Constraints to Strategic Default on Mortgages," Guiso, Sapienza, and Zingales, June 2009

ORTGAGE LENDERS are rightly terrified that more and more of the 22 percent of American homeowners whose homes are now worth less than their mortgages are going to exercise their borrower's right to default on them. At this point, most home defaults are still involuntary, but according to the paper cited above, more than one-quarter of them already consist of what the mortgage industry calls "ruthless defaults." And yet, why shouldn't homeowners be ruthless in their disregard for the financial interests of the home lenders when the lenders themselves have been utterly ruthless—and utterly stupid—in squeezing every last drop of potential demand out of the American public?

The housing crash was inevitable. The huge expansion in the number of home loans was an intentional attempt to expand the number of home buyers made possible by low interest rates, the widespread adoption of a risk-based credit model and political initiatives such as the Expanding American Homeownership Act. Of course, this short-term increase in the demand for houses drove up their price, which naturally led to an increase in the number of new houses being built. The problem is that this increase in demand was not sustainable for long, since there were finite limits on the number of homes that people who could afford them were willing to buy as well as the number of minorities in California who could make payments on the overpriced and predatory mortgage contracts they were actively lobbied to sign. (California was ground zero for the housing bubble, and by 2007 the median price of owner-occupied housing in California was 8.3 times median family income, nearly four times the national average in 2000.)

Once the limits of this artificially boosted demand were reached, the resulting excess supply of housing dictated the crash in prices that we are seeing today. The process has been a typical investment boom and bust, leading to a record number of American homeowners followed by a historic low of 41.4 percent in American homeowner equity and a record number of American homeowners in default.

The ramifications of the housing crash have been compounded by the corrupt and short-sighted decision of the Bush administration and the financial authorities to use taxpayer money to let the banks off the hook for the predictable ramifications of their reckless lending. As is so often the case with legislative intervention, the banking bailout has had unintended consequences resulting from the moral hazard it created, albeit less for the banks than for those who borrowed from them. Few Americans now see any reason why they should continue to pay the price for the negative consequences of their borrowing when the banks are being rewarded for the negative consequences of their lending. Nor should they. The banks were fully aware of the risk of potential default at the time they offered the loan.

The idea that a homeowner should continue to throw away a significant part of his income in a recession on a property rendered less than worthless by debt in the interest of maintaining creditworthiness is stupid for several reasons. First, creditworthiness is what got the homeowner into financial trouble in the first place. Second, reducing and avoiding debt should be a priority for all responsible Americans, so being unable to obtain credit is hardly a bad thing. Third, it is laughable to suggest that banks which recently offered 125 percent subprime mortgages to unemployed illegal aliens on houses that cost an average of $312,400 will not be willing to provide credit in the future to a duly employed individual with one home default on his record. Banks exist for the sole purpose of providing credit; that is how they make their money. So many Americans have already defaulted on their home loans that it defies both reason and statistical science to believe that banks will not be making loans readily available to past mortgage defaulters in the future.

The banking industry threw out the old rules in the ruthless pursuit of increasing short-term profits with the full approval of the government and the Federal Reserve. None of these parties are in any position to protest how the American public has been forced to learn to play by the new rules established by the banks. There is nothing new under the sun.

> *[W]hen [Cato] was asked what was the most profitable feature of an estate, he replied: "Raising cattle successfully." What next to that? "Raising cattle with fair success." And next? "Raising cattle with but slight success." And fourth? "Raising crops." And when his questioner said, "How about money—lending?" Cato replied: "How about murder?" From this as well as from many other incidents we ought to realize that expediencies have often to be weighed against one another and that it is proper for us to add this fourth division in the discussion of moral duty.*

> —Marcus Tullius Cicero, *De Officiis*

Irrational finance

July 6, 2009

ONE OF THE MORE remarkable things about the expansion of the subprime financial crisis into a general economic contraction is the Federal Reserve System's narcissistic focus on itself. In his speeches, Ben Bernanke spends more time talking about the Federal Reserve's balance sheet and how stupendously fabulous it continues to be despite the vast quantities of loans it is making to shore up various aspects of the financial system than he does about the unemployment rate or the expected effects of economic contraction on the public.

It's rather like a seeing a speeding school bus full of children smash into the school in front of the horrified eyes of the children's mothers. Then, after the crash and a subsequent explosion, the bus driver emerges from the cloud of smoke surrounding the wreckage and assures everyone he is all right, that, in fact, he has never felt better. But the health of the driver is no one's primary concern.

The Federal Reserve's myopic vision has been ironically harmful to the very member banks whose interests it is theoretically defending. In a 2008 speech entitled "Reducing Preventable Mortgage Foreclosures," Bernanke suggested a range of options to address the rising number of mortgage delinquencies and mentioned that despite the banking industry's distaste for loan writedowns, the combination of low equity rates and falling house prices meant that reducing the principle amount might increase the expected value of the loan by reducing the risk of default and foreclosure. However, neither the Fed nor the banks pursued this strategy of sacrificing reward to reduce risk, as the subsequent loan default statistics readily show.

Despite a government program that offers $1,000 to mortgage holders for each loan modification they make, the number of loan modifications has fallen by nearly one-quarter. In a recent study of subprime and Alt-A loans by

Wells Fargo, it has been shown that banks continue to prefer foreclosures and liquidations to loan modifications involving writedowns despite the fact that: a) the average writedown amounts to only 6 percent of the loan value, and, b) the average loss per writedown is only $13,077 compared to $141,953 per liquidated foreclosure. The average loss per liquidated foreclosure was 64.7 percent of the original loan balance.

This has serious implications for the value of the large quantity of mortgage-backed securities that are still held by financial institutions around the world even as the huge injection of taxpayer money into the banks are creating massive short-term profits that have recently seen bank bonuses rocket to levels exceeding those of the housing or dot com booms. This huge transfer of wealth from the public to the very banks that created the problem is economically irrational, demonstrably anti-democratic and extraordinarily foolish. The banks stubbornly refuse to understand that they are not the public's masters, but that their favored position in society will exist only so long as they are tolerated by the public.

As I pointed out last week, the American public can shut down the banking system in a matter of weeks by refusing to make their mortgage payments. And since state governments not only have the wherewithal to declare short-term moratoriums on foreclosures such as California recently imposed, but have the ability to make them permanent, the public can legally render the $14.6 trillion in outstanding mortgage debt essentially valueless by putting sufficient political pressure on the 50 state legislatures.

Such an action would be, as Cicero declared in *De Officiis*, both a subversion of property rights as well as ruinous to the public welfare. But an increasingly impoverished American public may not really care about the long-term implications of radical action, not if they are forced to watch Wall Street bankers pay themselves $700,000 bonuses out of their taxes as they lose their jobs and homes. If the chairman of the Federal Reserve is wise, he will accept congressional demands for an audit of the central bank and abandon the outmoded Finance First theory of economic development, for if he does not, he may well find the Federal Reserve System being burned down by an angry and irrational American public.

History's engine and the great bear wave

July 13, 2009

I HAD THE GOOD FORTUNE to attend a lecture given by Robert Prechter this weekend. Prechter is the originator of the fascinating neo-science of socionomics, about which I have previously written, and the purpose of his lecture was to update the Elliott Wave interpretations provided in his 2002 book entitled *Conquer the Crash*. His fundamental thesis is that the U.S. economy is now several years into a depression that will be an order of magnitude larger than the Great Depression of 1929.

Prechter's socionomic views are of particular interest to me at this time because the conclusions he reaches are virtually identical to those predicted by Austrian economic theory. Whereas Prechter's identification of a larger contraction stems from the forms of the Elliott Waves in the financial markets, Austrian theory guides one to examine the extent of bank credit expansion and the vigor with which the financial and monetary authorities are attempting to fight the subsequent contraction. While there is not sufficient space here to explain precisely why a Grand Supercycle wave is larger than a Super-cycle wave (I presume the nomenclature will suffice), the evidence in support of the Austrian position is easily summarized.

The extent of the credit expansion is significantly greater. The level of total U.S. credit market debt is now 375 percent of GDP, 44 percent higher than its 1933 peak. The amount of Japanese, European and Chinese debt also exceeds their historic levels. In 1930, it was the U.S. that launched a deter-mined, seven-year counter-cyclical fiscal program in 1930, thus deepening and dragging out the liquidation process that took rather less time in Europe and Japan. Unfortunately, all of the major economies are now following the U.S. historical model. In terms of GDP, Europe's collective stimulus package is a little less than half the size of the $939 billion Bush-Obama stimuli, while Japan's is approximately the same size, and China's is more than twice as big. Moreover, if banks continue to fail at the same rate in the second half of 2009 that they did in the first, the percentage of failed bank deposits to total bank deposits in 2008-2009 will be precisely twice as high as it was in 1930-1931.

Prechter's lecture went into great detail, exploring some of the more impressive successes of Elliott Wave Theory as well as its most costly disappointments. An interesting justification of one of the more notorious of the latter, the failure to predict the 2003-2008 stock market rally and coincidental housing boom, was a chart showing the divergence between the Dow Jones Industrial Average priced in nominal dollar terms and the same index priced in gold. His conclusion is that the current stock rally from March is likely in corrective wave B and will see one more wave upward into the fall before collapsing dramatically in a powerful third wave down. In contrast to nearly every economist and financial analyst who pays attention to the currency markets, Prechter also forecasts U.S. dollar strength in the medium term.

But the most fascinating aspect of Prechter's lecture was his formulation of the Socionomic Theory of Finance, which asserts that finance must be an entirely separate discipline from economics. I found this idea to be intriguing since I had independently determined that none of the major economic theories, including Austrian Business Cycle theory, appear to accurately describe the observed behavior of the financial markets. Prechter's brilliant insight is to note that the laws of supply and demand cannot be properly applied to financial markets because there are no producers to provide the supply curve required for establishing price equilibrium.

In a paper titled "The Financial/Economic Dichotomy in Social Behavioral Dynamics: The Socionomic Perspective" published in the *Journal of Behavioral Finance*, Prechter and Wayne Parker write: "But even to a casual observer, price equilibrium is obviously absent from financial markets.... If the law of supply and demand were regulating financial markets, prices and relative values for investments would be as stable as those for shoes and bread." Like many significant concepts, this idea is so retroactively obvious it borders on embarrassing. To make his case, Prechter showed a series of graphs demonstrating, in the case of the financial markets, an increase in price does not lead to a decrease in demand even though supply remains constant.

Neither prophets nor intellectual iconoclasts are often honored in their own time. It's clear that Prechter knows this, just as he recognizes the difficulty in overturning decades of scientific sclerosis even when the existing theoretical models have been repeatedly shown to be fundamentally flawed. Fortunately, as befits a man focused upon the future, Prechter has responded to this challenge by laying a solid, methodological foundation which can readily be built upon by others interested in following in his footsteps. Additional notes from the lecture and my comments on them are available at my blog.

'Get out of war free' card

July 20, 2009

THE CASE of the missing birth certificate grows more and more curious. It has been fascinating to see how quickly various news sites have been frantically altering their assertions regarding Obama's birth hospital ever since Jerome Corsi broke the news of Barack Obama's letter to the Kapi'olani Medical Center for Women and Children on July 6. This means that Obama was either born twice in Hawaii, or he was not born at Queen's Medical Center, as he claimed (or, more accurately, was reported by UPI to have claimed), in 2007 when he first announced his presidential candidacy in Springfield, Ill.

The attempt of the Obama administration to confuse the issue by substituting a computerized Certification of Live Birth for an actual Certificate of Live Birth—which contains information about the birth hospital as well as the signature of the attending physician or midwife—has failed, as *WorldNetDaily* had no trouble explaining the difference between the two to the American public.

While numerous attempts to clarify the historical record have been successfully fought by the administration's lawyers, the issue became much more serious when Maj. Stefan Cook, a U.S. Army reservist with deployment orders to Afghanistan, filed a lawsuit regarding his questions about the legality of a deployment order based on the command of a potentially illegitimate commander in chief. But rather than contesting the suit, the Army took the highly peculiar step of revoking the major's deployment order, suggesting that the Pentagon generals are not entirely confident that they can demonstrate the legitimacy of their purported commander in chief.

The doubts this action raised about Obama's legitimacy were further increased when Maj. Cook was almost immediately fired from his civilian job at a private defense contractor, reportedly due to pressure from a federal agency under the Department of Defense, the Defense Security Services Agency. Although the obvious purpose of revoking the deployment order was to render the lawsuit moot, the firing only provides Maj. Cook with additional ammunition for broadening the scope of his lawsuit now that he has suffered demonstrable material damages.

Maj. Cook has already been joined in his lawsuit by two other soldiers, a retired Army two-star general and an active reserve Air Force lieutenant colonel. But the potential consequences of the major's revoked deployment go far beyond the number of American soldiers with doubts about the legitimacy of orders from their nominal commander in chief. The Pentagon's decision to back down rather than risk exposing Obama's birth records to the public means that every single American soldier, sailor, pilot and Marine now holds a "get out of war free" card. Not only every deployment order, but every order issued from an officer in the line of command can now be challenged in the knowledge that the top brass are afraid to respond for fear that their commander could be exposed for a fraud.

Given the number of sea and barracks lawyers in the various branches of the U.S. military, it seems unlikely that it will take very long for servicemen who are disinclined to accept an unpalatable or dangerous order to figure out how to best make use of this useful little veto. If even a small number of soldiers elect to do so, the effect on military discipline could rapidly become catastrophic.

It is hard to comprehend why Obama has been so obsessively secretive about his personal records, but it is now time for him to call off his lawyers and show the American public his cards. It would be the height of irresponsibility for the commander in chief of the U.S. armed forces to be the source of destroying American military discipline. Permitting such an easily preventable situation to develop would very strongly imply that the man is not only ineligible for the office, but unfit for it as well.

The question about the Obama birth certificate is no longer one of conspiracy theory or hypothetical illegitimacy, as it now threatens to become a very serious military matter. Regardless of whether Barack Obama was born at the Kapi'olani Medical Center, at the Queen's Medical Center, in Kenya or in a manger, the issue will have to be conclusively settled in the near future.

It is one thing for Obama to deny the curiosity of the American public by hiding behind the courts. It is very much another for him to deny the right of the men and women of the Army, Navy, Air Force and Marines, who are sworn to risk their lives upholding the Constitution of the United States of America, to be certain their orders are legitimate.

Where is the birth certificate?

Economics of Obamacare

July 27, 2009

I T IS FASCINATING to see a second Democratic president immolating himself on the political pyre of nationalized health care. One would have assumed that with the original architect of Hillarycare in his Cabinet, Obama would have known better than to spend his political currency with the public in an area that has been such a major minefield for politicians at both the national and state levels.

If Obama is fortunate, his health care proposals will go down to defeat, he will regroup and turn his attention to more amenable matters. If he is unfortunate, he will manage to convince a sufficient number of skeptical Democratic senators and congressmen to vote for a plan that will not only ensure that he does not serve a second term, but may even preclude his winning the Democratic nomination in 2012. With approval ratings that are already plunging—the latest Rasmussen Reports show that his strong disapproval rating of 39 percent now exceeds his strong approval rating by nine percentage points—subjecting the entire United States to a health care regime that has hitherto been limited to the unhappy residents of Massachusetts.

On July 25, the director of the Congressional Budget Office sent a letter to the Democratic majority leader of the House of Representatives which stated: "The available evidence implies that a substantial share of spending on health care contributes little, if anything, to the overall health of the nation. Therefore, experts generally agree that changes in government policy have the potential to significantly reduce health care spending—for the nation as a whole and for the federal government in particular—without harming people's health. However, achieving large reductions in projected spending would require fundamental changes in the financing and delivery of health care."

ObamaCare Supply-Demand Curve

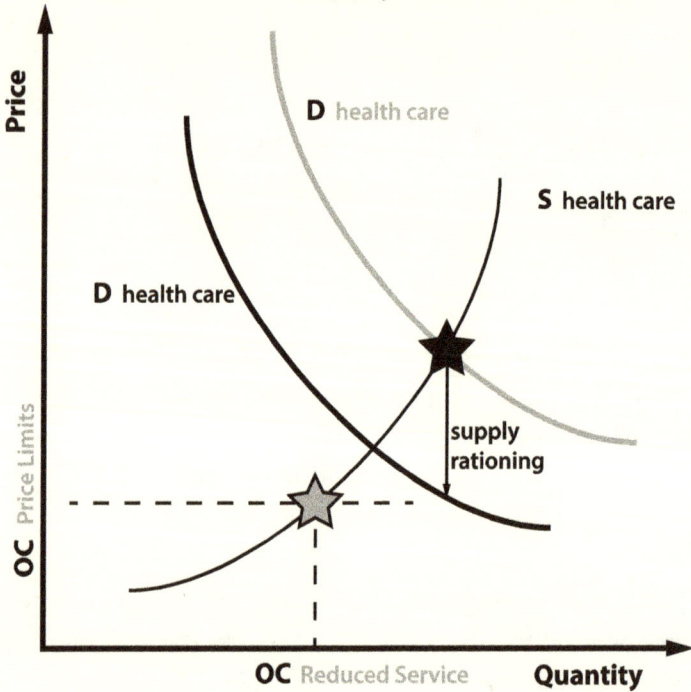

Of course, stasis in the overall health of the nation does not imply the same amount of treatment being provided on an individual basis today. The fact that the average American life expectancy remains static isn't going to be very relevant to you if you injure yourself and are unable to make an appointment to see a doctor for several weeks, as happens more than occasionally in countries with nationalized health care systems such as Great Britain and the Netherlands—because what the CBO means by "fundamental changes" in the delivery of health care is nothing more or less than the government-dictated rationing of health care services.

The stated purpose of Obama's health care reform is to extend health care coverage to 50 million uninsured Americans while simultaneously reducing the total costs of the health care system. Despite the rationalizations of economists such as Paul Krugman, who claims that economic laws don't apply to health care, Adam Smith's law of supply and demand makes it very clear that Obamacare will inevitably lead to not only government rationing, but a reduction in the level of services presently provided to those in the system.

The expansion of the health care market by 50 million uninsured is equivalent to shifting the demand curve out from the black line to the gray line. Normally, this would lead to an increase in both the price of health care as well as the supply at the point marked by the black star. This is problematic enough because the health care market is not free, and therefore the supply of necessary elements such as doctors and nurses cannot be readily expanded. But compounding this problem is that fact that Obama intends to make use of the government's lawmaking power to artificially suppress prices. As decades of central planning in numerous socialist economies have shown, supply does not magically obey government dictates. Some doctors will retire instead of taking pay cuts, some medical students will change their courses of study, and a percentage of current equipment suppliers will shift their attention to markets not subject to the health care regime. The supply curve will not move, but will shift back along the curve to the point where it intersects the dashed line marked by the gray star.

This combination of artificially expanded demand with naturally reduced supply is what produces the rationing that history shows is the consequence of nationalized health care. The triangle formed by the points marked by the blue star, the red star and the arrowhead represent the amount of supply rationing that will have to take place. This rationing is the result of interference with the market operations and has nothing to do with structural government inefficiencies, although those do tend to further compound the problem.

The U.S. health care market is already very inefficient due to previous government intervention in its operation. The additional intervention dictated by the proposed Obamacare program can only further reduce the average quality and quantity of care received by the American public.

'An Infernal Economy II'

August 3, 2009

Canto II

At the peak of a lofty precipice
A noisome stench wafted high in the air,
And yet my guide commenced to reminisce
As if there was no mirksome foulness there.
It was ever so at the cycle's peak,
He said with a rueful shake of despair.
Greed, whispered words, and an air of mystique
Brings the innocent lambs to the slaughter.
They hope to catch on to the winning streak,
Doomed, from the start, come hell or high water.
But justice they'll have, for here it is found,
Payback for each duplicitous fraudster.
He showed me a path that led further down,
Deeper into that corpse-scented chasm.
O Guide, do warn me what we'll find here bound,
What sort of odoriferous phantasm?
I know not how I shall hope to bear this
For much I feared an internal spasm.
Was imminent, given the foul abyss.
But I soon forgot my sense of affliction
As we looked upon the flowers of Dis.
For there was planted without restriction
An orchard such as none have ever seen,
Nor will see outside of hell's jurisdiction.
Displayed in a form well beyond obscene

The bodies of men, dead, yet living still.
Everywhere faces of treacherous mien
Staring at us with palpable ill will,
Flippers of mortgages, sellers of stocks,
Feeders of hedge funds, and then, the great shill.
I saw the mastermind, Ponzi's fox
Buried to his waist in the stinking mire,
His skin all covered by a weeping pox.
Is that who I think it is, my good sire?
Indeed, acceded the wise with grim smile,
Be glad we pass when the tide is higher
You would not fain see beneath the muck vile
Below is where the worms them devour.
We walked over stones along the defile,

Dark was the sky and late was the hour.
We passed chasms filled with human debris
Hearing screams of those in evil's power,
And still I shed no tear of sympathy
Nor did the master once slacken his stride.
Who could ever feel any empathy
For those accursed with such towering pride
Beyond we saw a great red-golden glow
Downward we strode and downward did we slide
Toward a gleaming pit through which did flow
The river of Midas in full advance.
Bubbling, boiling, burning and so
Scalding the servants of debt and finance
That they shrieked, and wept, and shamelessly cried.
The archaic current took its vengeance
On politicians from every side.
A fitting reward I had to admit
For the predicament they'd caused worldwide.
In silence we walked on past the dread pit
Sublime, it was, verily to behold,
And a prodigious heat did it emit.

Leaving behind that great river of gold.
Beneath my feet was no more stone but ice
Darkness descended and also the cold.
I shivered and hoped the guide would suffice
To ensure we were permitted to pass
This Fimbul-winter of devil's device
That Zero Kelvin would hardly surpass.
Then I saw two shades held in ice confined
A frozen embrace thus holding them fast.
Their eyes, tormented, showed madness of mind
And snow on the beard of one could be seen
Their arms were locked and their fates intertwined.
As none could hope to ever intervene.
Freezing though I was, colder my blood ran
Upon realizing that icy scene
Was Ben Bernanke and Alan Greenspan.
Entrapped in cruel bonds of hard liquidity
My guide gestured round with expansive hand
They damned themselves by their cupidity.
Live by the target, then die by the rate,
This is the consequence, naturally.
They sold for credit the soul of the state.
Finance first and foremost was their belief
Thus they encouraged assets to inflate
While withholding from the public relief.
Then we left the maestro and the scholar
In ongoing committee of boundless brief.
Not far now was the king of the dollar
Toward him, my guide urged. If your eyes avail
To espy him, go and see the squalor
Ere the last Trump and the epic fail
Of the king of the kingdom of despair
And out of the ice, at such mighty scale
I saw a giant beyond all compare
His ghastly visages were thricely florid,
Although mayhap they were once passing fair

Afore his constitution fell morbid.
Entrapped was he, by that which held the two,
Central bankers caught on that plain horrid,
Liquid flowed down causing ice to accrue
And held that monster fast about the waist.
Each of his three mouths endeavored to chew
What turned out to be an awful repaste.
Three great sinners now great evil endured.
The first called schoolmaster, now in poor taste,
His legs dangled as his head was tortured.
The second was once a president too,
Twelve long years a thief, his fate was assured.
The third morsel managed to so construe
A crisis as to hold nations hostage,
Arrogance such as the world never knew.
Look well on them, for this is the knowledge,
The fruit of the tree of economy
Which will in the end human action judge.
Man is not born into man's slavery
Nor may he be ruled, even in defeat,
Through the will of another's knavery.
Ergo the reliance upon deceit
By those who dare think to control the land,
Theirs is no more than the fatal conceit,
Oft shattered by the invisible hand.

Thus ends the second canto.

Obama and the 'B' Ark economy

August 10, 2009

T HE REMARKABLE THING about the "wildly popular" scheme to encourage American consumers to purchase more automobiles is not, as a few conservative commentators have wryly remarked, that the mainstream media finds it surprising that people enjoy federal largesse. It is, rather, that so many commentators have recognized that the program is merely designed to encourage tomorrow's consumption today.

This is remarkable because most of them had not hitherto been able to recognize a similar pattern that has been at work in the American economy since 1983. For you see, in media coverage of economic matters, one frequently hears that consumer spending accounts for 70 percent of the American economy, or as the economists put it, personal consumption expenditures make up 70 percent of U.S. Gross Domestic Product, or GDP. And while this is true, it is not the historical norm. From 1950 to 1983, consumer spending averaged around 62.5 percent, always remaining well within a four-point range between 60 and 64 percent. From 1983 onward, that percentage increased gradually until it reached 70 percent in 2002, which is roughly where it has remained since. (It appears to have peaked in real terms at 71.2 percent in the first quarter of 2009.)

The problem is that this increase in consumer spending correlates with the increase in household sector debt to GDP, which rose from its long-time average of 45 percent to 97 percent in the first quarter of 2009. So, the increase in consumer spending over the last two decades has been funded by borrowed money, very much like the "Cash for Clunkers" program. But regardless of whether one looks at the short-term auto sales program or the intermediate term rise in consumer spending, it is clear that what is at work is nothing more than a debt-funded shifting outward of the demand curve that will inevitably run up against the limits of demand in time.

That we are rapidly approaching these limits should be readily apparent to even the casual observer. As David Rosenberg has pointed out, nine years ago "0 percent financing" drove auto sales to a rate of 21 million vehicles per year. Four years ago, "employee discount for everyone" increased the annual sales rate to 20 million vehicles. Now, even with direct government involvement, "Cash for Clunkers" has only managed to inflate the rate to 11 million and has had to rely upon increasing both consumer debt and government debt to do so. This is significant because if the inability to further increase consumer debt causes consumer spending to fall back to its long-time historical levels, the decline would reduce real GDP by an additional $1,231 billion, or 8.7 percent. This reduction, on top of the 4 percent decline in real GDP that has already occurred, means that a mere return to historical consumption patterns will be a depression-sized event.

A debt-driven expectation of a collapse in consumer spending may explain the Obama administration's desperate attempt to quickly push through some form of radical health care restructuring. The percentage of GDP spent on health care has risen almost as fast as the increase in household sector debt, from 8.8 percent in 1980 to 15.3 percent in 2009. So, unless the government can exert enough control to force down the amount consumers choose to spend on health care, through rationing, cost-cutting or other means, an increasing percentage of declining consumer spending will be directed toward the health care services sector rather than toward more productive sectors capable of generating future economic growth. And a service economy that increasingly consists of doctors providing health care to other medical workers and health care bureaucrats is no more sustainable than Douglas Adams's 'B' Ark economy of hairdressers and telephone sanitizers.

Those who decry Obama as a socialist are more accurate than they know. The U.S. government is now engaged in central planning to an extent that few Americans are capable of comprehending, as the administration's planners attempt to effect major adjustments to entire sectors of the economy as they try to prevent the financial infrastructure from collapsing. Now that Fed Chairman Ben Bernanke's comparatively subtle finance first approach has failed, one can expect more ham-fisted attempts by the legislative and exec-utive branches to incentivize debt spending in some sectors while blocking it in others. The "success" of the automotive scheme suggests that we will eventually see some sort of "Cash for Casas" program and perhaps even a

"Dollars for Debt" offer wherein the federal government provides dollar-for-dollar matching contributions for federally approved purchases financed with consumer loans.

Interview with Ian Wishart

August 17, 2009

Vox Day interviewed Ian Wishart, author of Air Con: The Seriously Inconvenient Truth About Global Warming, *on Aug. 9, 2009.*

How did you end up deciding to write a book about the science of global warming? You're in New Zealand, after all, which few would consider to be at the forefront of the debate.

New Zealand is a perfect example for Americans of where this global warming issue is headed. The U.N. lobbyists pushing for a comprehensive emissions cap-and-trade scheme desperately want agriculture included in the mix, which is why the IPCC announced last year that greenhouse gas emissions from agriculture outweighed all of the industrial CO2 emissions caused by humans. However, the lobby groups know that they'll never get American farmers herded into that particular pen unless the rest of the world is lined up first, and unless America first surrenders its national sovereignty to an overarching international governance organization like the U.N.... Now, in New Zealand's case we've been a U.N. guinea pig for the last two decades, in the sense that we have strongly globalist political parties and a strongly globalist bureaucracy. We're often the first to stick our hands up to endorse various U.N. initiatives or ratify daft treaties. In fact, our last prime minister, Helen Clark, is now the No. 3 leader at the U.N., tasked with overhauling the agency for a bold new global mission. Helen Clark was a key figure in the leftist global organization Socialist International, alongside one or two people who are now President Obama's advisers. The fact that she's now running the U.N. Development Program and is tipped as a future U.N. secretary general should be sounding alarm bells. If the U.N. says "jump," our government's usual response is "how high?"

When you began your research for writing *Air Con*, were you convinced that global warming was taking place? Or were you always skeptical about it?

I've had an almost 28-year career in the mainstream media, from network television and talk radio to magazine and newspaper, but unlike many journalists I also served a stint as a political media adviser for a Labour administration briefly in the 1980s (like the American Democrats, only more left wing), so I've seen the news from the perspective of both the spinner and the spun. When the global warming issue first hit mainstream media in the late 80s, I accepted at face value, as I think most people did, that it seemed possible human pollution was overheating the planet. After all, we'd had the acid rain scare, the ozone hole and CFCs, we'd seen smog in Tokyo, L.A. and London, and we'd all watched the anti-nuclear movie *The Day After* which suggested pollution from atomic war would cause a mini ice-age.... I would say my journey can correctly be labeled "believer to neutral to skeptic." It wasn't until I began researching *Air Con* last year, however, that I gained the full appreciation of what has really happened and the agenda behind it.

You're a journalist. So, given that polls repeatedly find global warming to be of very little concern to the public—in *Air Con* you note that it finished 20th out of 20 concerns in a Pew Research poll of Americans—why does it always seem to be in the news?

It's in the news for a number of reasons. First, it's pictorially sexy: crashing glaciers, chuffing smokestacks, cute polar bears and penguins, charismatic politicians and earnest, eloquent and gamine environmental lobbyists warning of apocalypse now—these things make the essential ingredients of dramatic news coverage.... There's a further reason you get a lot of pro-AGW coverage in the mainstream media: bias. Most of us in journalism are not just reporters, we are idealists. We think we have a responsibility to change the planet for the greater good, and with the power of television and movies we think we can actually achieve those changes by manipulating public opinion. So at a newsroom level, you've had a subconscious buy-in on a whole lot of liberal agendas, including saving polar bears. Journalists are going to keep preaching human-caused global warming as a crisis because they genuinely believe it is, and they think they have a duty to educate you to believe as well.

The proposed solution, a global governance regime to save the planet and re-allocate resources, fits the academic, left-wing world view of many in the media like a hand in glove.

Activists seeking action on anthropogenic global warming/climate change repeatedly assert that the science is settled. Is this in fact the case? If the science isn't actually settled, then why is there an apparent scientific consensus declaring that it is?

Scientists are broadly agreed that Earth has been warming, but they are nowhere near broadly agreed on how significant that warming is or how much of it is caused by human influences. There are scientific papers flying back and forth like bullets on various aspects of alleged climate change; just last week there were stories about a scientific paper in the *Journal of Climate* that admitted that Greenland's supposed "extreme melt" of the past decade wasn't even a record for the past 100 years, let alone all time—the study found a warm period in the 1920s and 30s in Greenland was 33 percent higher than it is now, and for entirely natural reasons that have nothing to do with CO2. If there really were a scientific "consensus" on human-caused global warming, then activists on both sides of the debate wouldn't be able to accuse each other, as they currently do, of "cherry picking" scientific data to support their respective cases. If all scientific studies led to one conclusion, there would be nothing to cherry pick. The fact that we are having this debate, and that *Air Con* can be published with references to hundreds of scientific studies that cast doubt on aspects of AGW, is proof that the consensus is a fictional concept used by climate change fearmongers to scare the public and politicians into submission.

In the chapter titled "What Cars did the Dinosaurs Drive," you cite evidence that CO2 levels were much higher during the Paleozoic Era than they are today. But, doesn't that prove that the Earth was considerably warmer then and that the greenhouse effect is a potential problem?

What the data shows is that, despite the greenhouse effect, the planet's temperature has remained largely stable for most of the past 600 million years, and life of all kinds thrived in that warmer environment. It shows that after a certain atmospheric saturation percentage is reached, CO2 has no further impact on temperature. It also shows that CO2 levels have historically gone up and down without big impacts on temperature. In fact, the best data suggests the sun warms the planet first, and rising CO2 then follows around 800 years later, not the other way around. Perhaps most telling about the evidence in that chapter, however, is that the fossil record shows CO2 levels could shoot up, while at the same time temperatures plunged, and vice versa. So there's no obvious correlation between CO2 in the atmosphere and temperature, which is key to the current debate.

You're an investigative journalist, not a scientist. What is your response to critics who point out that you're not a scientist, let alone a climatologist, and therefore are not qualified to opine on a complicated scientific matter such as global climate change.

Yes, I'm a journalist. So is Al Gore by trade, although I have much more journalistic experience than he does. Rajendra Pachauri, who heads the IPCC and now also the climate change centre at Yale University, is a train engineer by trade. Nicholas Stern in the U.K. is an economist, not a climate scientist. Bill McKibben, who's pushing the 350.org agenda and whose work helped inspire Al Gore, is a journalist and Sunday school teacher. NASA's Jim Hansen is a politician masquerading as a climate scientist. New Zealand's self-appointed leading climate alarmist is actually a truffle hunter in his day job, and Leonardo di Caprio is a Hollywood actor. So my credentials are no better nor worse than many of the leading voices in the climate debate. What do I bring that's different? Probably a healthy skepticism and an inbuilt nose for detecting "spin" based on my experience in that field.

In conclusion, allow me to congratulate you. *Air Con* has been a No. 1 best-seller in both New Zealand and on Amazon in the Science > Earth Sciences > Climatology > Climate Changes category. I noticed that last week the top three books in that category, including *Air Con*, are all openly skeptical of global warming. Do you believe that we're approaching a tipping point in terms of the public's acceptance or rejection of the AGW/CC theory?

Yeah, I think we are, although I wouldn't underestimate the effect of the deluge of climate change scare stories that are going to hit us as we get closer to Copenhagen by the end of this year…. I'm heartened by the response to *Air Con*, which has been as high as No. 1 on Amazon's climate category on both sides of the Atlantic, because it shows people have found the book useful as a weapon to restore some sanity to the climate debate.

The FDIC is broke

August 24, 2009

T HE TWO HALLMARKS of the Great Depression were unemployment and bank failures. While the same economists who denied there was a recession for the first nine months of the economic contraction are now insisting that it is over and the recovery has begun, I am extremely dubious. Since the crisis became apparent, I believed that 2009 would be the equivalent of 1930, that being the year that everyone expected recovery to be waiting around the corner. But while there are some statistical green shoots, there are also numerous signs that the perceived recovery is illusory, and in fact, the economic situation is more dire now than it was 79 years ago.

In the first year of the Great Depression, unemployment reached 8.7 percent. The present unemployment rate is 9.4 percent. As I have shown previously in this column, bank failures in 2008 and 2009 are also worse than they were in 1930 and 1931 when measured in terms of bank deposits rather than the number of banks. Since that July column was published five weeks ago, 28 more banks have failed and driven the percentage of failed bank deposits up to one percent, which is more than I'd projected for all of 2009. At the current rate, bank failures over the last two years will equal 4.65 percent of total bank deposits, which is more than twice the two percent of failed deposits in 1930 and 1931.

Despite these widespread banking collapses, the American public has remained relatively quiescent, mostly because they believe their deposits are safely insured by the Federal Deposit Insurance Corporation. The problem is that the FDIC has now run out of money; the losses caused by the 81 bank failures this year has completely exhausted the Deposit Insurance Fund. At the beginning of 2008, the DIF had a balance of $52.8 billion. At the end of the year, during which 25 banks failed and caused $17.9 billion in FDIC-estimated losses, the fund was down to $17.3 billion.

At this point, I should mention that some observers of the banking system are careful to point out that it's not correct to simply subtract estimated losses from the reported DIF balance because the FDIC brings in money every quarter through the insurance premiums it charges. This is true, but on the other hand, it's even more important to remember that estimated losses reported are merely estimates. An examination of the last five quarters shows that the net impact of a bank failure on the DIF balance is approximately twice the level of the estimated losses. For example, the $2.3 billion in estimated losses from the 21 bank failures reported during the first quarter further reduced the insurance fund by $4.3 billion, to $13 billion. Over the last five quarters, projected fund balance reductions have been 1.94 times greater than the estimated losses.

While the FDIC does have the ability to borrow money from the U.S. Treasury, for the first time in its history, it has been forced to tap its $30 billion credit line. And while Congress can elect to intervene and bail out the FDIC as it bailed out the banks and other institutions, contrary to most depositors' assumptions, it is under no obligation to do so. An advisory opinion posted on the FDIC's own site makes it clear that the so-called federal guarantee is nothing more than non-binding reassurance made for the public's benefit.

> [A] joint resolution of Congress (H.R. Con. Res. 290) adopted in March 1982, which reaffirmed that the United States pledges its full faith and credit behind the federal deposit insurance funds, may have served as a moral pledge on the part of Congress to support the deposit insurance funds should they ever need it, but, because of its status as a non-binding resolution, did not serve to create any legal liability on the part of the United States Government to support the funds.... It is our opinion that Title IX of CEBA merely represents an expression of the intent of Congress to support the FDIC's deposit insurance fund should the need arise.

> —Full Faith and Credit of U.S. Government Behind the
> FDIC Deposit Insurance Fund

If there is one thing that has been made clear by the response of the monetary and fiscal authorities to the economic crisis, it is that they will not lift a finger to help the general public. When they could have spent millions to prevent homeowners with mortgages from falling into default and foreclosure, they instead chose to spend billions to reduce the impact of the failed mortgages on the giant zombie banks. If one looks closely at the mechanisms underlying the Homeowner Stability Initiative, the Making Home Affordable plan and the Cash for Clunkers program, one will see that they are not designed to help the homeowner or the car buyer, but rather the banks that finance the purchases.

Given recent history, it would appear to be most unwise to assume that the federal government will do much more than permit the FDIC to borrow the additional $70 billion by which its credit line was increased in May, especially should depositors become aware of the increasingly fragile state of the banking system and begin to withdraw their funds from it. Banking holidays and other restrictions on the public's ability to access its money are probably more likely than an outright bailout, especially since a bailout will cost around $225 billion merely to maintain the status quo if Meredith Whitney's calculation of 300 bank failures is correct. In any case, the ability to ask permission to borrow from an unpredictable institution already $11.7 trillion in debt and expecting a further $9 trillion in deficits is not insurance nor can it reasonably be described as a guarantee of any kind.

Liberal book banners

August 31, 2009

> *The issue was that the McCain-Feingold law bans corporate money being used for electioneering.... At the first Supreme Court argument in March, a government lawyer, answering a hypothetical question, said the government could also make it a crime to distribute books advocating the election or defeat of political candidates so long as they were paid for by corporations and not their political action committees. That position seemed to astound several of the more conservative justices, and there were gasps in the courtroom.*
>
> —*New York Times*, "Supreme Court to Revisit 'Hillary' Documentary," Aug. 29, 2009

FEW POLITICAL BOOKS have ever been published with more perfect timing than Jonah Goldberg's *Liberal Fascism*. Although Goldberg may have gotten the identity of the victorious liberal incorrect, his work has nevertheless proven to be a reliable indicator of the increasingly materno-fascistic behavior of the Democratic House, Senate and White House. The present Washington regime is the political version of the so-called helicopter moms who hover over their children at all times in an attempt to exert constant control over their decisions and behavior.

Whether it is forcing the young and healthy to buy unneeded health insurance, preventing the insured from seeing the doctors of their choice or dictating the unnecessary destruction of perfectly viable used cars, the collection of petty central planners in Washington are a direct and growing obstacle to the constitutional and natural liberties of Americans. To put it bluntly, they are a cancer on American freedom that has now grown to point that they dare to directly attack the Bill of Rights.

Intelligent observers have always known that the McCain-Feingold campaign finance reform law was an outrageous and blatantly unconstitutional assault on the First Amendment right to freedom of speech. But this went largely unrecognized by the American people for two reasons. First, the law was passed under the guise of protecting democracy from the undue influence of corporate wealth, which sounds reasonable to the average voter even if it is demonstrably false. Second, because the law was of great material benefit to the media by hampering the ability of non-media institutions and individuals to interfere with the political messages being pushed by the media, the greater part of the media wasn't terribly inclined to complain about it or draw attention to the probable ramifications.

Furthermore, McCain-Feingold was written to distinguish between broadcast, satellite or cable transmissions and printed formats such as books and newspapers. However, the distinction was a false and arbitrary one made to avoid the very PR debacle that appears to be developing, as there was no rational basis supporting it. Therefore, the decision of the Supreme Court to reconsider its 1990 decision, "Austin v. Michigan Chamber of Commerce," is extremely important, as if it does not, the federal banning of books will be only one of a series of deeply problematic consequences. As one liberal advocate of free-speech restrictions declared: "A campaign document in the form of a book can be banned."

That the liberal fascists are more genuinely fascist than liberal is not difficult to see in their constant struggle to seize the communications high ground and deny it to their ideological opponents. From the calls of House and Senate Democrats for the reinstatement of the "Fairness Doctrine," to the first pass at a media bailout known as the Newspaper Revitalization Act, to the continuing ramifications of McCain-Feingold and the proposed office of the national cybersecurity adviser, it is clear that the American Left will unhesitatingly sacrifice every principle it supposedly possesses to secure its control over national mass communications. This, too, was explained by Goldberg, as fascism is above all an eminently practical ideology.

No doubt this is why the mainstream media has become visibly nervous over the decisions of a few Americans to openly carry weaponry at a few recent political rallies. Because they are complicit in the federal government's attempts to eradicate America's First Amendment rights, it should be no surprise that many members of the mainstream media quiver in fear when they imagine at whom the exercise of America's Second Amendment rights will be directed, should such exercise one day become necessary in, as it has been written, the course of human events.

Glorious fall of a red czar

September 6, 2009

I AM OCCASIONALLY asked why I would ever choose to write for *World-NetDaily*. I am, after all, a columnist who has been nationally syndicated by Chronicle Features and Universal Press Syndicate. My scribblings have appeared in newspapers ranging from the *Atlanta Journal-Constitution* and the *Boston Globe* to *Pravda* and the *North Bay Nugget*. I was one of the first *St. Paul Pioneer Press* columnists to be syndicated in the paper's 150-year history, and I'm the only one who was ever syndicated twice, for two different columns. I'm considering either a gardening or a women's shoes column just so I can go for the trifecta. I don't know anything about either subject, but since Paul Krugman has an economics column, that can't possibly be a problem.

Meanwhile, according to its critics, *WorldNetDaily* is an unreliable and histrionic news source that is one step below the National Enquirer, which at least has a printed product. And while the National Enquirer likes reporting on celebrity alien abductions by surgically inclined extraterrestrials, WND rarely misses a story dealing with the antichrist, Harry Potter or other religious bugaboos. But this is merely flavor, and while it may be an acquired taste of sorts, it's no more meaningful than the flavor that accompanies major media institutions such as the *New York Times*.

One cannot honestly say that headlines like "Church bell 'noise' under attack—in America" are any more indicative of journalistic unreliability than the "Wither Gambia?" sort that P.J. O'Rourke accurately characterized as MEGO (my eyes glaze over), or those that accompany the "What you can buy in Slovenia for $250,000⊠ articles. The reality is that most church bells can freely ring, nobody cares what happens in Gambia or even knows where it is, and the only reason for publishing the European real-estate porn is so that readers of the Times can feel as if they're the sort of individual who just might buy a vacation home in Slovakia. Or Slovenia, whatever it was.

The superficial dressings are irrelevant. It's only the substance that matters, and it's here that *WorldNetDaily* has continued to go from strength to strength over the years. Its opinion columnists are smarter and better-looking than those featured by the mainstream media's standard bearer, but more importantly, they also cover a far greater range of the political spectrum. *WorldNetDaily* features liberals like Bill Press and Nat Hentoff, neoconservatives like Ben Shapiro and Michelle Malkin, conservatives like Pat Buchanan and Ann Coulter, and libertarians such as Ilana Mercer and me. The *New York Times*, on the other hand, has smart liberals like Nicolas Kristof and Thomas Friedman, less-smart liberals like Paul Krugman, Frank Rich and Maureen Dowd, and Republican liberals such as David Brooks and Ross Douthat.

WorldNetDaily more than holds its own on the news side as well. The resignation of Van Jones is the direct result of WND breaking news that the mainstream media attempted to bury by refusing to report it for five months. In its Sept. 6 story on his resignation, the *New York Times* referred to "weeks of controversy," which must have been news to readers of the Times because this was one of the first times the Times had mentioned that there was any controversy surrounding the White House's environmental jobs czar. This is far from the first time such a story has gone unreported; John Edwards' affair with Rielle Hunter and the hidden Obama birth records are similar non-stories that the media has unsuccessfully tried to keep from the American people.

It is amusing that a few very silly people with dubious right-wing credentials have begun to call for a boycott of WND because they claim it to be a part of "the lunatic fringe." This call is particularly bizarre coming from Megan McArdle, a blogger for *The Atlantic*; how can anyone take seriously advice on ideologically policing the right from an ersatz libertarian who not only supported the banking bailouts but actually voted for Obama! Now there is your true lunatic fringe—Keynesian libertarians for Obama: total membership, one. Back on Earth, the resignation of Van Jones and the increasing interest in proof of Obama's eligibility for the presidency clearly demonstrates that *WorldNetDaily* is neither lunatic nor fringe.

WorldNetDaily's reporting has forced one communist out of the White House, which is a lot more than one can say for the Republican Party leadership, whose main accomplishment of late is forcing Republicans out of Congress. The quixotic attempt to marginalize one of the Right's most popular news sites is not only counterproductive, but can only serve to increase WND's popularity among a conservative base that is angry with its leadership, appalled by the actions of the Democrats and deeply unimpressed by the Republican squish faction that believes a return to Rockefeller Republicanism of the '70s is a viable political strategy for the future.

Now, I don't agree with Joseph Farah on everything. I don't agree with anyone on everything. But the fact that *WorldNetDaily*'s leadership has the courage and the integrity to permit those on the liberal Left and the libertarian Right the freedom to write whatever they choose demonstrates its commitment to human freedom is genuine. And its steadfast reporting of the stories that the rest of the media ignore demonstrates a commitment to the truth that is just as strong.

On more than one occasion, I have been asked if *WorldNetDaily* can be taken seriously. In the future, I'll just tell them to ask Van Jones.

The false dawn

September 14, 2009

Composite Leading Indicators point to broad economic recovery. OECD composite leading indicators (CLIs) for July 2009 show stronger signs of recovery in most of the OECD economies. Clear signals of recovery are now visible in all major seven economies, in particular in France and Italy, as well as in China, India and Russia.

—Organization for Economic Co-operation and Development,
Sept. 11, 2009

T HE ECONOMISTS of the OECD are far more serious and credible than the likes of CNBC's Jim Cramer, who errantly announced the end of the recession in April. And, yet, they are no more likely to be correct about the economic recovery they are now forecasting than they were back in 2007, when they predicted 2008 GDP growth of 2.8 percent in the United States and 5.2 percent for the global economy. This is not to say that their optimism is baseless; there are a number of factors which tend to suggest that the economic situation has reversed and things are on the verge of improving soon.

The stock market has rocketed 50 percent higher from its March lows. France and Germany reported modest but positive GDP growth in the second quarter. U.S. plant capacity use has risen. General Motors has recalled 1,350 workers as part of a second-half production increase. According to the latest reports, retail sales have risen, and the Case-Shiller Housing Index showed higher housing prices. These are the realization of the green shoots that Federal Reserve chairman Ben Bernanke detected back in March. It should come as no surprise, although it will probably be covered as a major one by the financial media, when third-quarter GDP is reported back in positive territory. Therefore, one could be excused for believing that the massive global stimulus program enacted by the world's fiscal and monetary authorities must have worked, that the worst is well behind us, and that we can safely anticipate a prosperous future of strong economic growth.

Unfortunately, all of this good news is reliant upon a combination of statistical chicanery and a failure to correctly apply the very economic theory upon which the mainstream macroeconomic statistics are based. Both the chicanery and the failure could be expected, as the attempted manipulation of statistics is normal government behavior while the failure is the inevitable result of confusing the map with the land. Consider, for a moment, the composite leading indicators from which the OECD's economists have drawn their conclusions:

OECD CLIs are constructed from economic time series that have similar cyclical fluctuations to those of the business cycle but which precede those of the business cycle. Typically movements in GDP are used as a proxy for the business cycle but, because they are available on a more timely and monthly basis, the OECD CLI system uses instead indices of industrial production, or IIP, as proxy reference series.

In other words, the OECD's indicators are a proxy for gross domestic product, which was itself designed to be a proxy for the growth of the national economy based upon the principles of Keynesian economic theory. And over time, refinements to the proxy and the adoption of policies designed to address the proxy rather than the underlying economy the proxy is supposed to measure have enlarged the divide between the two. The focus of Keynesian theory was never GDP, national income or even economic growth per se, but rather employment. Indeed, the very name of Keynes's magnum opus is *The General Theory of Employment, Interest, and Money*, so the concept of a "jobless recovery" is an intrinsic contradiction in macroeconomic terms.

Due to the way GDP is measured, there are a variety of ways that GDP can increase and perceived economic growth can show up in the statistics without an improvement in the labor market. As I explained in a previous column, imports count against GDP, so if Americans stopped buying im-ported Mercedes and Nintendos for some reason, this would be reported as incredible economic growth and a vast increase in societal wealth. The reality, of course, is that a complete cessation of import buying would indicate that something has gone seriously wrong with the American economy and the

American consumer's ability to purchase goods and services. Another way is for the government to borrow and spend money, a third way is for the Federal Reserve to increase the money supply, and a fourth way is for the government to provide incentives for Americans to make purchases with consumer loans.

All four of these methods are presently being utilized, which makes the situation appear to be much better than it actually is. Imports are down, government spending is up, the Fed is desperately trying to increase the money supply and Congress created around $20 billion in new loans by handing out $2.75 billion to 611,400 car buyers. All of these results will show up in the macroeconomic statistics, and none of them are going to create new jobs or create legitimate economic growth.

Contrary to the belief of mainstream economists, economics is not a giant confidence game in which the government can fool enough people into feeling sufficient consumer confidence to generate a self-fulfilling prophecy of economic growth. Even as the composite leading indicators and GDP numbers turn positive, real measures of economic activity are pointing in precisely the opposite direction. International shipping has begun to slump again. After a three-month rise spurred by an aggressive stimulus program, steel prices have begun to fall once more in the world's largest steel-using country, China. Nearly 40 percent of the stocks traded on the New York Stock Exchange are the worthless stocks of four zombie corporations being propped up by the federal government, BAC, C, FNM and FRE. Total U.S. loans and leases are down 4.6 percent for the year, an initial sign that the inevitable deleveraging process has begun. The percentage of failed bank deposits in 2009 are rapidly approaching three times the percentage of failed bank deposits in 1931, and the FDIC has been forced to request a $500 billion credit line from the U.S. Treasury to stave off looming bankruptcy.

The map is not the land. The statistics are not the economy. This is not a recovery; this is the false dawn that precedes the darkness.

Bernanke's *Essays*

September 21, 2009

ONE OF THE BENEFITS of having an intellectual at the helm of the Federal Reserve during this ongoing economic crisis is that intellectuals tend to leave a paper trail. Bernanke, famous for being a student of the Great Depression, is without question very well-informed on the relevant historical issues. His book reveals an intelligent and scholarly mind that does not shirk from the details but, rather, leaps without hesitation into statistical analysis of the most technical economic minutiae. The book simply wallows in charts, equations and log changes; the net result is impressive, especially when compared with his predecessor's lightweight, revisionist chronicle, *The Age of Turbulence*.

On the one hand, it is reassuring to know that there is a genuinely intelligent man in full possession of the significant historical information at the helm of the monetary authority right now. On the other, Bernanke's *Essays* serves as a reminder that even the most brilliant man's abilities are limited by the conceptual models he is using to understand the situation as well as by the data available for plugging into those models. For example, on several occasions Bernanke resorts to utilizing proxies, and in one case, a proxy for a proxy, when the data required by the model cannot be found. While this is perfectly understandable, it necessarily raises questions about the reliability of his conclusions even if one assumes that his model is flawless. The Misean calculation problem does not only apply to socialists.

As one reads the book, four things about the present situation gradually become clear. The first is the recognition of the tremendous shock that the financial crisis must have given the Fed chairman. Because he places the greater portion of the blame for the Great Depression on mismanagement of the historical gold standard, it's fairly clear that he did not—and perhaps still does not—genuinely believe that another economic contraction of similar size is theoretically possible in its absence.

> *If the monetary contraction propagated by the gold standard was the source of the worldwide deflation and depression, then countries abandoning the gold standard (or never adopting it) should have avoided much of the deflationary pressure. This seems to have been the case.... In summary, data from our sample of twenty-four countries support the view that there was a strong link between adherence to the gold standard and the severity of both deflation and depression.*

The second noteworthy item is Bernanke's misunderstanding of debt deflation. He wrongly describes it as "the increase in the real value of nominal debt obligations brought about by falling prices." But he has it backward, as it is the refusal of borrowers to take on additional debt that collapses the demand required to support price levels. The Cash for Clunkers program was not enacted and the extension of the federal homebuyers credit of $8,000 was not proposed to decrease the real value of nominal debt obligations, they were designed specifically to increase those debt obligations and thereby increase both demand and prices. This misunderstanding indicates that Bernanke is unlikely to recognize the problematic nature of stopping the deleveraging process that has seen TOTLL, total loans and leases by the commercial banks, fall from $7.2 trillion to $6.8 trillion in the three months from June through August.

The third point is the explanation for Bernanke's focus on the banks rather than the consumer or even the private and commercial mortgage holders. While Bernanke follows Barry Eichengreen's lead in blaming the gold standard as the primary source of monetary contraction in 1930 and 1931, he views "sharp declines in money multipliers (reflecting problems in the commercial banking sector)" as one of the major causal factors responsible for extending the depression after 1931. While those who understand that the problem is too much debt, not too little money, will rightly be skeptical of both Bernanke's historical diagnosis and current prescriptions, this does explain some of his otherwise inexplicable actions in supporting loan modification programs that help the banks rather than the defaulting homeowner.

The fourth is the recognition that the Federal Reserve is not omnipotent and that Bernanke's ability to act is rigidly constrained by the economic circumstances. As the quoted paragraph about the Austrian banking problems of the 1920s shows, Bernanke is perfectly aware of the way that merging failing banks with still-solvent ones imperils the entire banking system, and yet the Federal Reserve and the FDIC have been addressing the failures of Bear Stearns, Washington Mutual, Merrill Lynch, Wachovia, and dozens of smaller banks in exactly the same way.

The fact of the matter is that the global economy is far too large and complicated for any one man, no matter how intelligent and informed, or any one institution, no matter how rich and powerful, to control. The debt deflation scenario must play out eventually, and the sooner that Ben Bernanke and the Federal Reserve accept this and work to speed up the process rather than fight it, the better off the American public will be. It is far too late to save the banks, as they sealed their fate when they increased the average amount of loans and leases per bank from $71.4 million in 1980 to $854.2 million today.

Evolution, economics and evil

September 28, 2009

The Mind of the Market: Compassionate Apes, Competitive Humans, and Other Tales from Evolutionary Economics, by Michael Shermer
Rating: 7 of 10

IT IS NO SECRET that I hold a rather low opinion of various books produced by a few well-known atheists. Without exception, they are riddled with factual ignorance, easily demonstrable illogic and fraudulent appeals to science. While Michael Shermer is every bit the atheist that Sam Harris or Richard Dawkins are, his scientific expertise happens to be applicable to his subject matter and his approach is entirely different. And unlike the New Atheists, Shermer makes intelligent use of both science and logic in utilizing various aspects of evolutionary theory to consider homo economicus.

A professor of economics with an active interest in a broad range of sciences, Shermer, who is also the founding publisher of Skeptic magazine, demonstrates the historical connection between classical economics and Charles Darwin's development of the theory of evolution by natural selection. He draws an interesting analogy between the development of an economy and evolution, suggesting that the sophisticated complexity of the former is the product of the same sort of bottom-up "design" process that evolutionists insist has produced living organisms. The implication that follows from this, which Shermer correctly makes, is that government intervention is no more necessary for a market economy than divine intervention is required for the origin of the species.

The text is eminently readable; in fact, the core of Shermer's case actually tends to suffer somewhat from the entertaining tangents in which he readily engages. For example, his exposition of the myth behind the dominance of the QWERTY keyboard is both detailed and fascinating, but it is largely extraneous to the larger subject at hand. And the history of the development of the two-wheeler, although informative, appears to have more to do with Shermer's abiding interest in the sport of bicycling than it does to do with either evolution or economics.

Where the book gets particularly interesting, if arguably even further afield, is when Shermer addresses the question of human nature, and specifically, the material problem of evil. He makes a rational case for refusing to come down on either the side of the dispositional theory of evil or the situational theory of evil, preferring instead to posit a materialistic dual-nature that is the evolutionary product of the intrinsic conflict between within-group amity and between-group enmity. This is an intelligent approach to the problem, even if it leads him to the same quasi-utopian conclusion that has plagued materialist philosophy for more than a century.

In the end, of course, people choose to be good or evil. We can change the conditions and attenuate the potential for evil, first by understanding it and then by taking action to change it.

Being a Christian, and perhaps more to the point, an individual who has read a great deal of recent literature pontificating on the subject, I tend to be more than a little skeptical about man's ability to understand evil, let alone attenuate his potential for it. But Shermer must nevertheless be praised for directly addressing the challenge of the human perception of material evil instead of simply resorting to one of the evasions customarily utilized by rational materialists.

It is a pity that Shermer does not direct more of his skepticism toward the evolutionary theory upon which he relies so heavily, as it is easily the weakest aspect of his case. This is particularly noticeable when he is making comparisons between economics and evolution as the evidence he cites for the former is always much stronger than it is for the latter. Shermer clearly recognizes that his stated goal of bringing together various new scientific fields together under the aegis of Evolutionary Economics "the study of the economy as an evolving complex adaptive system grounded in a human nature that evolved functional adaptations to survival as a social primate species in the Paleolithic epoch in which we evolved," is attempting to solve a really hard problem, but throughout the book I found myself thinking that evolution appears to need the benefit of economics more than economics needs evolution. In fact, the book itself would have benefited from more observable market realities and less hypothetical evolutionary conjecture.

But such criticism is somewhat beside the point, as Shermer's intention is clearly designed to stimulate thinking in new directions rather than provide conclusive evidence of anything. If one takes both natural selection and the free market as given, or as Shermer suggests, "factual realities of the empirical world," then his arguments are often sensible, even if they are not necessarily convincing in many cases. These arguments ultimately culminate in a laudable call for a positive approach to political and economic human freedom, which no libertarian can fail to appreciate. *The Mind of the Market* is an entertaining and stimulating book, and one that is definitely worth reading by anyone with an interest in either evolution or economics.

Ireland surrenders again

October 5, 2009

S O, IT WAS ALL FOR NOTHING. All the pain, bloodshed and sacrifice has gone for naught. The Rebellion of 1878, the Young Irelanders, the 1919 War of Independence, Sunday, bloody Sunday, the bombings in Belfast, the assassination of Lord Mountbatten, last year's "No" vote and every other aspect of the long and bitter struggle for Irish independence was to no purpose. On Oct. 3, 2009, the voters of the Republic of Ireland threw away their hard-won sovereignty out of fear, naiveté and greed for nothing more than the deceitful promises of the Eurocrats.

Only 15 months ago, the Irish rejected the Lisbon Treaty, which establishes the European Union as a sovereign, constitutional, supra-national political state, by a respectable majority of 53 percent to 47 percent in a national referendum. Since the European Union is less democratic than National Socialist Germany, where Adolf Hitler at least gave the German people the opportunity to express their will on important matters in four separate plebiscites between 1934 and 1938, the referendum yesterday will likely be the last time the Irish will be permitted to do so. In Europe's imperial bureaucracy, the masses are only allowed to vote until they have turned over sufficient power to the unelected European Commission to preclude any need for further voting.

This is not to say that Europeans will not be permitted to cast ballots for their national and European parliaments, of course. The superficial form of representative democracy will be preserved to deceive the former electorate into believing that the substance remains.

How were the Eurocrats able to turn around the vote so quickly, with 20 percent of voters changing their "No" vote to "Yes"? What could possibly have changed since June 2008? The answer, of course, is the Irish economy. Prior to the global economic meltdown, Ireland had enjoyed one of the biggest investment booms on the planet; housing prices tripled between 2000 and

2006. This investment boom was mostly the result of the usual expansion of bank credit, but subsidies from the European Union played a significant role in overstimulating the Irish economy as well. Since 1973, Ireland has received between 3 and 4 percent of its GDP every year in European subsidies. The equivalent, in U.S. terms, would be annually pumping an additional $494 billion into the economy.

As any Austrian economist could predict, and as those paying attention to Ireland did, the powerful boom was inevitably followed by a crash of similarly impressive proportions. It's far from over, of course, but in 2009 unemployment has risen 7.5 percent, GNP has fallen 12.4 percent, and its budget deficit has increased to 9.6 percent of GDP, the worst in Europe. This result was to send the newly prosperous people of Ireland into a panic… and straight into the jaws of the very European bureaucrats and central bankers who created the problem in the first place.

It seems that 453 years of British rule wasn't enough, so after less than a century of independence, the Irish people have now elected to be ruled from Brussels. Irish-Americans, next St. Patrick's Day, don't forget that the colors of Ireland are no longer emerald green, but blue and yellow.

A prize-winning presidency

October 12, 2009

U NLIKE MANY right-wing commentators, I had very high hopes for the Obama administration. Whereas most conservatives were wringing their hands about how Obama was likely to destroy the economy, I was confident that Ben Bernanke already had the task well in hand. Sure enough, Obama was content to continue where George W. Bush had left off, expanding the bank bailouts and quadrupling down on the $168 billion Bush stimulus package with his own $787 billion gambit.

Neoconservatives were afraid that Obama might not harbor sufficient enthusiasm for getting American troops killed in third-world hellholes of no possible national interest to Americans, especially when he failed to follow John McCain's lead in vowing to get them killed in second-world hellholes of no possible national interest to Americans near the Russian border. But here, too, Obama did not disappoint. He not only managed to get more American troops killed in Afghanistan in his first year than Bush did in any of his eight years in office, but even hinted at his willingness to order Americans to die in Pakistan and Iran, too. Unless Obama builds a pyramid in the Rose Garden and personally carves out the hearts of American soldiers before offering them to the great god Demoquetzocoacracy, it is hard to imagine a more useless sacrifice of American lives. This could only please the neocons, given their view of American blood as an irreplaceable lubricant for the global economy.

Social conservatives were deeply concerned that Obama might fail to make meaningless statements about the desirability of limiting the amount of unborn children murdered in America while assiduously avoiding doing anything that might prevent a single unborn child from being vivisected in the womb. Here his record to date is mixed; while he hasn't said much about abortion one way or another, he has, like every post-1973 Republican president before him, refused to make any use of the powers of the executive branch to save a single unborn human life.

Advocates of the Global Struggle Against Violent Extremists By Which We Mean Right-Wing American Christians With Guns were deeply concerned that Obama would rein in some of the more egregious encroachments on American liberties, such as domestic spying, warrantless wiretaps, and being held without trial. However, Obama vastly exceeded their expectations, not only defending the Bush administration's attempt to bypass the U.S. Constitution, the common law and the American judicial system, but also expanding the government's ability to interfere in the private lives of Americans by turning the Justice Department into the enforcement arm of the Recording Industry Association of America. And keeping everyone's favorite offshore prison camp open, no less!

Being a libertarian and therefore not wishing for a president to do much of anything except in the event of a Japanese naval invasion of the West Coast, my only fear for the Obama administration was that it would fail to live up to the comedic potential suggested by its leading man's hilarious performance during the campaign. Who can forget Obama throwing granny under the bus? And, uh, the, uh, adventures in teleprompting gave joy to, uh, millions. Around the world. Joy. Let me try this one more time. The hopetude, the changeosity, the Brandenburg Gate and the Temple of O in Denver all set a mark for unintentional comedy that it seemed no governing administration could possibly hope to surpass. My expectations were high and America's need was great, because in economic hard times everyone can use a good laugh.

But Obama showed right from the very start that no mere oath of office could cause him to abandon his destiny as America's comedian in chief. He managed to transform the gravitas imposed by the somber responsibilities of power with a wickedly subversive dry spin that makes even the most mundane executive action look like a pratfall. I had thought his sarcastic take on Bill Clinton's runway appointment with a hairdresser would be the high point of the year; who but the most gifted parodist would dare to use a theater-commanding general as the straight man in a short bit that required nine months of non-communication to prepare? But no one foresaw, no one could possibly have foreseen, the brilliant one-two of the Olympic failure, followed in quick succession by the Nobel Prize committee's hilarious announcement, and if anyone says they did, they're lying. The great ones never let you see the joke coming. For years, Americans have wondered if it was Eddie Murphy or Chris Rock who was the legitimate heir to Richard Pryor's comedy crown, but now it is clear that all three of them were doing little more than prepare the way for the greatest black comedian America will ever know: Barack H. Obama.

There is much ongoing discussion of what prizes Mr. Obama does or does not merit. All I can say is that if the man does not win the 2009 Grammy for best spoken comedy performance, they should stop giving out the award.

End the Fed

October 19, 2009

End the Fed, by Ron Paul
Rating: 10 of 10

> *The Federal Reserve System must be challenged. Ultimately, it needs to be eliminated. The government cannot and should not be trusted with a monopoly on money. No single institution in society should have power this immense. In fact, I believe that freedom itself is at stake in this struggle.*
>
> —Ron Paul, *End the Fed*, p. 11

IN 17 YEARS of writing game and book reviews, I can count on two hands the number of times I have ever given out the highest rating. True excellence is to be distinguished from the merely very good, and it is far rarer than the heavy use of superlatives in our everyday language would tend to indicate. *End the Fed* is more than a timely political polemic, it is also the story of the long and patient campaign by a small group of freedom-loving patriots to restore economic liberty to the American people.

Being a student of economic history myself, I was deeply impressed by Paul's knowledge of not only the Federal Reserve System's present organization and practices, but the way in which the system was surreptitiously created and inflicted upon an unsuspecting American people who had no idea what was intended for their money nor understood that the financial rapine of their descendants was being secured. Few of those who errantly believe that a central bank is a vital necessity to a national economy have any idea that Americans have shaken off the paper chains of a central bank three times in their history, much less know that the Fed's destruction of nearly 100 percent of the value of American money is entirely in keeping with the historical performance of its three predecessors.

Paul makes a strong case against the Fed by its own standards. He shows how it has not been successful in stabilizing the business cycle by citing the 18 recessions that the National Bureau of Economic Research records as having taken place since the establishment of the Federal Reserve System in 1913. He describes how it has failed to provide banking stability, and he demonstrates the way in which it has completely failed to control inflation with a graph that shows how 95 percent of the purchasing power of the dollar has been inflated away during the 96 years of the Fed's monetary monopoly.

Most importantly, Paul shows how the true purpose of the Federal Reserve System is to empower politicians to favor special interests while simultaneously enriching the financial elite who provide the politicians with that power. But because this parasitical system is not sustainable in the long term, it is guaranteed to break down eventually, most likely in a manner that will lead to a fascist system where profits are funneled to the influential special interests while losses are transformed into public obligations. Paul traces the seeds of this process back to Woodrow Wilson's planning state of World War I, seeds which have now blossomed into the financial industry bailouts and government takeovers of the insurance, mortgage, banking and automotive industries that we have witnessed in the last two years.

The most fascinating element of the book is Paul's personal interactions with three chairmen of the Federal Reserve: Paul Volcker, Alan Greenspan and Ben Bernanke. Of the three, he has the most respect for Volcker, while Greenspan comes off as a calculating pragmatist who knows better but goes along with the charade to get along. Bernanke is repeatedly slammed, as Paul wonders why, in light of his reliably incorrect prognostications, anyone takes his views seriously today. The most damning exchange in the book is the congressman's exchange with Bernanke on July 18, 2007, after he attempts to warn the Fed chairman about the unsustainability of the system.

Ben Bernanke: The Federal Reserve is committed to maintaining low and stable inflation and I'm very confident that we'll be able to do that.

Ron Paul: You're not answering whether or not you anticipate a problem.

Ben Bernanke: I'm not anticipating a problem like '79-'80.

Ron Paul: With your fingers crossed, I guess.

Paul adds, rather dryly, that the finger crossing must not have worked, as two weeks later the Bear Stearns hedge funds collapsed and kicked off the global financial crisis. Throughout the book, his tone is neither angry nor inflammatory, but instead reflects the bemused patience of an elder statesman who can no longer be surprised by the madness and short-sightedness of men. Indeed, Paul ends on an inspiring and optimistic note, as he clearly believes that for the first time in five generations, a sufficient percentage of the American people may be capable of understanding the system well enough to demand that it is brought to an end before it collapses in either global financial servitude or war.

End the Fed is a powerful indictment of the present financial system, and it is impossible to read it without concluding that the Federal Reserve System is doomed by its very nature and that it is therefore in the best interests of the American people to shut it down before it collapses. I suspect reading it will also be a bittersweet experience for many Republicans, as the contrast between the wisdom and integrity of the author and that of the bankers' minion who was more concerned with the fate of Wall Street than with the presidential election could not be greater. In writing *End the Fed*, Ron Paul has placed a fitting capstone on his legacy as a great champion of freedom, capitalism and the American people.

The Return of the Great Depression

October 26, 2009

E IGHTY YEARS AGO this Thursday, the Great Depression began. While the great stock-market crash of 1929 actually began on Oct. 24, it was the fourth day of the crash, Oct. 29, 1929, now known as Black Tuesday, that confirmed the severity of the four-day decline and alerted the world to the fact that not all was well with the U.S. economy. Those who appreciate historical rhythm will probably be aware that the most intense part of the subsequent depression was the four years from 1930 through 1933 that Milton Friedman described as the Great Contraction.

Although 1929 marked the beginning of the Great Depression, it is important to understand that very few people, let alone politicians or economists, recognized at the time that what they were experiencing was the Great Depression. People did not greet friends in the street and ask how they were surviving the Great Depression. In fact, it was not until 1931 that people gradually began to become aware that what was taking place was a larger-scale economic event than the Panic of 1921 or other previous depressions. As late as December 1930, Herbert Hoover was insisting that "the fundamental strength of the economy is unimpaired," a quote that should strike fear into the hearts of everyone who remembers John McCain declaring "the fundamentals of the American economy are strong" before the 2008 election. It was not until 1934, when Lionel Robbins wrote a book titled *The Great Depression*, that what was clearly a worldwide economic depression began to transform into the Great Depression.

When one browses the excellent News from 1930 blog, it is striking to see some of the same baseless optimism that presently pervades the financial media. Consider the similarities in these three pairs of statements each separated by 79 years:

Reserve bank areas forecast new year. Leaders in banking and industry throughout the country maintain an optimistic attitude toward the prospects for 1930.

—Jan. 1, 1930

Bernanke sees U.S. recovery beginning in 2010. Bernanke told the U.S. Congress in January that the Fed believes there is a reasonable prospect the recession that took hold in December 2007 will end this year and that 2010 will be a year of recovery.

—March 16, 2009

Col. L. Ayres of Cleveland Trust sees almost certain economic improvement from July to August and September; based on historical patterns and comparisons to earlier depressions (1907-08, 1920-21). However, recovery does "not promise to be emphatic"...

—Aug. 15, 1930

A panel of 45 U.S. economists expects a "modest" economic rebound to begin in the second half of 2009, picking up steam in 2010.

—May 27, 2009

The worst is over without a doubt.

—June 1930, James J. Davis, Secretary of Labor

Treasury Secretary Timothy Geithner said signs of economic recovery are "stronger" and have appeared "sooner" than expected...

—October 2009

I believe that just as the political and financial authorities were incorrect about the imminent end of the depression in 1930, their successors are incorrect about the imminent end of the depression today. Last Friday, British economists were shocked when the GDP numbers from the Office of National Statistics indicated further economic contraction instead of the growth that had been uniformly forecast, and I expect this to be the first of many such surprises to the downside. Mainstream economists did not see the economic crisis coming, they still fail to understand why it happened and they do not realize that, because the politicians and central banks have stubbornly refused to make any serious changes to the global financial system, the crisis is far from over.

It is not over. It has only begun. That is the central thesis of my book, *The Return of the Great Depression*, which will be published this Thursday, Oct. 29, by WND Books. Longtime readers of this column will recall that I correctly warned of the housing bubble and the threat it posed to the global financial system back in 2002. I even warned that the crisis was fast approaching in 2008, only six months before the crisis began. And now that virtually every mainstream economist and financial news reporter is declaring the crisis to be solved, the recession to be over and the recovery to be upon us, I am asserting that they are every bit as incorrect now as they were back when they were certain that the economy was strong and real estate was a safe investment.

I have compiled my reasons for believing the politicians, the media and the economists to be wrong again in *The Return of the Great Depression*, reasons based on my analysis of various economic theories as well as the economic history of the United States, Europe and Japan. I do not pretend to be a prophet or to have all the answers. I merely have the benefit of utilizing one of the only economic theories that accounts for what increasingly appears to be the most relevant factor in the economic equation, debt. I will readily admit the possibility that I am wrong; perhaps we are just months away from entering a golden era of unprecedented wealth and prosperity. But I don't think so. I really don't think so. I do think, however, that there is a strong case to be made for the idea that we are entering into a difficult period of history which promises to alter the fundamental character of the nation in much the same way that the Great Depression did 80 years ago. As the author of the book, I must leave it up to you to decide if *The Return of the Great Depression* is that case and if it is a convincing one. Unfortunately, only time can tell if it is a correct one.

Extend, pretend and defend

November 2, 2009

THERE IS ALWAYS a fraudulent aspect to democratic government. There are things the electorate does not want to hear, so any candidate who hopes to win their support quickly learns to avoid subjecting the voters to uncomfortable truths. Once safely in office, it seldom serves the interests of the elected official to tell the people whose interest he nominally represents anything that will highlight the divergence between what is good for the legislator and what is good for those who will be subjected to the legislation he helps create.

It is usually easy for government leaders to do whatever they want without the interference of the public. So long as their actions do not too greatly disturb the status quo or tread too clumsily upon the toes of the most powerful interest groups, the people are unlikely to trouble themselves overmuch with the deeds and decisions of the ruling class. However, in times of crisis, the people tend to find themselves belatedly inclined to begin paying attention, and occasionally a sufficient number of them will even realize that it is the past actions of their leaders that have brought them to their present, imperiled state.

This is what has begun happening in the United States. For generations, Americans have stood passively by as their financial authorities have slowly and methodically destroyed the value of their money in the process of erecting a prison of debt from which neither they, nor their children, nor their children's children can reasonably hope to escape. But now, as the system threatens to break down and collapse under the weight of the very debt it created, Americans increasingly find themselves beginning to wonder why the nation's fourth central bank should not go the way of its three hapless predecessors. The popularity of Ron Paul's bill to audit the Fed, with its 308 House co-sponsors and a powerful mass of public support, testifies to the significant change in American attitudes toward their present financial system.

Because the system is intrinsically unstable, with $14 trillion in annual economic activity now attempting to support $53 trillion in total debt, there can be no reasonable doubt that the status quo is bound to change because it is fast approaching the point at which it ceases functioning. No amount of extend-and-pretend, of subsidizing new loans or postponing fair value accounting is going to change the observation that the assets on corporate balance sheets are only worth around half what they are reported to be. Sweeping the worthless assets under the Fed's copious rugs at Maiden Lane accomplishes nothing but to delay the inevitable. To inflate or deleverage, those are the options.

It is unsurprising, though deeply unfortunate, that Barney Frank and other Democratic congressmen have elected to attempt trying to fool the American people into thinking they are taking bold steps to change the disastrous status quo when, in fact, they are attempting to defend it by preventing any substantive changes. But their attempts will fail, not due to any political groundswell of outrage, but because, to paraphrase Warren Buffett, the tide is going out and it will soon be readily apparent who has been swimming naked.

Sham and deception has become the order of the day. As congressional mandarins boldly rush to the barricades of Wall Street to defend the banks again, the administration careens wildly from one absurd public statement to the next; no sooner had it claimed to have created 640,329 jobs by spending $159 billion in stimulus money than it was asserting it had only spent $92,000 per job, not the $250,000 simple division would indicate. The federal government has reached a truly bizarre state of consciousness when it is attacking basic mathematics as "calculator abuse." And this Associated Press account of the administration's defense of nonsense serves as an amusingly apt metaphor for the way in which both the legislative and executive branches are desperately attempting to preserve the present financial system.

"[The White House] aggressively defended an earlier, faulty count that overstated by thousands the jobs created or saved so far."

The strategy of the political and monetary authorities is very clear. Buy time. Extend, pretend and defend. Exert the power of positive thinking, engage in happy talk and attempt to lift the public's animal spirits until the prophecy of economic recovery becomes self-fulfilling and rising asset prices return bankrupt balance sheets to solvency. It is not a good strategy. It will not be a successful strategy. But it is at least a coherent one. The problem is that they are fast running out of time. They simply refuse to understand that the real danger to the Federal Reserve system is not a political one due to the understandable fury of the American people or even an accounting one stemming from uneviscerated audit legislation, it is an economic one based on the simple fact that a fundamentally flawed system is once again approaching its inescapable reckoning.

Vibrancy at Fort Hood

November 9, 2009

I DON'T MIND ADMITTING that I mindlessly accepted the diversity propaganda when I was younger. Granted, this was before it became so frantic and overbearing that you couldn't walk onto a college campus without three very earnest people sitting down to lecture you upon the extreme importance of diversity at all times and in all places.

As a white 100-meter sprinter in high school whose primary competition was with black sprinters from the nearby inner city schools, I was a firm believer in the idea that all cultures were created essentially equal. Since I had friendly relations with the brothers from North, South and Roosevelt against whom I ran, I couldn't understand how anyone could deny the obvious truth that people are simply people regardless of their color, culture or creed. So, why should it be that you and I should get along so awfully?

Of course, when your grasp of history, psychology and social science is predominantly informed by sports and European electronic pop music, you shouldn't be too surprised when it turns out to be more than a little inaccurate. Since then, I have traveled around the world, have lived on three different continents and subsequently concluded that cultural relativism only lasts until you actually try living in a foreign culture.

My first inkling that perhaps all was not as it seemed was when my university, for no discernible reason, suddenly began preaching the diversity gospel during my sophomore year. This seemed a bit strange, as about the only diverse institutions on campus at the time were the track and football teams. Our sprinter-jumper-hurdler group was one of the most racially integrated groups on campus, and we all found ourselves bewildered by the vehemence with which the administration went about declaiming the joys of diversity to a deeply non-diverse student body.

The lady was protesting far too much. Racial diversity was a simple fact of life, not some sort of magical rainbow land where everything was better. To us, it made no difference if you took the relay baton from a white guy and handed it to a black guy, or vice-versa; a teammate was a teammate. It was simple, uncomplicated, and the coaches never made any accommodations for anyone on the basis of their race. Not a single race-related problem ever arose during a time when we won four conference championships together.

But, as both history and scientific studies have reliably demonstrated, social relations between majorities and minorities are largely dependent upon the existence of a strong majority culture. Most likely, things would have been equally easygoing if the university had been a black one and it was the white athletes in the minority. It is only when two or more cultures are numerically significant enough for there to be conflicts over the social norms and permissible deviations from those norms that serious difficulties begin to arise.

These days, the old problems of black and white racial relations in America that were once so problematic look downright simple compared to the complications introduced by the radical changes to U.S. immigration policy in 1965. Now, the very meaning of what it means to be an American has become a deeply complicated one, as evidenced by the murders of 12 American soldiers by a man who was born in Virginia to Palestinian immigrants, a major in the U.S. Army, and a Muslim. And while the shootings could merely be the last tragic act of a psychiatrist who went off the deep end—let's face it, the mentally unstable do tend to go in for the mind-related professions in disproportionate numbers—that's not necessarily the case. But regardless, the real question is not so much whether Muslims can successfully coexist with secular America; it is whether multiculturalism has succeeded in eradicating the essential concept of America. When the melting pot can no longer melt due to overfilling, is it still a melting pot? And was there ever a melting pot in the first place?

The great problem facing the U.S. in the future, of which the Fort Hood shootings would appear to be an early harbinger, is that the undermining of America's dominant European Christian culture has laid the foundation for what promises to be a long and bitter struggle for cultural supremacy. These struggles usually end one of three ways: division, expulsion or submission to a superior authority. Of the three, the latter would appear to be the most likely given the broad spectrum of global governance programs, but history seldom plays out according to the obvious scenario. Furthermore, economic downturns tend to play havoc with empires. The true tragedy of Fort Hood is that it could have been so easily avoided by rejecting the false promises of multiculturalism and mass immigration 44 years ago.

Fallacy of recovery

November 16, 2009

A one-time skeptic of fiscal stimulus, [German chancellor] Ms Merkel plans what amounts to a third stimulus package worth about € 7 billion ($10.4 billion), starting on January 1st.

—*The Economist*, Oct. 31, 2009

T
HE MAINSTREAM MEDIA is full of reports of economic recovery and an end to the recession of 2008, even though the Business Cycle Dating Committee of the National Bureau of Economic Research has not yet spoken its official word on the matter. The significant rise in the stock markets and a single advance GDP report has been enough to convince nearly every economist and financial analyst that the worst is past, that 10.2 percent unemployment is a lagging indicator, and that the primary concern at hand is now too much monetary and fiscal stimulus leading to inflation.

And yet, the actions of the monetary and fiscal authorities clearly belie their cheerful words. If the global economy is recovering, then why is Germany, whose 0.7 percent growth in the third quarter was widely cited last week as another proof of recovery, planning to embark on a third round of fiscal stimulus two quarters after the recovery arrived? Why is Paul Krugman declaring the need for the U.S. government to provide what he calls "a second stimulus," especially when those who can both recollect ancient history and count to two will recall that this would actually be the third U.S. stimulus package after George Bush's $168 billion stimulus plan of 2008 and Barack Obama's $787 billion stimulus plan of 2009. And why is the Federal Reserve still targeting an interest rate below 1 percent?

If the economy has recovered, then no further stimulus would be needed. Since further stimulus is required, it is therefore clear that the economy has not recovered.

True believers in the recovery theme will naturally point to the estimated 3.5 percent GDP growth reported in the third quarter of 2009 for the U.S. economy. But this doesn't actually prove anything. It only raises questions about the way GDP growth is calculated and the reliability of the measure's relationship to the actual economy. For example, if we ignore the estimates of government spending in the GDP report and look at the actual amount of money that the government has reported spending, it is quite clear that the relevant numbers do not add up.

In the second quarter, nominal U.S. GDP was reported at $14,151.2 billion. The second stimulus package was $787 billion, which represents an additional 5.6 percent of GDP being spent. This appears to indicate that instead of growing by 3.5 percent, the economy was actually continuing to contract by 2.1 percent, but that the contraction was masked by huge federal expenditures. Of course, economists and politicians will hastily point out that this analysis is too simple because it does not account for the fact that not all of the $787 billion had been spent by the end of the third quarter of 2009. And they would be correct to do so, because it does not.

ProPublica estimates that only 21.3 percent of what they calculate as a $792 billion stimulus has been spent, for a total expenditure of $168.7 billion. However, one must recall that to this must be added 78.7 percent of the 2008 stimulus, $132.2 billion, for a cumulative stimulus-to-date total of $301 billion, since if the 2009 stimulus is being spent in 2010, then obviously the 2008 stimulus was spent in 2009. This equals 2.1 percent of GDP; note that neither the 2008 nor the 2009 stimulus plans included the separate CARS bill, better known as Cash for Clunkers, which was passed four months after the $787 Obama stimulus. The Bureau of Economic Analysis estimated "added 1.66 percentage points to the third-quarter change in real GDP," so the net effect of these combined government stimuli comes to around 3.8 percent of GDP.

I expect even professional economists are capable of noticing that 3.8 percent is greater than 3.5 percent. Throw in the customary Keynesian "multiplier," and the situation looks even worse.

This is just an ad hoc analysis, of course, and there is no shortage of complicated theoretical models which purport to explain why a larger number is actually a smaller one, why spending more is really spending less, and why more debt is the answer to too much debt. But the salient point is that most of these models were wrong before the shocking economic contraction began and they remain wrong today. As you watch the news, remember that there are two possibilities with every economic report. The first is that the models used to produce the estimates are correct and accurately reflect the current state of the economy. The second is that they are incorrect and the increasing divergence between the reports and your observations indicates their increasing irrelevance with regards to the state of the economy.

As Steve Keen of Debtwatch has shown in detail, the two best leading indicators of reported economic growth are debt and government spending, and changes in debt are a more reliable indicator than changes in government spending. Since the amount of debt in the U.S. economy is continuing to contract at a rapid pace, this is a strong indication that the reported GDP growth is merely a temporary artifact of increased government spending, the economy has not recovered, and the desperate attempts to conceal its continued contraction will eventually fail at some point in the future, most likely before the end of 2010.

The global warming fraud exposed

November 23, 2009

I HAVE an old T-shirt that I used to wear from time to time during my techno days with Psykosonik. Eric Bloodaxe of the Legion of Doom created it in honor of the "Hacking for Jesus" tour, complete with a listing of ISP addresses that were supposedly hacked during the Legion's Internet World Tour of 1991. But last week, an anonymous hacker achieved a feat that will long be lionized by computer pirates, libertarians and genuine scientists alike, as he broke into the Climate Research Unit's computers, copied 172 megs of data, and then released it into the digital wild.

Information wants to be free. And this information desperately needed to be freed.

Upon perusing the searchable archive of the online data, most of which consists of e-mails being exchanged between a small coterie of climate-change charlatans who presume to call themselves "scientists," it soon becomes very clear why the anthropogenic global warming–climate-change industry has been so deeply and unscientifically secretive about the data they have used to reach their conclusions of imminent climate-based apocalypse. First, the data simply does not support their conclusions. Second, they know the data doesn't support their conclusions. Consider this amazing admission by Kevin Trenberth, head of the Climate Analysis Section at the National Center for Atmospheric Research and a lead author of the 2001 and 2007 Intergovernmental Panel on Climate Change's Scientific Assessment of Climate Change:

> *The fact is that we can't account for the lack of warming at the moment and it is a travesty that we can't. The CERES data published in the August (Bulletin of the American Meteorological Society) 09 supplement on 2008 shows there should be even more warming: but the data are surely wrong.*

The degree of intellectual and scientific malfeasance is simply astounding, and will shock even those who have been anthropogenic global warming–climate-change skeptics from the beginning. Jay Currie has chronicled how the e-mails offer substantive evidence of the following:

1. the suppression of data

2. the destruction of data subject to FOI requests

3. the organized subversion of the peer-review process

4. the blacklisting of a scientific journal for political reasons

Even worse, it is clear that the fundamental reason underlying their Chicken Little approach to the matter is not scientific at all, but ideological. As John Hindraker of Powerline points out, what these "scientists" are doing is politics, not science, as they are cherry-picking a few useful facts to reach a predetermined conclusion instead of simply collecting the observable evidence, examining all of it, and only then reaching conclusions. By their own admission, their science is "mission-oriented." But what is that mission? Another e-mail provides the answer:

> *One particular thing you said—and we agreed—was about the IPCC reports and the broader climate negotiations were working to the globalization agenda driven by organizations like the WTO.*

As climate skeptics such as Ian Wishart, author of *Air Con*, have warned, the hacked e-mails indicate that the climate-change industry is merely the pseudoscientific tool of the international fascists presently ensconced in various national governments who are seeking to evade the limits of national sovereignty by creating a post-democratic system of global governance. The fake science is supposed to provide an emergency which will justify the establishment of a system of global taxation and regulation, which will provide the means for the transfer of power from the sovereign nations to supranational organizations which have been formed to regulate economic and political activity in the name of saving the planet.

Ein Klima, ein Reich, ein Führer.

Even if the science behind the climate-change industry had been legitimate, it defies all reason and human history to attempt to argue that the only way to save the planet is to convert mankind into the hapless slaves of a global dictatorship. And since, as the Climate Research Unit correspondence shows, the science is rife with fraud and fiction, there is simply no excuse for viewing "climate change" as anything but the shameless propaganda arm of those who wish to crown themselves the kings of Gaia.

The dire sign of Dubai

November 30, 2009

I N 2007, the international financial elite knew very well that there were serious problems with the world's largest banks. Perfectly good loans were being called, long-standing corporate relationships were being cast aside for short-term benefit and there was a palpable perception of something wicked on its way. While news of the so-called credit crunch was duly reported by all the major newspapers, few outside the financial world had any idea that consequences such as the meltdown of 2008 were rapidly approaching.

But if you knew what to look for, it was fairly obvious that something big and ugly was developing, which was why I wrote that "the United States was fast approaching an interesting juncture" in my WND column published March 24, 2008. In a similar manner, what appears to be the minor matter of a Dubai-based corporation requesting a six-month moratorium on its debt payments looks very much like a warning that the next stage in the global financial crisis will be upon us soon.

Debt is the primary cause of significant economic shocks, both to the upside and the downside. This is because it magnifies profitable activity, and it multiplies losses. The following chart from Morgan Stanley shows the historical level of total debt compared to U.S. gross domestic product; note that the relative amount of debt was actually increasing from 1929 through 1933 as GDP shrank and governments and corporations attempted to stave off the effects of the contraction through debt-financed spending.

The spike in financial and government-sponsored enterprise debt that has taken place over the last decade is particularly problematic because it has only a tangential relationship with genuine market-driven economic activity. For example, Dubai World is a government-sponsored enterprise and its giant, gaudy projects have long been a byword for inexplicable and unsupportable excess. If the emirate does default on part or all of the Dubai World debt, this should serve as confirmation that the debt-deleveraging process indicated in the Federal Reserve's credit statistics has begun on a global scale.

It is no secret that many of the large banks around the world are technically insolvent. While accounting rules have been rewritten to permit them to continue valuing assets at elevated levels compared to what they could be reasonably expected to command if sold on the open market, this does not change the fact that the collateral supporting much of the world's public and private debt is worth less than the debt it theoretically supports. This can be seen in the FDIC's account of estimated and actual losses; I estimate that bank assets are only worth around 60 percent of their reported valuations on average despite the eight-month rally in the stock markets. This is why banks are increasingly unwilling to lend money despite the central-bank-suppressed interest rates that enable them to hold deposits at essentially no cost to themselves.

This is not a sustainable situation. There is presently around $3.75 in debt for every $1 in national income, whereas the historical chart indicates that the national economy can normally support around $1.50. Therefore, the elimination of a significant portion of the cumulative debt should be anticipated; in macroeconomic terms this indicates a decline in total public, private and corporate debt from $57 trillion to $21 trillion. This process of debt-deleveraging last took place during the Great Depression. The fact that the level of global debt is higher now than it was in the 1930s is why I believe that the consequence of the current deleveraging will likely be an economic event that is an order of magnitude larger.

It is important to remember that the signal event of the global Great Depression was not the stock-market crash of October 1929, but the failure of the Austrian Creditanstalt bank 19 months later, in May 1931. (In light of the FDIC's strategy of having "good" banks take over "bad" bank assets, it is probably worth noting that it was the Creditanstalt's forced takeover of the bankrupt Bodencreditanstalt that caused it to fail.) Is the feared default of Dubai World the modern equivalent of the Creditanstalt collapse? It is impossible to say at this point, but it is safe to assume that if Dubai is not the first in a wave of international debt-failures, it will be among them once another institution sets the long-delayed process in motion. And in any case, it is certainly a flashing red signal that the economic crisis is far from over despite the widespread reports of global recovery.

If you're interested in understanding more about the dependence of modern economies and the global financial system on debt, I would encourage you to take a look at *The Return of the Great Depression*, which describes both the system and the debt-deleveraging process in some detail.

Never enough

December 7, 2009

I N HIS BOOK, *Liberal Fascism*, Jonah Goldberg explains that the primary mechanism utilized by progressives in restructuring society to their liking is to disassociate every step in the program from the preceding and following ones. "It's just this one little brick," they explain to the conservative who is opposed to the idea of the proposed wall. "Don't be so paranoid… you didn't mean to take it seriously when we said we intended to build an entire wall. What's the matter with this one brick?"

Of course, the minute that the conservative foolishly accedes to progressive blandishments and allows the brick to be placed, the progressive immediately declares the pressing need to move on to the next brick in the wall. Climategate notwithstanding, Al Gore must feel that the present brick is being satisfactorily laid at Copenhagen, because he has already moved on to declaring the need to further handicap the global economy by reducing the carbon emissions 25 percent more than the climate agreement that will be announced next week.

Even if a deal is reached at the U.N. climate-change talks in Copenhagen next week, it will only be the first step toward the far more radical cuts that are needed in global carbon emissions, Al Gore, former vice president, told the Times last night. Gore said that to avoid the worst ravages of climate change world leaders would have to come together again to set more drastic reductions than those now planned.

He insisted that the present goal set for Copenhagen of stabilizing world emissions of carbon dioxide at or below 450 parts per million—enough to prevent a rise in average global temperatures of no more than 2 degrees Celsius—was insufficient and a safer target would be 350 parts per million.

This is insane from historical, scientific, economic and political perspectives. It is historically insane because we know the planet was more than two degrees warmer as recently as 500 years ago. It is scientifically insane because we know beyond any shadow of a doubt that the world is not warming according to any of the predictions based on models which are based on the idea that higher carbon-dioxide levels produce higher temperatures. It is economically insane because it strengthens the contractionary forces that are already in the process of plunging the world into the greatest depression of the modern era. It is politically insane because it reverses more than 300 years of advancing human liberty and democracy.

The global climate-change crusade is nothing more than the latest in a very long line of schemes permitting the governing elite to maintain and expand their power. It will likely succeed, since the larger part of the population that is in a position to stop the crusade is too fat, unimaginative and apathetic to have much interest in what their nominal public servants have in mind for them. The beauty and the curse of a representative democracy is that the people usually get the government they deserve, and what comes out of Copenhagen should accurately testify to what the last 50 years of European and American democracy have merited.

Republics, like empires, rise and fall over time. What we appear to be witnessing this week as the global leaders go through the ritualized dance of reaching a public agreement is a significant step toward the fall of the American republic and the rise of what increasingly looks like one of the mightiest empires the world has ever known. This is not the first brick in the great pyramid of the new state religion, nor, as Al Gore has made abundantly clear, will it be the last one. We can only hope that this new secular priesthood is more circumspect and less bloody-minded than their historical predecessors.

How to create skeptics

December 14, 2009

I T WOULD SEEM that the venerable magazine *The Economist* really believes the global economic crisis is over, since it is now turning the focus of its formidable expertise from economics to climate science. And by climate science, I don't mean the economic implications of the political policies of the eco-fascists in Copenhagen who are seeking to further cripple an already damaged global economy. No, the magazine has actually published an article attempting to examine the large difference between the raw data produced by Australian weather stations and the massaged version of that data subsequently published by the Global Historical Climate Network.

Now, I would have thought that *The Economist* would be rather more concerned about delving into the complete failure of its writers to identify the budding financial crisis of 2008 or to notice that the so-called economic recovery looks increasingly like statistical smoke and mirrors now that the Obama administration is making noises about what will be the third federal stimulus plan in two years. Instead, it has elected to play defense attorney for the climate-change charlatans in an article titled, Skepticism's limits, which encourages everyone without a Ph.D. to shut up and trust the scientists.

> *Why? Why do these people keep bugging us like this? Does the spirit of scientific skepticism really require that I remain forever open-minded to denialist humbug until it's shown to be wrong? At what point am I allowed to simply say, look, I've seen these kind of claims before, they always turn out to be wrong, and it's not worth my time to look into it? Well, here's my solution to this problem: This is why we have peer review. Average guys with websites can do a lot of amazing things. One thing they cannot do is reveal statistical manipulation in climate-change studies that require a Ph.D. in a related field to understand. So for the time being, my response to any and*

all further "smoking gun" claims begins with: show me the peer-reviewed
journal article demonstrating the error here. Otherwise, you're a crank and
this is not a story.

There are three problems here. First, as the skeptic whose work is being assailed points out in his response, the *Economist* article completely fails to debunk the criticism. While two trivial mistakes were correctly identified, neither error was sufficient to call the conclusions into question, let alone justify its dismissal. Second, one does not require a Ph.D. in a related field to correctly identify statistical manipulation. A background in mathematics or statistics will actually be much more useful in a forensic examination of statistical fraud than a doctoral degree in climatology or meteorology.

Third, peer review is not science. It is nothing more than the corruption of science by scientists. Consider the remarkable saga of professor Rick Trebino, a physicist at the Georgia Institute of Technology, whose attempt to publicly discuss the errors made in a paper published in a prestigious journal turned into an absurd 122-step tale of hypocrisy, political intrigue and abuse of editorial power that reads like something written by Kafka.

It has never been clearer that science is too important to be left to scientists. Climategate is merely the ice cube in the amaretto sour that the polar bear sitting on top of the huge iceberg is drinking. While the scientific method is worthy of trust, it is manifestly clear that many scientists are not. And scientists whose career and income depends entirely upon scaring the public into providing government grants should not be trusted any more than any other professional political lobbyist or used-car salesman. Scientists have no one but the numerous bad apples in their midst to blame for the public's increasing skepticism about science and scientists alike. And telling the public to place blind trust in the political process of peer review in lieu of actual science is only going to confirm the skeptics in their suspicions that something is very, very rotten in the present state of science.

As for *The Economist*, I expect we can look forward to reading numerous articles in the future agonizing over why it missed all the obvious signs warning of the return of the Great Depression.

Merry Christmas

December 21, 2009

THE COMMERCIALIZATION of Christmas has long been a concern for American Christians, and the overt attempts to secularize the happy holiday have been a minor annoyance in recent years. Even Garrison Keillor, no staunch right-wing Christian fundamentalist, recently complained about the continuing attempts of non-Christians to subvert, co-opt or simply join in the festive Christian spirit of Christmas. And while I can't help but agree with him on the aesthetic abomination of unitarians attempting to rewrite "Silent Night," I think it is a mistake to bar non-Christians from joining us in celebrating the birth of Man's Lord and Savior.

And if they don't wish to celebrate it, so be it. Let them go to work on Friday and pretend Christmas is a day like any other, if they like.

For we were all non-Christians once. Regardless of whether one is raised in a Christian home and played a starring role as Baby Jesus in the church nativity play or in an atheist house where the only shrines are to Karl Marx, Karl Popper or Chairman Mao, sooner or later one must make the conscious choice to humble oneself before the King of Kings and accept that he is, in fact, Lord and Savior. For most people, particularly successful and intelligent people, it is not reason, nor science, nor evil that stands in the way of accepting Jesus Christ; it is pride. And it is, I think, perhaps a little easier to humble yourself and repent of your misdeeds if you understand that the Prince of Peace was not afraid to humble himself so men might be saved.

In entering a beautiful church in northern Italy, one's eye is immediately caught by large letters embossed in the curved marble wall at the far end. E IL VERBO SI FECE CARNE E VENNE AD ABITARE IN MEZZO A NOI. The stark beauty of the message is enough to bring tears to many a non-believer's eyes. The Word became flesh and came to live amongst us. This is not only the true meaning of Christmas, it is the only meaning of Christmas.

The presents, the toys, the traditions and the joys are all mere reflections of that meaning.

There is no need to fear for Christmas. It will survive as long as man survives, for man cannot live without hope, and hope is precisely what Jesus Christ provides us. In celebrating the hope represented by his birth during a dark and evil time, we are reminded that no matter how dark our times may become, no matter how entrapped in evil our lives may be, even the smallest hope is capable of triumphing in the end. And there is no need to fear for Christianity, either. It does not matter if one billion or one dozen individuals declare Jesus Christ to be Lord; it is just as true in either case. As for the commercialization of the holiday, it does not matter if Christians celebrate Jesus Christ's birth by giving gifts of oranges or digital gadgets, for it is the same Savior whose birth we are celebrating on Christmas Day.

I wish a joyful, peaceful and Merry Christmas to you all.

2010: The year ahead

December 28, 2009

While the Great Depression is considered to have begun with the great stock market crash of 1929, the first mention of the words "great depression" was in a speech given by Herbert Hoover in late 1931. The first specific and titular reference did not occur until 1934, when British economist Lionel Robbins published a book titled The Great Depression. *This would neither be the first nor the last time economists influenced by the Austrian School would be the first to identify a major economic downturn in the making or to point out that the policies of the fiscal and monetary authorities were guaranteed to exacerbate it.*

What then, are the prospects of enduring recovery? It is clear that they are not bright. It is quite probable, if there is no immediate outbreak of war on a large scale, that the next few months may see a substantial revival of business. If the exchanges are stabilised and the competition in depreciation ceases, there is a strong probability that the upward movement, which began in the summer of 1932, will continue. If the stabilisation were made permanent and some progress were made with the removal of the grosser obstacles to trade, it is not out of the question that a boom would develop. There are many things which might upset this development. The basis of recovery in the United States is gravely jeopardised by the policy of the Government.

—Lionel Robbins, *The Great Depression*, Page 195

AT THE END OF 2009, conventional economists are claiming that the economic contraction which began in 2008 is over. Most government published statistics show growth and the stock markets have recovered half of their previous losses. While some of the wiser economists are hedging their bets by stating that they expect growth to be

Failed Banks % of Total Deposits
1929-31 vs. 2008-10

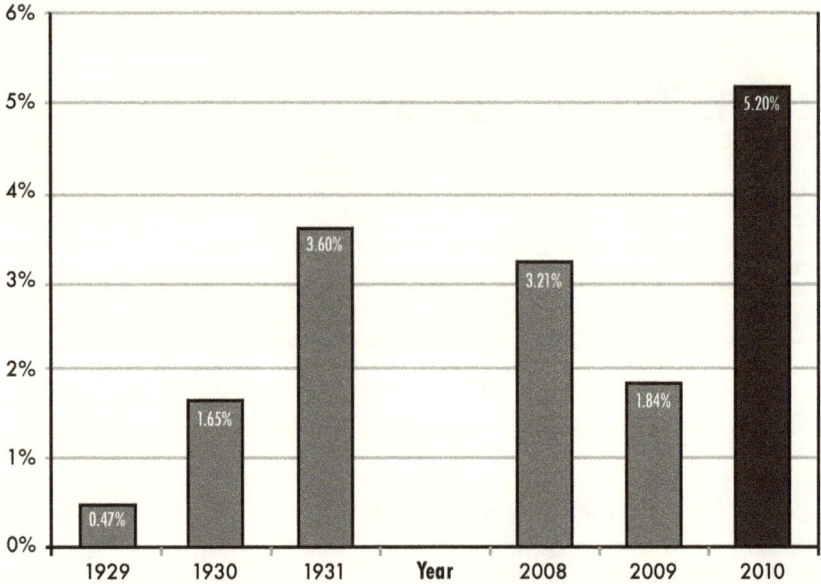

"sluggish" with "downside risks," there are no more expectations of market crashes, financial collapse or widespread economic contraction than there were at the beginning of 2008. The question is not one of growth versus contraction, but rather how much the economy will grow. However, the conventional economists are just as wrong to think the contraction is over as they were to believe that it was not on the horizon before.

While the Federal Reserve's statistics show that the debt-deflation process has not yet begun in earnest, the expansion of credit which is necessary to provide what passes for growth in a credit-based economy has ended. Total credit market debt remained essentially flat since the fourth quarter of 2008. Total loans and leases by commercial banks decreased 6.2 percent in 2009, which was six times more than the largest previous decline in 1975. The FDIC seized 140 failed banks in 2009; their $139.3 billion in deposits represented 1.84 percent of all of deposits in the U.S. banking system. As can be seen in the chart below, this was worse than either 1929 or 1930, and 30 percent worse than the 1.4 percent failure rate I projected in my book *The Return of the Great Depression*.

While it is not possible to predict precisely how many banks will fail in 2010, if we note the recent 1,600 new hires by the FDIC in conjunction with Calculated Risk's Unofficial Problem Bank List of 545 institutions with aggregate assets of $295.6 billion, we can make a rough estimate. In December 2008, there were only 204 banks on the list, so a similar Problem Bank/Failed Bank ratio would lead one to expect 374 FDIC bank seizures in 2010. This correlates well with the rumors of an expected 400 bank failures in 2010. Since the average bank that failed in 2009 had $1,229 million in assets and $983 million in deposits, we can calculate that 2010 will see failed bank deposits rise to more than 5 percent in 2010.

Since it is obvious that banks seized by the FDIC do not make new loans, we can expect the pace of credit contraction to increase in keeping with the number of failed banks. If failed deposits of 1.84 percent correspond with a 6.2 percent decline in commercial bank loans, then a 5 percent rate would tend to indicate a 16.8 percent reduction. This level of credit contraction would be completely unprecedented in the post-war period; one presumes it would also be catastrophic in terms of its consequences for the national economy. Moreover, it would not be something that the inevitable third or fourth stimulus plans are capable of curing, especially since the first two stimulus packages have done nothing more than partially prevent the public from realizing the true extent of the problem.

Lionel Robbins's fateful words, written in the summer of 1934, are as valid today as they were in the middle of America's Great Depression. Unfortunately, they demonstrate how tragically little has been learned in the intervening 75 years by our economists, politicians and monetary authorities.

> *It is true that there are some signs of recognition of the mistakes which have been made in the sphere of monetary policy. But as yet there seems little will to repair them, still less to face the wider economic consequences which such repair would involve. For the rest, so far from there being any recognition of the instability and confusion which has been caused by the policy of interventionism, the majority of the leaders of public opinion seem to have drawn from the events of the last few years the conclusion that more intervention is necessary.*

> —Lionel Robbins, *The Great Depression*, page 197

CASTALIA HOUSE

NON-FICTION
The Last Closet by Moira Greyland
Hitler in Hell by Martin van Creveld
Clio & Me: An Intellectual Autobiography by Martin van Creveld
Equality: The Impossible Quest by Martin van Creveld
A History of Strategy: From Sun Tzu to William S. Lind by Martin van Creveld
4th Generation Warfare Handbook by William S. Lind and Gregory A. Thiele
Appendix N: A Literary History of Dungeons & Dragons by Jeffro Johnson
The Nine Laws by Ivan Throne
Compost Everything: Extreme Composting by David the Good
Grow or Die: Survival Gardening by David the Good
Push the Zone: Growing Tropical Plants Beyond the Tropics by David the Good

FICTION
An Equation of Almost Infinite Complexity by Peter Grant
Brings the Lightning by Peter Grant
Rocky Mountain Retribution by Peter Grant
The Promethean by Owen Stanley
The Missionaries by Owen Stanley

MILITARY SCIENCE FICTION
Starship Liberator by David VanDyke and B. V. Larson
Battleship Indomitable by David VanDyke and B. V. Larson
The Eden Plague by David VanDyke
Reaper's Run by David VanDyke
Skull's Shadows by David VanDyke
There Will Be War Volumes I and II ed. Jerry Pournelle
Riding the Red Horse Volume 1 ed. Tom Kratman and Vox Day

SCIENCE FICTION
The End of the World as We Knew It by Nick Cole
CTRL-ALT REVOLT! by Nick Cole
Somewhither by John C. Wright
City Beyond Time by John C. Wright
Awake in the Night Land by John C. Wright
Back From the Dead by Rolf Nelson
Mutiny in Space by Rod Walker
Alien Game by Rod Walker
Young Man's War by Rod Walker

FANTASY
Iron Chamber of Memory by John C. Wright
The Green Knight's Squire by John C. Wright
City Beyond Time by John C. Wright